Susan J. Averill
153 W. Landon
355-7369

T5-DHA-445

EASY IN ENGLISH

EASY IN ENGLISH

AN IMAGINATIVE APPROACH
TO THE TEACHING OF THE LANGUAGE ARTS

by

Mauree Applegate

Associate Professor of Education

Teacher of Creative Writing

Supervisor of Practice in Elementary Education

Wisconsin State College, La Crosse, Wisconsin

HARPER & ROW, PUBLISHERS

Evanston, Illinois   Elmsford, New York
Pleasanton, California

1963

Copyright © 1960 by Harper & Row, Publishers, Incorporated
All rights reserved for all countries,
including the right of translation. 6824

To the children and the teachers of Wisconsin
who use "Let's Write"
and the directors of
the Wisconsin School of the Air
without whose help and inspiration
this book could never have been possible,
and especially to
Patricia Hall, Grade 8, Bonniwell School,
whom I have never seen, but whose cherished words
I use in dedicating this book:

It feels wonderful to give,
It feels wonderful to get,
And as long as you live
You'll do both of them, I'll bet!

Your over-the-air friend,

Mauree

Possible Goals for the Language Arts Program in the Elementary School

—to use words responsibly

—to think clearly

—to listen imaginatively

—to speak effectively

—to read thoughtfully

—to write creatively

—to use mechanics powerfully

—to regard good English respectfully

—to acquaint children with the best

CONTENTS

AN IMAGINATIVE
APPROACH TO THE
TEACHING OF THE
LANGUAGE ARTS

EASY IN ENGLISH

So that we may understand

each other better, will

you please read the

Introduction to this book.

Introduction

Today I named the book, the book that has been writing itself in my mind for four years, yet all but refusing to be harnessed into print.

I turned to the editorial page of a June issue of *The Christian Science Monitor*—one of those stacked and waiting for longer moments—and there it was—"Easy in English"—and I knew the book was named. I could feel the name settle down on my mind's ideas with a mother-notion, then become brooding and still.

It was Noriko, a young Japanese housemaid-student who gave the name to me via a delightful article by Nancy Nelson.

"I come to keep your house," Noriko joyfully announced to her prospective American employer, as she neatly removed her shoes in the hallway. "I come from the Y—— Agency because I am easy in English."

I said, "Thank you, Noriko, for the name," across the newsprint. "You do not know me, but you have helped me and I thank you."

Almost at once my mind began talking back to me about the name.

"You know very well," it pointed out sarcastically, "that 'Easy in English' is not the best of English phraseology. Whoever heard of a book on the language arts, and one for teachers at that, having an ungrammatical title?"—and here, if ever a mind snorted, mine did.

"If Shakespeare had had a mind like you," I shouted back, "his plays would have lacked life and verve. His characters used the English that said what they had to say whether it was in the book or not. That's exactly what I'm trying to do."

"Of course, you're no Shakespeare," my mind put in with a dark brown inflection, "and, by the way, just what *do* you mean by *Easy in English?*"

"The way I mean 'Easy' here," I explained, "means 'comfortable' —the opposite of 'uneasy'—'comfortable in English,' and there's nothing ungrammatical about that meaning!"

"If you mean 'comfortable,' why don't you say 'comfortable,' " my mind countered, "and be safe?"

"A book title can never be quite safe," I answered, talking more to myself than to my mind. "Safe things are sterile things. A book title must have life and unseen music running through the words like wind in wheat. The word 'easy' flows; the word 'comfortable' is full of padded bumps. *Easy in English* is the name of my new book—it says exactly what I want to say in precisely the way I intend to say it."

And that is that!

"For who today is easy in English?" I mused. Certainly not the teachers. Most of them are distinctly uneasy in English. Since there are so many conflicting ideologies about, the elementary teachers are seldom quite sure what they should teach in their language arts classes, let alone "how" they should teach it. Grammar or no grammar (and how can anyone teach part of grammar?), creative expression or correct expression? Are they at odds with each other? And which should win?

Thus, lacking insight and conviction, many teachers of the elementary grades build a curriculum as patchy as a squatter's shack.

Easy in English? Certainly not the parents, who too often judge their children's English efforts more by the misspelling than by the right-speaking, forgetting that the child who spells incorrectly is often the child whose thoughts and ideas are far ahead of his spelling book.

Easy in English? Certainly not the children in the classroom. For there too often they must speak and write of things about which they have no thoughts, or worse still, aimlessly fill in blanks like an old man working a crossword puzzle.

How does one get to be "easy in English"?

That's what this book is about. You'd better read it.

CHAPTER ONE

The Language Arts Are Our Business

Mother (to father at 11 P.M.): Turn off the television; we've got to do our English homework before we go to bed!

Father: I always knew that if we kept on criticizing the schools, something like this would happen.

. . . These are the days
When men forget the stars, and are forgotten.[1]

We lack the courage to be where we are:—
We love too much to travel on old roads,
To triumph on old fields; we love too much
To consecrate the magic of dead things,
And yieldingly to linger by long walls
Of ruin, . . .[2]

Edwin Arlington Robinson

MY BIG WISH

Some people want to be
A great big movie star,
Others want to buy a yacht
And travel off afar.

Others want to be,
A hero in time of strife
But my big wish is just
To lead a normal life.

Jim Merton, Grade 7

[1] From *Collected Poems*, "Hamilton" by Edwin Arlington Robinson. By permission of The Macmillan Company, publishers.
[2] *Ibid.*, "Octave XV."

There is one conversation in *Through the Looking Glass* by Lewis Carroll that I could swear must have been written about two teachers discussing curriculum making. Alice and the queen had been running like mad when Alice discovered they were still under the same tree they had started from, and looked around her in great surprise.

"Why, I do believe we've been under this tree all the time! Everything's just as it was."

"Of course it is," said the Queen: "what would you have it?"

"Well, in *our* country," said Alice, still panting a little, "you'd generally get to somewhere else—if you ran very fast for a long time, as we've been doing."

"A slow sort of country!" said the Queen. "Now, *here*, you see, it takes all the running *you* can do, to keep in the same place. If you want to get somewhere else, you must run at least twice as fast as that!"

There, do you see what I mean? If that last remark doesn't explain exactly why teachers dread starting to rethink curricula, I've never read anything that did. And I can't say that I blame them either.

Like Ogden Nash's "The Tale of Custard, the Dragon," each of us longs for a "nice safe cage" where everything will stay still long enough for us to get some teaching done. But the wonderland that is America right now won't allow for that kind of continuity. While we're right in the midst of an exciting teaching experience, the situation starts to swivel like the scenes of a New York stage-set, and the first thing we know, the scene that was on is off and one that was off is on, and we have to start all over again.

Yes, indeed, it takes all the running a teacher can do nowadays to stay in the same place, and if he wants to get anywhere else, he must run at least twice as fast.

Yet because that world stage rotates so fast, we must change the curriculum, since the times have already changed the scenery.

Except for the reading field, the language arts program especially needs overhauling right now; it's as patchy as a hobo costume at a masquerade. There's a little bit of everything in it, put together in a haphazard manner unworthy of the careful planning needed by a space age.

Some of you parents may be unacquainted with the term "language arts." (Things change so fast in educational circles that some of us teachers aren't sure what it includes either.) It was probably called "language" when you were in school and in actuality included writing, spelling, correct speech, a handful of grammar, and the study of great poems, stories, and pictures. Now what is actually taught in language arts classes is anybody's guess—the curriculum having bulged over the years like a waistline during the Christmas holidays. The basis of the present-day conception of the language arts is the four skills of communication: speaking, listening, reading, and writing. Formerly, reading was not considered as one of the language arts by the elementary teacher, and still is not in the thinking of many classroom teachers who are likely to consider reading and language as day-by-day classes rather than a part of the overall program of communication. It is a surprise to many parents to learn that "listening" is included among the language arts, and I can just hear some of you who so often give your orders to deaf ears saying, "—and high time!" Just as the era of cars hurried safety teaching into the curriculum, so the era of radio and television is necessitating the developing of the listening skills. *Eyes* were once our chief organ of learning; now *ears* are a close second. Yet what poor listeners most of us are; it is hard for a modern to listen long enough to get directions thoroughly or to remember the chief points of a speech. (Test yourselves sometime.)

More listening, of course, precludes more speaking—this is a world of voices—and practically everyone today influences others by word of mouth. Thus one can readily see that a language arts program today must, of necessity, be based upon the four skills of communication: speaking, listening, reading, and writing. If the language arts program stopped there, curriculum planning would be comparatively easy.

But it doesn't. What about thinking—a skill that must precede and accompany speaking, listening, reading, and writing? What about the classics and great poetry? Should we teach grammar to elementary children? Can we do something about the spelling problem? Can a child learn to write correct English by filling in blanks in a workbook? Does punctuation really matter, or is it something a stuffy English teacher requires because she was forced to the same punishment? Should schools tolerate slang? Just what to include in the language arts classes and just how to teach it constitute that un*easi*ness in English I was speaking about in the Introduction to this book. What! You haven't read the Introduction? Please do turn back and read it so you'll know what I'm talking about.

(Time out for reading the Introduction.)

Thank you for going back. Getting into a book without first reading the introduction is as confusing as walking in on a mystery movie after the first twenty minutes.

If such a definition were not as loose as a sack dress, we might define the language arts as the skills of living together, so thoroughly do these skills permeate the whole school day and the daily living of all adults. A better definition is that the language arts deal with ideas: their impression and expression in words. As a course in painting includes both the study of great paintings and the actual exercise of the paintbrush in self-expression, so the language arts, dealing in the medium of words, help a student to read and hear the best that has been written and said and at the same time help him to express his own ideas and thoughts.

While the language arts help people with something to say to say it better, it also helps people to have something better to say—or should. Unhappily, at the same time, it too often teaches those who have nothing to say to say it—at least so it sometimes seems. As a mountain woman so aptly commented, "School larns children to speak up, but not to shut up." (But my goodness, we're getting humorous again, and as the fifth grader said, "If it's funny, it ain't education.")

As usual, there's a good bit of sense in this nonsense. As parents and teachers, it is of utmost importance that we together plan our goals for the teaching of the language arts. The home gets "first dibs" on language arts teaching, and if that teaching is faulty, it takes years of correct teaching at school to change patterns learned at home. Schoolteachers and home teachers must get together on *what they want the children to get out of the language arts program.* For the *goals* of teaching make all the difference in the world in the *results* of the teaching.

If our goal in the field of speaking, for example, is to get children to express themselves, the results should be vastly more oral and less controlled than if we were aiming to help children to say better things better. Since our results and practices differ greatly from teacher to teacher, from school to school, and from home to home, we must first discuss together the goals of the language arts as needed for *our* day—a day vastly different from any day the world has yet known. These goals cannot be the goals of Yesterday, for Yesterday is gone. But we can learn from Yesterday. Neither can they be the goals of Tomorrow, for Tomorrow has not yet come. Yet we can and must anticipate Tomorrow by Today. Yes, we must carefully plan the goals of today's language arts. I have a firm conviction that a generation that lives skillfully today is in good condition for changed living tomorrow.

Possible Goals for the Language Arts Program in the Elementary School

—*to use words responsibly*

—*to think clearly*

—*to listen imaginatively*

—*to speak effectively*

—*to read thoughtfully*

—*to write creatively*

—*to use mechanics powerfully*

—*to regard good English respectfully*

—*to acquaint children with the best*

As you scan this list, you realize what up to now you may not have realized: that the language arts are not a mere school class any more; they are all of school and all of home; they are not a little segment of the school curriculum any longer but the whole world of ideas. *On ideas and on how they are taught hinges the future destiny of all nations.* On what men think, on what men read, on what men say and write, and consequently do, the future of the world depends.

In this list of goals lies a future of war or peace, of democracy or domination, of love or hate. These goals for children are identical to the purposes of the world of adults, and thus they should be.

Let us, then, consider each of these goals briefly before we go into a more thorough consideration of them in the chapters of this book. Since words are the medium of understanding in the home, the school, the church, the market place, and the world community, let us start with words.

—to use words responsibly

"His words are kind, Mother," a six-year-old said about a cross neighbor, "but his eyes look a different way—as if he wanted to choke me."

When you are talking with your neighbor, your words are supplemented by the look in your eyes, your bodily gestures, the tones and the inflections of your voice. But your neighbor today can be across the world from you as well as across the back yard. He hears your voice from the printed page and on radio across the miles, and judges you by your words and your inflections alone. Yet those words he hears he must first translate into a tongue foreign to him, and your words at best stumble down the corridors of his mind like rough shoes. If you use one word when you mean another, his feelings toward you and your country may be vastly changed. In this era, it is words, not cannons, that are the shots "heard round the world." Words are the heart's conversation—power pellets with real personality. As the modern poet, Joseph Auslander, says:

WORDS [3]

Words with the freesia's wounded scent I know,
And those that suck the slow irresolute gold
Out of the daffodil's heart; cool words that hold
The crushed gray light of rain, or liquidly blow
The wild bee droning home across the glow
Of rippled wind-silver; or, uncontrolled,
Toss the bruised aroma of pine; and words as cold
As water torturing through frozen snow.

And there are words that strain like April hedges
Upward; lonely words with tears on them;
And syllables whose haunting crimson edges
Bleed: "O Jerusalem, Jerusalem!"
And that long star-drift of bright agony:
"Eli, Eli, lama sabachthani!" [4]

The wonderful English language is full of words of understanding because that is the heart's direction of the country in which we

[3] Reprinted from *Sunrise Trumpets* by Joseph Auslander, by permission of Harper & Brothers. Copyright 1924 by Harper & Brothers, copyright 1952 by Joseph Auslander.

[4] Jesus' five words uttered from his agony on the Cross: "My God, my God, whv hast thou forsaken me?"

live. Our children must live with words—ours is a living, growing language—and we must learn which words ease the heart and which tend to clench the fist. We must be so ready with the right word that in our fumbling we do not use a word with unpleasant connotations. Our children must learn several languages; one never understands a country until he knows its language. How well Myra Perrings' poem explains why this is true.

ROOT AND BRANCH [5]

To learn your language, I must hear you speak,
not only with an ear intent on sound,
but with a tractored consciousness,
a well plowed ground
prepared for seed.

As one perceives
on first impression only outer leaves
of alien plants, I am aware
of unfamiliar verbal foliage,
exotic growth of syllables,
accents of color strangely placed
in fields of syntax seemingly untillable.

If I would learn your language, I must know
my own. Contrasting native flowers
in texture, shape and scent; comparing fruit
with fruit, the sour with sours,
the sweet with sweets among
the branches of linguistic trees,
pursuing difference of touch
and taste upon the tongue,
and tracing vocables down stalk and stem
how often and how happily
I come to common root.

To understand your words, I need to know
much more than words: I need to find
the heart of speech in the necessity
of mind to meet with mind.

Our children will be world ambassadors (of peace, we hope). World ambassadors must be well equipped with words that say

[5] By permission of the author and *The Christian Science Monitor*.

what the heart feels. We moderns are living in a world of words. It is sheer madness to have a lean vocabulary. Read Chapter Two, pages 23–39. It should interest you.

—to think clearly

Many books on the language arts do not include *to think clearly* as a goal of the language arts. Personally, I believe that thinking is the crux of any program of communication. The man who reads widely without thinking grows more and more confused every day. The man who listens to radio and television without thinking is at the mercy of a voice crying among the skyscrapers; even the man who is a close observer of what his own senses tell him may get a distorted vision of the world. "Think or perish" is the price of survival in today's complicated world. The Biblical promise that the meek shall inherit the earth may well mean just this.

The story is told that a genial hunter once met an affable bear in the woods.

"Where are you going this nice morning?" the bear inquired.

"I'm out to find myself a fur coat in the forest," said the hunter. "And you?"

"I'm out to get my breakfast," said the bear. "Why don't you come to my den and chat awhile? We have many problems in common, I am sure. Let's forget our purposes for a moment and talk."

Since the bear was affable and the hunter was genial, they sat down to have a summit talk together.

And may I report that real changes did come from this offhand conference. Within an hour, both parties had accomplished their purpose; the bear had had his breakfast, and the man was inside his fur coat.

Until our children learn to think, they will be at the mercy of every bear in the political and diplomatic woods. It does little good for the lion and the lamb to lie down together unless both have a common purpose in their hearts. But thinking without developing the attitudes of peace and tolerance merely exchanges cold wars for shooting wars. Right attitudes must accompany clear thinking. We must prepare our children for a world in which wrong thinking is a greater enemy than an inimical country. In today's world, ideas are more dangerous than atomic weapons. Any skill as necessary to peace and natural living as thinking is should certainly be included in a language arts curriculum. See Chapter Three, pages 49–77.

—to listen imaginatively

For the first time since magazines and newspapers became common, one may become as thoroughly conversant with current problems as much through listening as through reading. Yet as any elementary school teacher can and will tell you, the modern child:

1. Will not listen to what he thinks is uninteresting.
2. Is influenced more by the dramatic than the logical.
3. Has a short listening attention span.
4. Does not know how to separate the essentials he hears from the nonessentials.
5. Is influenced more by voice than by truth.
6. Has a tendency to believe everything he hears from a machine.

An adult reading this list will be struck by the realization that those six comments describe his listening habits as well as the child's. The skills of listening can be acquired through self-direction and self-discipline, but they are surest to take hold if they become habits in childhood. A skill is effective only if its use becomes habitual.

Except for an occasional lecture and the Sunday sermon, until radio and television became part of our lives, few people needed to learn the skills of listening; they were glad to listen to anything that changed the tedium of regular living. Now even a child in kindergarten hears so much from "up-time" to bedtime that he turns off his mind to everything he doesn't care to hear, a trick husbands of garrulous wives learned long ago. My niece, at the age of three, cut off her mother's reprimand with a terse, "You don't need to say that, Muh-er, as far as I'm toncerned." And so think all children when their parents begin to reprimand them.

The story is told of a first grader who was taken to the doctor for a hearing checkup by his mother whose talk had no terminal facilities. She went on at a great rate telling the doctor about her son's apparent deafness so that the doctor had trouble getting into the conversation. After completing the test and before reporting that the child's hearing was normal, the doctor asked the boy if he had trouble hearing. "No," the little fellow replied, "I just have trouble listening."

These are "listening" days, and most of our ears are surfeited with listening. Children are learning to turn off their attention as they turn off television. Schools and homes are going to have to teach not only the skills of listening but how to be more discriminating in what we listen to. Read Chapter Four, pages 85–125.

—to speak effectively

> "Speaking is silver
> Silence is gold,"
> Teachers all said
> In the school days of old.
>
> But why can't we get
> Through a modern child's cranium
> That to know *when to talk*
> *And keep still* is uranium?

Many teachers can remember how hard we worked "way back when" to get children to express themselves. We socialized and motivated until we finally got a class to carry on as fluent a conversation as is held at a ladies' aid or a men's night out. Then, guess what our next problem was! *We couldn't get them stopped.* Now a primary class wants to "tell" all the time a teacher is trying to teach. One of our major tasks in the language arts is to help children to know when to talk and when to keep still. The art is at present a rare one. But one thing is certain—the children can never learn it from us adults. How could they?

A second need in the speaking field of the language arts is the need to work on the skills of conversation. Conversation is coming back into the American scene in spite of television. In fact, a number of programs current today are capitalizing on the conversational idea. Directed conversation, which is being used in college communications classes to advantage, must, I believe, be started in the intermediate grades. In the college setup an entire class reads on one controversial subject such as integrated schools, competitive sports, college dating habits, or any subject vital to young people. A small group plans some points to be discussed and starts the conversation rolling for the six to eight people on the committee. As each topic or the discussants are exhausted, the rest of the class takes over the conversation.

I believe that if directed conversation is introduced in the intermediate grades and in junior high school, the topics should be informational rather than controversial, as they often are in college classes. The discussion of outstanding musicians, artists, actors, statesmen, doctors, and sports personalities is enlightening and interesting to any group of young people. The children of the elementary grades are interested in discussing live people and live issues. Did you ever stop to think how often discussions center around dead heroes and past issues?

The greatest challenge in this section of the language arts is the increasing tendency to write and read reports rather than to plan them and speak from one's notes. Many speakers with much to give lose it on paper. A paper that must be read rather than talked by the speaker had better be read than listened to by the audience.

Before you turn to Chapter Five, page 141, make a list in your mind of the present-day needs that come under the topic "to speak clearly" in today's living. One of them is sure to be the ear-annoying English used by many of one's associates.

—to read thoughtfully

The reading needs of this generation differ greatly from those of any preceding generation. Reading used to take the place of experience. Today experience for many persons takes the place of reading. Learning to read at the age of four, five, or six used to be the Open Sesame [6] from the workaday world of monotony into the fascinating world of experience; now any three-year-old can get quicker results by turning on television or accompanying his parents on a trip. Reading to find out does not appeal to children in the way it did; they feel that they already know, and frankly, the adventures of Alice and Jerry and Dick and Jane seem slightly limited to many of them. A professor friend of mine, who was attending an educational meeting in St. Louis, visited a first grade one morning. She became especially interested in a youngster who was reading third-grade material to himself at his desk.

Anxious to talk with the little fellow, Dr. F—— asked the teacher if the lad might read to her. She graciously assented, but like most primary teachers, fearing that a strange situation might disturb the boy's reading, she handed him a primer rather than the third-grade material he was reading with apparent understanding.

The child read without comment through several pages of limited vocabulary about the adventures of the dog Spot. After a page on which the dog's name was used a number of times, he turned to the professor with a bored twinkle and remarked, "This page needs Spot remover."

[6] Sesame (ses'a-me), the word Ali Baba used to open the door to the robber's cave in the story of "Ali Baba and the Forty Thieves" from *The Arabian Nights.*

The drive to learn to read in order to find out has been lessened considerably since the advent of radio and television; yet the need for thoughtful reading is greater than ever. It is not the amount of reading I am referring to here; librarians report that school children are reading more books rather than fewer since the advent of television, and on a greater variety of subjects. In today's world, reading does not so much add to a man's world as it simplifies and clarifies it. Surrounded by more stimulations than he can possibly respond to, a modern man is in much the same position as the Korean orphan, adopted by a rich family, who went from no toys to so many that he was bewildered into shocked withdrawal.

It seems to me our chief reading problem in the schools of today is not only to teach a child to read but to teach him what to read and how to change his type of reading to suit his particular purpose. A child must realize before he enters high school that reading helps him to make up his mind intelligently, aids him to feel comfortable socially, and protects him from false and misleading doctrines that assail him from every billboard, neon sign, and television voice. Reading, which used to be the door to experience, is now the Geiger counter detecting the grains of truth in whole mountains of baser metals.

The elementary school is no longer merely a place where a child learns to read but where attitudes toward reading are as important as the reading itself. That habits of and attitudes toward reading are largely set before high school is a truth parents and teachers would do well to ponder. The number of citizens who believe 100 per cent what they read about education in national magazines and hastily whipped together popular books without ever checking their local school systems for the truth of general statements is astounding. I am a little weary of people who read nothing more than the daily newspaper, a popular magazine, or a trade journal, complaining that nobody in the public schools can read. When the public begins to realize that as many or more of the reading problems from which the schools are now suffering come to school with the children, we may be able to solve more of our school reading problems. Emotional problems, lack of attention, overcrowded classrooms, overstimulated children, and the willingness to hire mediocre teachers account for many of our reading problems. Let's talk it over together in Chapter Six to our mutual benefit.

The same thing is happening in the field of reading as in listening: the sensational and the exaggerated are claiming the eye as well as the ear of the citizenry. I suppose that condition has always pertained to a degree, but the propaganda to which a young person is subjected in a single day is truly frightening. It is doubly dangerous these days to believe all that one reads. Half-truths masquerade as truths, and pictures whisper insinuations that the text might not dare carry.

What is more dangerous is that half-truths distort the picture of what is going on in the world. Unless Americans learn to read thoughtfully about their international problems before they become international crises, they can hardly back the right moves in the UN or vote for the right people. We must teach our children to read between the lines. —

I'm positive that there are better ways to get children interested in thoughtful reading about world problems than we are now using. Better educational television and more movies of actual conditions may be the answer, but I believe that our reading problems go deeper than visual aids. Good old family discussions around the family dining table would help, but that would interfere with each individual's favorite television program and that would never do. Maybe a much wider reading of current magazines, especially by the highly intelligent in our classrooms, followed by a directed conversation on the subject would kindle a real afterschool interest in world happenings. Perhaps we need to add still another class to our daily schedule—but we can't get in the ones we have—so . . .

Oh, there's a great deal of thought and analysis that must be done by both parents and educators in the reading field. Chapter Six, pages 191–215, may help you to a clearer picture of reading in the whole mosaic of the language arts. Let's think it through together—it's our problem.

—to write creatively

The thesis of this book is that creative imagination is the chief tool of a closely-knit world. Men cannot live well together in one world until they learn how to "walk in one another's shoes." They must not only know facts about each other but must learn to crawl into each other's hearts and get the feel of one another's problems. Cold bare facts change few men's opinions and attitudes; true empathy comes only to those who *go and see* or *see and feel* through the eyes of imagination.

Partly from an awakening sense of world responsibility and even more from the fear of a communist-dominated world, America is sharing money and technical experience with countries, many of which we taxpayers cannot readily locate on a map. Such abstract sharing will hardly get concrete results. There's as much truth as poetry in this quotation from James Russell Lowell's "The Vision of Sir Launfall," on which many of us older ones cut our classical teeth in the eighth grade:

> Who gives himself with his alms feeds three,—
> Himself, his hungering neighbor, and Me.

Dole-giving is not the answer to a need for a democratic world, but sharing may well be. Without creative imagination to help us to know the neighbor we cannot see, there can be no true sharing. As the first Cinemascopes took us into the awful chasms of the Grand Canyon, so must imagination take us into the homes of the poor of India, where personal dignity can abound without sufficient vitamins. Applied imagination can help us to appreciate why an Arab prefers want with freedom to soft living without it. The wings of the creative spirit can penetrate the iron curtain countries and help us to feel the Russian's thirst for knowledge which can hardly be slaked. Creative imagination can surely take our hearts where minds alone cannot penetrate.

This tool of democratic living will not *just happen;* it must be sharpened through use just as any tool of learning is sharpened. Imagination puts a keen edge on all the goals of the language arts. For how can we use words responsibly if our minds do not run ahead to hear them with the ears of those at whom they are directed? What is thinking, pray, but a shuffling of imaginary cards in the air to find the highest trump? What is speaking over the air but sending out, in fancy, carrier pigeons with a message to the world that may never take it in? And listening! What is listening but the constructing of a face and a mind for a voice and the giving of a home to an idea so that the listener can become acquainted with it?

Other than thinking, writing is the most imaginative of the arts of communication. In order to write intelligently, one must write imaginatively. To write an intelligent letter, for instance, one must visualize the person he is writing to, whether he knows him or not. Both notes and letters are imaginary conversations between two friends or acquaintances. If one writes imaginatively, he will rarely offend; if he thinks of his written conversation as a one-way process, he may, because of his unawareness, handle his friendship with clumsy hands. It is this imaginative quality that makes a good letter writer; a person whose writing is just talking written down is a natural writer.

Our children will probably use these on-paper conversations more than our generation has. More and more young people will be scattered over the face of the earth—in the armies, in Point Four programs, in industry and trade as well as in diplomatic circles. Natural, imaginative letters can bring home and stability to sons or daughters a world away, and young people who learn to project their personalities onto paper will be the ones to hold the interest of fiancées or friends across the sea.

Business letters, probably the worst examples of unimaginative writing unless it is government pamphlets, could be doubled in effectiveness if only the writers would conjure up real persons to write to, imagining their possible answers and reactions to the writer's sales talks. A generation that will do business with the whole world will need to write imaginative business letters. These businessmen and women of the future are in our schoolrooms right now. They will need to learn more about imaginative writing than they can learn by filling in blanks in a workbook.

What about the writing of stories and poems? Should they be attempted by anyone but the gifted?

Approximately 50,000 children listen to my creative writing program, "Let's Write," over the Wisconsin School of the Air out of the University of Wisconsin at Madison. For six years Wisconsin's elementary school children in grades four to eight have been writing creatively, following my weekly broadcast of fifteen to eighteen minutes. The best efforts of the children are sent in. This book is full of their writing, which, I believe, speaks for itself. As a result of weekly creative writing lessons, ordinary children are improving in vocabulary, in imaginative ideas, in sentence structure, in picturesque speech, and in generally good writing habits. Furthermore, more children every year are getting excited about writing, and those who get really enriched by writing will have enriched their generation. Incidentally, I learn more from what these children write than they probably learn from me.

At least once each week brings a letter from a teacher with a "chuckler" in it. Here is one that came from a fifth-grade teacher near Madison:

I was afraid at the beginning of the year the group would be unimaginative and **dull** but with your help they're starting to perk.

After "Columbus Secundus" [a program about being the first man to reach another planet] maybe my own desire for forceful words really paid off. This is a line from Louis's discovery of a new planet: " . . . off with one hell of a roar."

The funniest one I ever got isn't very nice. A teacher enclosed this gem written by a fourth-grade rural child, who truly loved her teacher:

My teacher is pretty with white curly hair that always looks just so. She wears glasses with pretty sets in the rims, and nylon stockings and wedgie shoes. She has beautiful brown eyes, just the color of manure.

(Forgive me, please, for putting this one in, but it was too humorous *not* to mention.)

If you wish some of my enthusiasm about writing as well as some helpful ideas to rub off on you, get acquainted with Chapter Seven, page 227, on the writing of poetry, Chapter Eight, page 275, on story writing, Chapter Nine, page 319, on practical writing, and Chapter Ten, page 389, on letter and note writing.

Learning to write imaginatively will pay real dividends in this coming era of creative imagination, will pay in everything from foreign policy to a thank-you note.

—to use mechanics powerfully

Do you teachers feel discouraged about children and mechanics? I believe every elementary teacher is frustrated by the modern child's shrugging off whatever he sees no sense in—punctuation, spelling, indenting, and the like.

We parents and teachers do not always realize how intensely practical the modern youngster is; he just doesn't believe in doing anything in which he sees no benefit.

I used to feel the same way about mechanics. I once told my sixth-grade teacher that I thought it was dull and uninteresting to spell a word the same way every time and was promptly slapped across the mouth for my opinion.

It seems to me that it is our salesmanship that is lacking in this area, not our teaching of mechanics.

My personal opinion is that we teach old things in an old way rather than old things in a new way. I have never seen children resent the teaching of punctuation marks as the traffic signs of the reading road: a period is a full stop; a comma, slow; a semicolon, bridge out; an exclamation, danger; a question mark, road which way?

As a child begins his first reading, teach him that the punctuation directs exactly how the story writer wishes his story to be read. A child who gets his punctuation first through reading will have little trouble with punctuation in writing.

Chapter Eleven of this book, page 443, should help you teachers convince children that the mechanics of writing equip our meanings with safety devices, thus ensuring speedy understanding.

One must speak to a generation in its own language.

—to regard good English respectfully

One of two things is bound to happen to English in the United States: either the speech of the people will improve, or slouchy English will become the accepted speech. The people, not the dictionary-makers, determine finally the English standards of a country. I do not believe that the American people will allow their speech standards to drop to the level heard on every bus and street corner: "I seen," "My aunt, she," "I done it," "I sez to him," and "I laid down and slept."

Speech patterns are set at home before the child comes to school. There are many reasons for poor speech at home: carry-overs from speech patterns in a foreign language, parents exposed every day to inaccurate speech during their working hours, genuine ignorance of what correct speech patterns are, personal carelessness that carries over to speech, and the poor speech patterns of many classroom teachers.

A person's speech patterns begin with him; he need not retain the inaccuracies to which he was born. A parent soon finds that he cannot change the family's speech through nagging but through adopting better speech patterns for himself and expecting better speech from his children.

Teachers cannot change the faulty speech of youngsters by embarrassing them in front of their contemporaries or peers. Speech patterns are changed only when pride in correct speech is generated in a child's heart.

Both the home and the school have a part in improving the speech of America. Let us think together how each of us can do our part in giving America's citizens a real respect for good English.

—to acquaint children with the best

Remember, in the definition at the beginning of this chapter, we suggested that the language arts were the impression and expression of ideas in words. Of these two divisions, I have a feeling we parents and teachers are working harder to develop the *expression* than the *impression.* Let us think about this together.

— I believe that most of us would concede that what we live in our hearts every day we become. Certainly, almost everyone wants the best for his children, but we differ so in what we mean by the best. What *do* we mean by the best? Is it the best books to read? Is it the best music, the best people to associate with, the best paintings to look at, the best plays to enjoy?

Did you ever make an inventory of every hour of your day for a week's time? How much of that time was spent with the above-named Best's?

You and I are so busy making a living that we often forget the Best's. If children spend as little time with the high and the beautiful as we adults do, how will they put away in their hearts' storehouses golden coins for the day when they have little time for the Best's? Truly none of us can live on a high plane all the time; life tends more to tablelands than peaks, but what will happen to those who have no mountain peaks in their childhood? I wonder and wonder. I like to ponder on Lionel Stevenson's "In a Desert Town."

> We have a mountain at the end of our street,
> Changing from day to day;
> Sometimes it is prim and distant and neat,
> Vestured in sober gray.
>
> Sunset bewitches it to drift and glow
> Like a castle with opal walls;
> Winter transfigures its cliffs with snow
> Into spell-bound waterfalls.
>
> We have a mountain at the end of our street
> Where other towns have a church,
> Promising refuge from the clamor and heat
> Like the goal of a weary search.
>
> .   .   .   .
>
> Certain that beauty is lingering to greet
> Our homecoming from any place,
> Having a mountain at the end of our street
> We do not lack for grace.[7]

[7] Reprinted by permission of the author.

I have a feeling that there is much that schools and homes can do to put mountains in the minds of our children. They must not always wander on the flat plains of second-rate television shows and in the Death Valleys of cheap magazines.

And now we have outlined and discussed briefly some possible goals for the language arts course in the elementary schools. Four realizations, I am sure, have come out of this brief overview:

1. Parents and teachers must have the same goals if they are to teach the language arts effectively to elementary children.

2. The language arts no longer belong in one single class; they are a part of the whole school program.

3. The language arts deal with ideas: their impression and expression in words.

4. Although a text can help us with ideas and methods, the real language arts book for elementary children lies in their particular needs in their environment and in the times in which they live.

Slow, slow,
Mind tendril grow
Toward what we need
To what we know

Read,
Heed,
Listen,
Learn,
Ponder,
Wander,
Think,
Yearn,
Choose,
Spurn,
Use.

Slow, slow,
Mind tendril grow,
Yet we never know
Never ever know.

CHAPTER TWO

Words Make the Difference

1st First Grader: Our preprimers are sure a mess of little words.

2nd First Grader: You really can't blame 'em; they forget we were born in the space age.

They cross on the ether now.
They travel on high frequencies
Over the border-lines and barriers
Of mountain ranges and oceans.
When shall we all speak the same language?
And do we want to have all the same language?
Are we learning a few great signs and passwords? [1]

Carl Sandburg

WHAT PEACE MEANS TO THE PEOPLE OF MILWAUKEE

I am a Jewish girl and we, the Jewish people, have a word for peace, too. It is "shalom." It means hello and goodbye and peace. Not just the Jewish people know what peace means but all of us do. It means freedom and friendship. If all of us were like a big family, our America would be a greater one. Love one another and keep it up.

Diane Cohen, Grade 4

[1] From *The People, Yes* by Carl Sandburg, copyright, 1936, by Harcourt, Brace and Company, Inc.

An imaginative child can look at a globe and see a world, a world of history and geography and ideas, but few children can conjure up the world of words without the help of a teacher.

The world of words, like the globe, shows broad continents of conversation, occasional peaks of poetry, sunny meadows of thought, sharp chasms of conflict, and almost unexplored oceans of understanding. A child looking at the world of words sees only language lessons. Words are his world, but all he sees is a more-or-less isolated blueprint of a lesson in a book or a number of alien spaces to fill, willy-nilly, with words not of his own choosing.

Many an elementary teacher, curdled with curriculum changing, sees little more than the drudgery of coaxing casual commas to heel; the military task of putting capital letters in charge of straggling ideas; the mummery of "Read like talking now," or the useless "You forgot the rule here."

Words are our worlds, but we see them as dead symbols, not creatures of breath and blood, and thus keep them forever flattened on a page when they were meant to rise up with wings.

To give children, through their teachers, a more personal vision of the world of words is the purpose of this book.

Words Are Voices and Lips

The arts have forever been the voice of the people in a world of many voices. We look at the paintings of any age, and they speak to each in his own tongue. We look at the vast machines of modern times, translating clumsy pig iron into flowing steel, and catch new rhythms of living.

All the arts of man speak, but the language arts—thinking, speaking, listening, reading, and writing—are at once the voice and the lips of all art, thus doubly important to our lives. We listen; we read; we think; our tendrils stretch out and take in. A thousand rivulets of sensation feed the rivers of our experience and flow out again through the broad fields of speaking and writing. No wonder the language arts are sometimes called the arts of understanding; they interpret the world to us and us to the world.

Words Are Powder and Peace

Words are both our war and our peace. I learned not long ago that the same Alfred Nobel both invented commercial dynamite and established the Nobel Peace Prize; in fact, he used the proceeds of the one to finance the other. War and peace, too, have a common source. Words can explode into bombs that destroy the world or into friendships that bring it together. Words have ever been superior to gunpowder as a weapon and a tool. A simple "Where have you been?" turns from peace to powder with a change in inflection. The phrase "husband-stealer" said in a playful voice is a peace word, but said in malice is a deadly weapon to a woman. A mere change in the voice, a look in the eyes, and the turn of a phrase change peace words to powder words.

Words written are so much more volatile than words spoken. The moment words stiffen into permanence with no facial and bodily expressions to clarify and extend their meaning, the quicker they trigger. Have you ever made the most innocent, offhand remark in a letter (innocent in intent, that is) and found it set off a whole circuit of family feudings?

Indeed, there is nothing safe about words; they are the most explosive things in the world. Of course, this is because our words are our thoughts, and our thoughts, like our breaths, become visible when warm friendliness meets a cool reception. When our thoughts snarl, we speak snarl words, and we have so many of them; but so often when we think peace thoughts, we have so few peace words, and while we search for them the moment for words passes and is gone. Indeed, we must get more peace words ready for more peace thoughts. As Sandburg says:

So long as we speak the same language and never understand each other,
So long as the spirals of our words snarl and interlock
And clutch each other with the irreckonable gutterals,
Well . . .[2]

The rest of this book lies unsaid in that word "Well . . ."

Since our words are only the labels that our thoughts bear and that presumably tell people whether our thoughts passed the Pure Thoughts and Drugs Act of the Highest Congress, perhaps we teachers had better do even more to help children get inner peace

[2] From *Good Morning, America,* copyright, 1928, 1955, by Carl Sandburg. Reprinted by permission of Harcourt, Brace and Company, Inc.

than to worry about the words they say. For when we think Grand-Canyon thoughts, we cannot speak Death-Valley words, and when our thoughts go down as deep as the earth's middle, we can hardly rattle off dry-gully words.

How much time do you and your pupils spend every day, teacher, living together with the high and beautiful in the schoolroom? Oh, I know it isn't in the curriculum—so many minutes to spend every day at 11:15 thinking only high thoughts, but many children never get any higher than the grocery list at home or the price of a new high-priced low-priced car. Somebody has to see that these children have a chance to have some sky ideas to think about when prices go spiraling up and income goes slithering down. Even if we get to the moon pretty soon, little men are still going to have big problems, and there's nothing so good for problems as a little sky thinking. Yet how can men think sky thoughts without sky words? Oh, we'd better hurry, teachers. It's getting later all the time.

Words Have Many Lives outside the Dictionary

The dictionary, that "Who's Who of Words," cannot keep up with the connotations words gather as they age. Take the word "curriculum," for example; it used to be as innocuous as orangeade. Now teachers, hearing it, remember the bone-deep weariness of still another afterschool meeting and the unread and unready discussions that live on long after they die, whereupon many teachers, when the word is mentioned, develop definite symptoms of curriculum allergy: goals before the eyes, a slight nausea, a curving of the fingers of both hands, accompanied by a violent desire to choke somebody (the curriculum co-ordinator, preferably). In fact, I hear M.D.'s will soon be working on a new educational antihistamine designed to keep teachers on curriculum committees from developing hives. Probably better than an antihistamine, though, would be a serum developed from the blood of Ph.D.'s; they've lived through so many dull meetings that they no longer get excited about anything.

In the elementary grades teachers usually have more trouble with good taste in words than they have with word connotations. It is hard for a young child to realize that some words are for use in the living room and that others should never leave the privacy of the bathroom; that some words should go to parties and others should always stay at home. If the same standards of suitability were always used at home as are acceptable outside, children's boners would cause fewer red ears. I have an honest conviction that home should be a place where members of a family can "let down their hair"— even with words. Besides, such "company" standards at home would cheat us all of many healthy chuckles, and chuckles help to make better homes and us to be better people. Paying too much attention to good taste in words often makes a child's writing anemic. Personally, I think fifth-grade Judy's poem entitled "With a Thump and a Bump" is enhanced rather than weakened by the use of the good old Norwegian "rumpe," though the English version should seldom, if ever, go to parties, my mother explained to me long ago, and Webster definitely restricts it to the rear end of an animal.

With a Thump and a Bump

I don't know how to slide,
On skates, I can't glide.
If I try I go down with a thump and a bump
I get a sore rump.

I am not a quitter,
But when I try again I'm a sitter,
Because I fall with a thump and a bump
And get a sore rump.

Judy, Grade 5

I note with laughter that Webster's third definition for Judy's word is "fag end," and just isn't it, teachers, by Friday night after a hard week!

Yes, indeed, words have many lives outside the dictionary, and some of them are more delightful than those within. It is a warming thought that one can get more out of a dictionary than Mr. Webster ever dreamed of putting in—or did he?

The Right Word Is a Deep Satisfaction

Mark Twain once pointed out, "The difference between the right word and the almost right word is the difference between lightning and the lightning bug."

How can we help our children to experience the real satisfaction in the finding of the right word—the word that when it settles into a sentence, immediately makes it whole? To a lover of words, the finding of that right word is a barbaric joy, a sensuous, personal excitement that can hardly be described.

The situation here is analogous to the experience of the elderly minister instructing a class of ten-year-olds in catechism.

"What is the first step to the forgiveness of sin?" he asked, expecting a routine answer.

For a minute there was a bumpy silence. Finally one intrepid youngster burst out, "Well, first you gotta sin!"

Exactly and reversely! If we would teach children to find joy in the right word, we must first lead them to love words—in the small boy's pattern, "First you gotta love!"—and may I add, "First the teacher's gotta love." Many an elementary teacher remembers her college English classes as being less medical than surgical (explained by one small boy to another with this question: "Were you sick when you came, or did they make you sick after you got here?").

Getting children to love words without hating English and school in general (along with the teacher) is a delicate aspect of curriculum surgery. Language arts teachers have used the red-pencil scalpel for years, and too many of the patients have died in the chair or have never wakened from the anesthetic.

I believe in neither "catechismic" nor cataclysmic methods in the teaching of the language arts during the first six years of a school child's life: in death neither by rote nor by scalpel, but rather by a gradual association with the best, a child becomes easy in English.

One of our fourth-grade "Let's Writers" two years ago, in writing an evaluation of what he liked about the program, said, "Why, we don't have to be just *mad* any more. We've learned new words, and now we can be *angry, frustrated, irritated,* or *furious.*"

Yes, it's truly wonderful to have the right words to be mad in, and still more wonderful to have the exact words for the measuring of our delights.

"Speak," says Sandburg, "choosing your words, sir, like an old woman over a bushel of apples."[3] Carl Sandburg speaks a whole book in every sentence he writes. What might he be telling teachers about the right word as well as about the choosing of apples?

It is just possible that, in translating apple-choosing into word-choosing, he might say something like this: Only the word-experienced are adept at word-choosing; the nonexperienced will buy the

[3] From *Smoke and Steel* by Carl Sandburg, copyright, 1920, by Harcourt, Brace and Company, Inc.; renewed by Carl Sandburg. Reprinted by permission of the publishers.

best advertised words or whichever words are out on the counter at the time he needs words. Everybody doesn't like the same varieties of words, and a few have no feeling for them at all; we teachers must provide a wide choice of words for all kinds of people. No coercion, please, and advertising must be as subtle as the perfume of winter apples in the fall.

As old ladies, a bit arthritic in the knees, will choose apples oftener if the basket is kept in the utility room than in the basement, so a child with mind-points a little stiff as yet from unuse will sooner choose his words from any easier place than a dictionary. Only the apple-hungry go to the basement, and only the word-lover or the teacher-driven goes to the dictionary. It seldom takes seven years of living with word-lovers before a child becomes a word-lover; *one* year is enough if the lover is lover enough.

Excuse me, Mr. Sandburg, for explaining to these teachers what you may have meant by your one sentence about apples and words. You see, Mr. Sandburg, it is hard for many teachers to translate apples into English, since they have no apples in their background. Besides, many elementary teachers with a good English background know very little about children, and many others well trained in child growth and development are not very "easy in English," so there you are, Mr. Sandburg.

My weekly radio program "Let's Write," one of the University of Wisconsin's many FM classes for elementary school children over the Wisconsin School of the Air, is dedicated to the right word for the right child at the right moment. Several hundred papers come in every week from children in grades four to eight for whom the program is prepared. Each program has three parts: a discussion period to interest children in writing and to tie the program to their experience, oral reading of prose excerpts and poems that stimulate thought and attune the ear to rhythmic writing, and teaching a few words that might enrich the thinking and writing for the day.

The teachers report, and the children's papers reaffirm, that the use of picture words and strong verbs and nouns has more than doubled during the six years the program has been on the air. Many of the teachers send in notes on the papers telling how a child has improved in word power. A fifth-grade teacher rejoiced when Gerald, with whom she had been working for months without a spark, called his story about rabbit-hunting "He Got Away" and wrote that the rabbit he had scared "dashed out like a football player."

I am convinced that almost every school child has the power to "grow" a true enjoyment of words. Radio and television programs can spark and foster such a love, but only the teacher and the parent can create the climate wherein children grow in the discriminative use of words.

If the climate of the room is such that correctness is paramount to discovery and exploration in word use, a teacher or parent will kill the very thing for which he seeks. A wise adult welcomes a child's using a new word even if it is misused or misspelled or both. Handle the misuse of a word as carefully as you would handle a touchy parent at a conference. (Thank goodness, most of the parents are more at ease at conferences than the teachers!)

Fifth-grade Jim (B.I.L.—before I learned) once remarked to me that he was never going to use any big words again for me in a piece of writing. Of course, I inquired why, as he had intended that I should. "Because when I try long ones," he said firmly, "they're apt to be spelled wrong, and you mark them out in red. It's cheaper to use small ones for you and spell them right." (Who was it said a few pages back that teachers killed children's English efforts with the red-pencil scalpel? I should know; I've left many corpses behind me in the English room at the educational morgue, and the weapon I used was a red pencil.)

I have even said to a child (B.I.L.), "Oh, but there is no such word as that!" What if fifth-grade Judy's teacher had stopped her from using this lovely word "wondery," which she coined in her reverent little heart?

> Once I saw a snowflake,
> Moving slow as slow can be.
> When I caught him with my hand,
> He looked at me with wondery.
>
> I wondered why he stared at me,
> So I asked him gently,
> "Why do you always stare at me?"
> Again he looked with wondery.

Judy, Grade 5

(Forgive us our sins, O Lord.)

In the early stages of any sort of teaching, climate is far more important than excellence. Until the child takes the goals of the teacher as his own, the teaching of anything must be coupled with the feeling of accomplishment rather than defeat lest the only lesson learned is despair. I think sometimes that our teachers are too narrowly educated. I wonder if any teacher should be trained to teach one age group only. If each teacher recognized the growth patterns of *all* children, we would not defeat our own ends by using secondary methods in primary school and primary methods in secondary. Mistakes that are natural in the growing patterns of young children may be actually stupid in the training of intermediate and junior high school young people. A teacher who puts more emphasis on the spelling and the correct use of words than on the joy of discovering them may find that she has taught more distaste than love of words.

Besides, what would we markers-of-papers do if there were no mistakes on the papers to give us an occasional laugh? I chuckle to remember a former eighth-grade pupil of mine, who while studying "The Legend of Sleepy Hollow" was required to look up the word *coquette* in reference to the plump Katrina. He confused the word with *croquette* and came up with "a coquette is a meat ball." I have often wondered if the lad were ahead of his time. I had a summer school student in a workshop a few years ago, who, when she wrote an evaluation of the shop saying that my lectures "added greatly to her infirmation," may have unwittingly spoken the sentiments of the whole class! Another student reported via her weekly theme that her boy friend took her "for granite." After I wrote on her paper, "Why be so hard on him?" she laughingly told me that she had heard that phrase incorrectly all her life.

The most hilarious mistake I ever knew of a student's making was the one told me by an English professor at a small college. In a short story about a minister's wife who had received a great scare, a freshman confused the words *prostrate* with *prostitute* and wrote: "The woman lay prostitute upon the floor." Whereupon the professor wrote in the margin of the student's paper, "Was this woman temporarily or permanently fallen?" (Score one for the professor that time, say I.)

Yes, there's no doubt about it, the wrong word is sometimes the right word—for a chuckle. On and on throughout the total school years, taste in the use of words keeps building, through constant association with the best: stopping to discuss a challenging word discovered in the reading; a wonderful paint-mixing period before any creative writing is done by a group; a frank discussion of words that should be invited to parties and those that should stay at home; frequent half-hours spent discussing the fascinating biographies of words and how their meanings have changed with the years; [4] getting together every week for a family reunion of words with a common stem; and, oh yes, finding in social studies class the chief words that have found their way into English from lands across the sea and the source of which the thoughtful Noah Webster jotted down for us in the dictionary.

Since words make all the difference, children should meet them in such pleasant ways that they will welcome new words as new worlds. From many words to the right word is a natural step, especially if the primary teacher has, from the first, helped children to go back over their first story charts to find together better ways of saying what they want to say.

From class-searching to self-searching for better words should be the normal growth pattern, and those who have a natural love of words will, of course, find the right word soonest. Even very young children who live in homes where words are important begin early this search for the right word. A less than three-year-old child of my acquaintance was down on his hands and knees watching the kitten lap up her milk. "The kitten is wrapping up the milk," he commented; then he frowned, "No, that's wrong, it's 'lapping,'" he added, but here he bent down again to watch that busy pink tongue. "She's really wrapping it, you know," he said gravely, and of course, he was right.

How much one respects the child seeking the right word to say what is in his heart!

A third-grade child, among a group of rural children visiting our local children's library, impressed with what seemed to him an immense number of books, said gravely to the head librarian as he left, "*Wonderful* isn't a good enough word for a place like this!" How often our deepest feelings defy finding that right word.

— Parents are the best English teachers. Even when their teaching is wrong, it is almost impossible to change the learnings. What one learns at home sticks—and just won't unstick.

Sixth-grade Neil may not have his mechanics of writing correct as yet, but he has reached for the right words in his poem and found them. If he gets the right words first, a child can easily be led into proper mechanics. Only when there are no ideas on a page and no right words to express them need an English teacher despair.

[4] On word origins see the following books: For teachers—Wilfred Funk, *Word Origins and Their Romantic Stories* (Funk, 1950); for children—Margaret Ernst, *Words; English Roots and How They Grew* (Revised 1954) and *More about Words* (1951) (Knopf); J. Newton Friend, *Words: Tricks and Traditions* (Scribner's, 1957).

My Garden

My garden is so gorgeous
With its sun-bloomed roses.
Its rain-drenched daffodils.
The hail-hammerd violets
Have almost lost there purplenes.
My flowers are like gems to Me.
My sister thinks they are the epitomy.

Neil, Grade 6

To one who is a friend to words, a right word is one of the most personal satisfactions in life. (Thank God, a feeling for words can be learned, and so can be taught!) ✓

Specific Words Are Terrific Words

Sandburg warns, "Be careful of abstractions: they become bright moths." [5] Yes, your facts may fly away and tempt your meanings to follow them unless you learn to fasten down your facts with specific words: action words that act, picture words that picture, nouns that name; grammar in action—that's all good writing and talking is, each word doing the job it was meant to do and being cast out if another word can do it better. (There luckily is no union protection for inept words.)

Action Words That Act

Let's notice sixth-grade Eileen's four lines spelled as she spelled them.

My Dog

He slops up his food,
Then pleads for more,
He cleans out his dish,
But dirtys the floor.

Eileen, Grade 6

[5] From *Complete Poems*, copyright, 1950, by Carl Sandburg. Reprinted by permission of Harcourt, Brace and Company, Inc.

Four magnificent lines and four specific verbs—*slops, pleads, cleans, dirties.* Eileen, you can write; yet all some teachers would see on your page would be that one misspelled word and the one unnecessary adverb, which isn't really so unnecessary, after all.

Fifth-grade Carl may not be elegant, but he is certainly effective; he not only uses specific verbs, but he has learned the cartoonist's trick of slight exaggeration:

My dog is a large husky muscular dog. He is full of pep. Usually he isn't fussy about what person's leg he chews off. He loves to steal hats. Then he rips and tears them to shreds. Also he likes to mangle things. When he eats he doesn't fool around . . . He just slobbers it down.

Carl, Grade 5

Strong specific verbs intrigue even a young child if a teacher will introduce the two. Children like strong specific directions, too; they do not appreciate subtleties either in direction or language. Praise and display on bulletin boards will bring out a veritable rash of specific verbs on the written papers. These are typical:

The caterpillar *curlycues* up a tree.

The cold wind *whistles* and rudely *talks*.
While *swaying* the trees like old cornstalks.

Earthworms are *stranded* in the rain.

Caw-Caw, my pet crow, is as black as Halloween. When I am walking in our woods, Caw-Caw *comes diving down* like a bolt of lightning. All of a sudden he *pulls up* and *scoots* into space; then he *will dive down* and sit in front of me and say "Caw-Caw" laughingly.

One can hardly think of specific verbs without chuckling over this conversation from *The People, Yes.*

"Yesterday," said the college boy home on vacation, "we autoed to the country club, golfed till dark, bridged a while, and autoed home."
"Yesterday," said the father, "I muled to the cornfield and gee-hawed till sundown, then I suppered till dark, piped till nine, bedsteaded till five, breakfasted and went muling again." [6]

[6] From *The People, Yes* by Carl Sandburg, copyright, 1936, by Harcourt, Brace and Company, Inc.

When we laugh, we are beginning to understand. Yes, specific verbs are terrific verbs.

How can you get your children to use action words that act? Begin in kindergarten to notice actions, actions in stories read, actions in pictures, live actions especially: a fat puppy waddling down the street, a squirrel spiraling a tree, a baby choosing his steps, an uneasy leaf trying to balance itself in the air. The six steps of teaching specific verbs to any age of school child are:

1. Observe the action.
2. Decide together the word that exactly says the action.
3. Write the word.
4. Act out the word.
5. Record the word in a personal list.
6. Use the word as often as you can. (If you do, the children will.)

In the schoolroom, on the playground, at home, and on the street, we live in the middle of an animated dictionary and know it not.

Picture Words That Picture and Nouns That Name

Teach your school children the value of a quick word picture of the person or thing he is describing. I found these in the papers of intermediate pupils:

My calf, Arlene, is a piece of bread with a few spots of butter.

My golden colored leaf (my dog) is a cocker spaniel with freckles on his nose.

My cat looks like a marigold cluster.

My dog licks me in a Morse code all his own.

A caterpillar is like a regiment of soldiers marching along—its head is strongly ordering its feet to get in step. [I love that "strongly ordering."]

My calf, Taffy, has her tail a-flying like a flag in the morning sun.

The brown leaves are little shoes walking away.

Why tell a child to use fresh new expressions instead of clichés? He won't know what you are talking about. All expressions seem fresh and new to a child because he is fresh and new himself. Besides, many children are doing well to include even one word picture in their writing; we teachers forget that writing and speaking are expressions of *self* and what is a cliché for one child is the top step to another.

How can teachers get children to think, talk, and write in word pictures? It is easy enough if the kindergarten teacher starts and the skills develop with the children. Chapters Five and Seven are alive with practical ways of accomplishing this important part of every child's education. One sentence of "how" is sufficient for this introductory chapter: Whatever you wish children to use and appreciate, let him live with every day. Our appreciations are only the loves we have lived with and listened to. What a teacher would encourage, he makes popular through praise, posting, and a positive approach—be it words or wars.

Picture words that picture, nouns that name, action words that act—grammar in action; truly specific words are terrific words.

"Which Word?" asks Rachel Salisbury, then answers her questions in words that should be required reading for every American.

> Words make all the difference—
>   words written and read,
>   words spoken and listened to.
>
> From the vacuum tubes of an electronic age
>   words flow in hypnotic rhythm:
>   they tumble and ooze,
>   they tinkle and boom.
> From the gaping mouths of gluttonous presses
>   they spew in continuous flow:
>   captives in ink, inert and mute,
>   words of fear—words of faith,
>   they wait to be resurrected
>   a moment or an eternity hence.
> From the glittering marquees of industry and amusement
>   they stab in neon brilliance
>   deep into the long-remembering subconscious:
>   they coax and wheedle,
>   they lure with curved, exotic line,
>   they tempt with the prospect of profit,
>   they promise and promise and promise!

From platform and pulpit
    in rolling cadence or power-packed phrase
    words reach for the minds and hearts of men:
        sincere, seductive,
        fervent, feeble,
    they fill us with doubt and hope,
    they stir us to thought and action.

Words fill our waking hours.
We surfeit in verbal abundance.

With today's words, the destinies of nations are forged.
Words slink through the smoke
        of political anterooms,
    they breed in the dust
        on the cluttered desks of bureaucracy
    they ring on the resounding anvils
        of statesmen's tongues,
    they march in dignified ranks
        through the echoing corridors of diplomacy.
The word today is a fighting word,
    newly inducted into the strange war of ideologies,
    fighting on every world frontier:
        holding closed ranks in the councils of the mighty,
        spying in obscure dens of intrigue,
        revolving Janus-faced in the treaty chambers,
    by distortion, enslaving the unwary and the innocent,
    by suppression, terrifying the faceless, voiceless peoples.
Day by day, word by word, the battle line advances
    and retreats
        and advances again.

The Word that is The Lie
    is in a death struggle with
The Word that is The Truth.
Words make all the difference—
    words written and read,
    words spoken and listened to.[7]

Yes, "Words make all the difference—words written and read;
words spoken and listened to"; yet the child and the teacher and the
man on the street go about their daily business as if words were as
harmless as exploded shells, handling them as carelessly as if they

[7] From *Current Thinking and Writing*, Third Series, by Joseph M. Bachelor,
Ralph L. Henry and Rachel Salisbury. Copyright © 1956, Appleton-Century-
Crofts, Inc.

had not the power to break hearts or create enmities or to make desert lives bloom with joy. We daily hear college graduates overworking a few man-of-all-work words when a dozen experts are theirs at almost no cost in time or energy. Should one pick dandelions for his silver bowl when he could have roses, roses that can bloom any month in the year?

PROPER TIME [8]

Touch a word lightly.
Ever and ever,
nurture it fondly.
Hurry it never.

Let it come slowly.
Find what is needed
after a living
language is seeded,

after the patient
bountiful sowing;
see in the morning
all that is growing:

leaves that were hidden,
green in the shower;
words as awake as
the crowing hour.

Joseph Joel Keith

Should there be safety rules for weapons and not for deadly words? Shall we English-speaking people allow the beauty of our lyrical language to be lost to our children because we just don't care?

Words make all the difference—
words written and read,
words spoken and listened to.

[8] By permission of the author and *The Christian Science Monitor*.

CUPBOARD OF IDEAS for Chapter Two

Words Make the Difference ❖ ❖ ❖ ❖ ❖ ❖ ❖ ❖ ❖ ❖ ❖ ❖ ❖ ❖

Pretty Miss Hubbard
Went to her school cupboard
Some fresh teaching aids to locate,
Though her cupboard was bare,
She found ones more rare
In the cupboard of M. Applegate.

Primary Shelf

Word Folders (Advanced Gr. 1–3)

Keep folders of words that a child might want to use in writing a story. Call one folder "Fun at a Picnic." On one side of the folder, paste a picture of a group of children or a family having fun at a picnic. On the opposite side print a dozen or so picnic words usual to your community.

Other folder titles might be "I Went to the Zoo," "At the Circus," "My Visit to a Farm," "I Visited Toyland," "I Have Fun with My Grandfather," or "My Dog, Spot." These folders are indispensable for children who delight in using new words. Many teachers use similar folders with each word illustrated but no big pictures, labeling them, for instance, "Farm Words," then allowing the children to use the words either in a story or in sentences.

Play It and Say It (Kdgn.)

Have children dramatize various actions noticed on the way to school; after watching, the class chooses the word that best describes the action. Kindergarten children love this game.

Fruit Basket (Advanced Gr. 1–2)

Give each child a piece of manuscript paper with a picture of a fruit they know pasted in one corner. Put on the board words to describe the looks, the smell, the feel, and the taste of fruits generally. After explaining the words, ask the children to write about their fruit in as many sentences as they can.

Looks	Feel	Smell	Taste
yellow	smooth	delicious	sweet
round	bumpy	sweet	sour
red	cool	winy	bitter
like a ball	rough	mellow	spicy
like spears for hair	waxy	tangy	
	like leather		

Weather Rhymes

Put a rhyme on the board each morning in the weather corner:

> This is an umbrella day—
> I'm *afraid* that we can't go out to play.

Or

> The snow this morning *splishes* and *sploshes*
> I hope you children all wore galoshes.

Stop to look at and talk about the word you have chosen for that morning; bring it alive to the children. If you can't rhyme, perhaps the teacher across the hall can, or perhaps your poem books can help you.

Action Words

On a corner of the board, write an action word that you observed in the hall or on the playground during the day: *dribbling* a ball, *echoing* back, *shuffling* along, and so on.

Hard-to-Remember Words

Make up games for hard-to-remember words.

1. Make word cards for *where, what, when, why,* and *how,* and arrange them on the chalk tray. Each child asks a question of another who, as he answers, takes the proper beginning word from the chalk tray.

2. Fasten a blue triangle of construction paper at one end of a thread and a red triangle at the other. Slip the thread through a large bobby pin taped to the board. In demonstrating the words *up* and *down,* have the pupil state his actions as he chooses the right word from the chalk tray: "I pulled the blue one up"; or "the red one is down."

3. Make control charts of the words that many children fail to remember.

4. Picture every outstanding vocabulary word discovered in a unit of study. Words before the children's eyes become words in the children's minds.

On-the-Spot Vocabulary

Even in kindergarten stop any time of day to bounce lovely rhymes or get a word for any exciting happening: "The puppy *pled* to stay." "John looked so *astonished* when he fell down." "The principal looked *stern* as she told us about sliding in the street." "The leaves are sliding down the *banisters* of the wind."

After a story is finished, talk together about the wonderful words in it. Try to use them sometime during the day.

Make a list of Halloween words, Easter words, and so on.

Intermediate and Upper-Grade Shelf

Translating Pictures into Words

Give each group of three to five students a color scene from your picture file. Let each group try to say in words exactly what the picture said with color or form. This is a real challenge and popular with up-and-coming groups.

Use picture post cards of a group of states. Allow the children to work alone or in pairs to make one good sentence summarizing and describing the pictured scene. From a good group you will get such sentences as "Ouray, Colorado, viewed from the air resembles a handful of marbles in a giant's pocket." "Ouray, Colorado, is at the bottom of a well of mountains."

If your children are "lean" in words, why not work on the same cards using an opaque projector so that everyone can see? Another day reverse the process and let the class paint pictures to match their own descriptive paragraphs.

Similarly have children translate action pictures into action sentences—it's fun. Once a year many magazines have a cover literally filled with small definite actions. This makes a wonderful exercise.

Color Dictionaries

Have children work in groups to find exact words for the shades and hues in any color area, illustrating each color with a square of cloth, paper, or water color. These color dictionaries are of great help in making general descriptions specific.

Hobby Verbs

When the class studies verbs, have each person choose a hobby he is interested in and see how many verbs he can list that he uses in working at his hobby. This is only a beginning of the list one might make for *camping: motoring* to the spot, *hiking, locating* the camp site, *setting* up the tent, *fishing, finding* worms, *baiting* a hook, fish *tugging* at a line, *nibbling* bait, *scared* of noises at night.

Dictionaries of Hobbies and Occupations

Let each child gather vocabulary words used in connection with his hobby, such as stamp collecting, 4-H, tennis, gardening, farming, and so on, defining and illustrating each.

As the class studies foreign countries or states of the United States, do the same for occupations: the vocabulary of creameries, air-conditioning plants, paper mills; names of tools, machines, processes, workers. The results are simply fascinating. Advertising booklets and encyclopedias can be used as source books.

Area Words

As each state or country is studied, keep a class list of words indigenous to that area as to scenery, geography, weather, industries, and so forth. The North Central states might have dairying, rounded hills, rolling land, wide fertile valleys, silos. A good summary is to give each student three or four of the words gathered and have him write each into a descriptive sentence.

Vocabularies of Vocations

In like manner have each student keep a list of every word that has anything to do with his present choice of vocation, listing them under the three headings: *nouns, verbs,* and *adjectives.*

What Else Can You Call It?

Children in the early intermediate grades have trouble using a variety of synonyms for their overworked nouns. In writing a paragraph about an elephant, show that it may be referred to as *he, him, this huge beast, this great lumbering creature, the pachyderm, animal,* and *beast.* For John: *he, him, boy, lad, little fellow.* This sort of word choice must be made together in class several times before a teacher can expect results from the child alone.

A Dictionary of Towns and Cities

As a word project, write to the mayor, town chairman, or village president of communities in your state with peculiar names, and try to trace down where the names came from and compile them in a book. This is a fascinating project.

Word Histories

Using the source books listed on page 33, let committees find the stories behind favorite words or phrases that have to do with sports, food, music, business, the boudoir, emotions, houses, garden, animals, war, science, and so on. (No intermediate teacher can afford not to keep Wilfred Funk's *Word Origins* on his desk at all times.)

April Fool Ads

Children love to search for antonyms. Pass out enough clothing ads so that each has one with a few interesting words such as intriguing, luxurious, and glamorous underlined. Let each use the dictionary to find antonyms of the underlined words and then rewrite the ads humorously using the antonyms—April Fool style.

Vacation Ads

Resort advertisements in the Sunday papers make wonderful word study materials on Mondays. Make notebook lists of words that beckon, words that lure, words that frighten, color words.

Tell-a-Television

Post words that intrigue your children on television programs, discussing and characterizing each as to usefulness for them.

Meanings within Meanings

Children are unaware that synonyms cannot be used interchangeably. On a dictionary discovery day, give intermediate students such a simple word as *foam* to look up. Add to their findings synonyms listed in *Webster's Dictionary of Synonyms*. (This book should also be on every teacher's desk.) You may end with this list:

1. *foam*   liquid topping having small bubbles
2. *scum*   film that comes on top of liquids
3. *spume*   liquid from agitated water
4. *froth*   both foam and frills
5. *lather and suds*   soapy foam

In junior high school try such a word as *follower* and discover that each synonym has a slightly different meaning:

adherent   believer in ideas and doctrines such as democracy and communism

disciple   master-follower relationship as in the case of Jesus, Plato, Ghandi, and Mohammed

henchman   subservient follower of a political boss

satellite   a follower deeply devoted to a person (small boy a satellite of an older one)

If the words studied are current, they become twice as potent. Connotations are hard for any but the brightest to discover by themselves. Keep one spot on the board for words students ask about; then assign them to word scouts to trace down in extra time.

Getting Words for Specific Ideas before Writing Time

1. Do buildings talk to you? Have you noticed any like these on some of your walks?

A house that resembles an old tramp in the sun
A new barn bursting with hay and pride
A white church tiptoeing toward a hilltop
A tiny doghouse for an oversized dog
A tumble-down house hesitating at the edge of a cliff

What do they say? Today in writing time have pupils describe a building that to them seems to be alive. In order to help them to a better choice of words, give this exercise a day or two ahead of time: Use the dictionary to find the meaning of the following words and phrases: weathered, shingles, sagging ridgepole, dangling eaves spouts, flapping shutters, warped floors, cracked ceilings, mildewed walls, dilapidated porch, and knock-kneed fences.

You might list together words for some of the expressions houses seem to wear: sheepish, exultant, cowering, discouraged, joyful, secretive, menacing, surprised. Before the children write, work with synonyms for the general word "talk." Review ways to achieve good characterizations. Use imagery; use adjective comparisons, but don't string adjectives together like beads; use a few good ones. Let the conversation and actions characterize.

Mechanics. List and learn to spell all the vocabulary words that belong with houses: doorsills, beams, rafters, gables, garret, attic, basement, foundation, louvers, dormers, ridgepole, and the like.

2. So often the picture windows in houses frame ugly pictures. But this golden autumn day we're after beauty. We're going to use the two portable windows nature gave us and frame our own lovely fall pictures.

In the park, on the farm, in the woods, from a hill, perhaps only in a snapshot in our memory book, there is one golden spot just the size to see with one look through our portable eye-windows. Today we're going to learn to describe the nature pictures we see almost daily.

Get out your mental paintboxes. What color words we're going to use today! Vermilion, bronze, scarlet, and living gold! What action words we will have to find in order to express how the clouds travel across the sky and how the trees climb up the hill. What verbs we'll need to describe how bushes huddle in clumps or get their heads together in thickets. This truly will be a word-learning day when colorful vocabulary will fill our lines with dancing gaiety.

3. Go down far into the water on an exploring trip. Examine that quiet world of magic down under. Think of the colors you'd see there: lapis lazuli, jade green, topaz, and violent orange.

Think of words to describe the way the water weeds sway in the current. Think of the little comedies and tragedies taking place on the theater stage of that silent, intense world. Think of the fish that will be gliding around in the water in slow motion. Before writing time, help the students with the vocabulary of each of these "thinks." There are so many kinds of vocabulary to work on, probably you'd better begin several days ahead.

What would the life of the creatures be? Would there be families doing the things that families do on the ground? What kind of games might the "children" play? Would the children have the same problems down there that we have?

Mechanics. Work on short, phrase-like sentences to match the wave lengths of water ripples.

4. As you listen today to the lullabies, think of a lullaby you'd like to write: perhaps a mountain's lullaby to the hills at its feet, perhaps the soft voice of the snow covering the sleeping flowers to keep them warm. Perhaps you will write a lullaby to a baby animal —a little chipmunk, for instance; or even one to a tired child who has been naughty during the day.

Lullabies need soft words. Lullabies tiptoe in soft words. Work together on lists of sleep-producing words: hush, lull, quiet, soothe, sleep, relax, feathers, billowy, comfort, soft. Because of the soporific effect, lullabies require a quiet form of verse, slow-moving and regular in form. Read such poems to your pupils and listen together for the steady flow of the rhythm.

In writing lullabies, try to think of the child you are singing to. What words would quiet him? What ideas would comfort him? Is there a specific pattern or rhythm that begs to be used?

Later this year some of you will want to write lullabies for babies of different countries as you get acquainted with the home life of the people.

This is December 12. What a privilege to work today on a lullaby to the Infant Jesus! Why not study in reading the outstanding lullabies you can find together with pictures of the Madonnas? Our songbook has several in it this year.

CHAPTER THREE

Thinking Makes Sense

Teacher (in year 2000): Will the class in remedial thinking please orbit?

Our problem for today is this: What would have been the probable result to civilization if the inhabitants of the world had learned about "inner" space before they tackled "outer"?

THE DINOSAUR [1]

Behold the mighty dinosaur
Famous in prehistoric lore,
Not only for his weight and length
But for his intellectual strength.
You will observe by these remains
The creature has two sets of brains—
One on his head (the usual place),
The other at his spinal base.
Thus he could reason "a priori"
As well as a "a posteriori."
No problem bothered him a bit:
He made both head and tail of it.
So wise he was, so wise and solemn
Each thought filled just a spinal column.
If one brain found the pressure strong
It passed a few ideas along;
If something slipped his forward mind
'Twas rescued by the one behind.
And if in error he was caught
He had a saving afterthought,
As he thought twice before he spoke
He had no judgments to revoke;
For he could think without congestion,
Upon both sides of every question.

Bert Leston Taylor

Sometimes I wonder,
When I slumber.
Why eggs hatch,
In a patch.
My mother says, "Natch."

Susie Isensee, Grade 4

[1] By permission of *The Chicago Tribune.*

NATURE'S HELICOPTER

I wonder how a hummingbird
Can hover in the air,
And flap his wings with all his might
And not go anywhere?

Tim Tillotson, Grade 5

I don't want to think, Grandmother, I'm allergic to thinking," a first grader recently told his schoolteacher grandmother.

"Allergic to thinking! John, what do you mean?" his grandmother exclaimed.

"Why, Grandmother, don't you know what allergic means?" the little sharpie demanded. "It means that you're sick to something. Some people are sick to bananas and some are sick to raisins. I'm sick to thinking."

Mrs. D——'s six-year-old grandchild seems to have hit on a national allergy. As an eighth grader of mine once said, "I never think unless I have to—it's so much easier to be told what to do." Yes, and there's always one of us parents or teachers around, glad to oblige at this telling-what-to-do-business; we're born bosses, we adults.

Of course, thinking *is* dangerous—dangerous to a safe, undisturbed type of home and schoolroom. If we allow children to think for themselves in one area, they'll pop up with original ideas in areas we believe belong exclusively to us.

And some areas do belong to us—that's been the trouble; we parents and teachers, in our efforts to be democratic, have handed over most of the prerogatives of our departments to the children. A democratic government does not operate in this way; each department has its own exclusive rights and privileges and others that each citizen may share. There is definitely more to democracy than voting, though one wouldn't realize that fact from observing homes and schoolrooms where the children run everything but themselves.

To tell the truth, voting is one of the few democratic procedures that the government postpones until citizens grow old enough to think for themselves. But a voting citizen who has had no choosing in his background is in a sorry way.

I chuckle to remember an episode that happened in a first-grade room in North Carolina. The children were having fun with a stray cat that had wandered into their classroom when one of the boys asked the teacher if the cat were a boy or a girl. The teacher, not wishing to get into that aspect of the case, turned the remark aside lightly, but the boy persisted. "I know how to find out!" he declared.

The teacher gave up. "How?" she asked curiously.

"We'll vote on it," the lad suggested gravely.

Besides being genuinely funny, that story has a terrific impact. Are you allowing your children to vote in areas beyond their experience? Unless children learn how to choose when they are young, they will not be ready to vote when they are technically ready for voting. Young children, however, are rarely ready to make choices except within a parent's or teacher's framework.

What do we mean by that statement? The wording of parents' questions narrows the field of answers and saves unnecessary quibbling. Notice the difference between the latitude allowed in these two questions asked of children on a rainy day. "Which would you rather play, Squirrel and the Nut or Button, Button?" "What do you want to play today?" Or this one: "Which shall we do this evening, watch television or ask the Joneses over?" "What shall we do this evening?"

Even very young children can choose within a framework set up by their parents or teachers. But a broad "What are you ordering for lunch?" is sure to elicit the most expensive, indigestible item on the menu, as any parent will affirm, while a narrower "Would you prefer a hamburger or a hot beef sandwich?" can save on wear and tear in a public place. Allowing a young child no choices at all, even within a framework, is worse than too much leeway.

I discovered just such an interesting situation last year in a first grade. Eva had a distinct case of negativism. She had been refused so many of her simple requests at home and had been bossed so much without ever being consulted that any request at school, however gentle, was met with a definite "No." No, she wouldn't come to class. No, she wouldn't do her reading seatwork.

Eva's teacher was wise. "You may have a choice, Eva," she said firmly; "either choose to come to class and learn to read like the other boys and girls, or stay at your seat and not learn how to read."

After a week of open rebellion with no commotion or nobody's apparent caring whether she came to class or not, Eva chose to learn to read and has been choosing to learn ever since. By spring, the stubborn lines around the child's mouth had eased away, and Eva was a good helper.

It pays to allow little children to make many simple choices within a framework set up by adults. Nothing is more dishonest, however, than asking a child to choose, then compelling him to keep on choosing until he chooses what the adult had already chosen for him. Thinking itself is a series of choices and a discarding of each as one finds it unworthy or impractical. Long before preschool children can think for themselves, they can think through problems orally with their parents.

Let us say a three-year-old has played with his brother's model airplane without permission and broken it. This is a serious offense and must not be passed over lightly.

"Let's think this through together," the mother of the three-year-old says to her small son. "Let's face it; you've taken someone else's toy without permission—and that's bad; you've broken it—and that's worse. Now it's up to you to figure out what *you* [not *we*] can do to make things as right as they can now be. I'm going to put you in your bedroom alone to think quietly about how you can make peace with your brother. It was you who did the wrong and you who will have to try to make it right. Right now both you and I are upset. While you're in your bedroom, we will both settle down; there's no use trying to think when we're upset."

Three-year-old will, of course, not want to be alone, and he may, during his isolation, think about everything else but the wrong he has done, but he will have been exposed to the first steps in thinking a problem through:

1. Face your problem squarely.

2. Realize that it is the doer of the wrong who is responsible for his own actions.

After an isolation period of ten minutes or so, mother and child are ready for the next step: thinking through together the various steps in attempting to right a wrong.

"There are two ways to handle this situation," mother points out to three-year-old; "either you can be a cheat and hide the toy you've broken and wait until your brother finds out about it and gets angry. Or you can tell your brother what you have done and that you're sorry. Which would be right to do?"

If three-year-old doesn't commit himself, mother might ask quietly, "If your brother broke one of your toys, which would you rather he did to you?"

Three-year-old can usually be guided to the right decision, but there is still another step: suggesting to him that he take money out of his bank to give to his brother for a new airplane. If the parent furnishes the money, three-year-old may fail to feel any remorse whatsoever. Who cares if a parent has to pay out money? A child should learn before he starts to school that he must take the responsibility for his own acts. —

Learning to think through a problem with a preschool child, then, allows the parents and child to (a) face the problem squarely; (b) think through the problem in isolation, trying to make plans about what can be done to make it right; (c) talk over the various means of meeting the problem, guiding the child to make what seems to be the best decision for him.

Three-year-olds, in many cases, may be too young to really think, but few of them are too young to be introduced to the thinking process. Notice how many right attitudes a young child is exposed to in this thinking-aloud process:

1. There should be a quiet time before decisions.

2. People cannot think when they are angry or upset.

3. One must always think of the other fellow's point of view.

4. The one who does the wrong is the one who is responsible for attempting to right it.

5. A person usually feels better when he does the right thing.

How can one be a successful adult in this complicated society of ours without such attitudes? Our attitudes come as a result of experiencing, not from being lectured to.

Learning to think is a long, slow process begun in the home long before the child understands what he is learning. I know of no expenditure of time that pays such dividends of improved behavior as does thinking through a problem with a young child. Most adults tend to underestimate a young child's ability both to think and to draw conclusions.

Betty, a young friend of mine, is distinctly thorny early in the morning. Once when her not-quite-four-year-old son was almost as unpleasant as his mother, she told him that it would be well to pack his bag and find a family he could get along with, since he didn't seem to like living with his own. A few mornings later, Betty was at her worst. Nothing any of the members of the family did was right. Finally, her son looked at her firmly and remarked with an innocent expression, "Mommy, I think you'd better pack up your bag and go hunt a family who wants a cross Mommy. We don't need one here."

Touché!

The steps in thinking through behavior problems with older children at home and at school differ in only one particular from those used with preschool youngsters: one does not have to suggest possible courses of action; the child can usually think of them for himself. Children who learn to think along with an adult learn the techniques by which they can later approach and conquer their own problems.

A young primary teacher said to me recently, "I find myself automatically making decisions for the children that they probably should make for themselves. But teacher-pupil planning is so slow, and there's so much to do in one day!"

Perhaps we can answer Miss Adams' problem in this way: "Decide ahead of time which decisions belong in your department and which belong to the children. Be sure that the children recognize the difference between rights and privileges, between your area and theirs." In planning a trip to the post office, for instance, the arrangements, except perhaps for the initial ones, are in the hands of the class and the teacher planning together, but *more* in the teacher's hands. The safety precautions on the way, the walking formations, or the bus regulations will also be arrived at together as will the children's planned questions. Their actual behavior and good manners on the trip are of the children's doing until they show the teacher they cannot operate successfully under the standards they have decided upon together. I think it is well for children to understand that when their discipline of the group breaks down, the teacher takes over with no arguments.

If evaluation by the children under the direction of the teacher takes place after all major group actions, children eventually learn to think better. Every school child has the right to know just where his privileges end and his responsibilities begin. When there is unsureness about such matters, and when boundary lines between "teacher's" and "ours" change from day to day, a child would be a mouse not to gamble on the chance that this is the teacher's *soft* day and to operate accordingly.

Many misbehavior problems are the direct result of the lack of road markers, the "Good fences make good neighbours" policy.[2]

We can probably clarify Miss Adams' perplexities by suggesting that most questions of thinking things through in a primary room

[2] From *Complete Poems of Robert Frost*, "Mending Wall." Copyright, 1930, 1949, by Henry Holt and Company, Inc. Copyright, 1936, by Robert Frost. By permission of the publishers.

lie within a teacher's framework. But it must be clear to every child in the room just what he is privileged to do. Most children can be brought to see the justice of rules and regulations if they have had a part in making them.

Probably the most misunderstood idea in the field of child management concerns rules in the home and at school. When people live together, there is certainly always the need of rules. But the modern child feels about superimposed rules that he has no part in making as the early colonists felt about British taxes, that "Taxation without representation is tyranny."

The first plank, then, in the smooth governing of home or schoolroom is *to make the rules of government together with the children involved.* Let us consider together one such instance worked out carefully by a thoughtful mother of four lively children.

It was spring and the youngsters—six, eight, twelve, and fourteen, respectively—were tramping mud onto the kitchen and living-room floors at a great rate. The mother felt that she was having to redouble her housework, while at the same time she was the only one not contributing to the cause. Accordingly, a notice on the family blackboard called a meeting to be held immediately after dinner in the living room. (Anyone in this particular family who felt he had a grievance on a matter of importance had the right to call a family meeting.)

At the meeting, the mother stated her grievance and asked the family for suggestions. The following were proposed by various members of the family:

1. That each member of the family must wear rubbers in muddy weather.

2. That the offenders should do the cleaning for the week.

3. That offenders' allowances be docked for infractions.

4. That offenders lose privileges.

After a vigorous discussion, it was voted to adopt suggestion 4, and if conditions failed to improve from this democratic procedure, the mother reserved the right to put suggestion 2 into action.

The family members did take greater care after that, but guess who had to be disciplined by the group—the father and the fourteen-year-old.

Group discipline is fairly effective at home and at school if the group members make their rules and their evaluations together and if the adults in charge reserve the right to take over if group discipline breaks down. Parents and teachers must remember, however, that individual misbehavior is a personal matter and must not be decided by the group only, but by the offender and his adult guide together.

The second plank in the smooth governing of home or school-room is *to use every opportunity to teach children to think through problems.* A good primary teacher uses every opportunity at hand to get her children to think through not only behavior problems but problems the children bring to school from home and the street. Such questions as estimating distances, weight, and height take thinking and comparison, so the teacher thinks aloud with her brood as to how one goes about figuring out an estimate. "How much does Johnnie in the next room weigh?" is the query. In their own room they weigh Charles, who seems most nearly to approximate Johnnie's weight. Instead of wild guessing, the teacher leads the children to estimate and arrive at approximate answers.

Such questions, however, sometimes bring as many chuckles as information. I recall the story of the teacher who, in connection with a story she was reading to her second grade, was trying to get her children to estimate distance and time.

She asked each child how far he thought he lived from school and how long it took him to get home from school at night. She couldn't help smiling at one little boy's answer.

"I must live pretty close," he said seriously, "because when I get home, my mother always says, 'Good grief, are you home already?' "

Outside of teaching children to read, one of the most valuable attitudes a primary teacher or young parent can develop in a child is this: "I have a problem. What are the several ways I can solve it? Which answer is the best?"

A young couple of my acquaintance had a timid child in first grade whom a bully from second grade met every night on the way home from school and knocked down. The parents and the child Jimmy talked the matter over and thought through these possible solutions. (Of course, they had to do most of the actual thinking, but they included the child in their planning.)

1. The mother could come to school to get the child each night. (Discarded, since the other children would certainly think the child was a sissy if his mother had to escort him home.)

2. Jimmy should tell the teacher of the second-grade boy. (Discarded, because the teacher had neither the authority nor the time to look after the children on the way home from school. Besides, two teachers were involved here.)

3. The father should teach Jimmy how to fight so that he could scare the bully away. (Discarded as impractical, since one boy was so much bigger and stronger than the other.)

4. This seemed to be more a school than a home matter, so Jimmy asked the principal for a conference and explained his difficulty; the principal talked to the second-grade boy, and that was the end of that. The principal became interested in the second-grade lad, however, and gave him jobs, and the lad gradually got over trying to bully younger children.

This method of settlement was handled by the child as much as possible and through the channels best suited to this particular case. Jimmy learned a great deal about how to take care of himself and what procedures to take when in trouble. In fact, both boys were helped, Jimmy not least of all by the parent-child planning that brought a solution that worked.

The effectiveness of guiding children to think depends on skill in asking questions. A question that implies the answer is of no help in teaching children to think, and yet how often do we phrase our questions so that the answer is implicit in the question?

Does this picture show how cotton is made? (What parts of the cotton-making process are shown in the picture?)

Did this film strip tell us that Indians have a long house? (Explain how the woods Indians used the long house and compare it to a cafeteria as we know it.)

In leading children to think, phrase your questions in such a way that a child will have to think in order to answer them. Thought-provoking questions must be carefully worded.

1. List and explain the reasons for the climate of England.

2. How do the United States and Russia compare in regard to shipping opportunities?

3. In what ways are England and United States alike? In what ways different?

4. Why is the number of farm workers in the United States decreasing? Explain.

5. Prove, if you can, that a longer noon hour would be beneficial to the pupils of Webster School.

6. List the reasons for and against holding our school picnic in Myrick Park. Be ready to vote at ten minutes to four.

7. Think through this statement: Every American should vote, or his right to vote should be taken away from him.

8. How would you evaluate the truth of this statement? We are all born free and equal.

9. Look for the fallacy in this statement: Everyone should do what he thinks is right.

10. How would you go about finding out whether or not water is heavier than air?

Guidance in thinking not only requires skillful questioning; it also requires time enough in which to think of the answers. No wonder only the children with the quickest minds answer our thought questions. A slow-geared mind is not necessarily a poor mind. Many slow, deliberate children are fine thinkers, but we hurl questions at a class at such a rapid pace that only the fast are geared to answer. Thought questions must be either mimeographed or written on the board far enough ahead so that all children have time to answer them. Many children with good minds are more visual- than auditory-minded and have a harder time grasping spoken questions than written. It is wise to write questions for class discussion of policy on the board early in the day, but have the discussion during a later period. To think things through takes time. I believe that we have been gearing our questions too much toward mediocrity but slanting our time toward the brighter children.

Just how does a teacher guide children to think—in the social studies, for instance? Both the questions and the answers are right there in the text, and it is surprising how one can earn a fairly good grade in the social studies without doing much actual thinking. No, the reading and the regurgitating to the teacher of the contents of a single text do not necessitate using the thinking process at all, but they can. Many of the faults laid to a textbook are often due to a teacher's lack of understanding of the purpose of the book he is using. Even a manual cannot tell a teacher exactly how to teach. A manual is to a teacher what a medical treatise is to a doctor. It acquaints him with his subject, but he must act as the middle man between new material and his own patients. Because many manuals attempt to explain every breath the teacher draws, many primary teachers have become mere direction-followers who fail to shake well the manual mixture with common sense and a knowledge of his own pupils, before using. If the colleges want prescription teachers, they must not train direction-followers. The surest way to get teachers not to think is to prescribe conformity with too minute directions. Minds not used are easily lulled into sleep, and I for one do not want to trust children to trained automatons. Many

teachers confuse the purposeless memorization of facts with the conclusions drawn through setting up questions and answering them.

Notice the difference in the plans of these two teachers: the first a
student teacher groping her way toward teaching, the second a
master teacher; both were introducing a unit of study on Russia to
a sixth-grade social studies class.

The first teacher—let's call her Miss A.—began with Russian
names in the news, and the meanings of Russian terms, such as
communist and *soviet*. After considerable conjecture and discussion, Miss A., eliciting her questions by the tweezer process (what
else do you want to know?), asked the children what they would
like to find out about Russia; the children, used to the formula
from other unit studies, dutifully piled up a list of topics they knew
they had to study anyway.

The second teacher, Miss B., had an entirely different approach.
Across a great bulletin board this lone question challenged the students: *What baffles you about Russia?*

On different tables in the room were piles of pictures and post
cards, a scrapbook of newspaper clippings about Russia, a stack of
magazines, a number of books arranged temptingly as well as a few
maps, a globe, and encyclopedias.

First, the teacher cleared the meaning of the word *baffles*. A
group of students was assigned to each table with this injunction:
"Read and examine as many of the materials at your table as you
can in twenty minutes. This is a thinking time for each of you;
work alone but as a sharing member of a group as far as materials
are concerned. As you read and look, jot down questions about
Russia that baffle you, that you don't understand, or that you wonder about. When the bell rings, get ready to share your individual
thinking with that of the class."

In group discussion time, the children came up with these questions they wondered about:

1. Is Russia really going to make war on the United States?

2. How did Russia get so advanced in science all at once that she got
ahead of the United States? How much ahead is she?

3. What are the Russian people really like? Are they interested in
the things we are? Are they warlike, or is it just their leaders?

4. Actually how big is Russia in comparison with the United States?

5. How come there's the Iron Curtain and just how iron is it? Some
people get in.

6. I found in a book that most Russians are not communists. How
come? I thought they all were.

7. What does communism mean? In what ways is it different from our government?

8. Just how held down are the Russians? Can they still be sent to Siberia? Are there really secret police to spy on you all the time?

9. I want to know—do women work at men's work in Russia? Don't they wear nice clothes or lipstick or anything?

10. Why did Mikoyan come to America? Should we have treated him so "good"?

11. I want to know what does communism do for people—common, ordinary people?

12. How can Russians say that they are democratic? They're always saying that.

13. What I wonder about is, is there an underground in Russia, and will they revolt?

14. I read that communism is against God. Don't Russians have any religion?

15. The Russians don't keep their promises. Is that because they have no religion?

16. If Russian schools are not democratic, how come they have good scientists?

Whenever the questions stopped flowing, the teacher read a news article, discussed a picture, or spoke of a happening, and the flow began again.

When the time was nearly up, the teacher made this assignment for the next day: "Tomorrow at eight-thirty, I'll hand you each a copy of these questions that you have made about Russia. Look them over carefully before class if possible, and add to them. In what other ways is Russia an enigma to you? (Here she put the word *enigma* on the board and explained it.) In class we are going to reword these questions and organize them into topics. We want to get some order to our questions so we can get some order to our study. Some of you always have extra time. After your other assignments are done, browse through this material on Russia arranged on the tables, add to your questions, and begin to reword and reorganize them. Someday we hope that the United States and Russia, different as they are, will be living at peace with each other. Russia can be a friend or an enemy, but in either case we must *know* Russia."

Let us analyze together why the second teacher got a better brand of thinking from her planning than the first.

1. She stimulated the children to ask questions through pictures, through having them examine magazine articles, newspaper

clippings, maps, and books. She didn't expect thought-rockets to be launched without launching platforms.

~ 2. She so worded her main problem that it intrigued the class: "What baffles you about Russia?" How different that question is from "What do you want to know about Russia?" One question draws the particulars; the other, general information.

A teacher gets just about the type of thinking his questions ask for. This means that a teacher who wants to get all the children thinking must do much of his thinking ahead of time. What thinking had this teacher done before class started to provide for individual differences?

~ 1. Miss B. assigned the poorest readers to pictured material and the best readers to books and difficult magazine articles. She did not ask for volunteers for different tables; such a procedure is upsetting both to children and to a teacher's plan. This part of the planning is a teacher's prerogative, not the children's. Choices come later in the unit when children are well launched into the material. (Besides if children are always allowed to pursue only what they enjoy doing most, they are scarcely ready for reality. Imagine that procedure taking place in the average office, factory, or school system!) A twinkly-eyed old school superintendent once said about a new teacher, "That woman gets into such tangles being democratic that she's always having to turn policeman to quell the riot caused by badly organized democracy."

2. Miss B. informed me that she had chosen an advanced group of children to help her locate the materials on the tables, and that oftentimes such a group did all the gathering without direction from her. She said, also, that sometimes such a committee rewords the questions and organizes them so that the children will not become bored with the same routine unit after unit.

~ (The teacher who thinks through the preplanning of a unit of work in terms of the several abilities of her children avoids considerable time waste.)

How Can a Teacher Stimulate Children to Think?

Miss B. used a challenging, over-all problem encompassing her entire unit: pictures, current magazine articles, newspaper clippings, book and article displays, and thought-provoking questions.

She pointed out to me that later in the unit or in subsequent units of work she planned to use these further thought-stimulating experiences:

Being Map Detectives

The climate, the trade, the crops, the progressiveness and temperament of the people, the size of the cities can each be approximated from map study before the text is even consulted.

"Here is a country approximately in the same latitude as Wisconsin. On studying the map, what conditions would you think could change its industries and its farming habits from being like ours?"

"You've been looking at this physical map of _____. Can you see any reason for this country's backwardness?"

Delving into the secrets of maps together will give individual children an entirely different point of view on what facts we can get from maps if we are willing to do a bit of thinking. I have heard teachers call such exercises "Sleuthing through Asia," "Sherlock Holmes at Work in South America," "Whatsit?" "Howsit?" and "Whysit?"

From a map study to text study to see how right our conjectures are is the next natural step, of course, to map sleuthing.

Educational Films

Miss B. says that she uses educational films in three ways:
  — 1. To launch a unit of study
  — 2. To enliven the halfway sag in a unit of study
  — 3. To summarize facts learned
She pointed out that she prefers the first two uses of classroom films; since children like them especially well, films are equally good as thought-provokers or mid-unit stimulators.

The modern child is restless and highly stimulated; we cannot hold his interest with flat teaching. Films animate information and stir the child to thinking. Visual aids do to a modern's thinking what books did when they were a scarce commodity and can still do if they are dramatically written. To interest a child, school must at least be as interesting as home.

Most of the educational value of films is lost by the teacher who shows them without previewing and giving the children directives of what to look for, directives worded so that the student will have to think as he looks.

Turning a class loose on a film without preparation and definite directions usually produces about the same results as would a woman's directing her husband to the supermarket with this suggestion: "Oh, just buy anything that looks good to you."

And the sad part of this story is that the teacher who gives the loose directions is the one who will criticize loud and long the resultant lack of learning. Educational films can be one of the most potent tools of thinking in the hands of the thinking teacher, but just another wasted half-hour to the teacher who does everything but think.

Film Strips

Film strips are the answer to the teacher's request for material at the interest level of her children but beyond their reading level. Film strips are not mere entertainment, but concentrated, animated information hard to come by in book form. To children at all grade levels, film strips introduce ideas, clarify concepts, introduce vocabulary, picture facts, promote thinking, and summarize learnings.

But all film strips will not do, and are not meant to do, all these jobs; a film strip must be chosen with the teacher's purpose in mind. If the film strip suggests questions and answers them, an astute teacher, in order to get the children to think, will gather from them their ideas before they read the answers on the film strip. If he realizes that a concept the film strip teaches is beyond the mental grasp of most of the children, a teacher will, of course, bring the explanation down to their level of understanding. For a teacher to attempt to use a film strip without previewing it is as risky as buying supplies before one estimates how much room he has in the freezer.

Is it ever good sense for the teacher to read a film strip to a class? What do you think? If the pictures in the strip are necessary to the understanding of the children, this might occasionally be necessary, but it seems hardly worth the time and effort to darken a room for showing a film strip as a mere listening lesson. Better, in my opinion, to use less condensed material for listening lessons. What use to look for outstanding points in material that is in itself little more than bare facts? Know your educational tools, know your children, and know your purpose—these three *know's* would save dozens of hours of educational time. My pioneer grandmother used to put it this way: "Don't use an ax if a hatchet will do." Know your educational tools: your books, your workbooks, your visual aids, and most important of all, know yourself.

Bulletin Boards

School bulletin boards can sell ideas as well as any expensive advertising caption on a billboard. Imagine the impact on thinking that would come from such challenges as these:

Grade 1   **We Grow Up All Over**
                        (illustrated with pictures)

(girl on scales being   (child reading from   (boy helping
measured and weighed)   a large book)   small child)
  our bodies grow   *our minds grow*   *our actions change*

                        (boys fighting)
                        our judgments change

                How different we were in kindergarten!

Grade 2   **Is Your Home Arithmetic Plus or Minus?**
                (illustrated with stick drawings)

Do you have to be pried out of bed?   Do you do your jobs cheerfully?
Are you a grouch at meals?   Do you ever compliment your parents?
Do you take care of your pet?
Is your mother glad to see you leave for school?
Why?
Do you share TV with the rest of the family?
Is it a major operation to get you to help?

Grade 3   **"There Must Be Magic**
                            Otherwise—"
                        (illustrated with drawings)

Where does water come from?   Where does water go?
                Where do clouds come from?
How does water get on the outside of a cold pitcher in summer?
            How does fog come so quickly?
            How can the sun draw up tons of water?

Grade 4   **Today's Aladdin Doesn't Need a Lamp**
            (illustrated with children's water-color drawings)

        Jet Planes   *Television*
        Electricity   *Penicillin*
                World Communication

Grade 5   **Well People Tend to Be Happy People**
(filled with pictures of people looking happy as they work)

Grade 6   **Science Values Your Body at about $1.00**
What Are You Going to Be Worth to the World?
(This space was left blank for a week, then filled with imaginative stories from the future vocational lives of the children: "An Exciting Episode in My Life as a Pilot," or "A Day with Stewardess Hanley," or "I Saved a Child from the Fire."

When should a teacher plan a bulletin board, and when should the students do the planning?

Since it is the purpose that determines the procedures (a whole teaching course is contained in that sentence), ask yourself the question, "Why am I having this bulletin board? Is it to stimulate thinking in a new area?" Since you are the only one who is aware of your aim at this point, who better than you could make a challenging bulletin board?

Is your purpose to get rid of the mid-unit sag? By now your class must surely be aware of their direction. Why not use the best thinking of a group of up-and-coming students to accomplish this uplift? Lacking those, why couldn't some good performers carry out *your* idea? There is room in the world, too, you know, for good "carry-outers" of others' ideas.

Is your purpose to summarize unit learning? Whose business is it to summarize learnings? Those who have done the learning, of course. The children must, then, work out a good bulletin board to summarize what they have learned in a unit of work.

The purpose of a bulletin board certainly determines who makes it—if any thinking is to go on, that is.

Role-Playing

Have you tried role-playing as a method of getting children to think? Role-playing, because it gets to the mind through the emotions, works faster and deeper than most classroom methods.

What is role-playing? It is that type of creative dramatics in which the players take on the characteristics and problems of members of other groups outside themselves. The purpose of role-playing is to get people to feel the other fellow's point of view.

Let's say that the problem is a local one. Many new pupils have entered your school of late. The present student body is ignoring the newcomers, leaving them alone for the most part so that they feel unwelcome and unwanted.

Either an astute teacher or a local group of students decides measures must be taken. An assembly meeting is planned at which interested students (*a*) pretend to be newcomers and talk over the situation; (*b*) plan a skit bringing out this problem and how the other fellow feels about his treatment, and offering a possible solution; or (*c*) find a story such as "The Hundred Dresses" by Eleanor Estes, in which sixth graders actually meet such a problem, and dramatize the story before the whole group.

Role-playing works best if the problem to be presented is one about which there is considerable emotion, and the players assume the roles of distinct stereotyped characters: the girl who wants to show she's the leader through making others feel inferior; the boy who obviously flaunts the fact that he has money; the girl of good family who is ashamed of the group's action toward the newcomers; the popular girl who is a natural leader, but not snobbish; the boy who feels inferior and curries favor by "yesing" the snobs; and the boy who not long ago was a stranger himself.

Because children can easily assume roles, they will usually get more excited talking for others than if they were talking for themselves. I have not found role-playing of local problems to be effective before fifth grade, but from then on it can influence group thinking more than any method I know. Role-playing is especially effective in feeling the problems of history. The elementary teacher who uses role-playing at intervals gets the children to feel their country's past. Think of what an experience it would be for children to assume the roles of those characters living in the 1700's when the colonies were planning to break away from England: the man who is amazed that colonists would even consider breaking away from the mother country; the fiery patriot who thinks that not to revolt is heresy; the man who inclines toward staying with the colonists, but is afraid to take a stand; the king's spy; the man who wants to send a delegation over to talk to the king; and the man who constantly feels that his property may decrease in value if he joins the rebels.

Role-playing gets children excited about history and helps them to realize that history is going on now. Most important of all, children learn from role-playing that live issues always have at least two sides.

Such current political questions as "What Shall Be Done about Germany?" make excellent subjects for role-playing if the children are well grounded in the facts. Needless to point out, role-playing must always follow a thorough knowledge of the subject, and in the case of historical questions, wide reading on both sides of the question. (See pages 81 and 185 in the Cupboard of Ideas for further role-playing suggestions.)

Educational Television and Radio

What a great day it will be for thinking in our schools when educational television can lend still another dimension to our teaching. But there must be much experimenting before television will be other than a new gimmick to intrigue children.

Much of the experimenting being done, I believe, is in the wrong direction—in vocabulary teaching, for example. Vocabulary can be better taught by a teacher than by a machine, taught more quickly and with more variety in the teaching. Nor am I at all sure that I believe in teaching classical literature with television. One of the delights of reading is the flashing of personal pictures on the inner screen of a reader's mind. Will it stifle creativity to have everybody see the same pictures as he reads? What one gets out of a classic is what he wrests from it singlehanded or gains from class discussions. I'm not at all sure that what television can give to a classic will do for a thinking child what reading a classic could do for him. The pictures will tell the story, but can they put into the secret pockets of children's minds those golden pennies that reading can give? The answer to that question remains to be seen, and I shall be glad to be convinced.

Television, I believe, would be good in a teachers' meeting to teach teachers how to perform experiments in science. But teach science by television? Would the children then have the feeling of finding out that they get with performing experiments for themselves? I doubt it. If finding out through the eyes is what we are after in science, then television can be an expensive way to present scientific facts. If real learning is what we are after, then television will be only a superficial teacher and an expensive one at that.

In the field of social studies, educational films bring other countries alive to us. They acquaint us with our world neighbors as we *must* get acquainted with them in this shrinking world. But television could bring right into our classrooms outstanding personalities from these countries. Until foreign people come into our daily lives, they will hardly come into our hearts.

Television could bring outstanding discussions to the ears of children who need to get a feeling for the other fellow's problems. It seems to me television's greatest contribution is going to be in the humanities where the most thinking needs to be done. Until "live" television can take us to faraway places and people, thus becoming our magic carpet, it must bring the world to the classroom, for children must meet the world if they are to understand other peoples and their problems.

In the field of social studies, television could make historical questions and times real to children through dramatizing them. Many teachers have not the power to teach three-dimensionally. But to make such television shows other than a cheap farce would require talented actors costing mints of money, and the public has a wary eye on the taxes.

I believe that it is in the field of economics and government that television can make a real contribution. Television charts in the hands of a clever teacher could get children to see relationships between forces that are dark secrets to most voting citizens—the myth of higher wages, for example. Yes, television as a means of getting children to think, to reason, to explore needs experimentation.

Perhaps I believe more in the future of television because I have seen what state-controlled radio has done for Wisconsin. For almost thirty years it has gone into schoolrooms and changed teachers and children and whole communities. Its adult programs strengthen and extend those for children. I have seen state radio, with its carefully planned programs and teachers' manuals, be a genuine moving force in Wisconsin's thinking. In fact, it is radio that makes me have faith and hope in the future of television. But both radio and television programs, like educational films, must be prepared for by the teacher. It does little good to set children to listening and looking without definite directions as to what to listen and look for.

Experimenting in the Areas of Science and Health

School experimenting stirs up more questions than a teacher's coming home at two in the morning, and certainly provides more scientific answers. Oversized classes and the fear and unsureness of many elementary teachers in such fields as electricity and chemistry keep the teaching of science in the elementary schools a mere shell of what it might become.

Nothing more suits the modern child's temperament than the study of science. A child's whole life, if it be a natural one, is a series of experiments, a finding out if this is true, if that will work, and what will happen if he mixes this and that. Oh, one can get the answer from an adult or a book in five minutes, but *who wants answers? It is the finding out that intrigues a child*. It is definitely hard, sometimes, to make history alive to children, but science is already alive if a thoughtless or hurried teacher doesn't kill it.

Health—a subject for old ladies (a child thinks) —who's going to be sick anyway? Experiment with white rats or hamsters to find out whether milk is necessary? Whoopee! That's different; that isn't school, that's fun.

Experiment with nicotine on plant life to find out how tobacco affects growth. Experiment with alcohol on animals to determine what happens to a befogged mind. Experimenting will save more modern youngsters than "scare" literature or highway posters. The way to a modern youngster's mind is through experimenting.

Set up experiments to trigger his questions; set up experiments to find out the answers. If science is hard for you, ask help from boys and girls in an upper grade or gifted children in your own grade. Why not get help from experts? You have a group of them in every grade from kindergarten on. For that matter, the modern science books are as foolproof as a Betty Crocker cake mix. An experimenting teacher can hardly fail in his experiments nowadays. You notice I said "hardly fail." It is organization of a large group of young children into experimenting groups, to my mind, that is the hardest thing about teaching science in the elementary school. If you have trouble with organization, ask your principal or the custodian to help. Call on the experienced teacher who is noted for expert organization. (See page 82 in the Cupboard of Ideas for suggestions as to desk arrangements during experiments in science.)

Taking Field Trips

Teachers are still studying about trains from textbooks and pictures with the railroad yards just across town—a rather silly procedure when one stops to analyze it.

Yet many school systems make it as hard as possible for an elementary teacher to take her brood to the real source of knowledge. The more red tape is wrapped around a field trip, the less a teacher is inclined to take one. Many worth-while activities are strangled by red tape. School busses stand empty all day when they could (with written permission from parents) be transporting children to firsthand sources of knowledge.

Try the idea on yourself. Read a pamphlet explaining just how a product is made; then go to visit the factory. Ah, the difference after that trip. Before the trip you imagined and conjectured; afterward, you knew. Like Chicken Little in the old folk tale, "You *saw* it with your eyes, you *heard* it with your ears," and to change the text slightly, "a piece of it got into your head."

Many parents are the chief offenders in condemning field trips. "All nonsense," some say, "to have anything but essentials taught at school."

Essentials? What are essentials? To understand our complex economy is an essential. How your own lives have been extended by television! How much more extensive would that experience have been had you actually gone to the places you visited via the silver screen. A parent should welcome any service that, under the expert supervision of the teacher today, increases his child's experience.

Thinking? A visit to an airport, a railroad yard, a boat dock, a factory, a cannery, an assembly line, or a museum engenders more questions than a locked closet door at Christmas time. Whenever I hear either parents or teachers talking against real experience in favor of vicarious living from books, I could cry out and say, "Your children will someday visit the moon. Will you deny them a trip to the rocket factory?" Are you, like the teacher in Walter de la Mare's poem "The Dunce," going to scold your children for asking "How?" "When?" and "Where?" of life instead of finding the answers in a book? Books should never be a substitute for life; they should be extenders of experience; the places we go to when we cannot have life experiences.

I shall never forget the first time I saw a paper mill and followed the process of converting a live tree into a giant bolt of paper. What thoughts were mine that day! I was older and my thoughts were different from a child's. As I saw the tough wood fiber eaten by acid, pounded and shaken by great beaters, then flooded and washed by literally gallons of water, pressed between heated rollers, then finally emerge a useful product, it wasn't paper I really saw. I could see man—tough, fibrous, resilient man being pounded and beaten into a civilized state by the urgencies of life and finally becoming useful to his fellowman—a cog in a great wheel, losing his identity in the process of service.

Oh, I did a great deal of thinking that day I saw a tree get civilized in a paper mill. And, believe it or not, there was thinking going on in the heads of the children who went with me that day. How do I know? I listened to their questions when they got back to the classroom. But their deepest questions were asked only with the eyes and the changed moods. A firsthand experience with a first-rate teacher is indeed education of the finest kind.

Before we pass on to the next point, may I tell you the best field-trip story I ever heard.

A young third grader with a speech defect had gone on so many field trips that she fairly hated to see the bus arrive. Were these trips not always followed by writing or drawing of some sort or other? Were these trips not weak excuses for reading still more books?

Finally she grew desperate. Upon boarding the bus for still another trip, she whispered loudly to the other children, "Don't wook! If you wook you have to wead, and if you wead, you have to wite. Don't wook!"

When you get through laughing, think of the two very important things in that story for a teacher to think about. Maybe you'll even be sorry you "wead" it.

Expressing Ourselves through the Creative Arts

Many teachers seem to be under the impression that the creative arts promote feeling, but not thinking.

Let us think through a creative writing lesson I tried recently over the Wisconsin School of the Air and, from a few of the papers received, get some data as to whether or not creativity produces thinking.

The name of the program is "The Beat of the Unseen," and is based on the idea that each different sound, like the beat of unseen feet, has its own particular rhythm.

First the children listened to recorded sounds—an evening in the country, birds in the morning, noises at a baseball game—and tried to recognize the sound patterns or musical phrases each suggested. From there, the natural step was to read sound poems in which the music of the lines matched the rhythm of the thoughts expressed: James Tippett's poem "The Sleet Storm," which begins "Tic-tic-tic . . ."; a train poem in which the words rush along the lines as a train beats its way down the track. Illustration after illustration was used to show that a sound poem naturally writes its own tune. Then the children were asked to write either a poem or a paragraph telling about their favorite sound, with the lines beating to the same rhythm as the hidden tune of its song.

Let us examine together several of the results sent in.

TRAIN SOUNDS

The clickety-clack of wheels on the track
Like one-hundred twigs all snapping.
The constant rhythm of clickety-clack
Is music which lulls me to napping.

The clickety-clack of wheels on the track
Rolling along from village to town
Clickety-clack, clickety-clack, clickety-clack
That is the train on the track.

Gregory, Grade 7

ROCK 'N ROLL

That crazy beat of rock 'n roll
Makes my shoes and rubber soles
Go clickety, all around the room
If I haven't got a partner, I'll use a broom.

Sandra, Grade 5

CARNIVAL SOUNDS

The carnival bells are ringing
The merry-go-round is singing
The crowds are cheering
As their favorite animal is nearing.

The horses are rearing up
The pouring of orange pop in a cup
The ferris wheel whirring around
I like all of those sounds.

Tom, Grade 5

SOUNDS

It's a real nice sight
When on Friday night
My father comes up the stairs
When we hear the beat
Of his sturdy feet
We know he is there.

Kenneth, Grade 5

OCEAN WAVES

Down on the sandy and rocky beach,
On a cold and breezy day,
The blue-green ocean waves
Hit against the rocks and seem to say,
"Hi and good-bye, for the wind will blow us away."

Janet, Grade 6

MY NURSES

My nurses are the streams;
They sing me to sleep with their verses;
Washing and caressing the pebbles tenderly;
Twinkling, twinkling softly in the woods;
They seemed to tell me lovingly,
"Sleep, my child and rest."
Flowing, flowing in the woods;
Sometimes they sounded lonesome;
And seemed to say,
"Come and be my companion."
Floating, floating, silently away.

Betty, Grade 5

The Beat of the Unseen

What's that I hear so early in the morn?
Why, it's the whimpering of puppies that have just been born;
Huddling and cuddling closely together,
Why were they born when so cold was the weather?

Quickly, quickly, I got dressed;
To play with the black one, and all of the rest;
Huddling and cuddling closely together,
Why were they born when so cold was the weather?

Christina, Grade 8

Creativity is a translating of experience into another medium—in this case, rhythmic verse. As you read each of these seven pieces of writing, you can almost see the steps that went on: first, the feeling of the various sounds as they were recalled through playing the recordings and reading the poems. Then came a choice as to the favorite sound, the selection of the ideas to be expressed, the fitting of the rhythm to the sound. Almost the same steps would have been traveled to get "The Beat of the Unseen" idea into art or creative music. Feeling may engender creativity, but thinking and experimenting create the final product.

I am convinced that whatever we wish our children to think about, we must get them first to feel, then to express creatively. Especially is this true if the child pretends to be the thing he is writing about; then he truly thinks.

Any expression of a creative art takes thinking—a personal, contemplative type of thinking, the kind every child needs to do in order to grow.

We hear a great deal these days about a returning to the essentials of education in order to get ahead of Russia. The essentials of education can never be returned to; for what were the essentials in one area will probably not be the essentials of the next. A free, growing America must always find its essentials by moving forward. —

Furthermore, may I be so bold as to state that if countries react to being "best" in the same manner as personalities do, then I deeply hope that America may never be first in everything. Human beings who always excel have a way of forgetting how those who do not excel feel, and that is a sad state indeed. It always makes me think of Carl Sandburg's story of the maggots.

Furthermore, I believe that in the things that really matter America is already first. "Ah," but you say, "we must be ready to conquer our adversary in case of a war." In case of a war, is it always the side with the most weapons that wins? Not if I know my history. In the final analysis, people win wars with their heads and their spirits—sometimes even without guns.

I believe that teaching our children to think is an absolute necessity. Too bad that life cannot issue a manual so that we teachers could teach our children to think without having to think ourselves.

Essay Tests

Children who enter high school without having written essay tests are greatly handicapped. Objective tests are excellent for two reasons: they answer the student's question, "How am I doing?" and the teacher's question, "How well am I teaching?" Objective tests are directional tests; they point out to the teacher his next step: reteaching assignment of enrichment material to advanced students, special help for weak students, or group work for students ready to work together. For this reason objective tests should take the form of short daily quizzes or weekly status tests, but not terminal examinations. At a unit's end is a poor time for finding out what the next step should be. An end-of-the-unit test is given for a purpose entirely different from that of an objective test. It is not a checkup but an exercise in organization, a thinking skill highly useful in the modern business and technical world. I have been a bit troubled by the inability of so many college freshmen both to organize or summarize, both skills that children in the elementary school should grow up with and really master before entering high school.

A fifth grade that has completed a unit study of a group of states should be ready for an organizational test based on such thought questions as these:

1. What are the reasons for Wisconsin's developing as a dairy state? Explain each reason.
2. Name the difficulties Kansas has met and conquered as an agricultural state and explain each.
3. Why did the New England states become noted for manufacturing rather than farming? Explain.
4. In what ways are the school problems of Iowa and Mississippi different? Explain.

5. Name five of the largest cities of the United States, listing the reasons for the growth of each and naming the chief product for which each is noted.

It takes thinking to write a good essay test; it always takes thinking to discern a living outline in a body of facts, then to be able to develop that outline again into a summary. There is a tendency among elementary teachers, I believe, to teach for small objective facts rather than to seek for the answers to large inclusive questions. Which is better for a pupil to retain from a unit study, broad sweeping vistas of understanding that come from a study of cause and effect or trivial answers to objective questions that will be forgotten in a year's time?

If history, geography, and science are taught as a series of problems to be solved, tested often with short-answer quizzes, later outlined in review and often summarized in problem style, then finally tested with organizational tests, a teacher can really measure a student's ability to think. An objective test often measures only his retention and his ability to guess correctly.

Although it takes longer to read essay-type tests, a teacher is less likely to go to sleep during the process. We have too many students memorizing the book and too few thinking through the problems involved. A student who enters college without ever having learned how to organize a body of knowledge is handicapped from the day of entrance. Elementary schools must teach youngsters this skill as soon as they are ready.

Thinking makes sense for children; makes sense out of the chaotic mass of facts to which they are subjected in the elementary school; makes common sense, too; action that is born of thinking is likely to be better than precipitous action.

But thinking is a learned skill—don't forget that. It must be taught consistently by the home and the school if it is to be used. As Robert Frost says, "It's knowing what to do with things that counts." [3] Facts are not enough; children must use facts to think with and learn how to think with their facts.

---

[3] From *Complete Poems of Robert Frost*, "At Woodward's Gardens." Copyright, 1930, 1949, by Henry Holt and Company, Inc. Copyright, 1936, by Robert Frost. By permission of the publishers.
This poem is reprinted in full in Chapter Thirteen, page 546.

CUPBOARD OF IDEAS   for Chapter Three

Thinking Makes Sense ❖ ❖ ❖ ❖ ❖ ❖ ❖ ❖ ❖ ❖ ❖ ❖ ❖ ❖ ❖ ❖

Primary Shelf

I. Thinking in Social Studies and Science (Gr. 1–3)

On the blackboard keep a list of the questions children ask that are too involved to answer in class. Once a week use these questions as a basis for your social studies or science classes. Always let the children try to figure out the answers from the known facts first. From there go to books to verify the conjectures. In third grade assign a committee to work on each question to try to locate the information. Each committee may have about three children of different types. In first grade do considerable listen-to-learn type lessons to get questions answered, or send children to interview older children whom you have notified ahead of time. Show primary children how to find pictures in an encyclopedia by looking for captions under the right letter and hunting from there on for right pictures. Parents know so much these days that children are getting lethargic about finding their own answers.

II. An Atmosphere of "Why"

Make "Why" the motive power of your primary grades. Encourage the children to bring their *why's* to school.

Show as many question-producing movies and film strips as you can find. A good movie should produce as many questions as it answers. Post class charts of the questions suggested but unanswered by a movie. By the end of the primary grades children should realize that life is a continuous finding out and adding to and changing of ideas.

III. *The Opaque Projector Promotes Thinking*

The opaque projector is a necessity in the primary room. It enlarges pictures and maps in books so that children can find answers to their questions and raise more questions from their answers. Passing pictures around is time-consuming and unsatisfactory. The opaque projector focuses attention of all children on the same picture at once. Pictures can be more conducive to thinking than anything read aloud in the primary grades. Most of early childhood is "We look and see," "We listen and see," or "We go and see." See that pictures ask questions of your students' minds.

IV. *We Go and See and Think*

Nothing produces thinking quite like going and seeing: a walk to the neighbors who have the new puppies, a bus trip to a dairy farm, a hike to a bakery or a greenhouse produce more questions than Santa Claus, and questions start the youthful questioners thinking.

V. *Living Questions in the Classroom*

If there is something alive in your classroom (besides you and the children, that is), make that bit of life get your children to thinking. Place a question on the canary's cage, "Why is our Benny molting?" a question beside the goldfish bowl, "Why is Herman blowing bubbles?" or a sign by the painted turtle's hideout, "How do people act like turtles?"

VI. *The First Arithmetic Is Lived* (Kdgn.-Gr. 1)

If the kindergarten and first-grade teachers in a school system would together make a list of all practical experiences with numbers that could be met and figured out naturally in these two years and would meet them systematically and thoroughly, children would arrive in second grade with a real feeling for number concepts. It bothers me that too many children get their first contact with numbers in an arithmetic workbook. The first arithmetic should be lived, not flattened out on a page.

VII. A Thinking Moment

I know a primary teacher who takes a few minutes before dismissal time to think through these questions (with children's heads on their desks).

A. Did I fail to do anything that I promised to do today?
B. Did I do somebody wrong today that I didn't try to make right?
C. Did I forget any of my wraps on the playground?
D. Did my mother give me any directions about hurrying right home?

(Mothers report that there is a real carry-over from these few minutes to collect scattered thoughts.)

VIII. Thought for the Day

Keep a corner of the board for a daily thought to be discussed at the day's end. Use such questions as: If your mother doesn't act like herself and seems sick or troubled, what can you do to help? If you find yourself losing your temper easily, how can you get better brakes for your temper car? If you need friends, how can you get them?

IX. Writing One's Thoughts (Advanced Gr. 1–3)

Second semester first graders and second- and third-grade youngsters enjoy writing out one thing they were thinking about during the day or in bed the night before. (See page 245 on poetry for a nice example.)

X. Creative Seatwork and Thinking

Creative seatwork is not only a restful change from workbooks but even provides a challenge to imaginative children.

A. After a unit of farm or city stories in their reader, have children write either a true or imaginary experience that might also have happened. This will enable children to use a number of vocabulary words in the glossary.
B. Write the letter the visiting child might have written to his home telling about his visit.
C. In a story where an animal is one of the characters, such as a goat's adventure in a grocery store, let a third of the

class write what the goat told his nanny when he got home; let another third tell what the grocer told his wife, and let the remaining third tell what the boy reported to his mother about the happening. If some members of the class have trouble writing, let them draw the story, actually writing only a line or two.

XI. *Safety Lessons Must Make Children Think* (Gr. 1–2)

Teachers have a tendency to make safety units too long. An occasional well-timed lesson dramatically taught is better than a long unit of study. Confront first- and second-grade youngsters with imaginary situations; then have them acted out by the class.

A. You start to cross the street and suddenly cars are coming from both directions. With miniature cars and dolls act out what you would do; then explain why. (If the child chooses a poor answer, such as hurrying across, call on another child to try another answer.)

B. If you must ride a bicycle at dusk, what can you do to ensure your safety?

C. Show us where you would ride your bicycle in a line of cars.

Creative dramatics, followed by discussion and then by the making of catchy rhymes or posters, impress primary children with the importance of safety. A high table with paper cover on which roads and intersections are blocked in and a miniature traffic signal set up makes safety real to children and helps them to think through situations presented by the teacher.

XII. *Ideas in Ethics*

Acting out imaginary situations sometimes helps children to make right decisions.

A. You accidentally break a dish at a friend's house, but his mother didn't see you. Act out the scene as you imagine it.

B. On the playground one of your classmates trips you and makes you fall into the mud. How will you handle this situation?

C. A little girl has asked you over to her house to supper, but you're not sure if her mother knows about your being asked. How can the situation be handled best?

Intermediate and Upper-Grade Shelf

I. *Organization in Science Aids Thinking*

Teaching science is largely a matter of leading children to find out. Success depends on organization. Be sure your seating arrangements serve your purposes. When children are experimenting in small groups, arrange the chairs in groups of four, turned together to form a table; when you or a child is demonstrating before the class, arrange the chairs in a large circle so that all can see and hear.

Appoint a strong leader for each group when experimenting, after having worked out together in class a list of the characteristics of an effective group leader:
A. Challenges and works with, but doesn't dominate the group.
B. Leads group to find the answers to its assigned problem.
C. Checks early on all needed materials in time to get them if committee members failed in their assignments.
D. Meets inattention with dismissal from group. (Science, like arithmetic, is a formal class, and no waste of time should be tolerated. Children always do what they are allowed to do.)
E. Appoints one or two persons to report on the results of an experiment.
F. Sees that materials are put away and desks restored to order after the class is dismissed.

II. *Thinking through a Subject*

A. **Space travel.** (Gr. 5–8) Let each child choose any subject in which he is interested: fishing, amateur boxing, water skiing, his favorite ball team, tennis, mystery stories, swimming, and so on. Give the class from seven to ten minutes to think through the topics they choose, and make a simple outline. When the time is up, have each youngster choose the first and one other topic in his outline and develop each into a well-written paragraph using any of the different ways of developing paragraphs learned earlier: piling up details, giving examples, explaining with stories, expanding definitions, comparing or contrasting ideas. (See Chapter Eleven, page 458.) On other days have each person expand one topic orally, paying particular attention to relevance of material.

A good preparation for this type of thinking exercise is to have each student read through one article in a *Reader's Digest* on his own reading level. As soon as he is finished, each tries to reduce the paragraphs in the article to one sentence.

Another good preparation for the first exercise is to use the science or social studies text as a base and reduce a paragraph to one sentence. Work together until the top half of the class has learned the technique; then let those children go ahead on their own while you help the others.

B. **Deep-sea diving.** For the top half or third of the class this is a fine exercise in memory and organization. Each reads an article through carefully once, then lays it aside, and from memory makes an outline of the content; using that outline, he sees how much of the article he can rewrite. In other words, he dives deep and *fights* his *way* back up. If we are going to get the most from our good minds, we definitely must have more exercises of this type. However, we must not expect too much at once. Lead up to this type of thinking exercise gradually, and the bright children will enjoy it. It challenges them.

C. **Brains on review.** When pupils have finished studying a subject in the intermediate grades, make a sentence for each topic on separate strips of paper and put them into a box. Let each student draw one slip which he uses as a topic sentence to expand into a written paragraph (a good test procedure) .

D. **Life lines.** Intermediate and junior high youth need to read many biographies. Make a life line or two for each biography, and ask each reader to expand these into paragraphs. A life line is a summary sentence, such as:

1. Hans Christian Andersen was the original ugly duckling of his own fairy tale.
2. George Washington Carver's life was one disappointment after the other.
3. Daniel Boone was always needing more elbow room. Or Daniel Boone was quick-witted; he was wily.
4. The Wright brothers were always tinkering from the time they were small boys.

E. Book reports that require thinking
   1. After a unit on biographies is finished, ask each reader to make five life lines that together sum up the contributions of the hero's life.
   2. In one large comprehensive paragraph, prove that the person you have been reading about *was* or *is* a great man or woman.
F. Thinking through contrasts makes a clear picture
   1. As each nation of Europe is studied, note the handicaps —poor soil, lack of good harbors, poor or no natural resources, small size—and study how each nation has struggled to overcome each handicap and with what success. As one point in the unit examination, include a paragraph contrasting one nation's methods and success or failure in overcoming handicaps with another's. Especially must this be done in studying slow-developing countries.
   2. Let groups study and compare such subjects as sports and recreation in different countries, and write paragraphs contrasting them. When the fifth graders are studying the states of the United States, let each two children select one state to contrast with one already studied. The two must study separately but make an outline together of the points of contrast and then work out their contrasting paragraphs together.

III. Teaching Children to Think in Arithmetic Class

A. Have an occasional class for estimating answers after analyzing story problems.
B. Use newspaper advertisements to concoct original arithmetic problems for each other.
C. Get children to work out for themselves any arithmetic problems arising in the social studies, such as number of people to the square mile, estimated distance between cities, and the like.
D. Have a Math Shark Club for students who are far ahead of the class. Let them meet during the arithmetic period in a corner of the room and there work quietly under a chairman having a "whale" of a time working difficult problems.

CHAPTER FOUR

We Need Disciplined Ears

First-Grade Ike: The teacher gave us something new today: creative directions.

Second-Grade Mike: What's creative directions?

Ike: First the teacher tells you what to do, then you do as you please to end up with.

Mike: Pooh! There's nothing new about that. My mother always gives my father that kind!

I Hear America Singing [1]

I hear America singing, the varied carols I hear;
Those of mechanics—each one singing his, as it should be, blithe
 and strong;
The carpenter singing his, as he measures his plank or beam,
The mason singing his, as he makes ready for work, or leaves off
 work;
The boatman singing what belongs to him in his boat—the deck-
 hand singing on the steamboat deck;
The shoemaker singing as he sits on his bench—the hatter singing
 as he stands;
The wood-cutter's song—the ploughboy's, on his way in the morning, or at the noon intermission, or at sundown;
The delicious singing of the mother—or of the young wife at work—
 or of the girl sewing or washing—Each singing what belongs to
 her, and to none else;

Walt Whitman

Workers on Parade

The cobbler mending shoes on his bench,
The plumber mending pipes with his wrench,
The fireman spraying water with a hose,
A doctor patching a cut on the nose.
They are all singing
  merrily
    merrily
      merrily
        merrily
          merrily
            merrily.

Lynn Schneider, Grade 7

---

[1] From *Leaves of Grass* by Walt Whitman

If Mark Twain were living today, he might define listening as hearing with a college education—but not if he had been teaching college classes lately. Will Rogers, with that wry grin of his, might have said that listening is what a woman does when she's not supposed to hear. Bob Hope might quip that listening is what women do before marriage, men afterward. A college professor might define listening as purposeful hearing, thereby demonstrating the reason why his students have trouble listening to his lectures. But the most modern definition of listening I have ever found comes from a sixth-grade boy who wrote, "Listening is tuned-in hearing."

Let any group of teachers from kindergarten to college get together informally of late, and before the meeting is over, the problem of listening comes up.

"We lose minutes every day having to repeat directions," the sixth-grade teacher fumes.

"They sit there with interested looks on their faces," the high school teacher complains, "but they haven't the vaguest notion of what I'm saying."

"They take notes in their sleep," a college professor moans, "until I find myself talking in mine."

So exercised about this matter of listening was a teacher friend of mine that she asked the parents of the third-grade children in the suburban community where she teaches to keep a record for a week of how many times they told their children to go to bed before they got results. The parents themselves were astonished to find that the average was five times and that one mother had taken fourteen tries before her suggestion paid off. This same teacher wondered how many times on an average she repeated the directions she gave these same children in the schoolroom and, on checking, found that she usually gave each direction three times and sometimes four.

That was enough for her. She got her class interested in educating their hearing, and the experimental listening going on in that third grade this year is already yielding results. Now the whole school is getting the idea, and the parents are seeing how they can improve on direction-giving at home. One mother reported laughingly that her methods worked far better on her children than on her husband. In fact, anyone who is at all concerned with today's listening problem finds that adults have the same listening habits as the children; it's hard to get their attention in the first place and even harder to hold it with anything less than a Western or a joke.

Many classroom teachers find themselves in the position of the man from Missouri who paid a high price for a mule guaranteed to be an outstanding field animal. But as to whether or not this was true, the new owner never could determine; he just couldn't get the mule to move. Finally in desperation he sent for the former owner and complained. Immediately the man began to beat the mule over the head with a two-by-four, whereupon the mule at once began to pull the harrow to which he was hitched.

"There! You see he's just what I guaranteed him to be," the former owner said, turning to the other man. "You just have to get his attention before he'll get to work."

And, indeed, that's all that's the matter with the modern youngster—you just have to get his attention before he'll get to work. But how to do it . . . ?

I asked an unculled, unsquelched group of sixth graders one day to write down what they thought was the reason for their poor listening habits at school and among the usual, found these nuggets in the rough:

1. I never can listen long to one thing. My mind goes wandering off and by the time I get it back, the place it was, is lost, too.

2. It's so noisy at home with all the kids yelling and fighting, I just get used to turning everything off.

3. Our teacher always repeats her directions three or four times, and I make a game of betting with myself which is the one she's going to stop on. Then I listen.

4. When there's anything interesting to listen to, I listen. School is just the wrong station for me. School is dead stuff.

5. I mean to listen, but my thoughts sneak out on me. I do try, though, but thoughts are "slipperyer" than a catfish.

No, we can't put it off any longer: we must teach our children to discipline their ears, and we must learn to discipline our own. What was once left to chance and to inclination is now the joint task of the home and the school. By means of the radar of definite direction and purpose, we must get children out of this babel they dwell in.

How Shall We Go about Teaching Better Listening Habits in Our Schools?

By exploration and discovery, of course, the way we shall discover and uncover new worlds within and beyond the world we now know. The children of the elementary grades can become excited about overcoming the obstacles in the field of listening as they already are about surmounting the obstacles to outer space. Children are already in another world and another time.

How well Peter J. Henniker-Heaton sketches this world to come!

POST EARLY FOR SPACE [2]

Once we were wayfarers, then seafarers, then airfarers,
We shall be spacefarers soon,
Not voyaging from city to city or from coast to coast,
But from planet to planet and from moon to moon.

This is no fanciful flight of imagination,
No strange, incredible, utterly different thing;
It will come by obstinate thought and calculation
And the old resolve to spread an expanding wing.

We shall see homes established on distant planets,
Friends departing to take up a post on Mars;
They will have perils to meet, but they will meet them,
As the early settlers did on American shores.

We shall buy tickets later, as now we buy them
For a foreign vacation; reserve our seat or berth,
Then spending a holiday month on a moon of Saturn,
Look tenderly back to our little shining Earth.

And those who decide they will not make the journey
Will remember a son up there or a favorite niece
Eagerly awaiting news from the old home planet,
And will scribble a line to catch the post for space.

What a wonderful way to catch the imagination of children in the teaching of history:

Once we were wayfarers, then seafarers, then airfarers,
We shall be spacefarers soon,

[2] By permission of the author and *The Christian Science Monitor*.

In the same way we can kindle visions in our youth with that equally wonderful story of the lengthening of man's voice and the strengthening of his hearing.

First the savage listened to the music of the elements: the casual conversation of the little winds in the evening leaves; the wild arias sung by the waterfall at midnight; the wild sucking roar of the windstorm using pines as playthings. These sounds man translated into his earliest song-poems and into the moving rhythms of his dance. The tribe looked on and listened, and the words within men's minds grew and enlarged and reached out. In like manner the wise men of those times listened to the still voice within their minds and piece by precious piece fashioned a savage's conception of God. And each generation added a living bit to that picture; for as men listen and learn and grow, so does their conception of all good grow.

For centuries man's voice was a pygmy voice, walking only as many miles as he walked and returning with him to his dwelling place at nightfall.

For hundreds of years—yes, even thousands—man's voice took short steps indeed, but listening to the wisdom of the old men and of the prowess of past heroes carried each generation not many steps forward.

Then in the middle of the fifteenth century a German named Gutenberg whittled out movable type, and the first mass production of books became possible. While man's thoughts and ideas traveled over all the world in books, his voice still got no farther than his own person. If he would speak to the world, a man must, perforce, be always a traveler or have his works speak for him.

Suddenly, in 1876 Alexander Graham Bell, while he was seeking to make a hearing aid for the deaf, quite by accident stumbled upon the principle of the telephone, and man's voice for the first time crossed space without him.

In the next year another man, Thomas Edison, invented a device for capturing the human voice and reproducing it on a rubberized disk. Thus, one of the world's most original inventions made the voice of man immortal.

Twenty years later Marconi, an Italian, discovered the wireless upon which our radio and television are based, and a man's audience became the whole world.

Then in the spring of 1959, the unbelievable again happened; President Dwight D. Eisenhower sent greetings to Canadian Prime Minister John G. Diefenbaker via the moon. The voice of

man has penetrated even into outer space, his voice traveling 480,-
000 miles to the moon and back in 2.7 seconds.

"Quo vadis?" we ask ourselves and wonder as we ask.

Truly the story of man's rise from barbarism is the story of the
length of a man's voice and the strength of his ears. Never in all
the world's history, we must impress upon children, has the human
voice had such potential for good and for evil as it has today. The
warmonger who used to whip his group into tribal frenzy now has
a tribe of millions, all of whom can both see and hear him better
than if they stood on the outskirts of the crowd he is addressing. The
silken voice of the advertiser strokes our tenderest spots promis-
ing us new sensations for old in true Aladdin style. The voice of
evil, disguised as the voice of a friend, has never in the world before
sought and found so many ready ears. The problem of our generation is truly a problem of listening. To which voice shall we listen?
To which doctrine shall we give ear? From the great babel of many
voices how shall our ears sift and choose the best? The listening
problems of today are training problems: How to choose wisely
what to listen to; how to discipline listening to get the most from it;
and how to listen creatively to the man behind the voice?

Since more than 45 per cent of a modern's communication is
listening, as contrasted with the 16 per cent spent in reading, perhaps parents and teachers should be more concerned with "Why
Johnny can't listen" than with "Why Johnny can't read." Or perhaps, since modern life evaluates more than it teaches and presents
more problems than it provides answers for, we should save both
time and newsprint by calling the next diatribe against the schools
simply "Why Johnny Can't."

Be that as it may, to fail to train today's children in the three
problems of listening—selection, discipline, and analysis—would
be as futile as to let nature take its course in the breeding of corn
and cows.

This chapter, then, will attempt to think through with you
how to educate the ears of America as to what to listen to, how to
listen, and how to tell the true from the false in what is heard.

Youth Must Approach the Listening Problem Scientifically

In Russia education is a problem of telling children what to
study; in America it is a problem of selling children on the ad-
visability of learning, a much harder job.

Every teacher in America will do this selling job in a slightly different way, but these steps will be common to all teaching of the listening skills:

1. Interesting children in wanting to learn
2. Experimenting to find out how they rate as listeners
3. Improving the listening skills

Our First Job Is a Selling Job

We have already sketched the epic of man's strengthening his ears, a subject of vital interest to most children. Intermediate and junior high school teachers may best establish this concept through making an epic poem of this development and using it later with a voice-choir.

But primary teachers must use a different approach to our need for better listening habits. Little children are not interested in long, sweeping vistas of progress; they are interested in the "now."

One kindergarten teacher I know used the rabbit approach. After the children had entertained (and loved) a rabbit for two weeks, they showed a keen interest in how the rabbit listens both with its nose and ears. The teacher put up a bulletin board, featuring an enormous three-dimensional rabbit, with this rhyming caption in raised letters:

> A rabbit with ears as pink as a rose,
> Gets answers with his ears
> And questions with his nose!

Then followed some excellent ear-training devices:

Listening to answer questions. From the children's interest in cherry blossoms, questions about seeds arose, and the kindergarten teacher said they could learn the answer by listening. She told the children that she was going to ask three questions after they had listened; then she read these paragraphs:

Most garden vegetables grow from seeds. Fields of wheat and corn grow from seeds. Cherry trees and other fruit trees can grow from seeds. Even the largest trees in the world started from small seeds.

Seeds are many different shapes and sizes. Some seeds are very, very tiny. They are so small you can hardly see them. Some seeds, like the coconut are large.

Seeds are different colors, too. Some are red. Some are yellow. Some are brown. Some are all different colors.

After reading the paragraphs to the kindergarten group, she asked these questions:

1. What is the name of the fruit tree in the story which grows from a seed?

2. Give the name of a large seed.

3. What colors can seeds be?

The results of this exercise and ones similar to it were excellent. The teacher plans next year to have a great many of such learning and listening exercises in kindergarten in answer to the children's questions.

Listening for rhyming words. This kindergarten teacher made a foot-high rabbit with jointed ears, nose, and legs out of construction paper. While she manipulated the movable parts, she made suitable rhymes for which the children provided the final rhyming word. (See the Cupboard of Ideas for the poetry chapter page 267.)

> I asked a silly question of my funny Mr. Bunny;
> He cocked his ears and twitched his nose,
> And oh, he looked so *(funny)*.
>
> My little white bunny nibbles the grass,
> And watches the go-down-the-street people *(pass)*.
>
> My pretty white rabbit has just run away,
> I'm hoping my Daddy can find him *(today)*.

Making new verses to a known tune. After a visit to a farm, the kindergarten children composed two stanzas to the song, "I'd Like to Be a Farmer." This was the first one:

> I'd like to have a rooster
> I'd have him for my pet
> He'd wake me in the morning
> When I could hear him crow.

Teachers at every level will find ways to interest the children of their grade. A first-grade teacher of my acquaintance discovered that the fathers of many of her children were going hunting. Accordingly the class got interested in the subject of training hunting dogs. From there it was an easy step to training their own ears so they could go right after ideas in school. This same teacher had a bulletin board with the caption "Alert Ears? Lazy Ears?" illustrated with a padded paper pup. By means of a string arrangement like the cord on draw drapes, she could pull the pup's ears up when she wanted the children to listen intently. That device was worth a dozen admonitions to "Listen well now." (See Cupboard of Ideas following this chapter, page 126, for other listening devices.)

How Well Do Children Listen?

Every teacher will have to discover for himself the best way to interest his class in listening. Why not experiment? Especially if your children have just begun to get interested in how well they listen, why not conduct a series of informal experiments in some of these areas that are at present practically untouched in the elementary field?

1. How can listening be motivated?

2. What relation, if any, is there between listening ability and the I.Q.? between listening skills and reading ability?

3. How much does definite and regular work on listening skills change the children's ability to listen?

4. Does listening ability change from grade to grade and how much?

5. How much does the attention span of listening change between grades?

6. How does the listening ability of creative children compare with that of the less creative?

7. What part does interest play in sustaining listening?

8. Which types of listening exercises are most challenging to each grade level?

9. Is there better listening when pictures and script are used together? How marked is the improvement (if any)?

10. What better tests and exercises can you work out for increasing the listening ability of the children in your room? (Your school could make a great contribution here, and think what an entire school system could do.)

Change Interest into Action

After interest has been aroused and experimenting to find out just how well the children listen has been done, the third step is doing something about it. "How well do I listen?" is a real challenge to a modern to find out just how he rates. Interest-experiment-action—this is the sequence in any area of communication.

Homemade, informal testing exercises are almost better than commercial ones in finding out how well children listen. Such exercises may be worked out with fresh, informational material on the subject of current interest or the unit being studied. Whatever children are interested in, on a reading level one or two grades above their own, makes good material for a listening exercise.

For those teachers who need help in working out listening exercises, a few suggestions follow. Although in the classroom, a selection is seldom used for more than one exercise, to conserve space here I am using the same material for several types of tests.

THE ANTS [3]

Among all the insects, the ants probably come closest to being human. Their ways resemble ours in a surprising number of instances.

They go to war, often marching in columns and attacking in unison. They keep cattle in the form of smaller insects that give off honeydew, milk them regularly, and, in some cases, even build barns to shelter them. Some ants plant fungus gardens and gather crops like farmers. Others harvest grain and store it in granaries. Still others have servants and slaves to wait on them. Many ants keep pets in their homes. In fact, it is said that the ants have domesticated more different kinds of creatures than man has!

Sometimes, tropical ants live in great cities that contain half a million inhabitants. Their nests have been known to occupy as much as three hundred cubic yards of earth. Finally, like man and unlike most insects, ants live for years. Workers have a life span up to seven years and queens have been known to live eighteen years. The same underground cities are sometimes occupied for half a century, one generation of ants "inheriting real estate" from the generation before.

The life of the ant colony begins with the swarming of the queens and males. This usually occurs on some still and sultry day. Sometimes, the flying ants will appear in such numbers they seem to fill the sky. A few years ago, in southern California, so many billions of the winged insects appeared over the Malibu Hills they formed a black cloud which was

[3] From *The Junior Book of Insects* by Edwin Way Teale. Copyright, 1939, 1953, by E. P. Dutton & Co., Inc. Reprinted by permission of the publishers.

mistaken for smoke from a forest fire. Rangers rushed to the spot and found the air swarming with the insects.

Certain weather conditions stimulate the ants to make their mating flights. This assists in producing cross-fertilization, as the inmates of many nests of the same kind take to the air at once. There are 3,500 species of ants and none of them mate with other species; all breed only with those of their kind.

The workers, which make up the great bulk of the colony, cannot fly. Only the queens and males have wings. And they use them but once, the time they soar into the sky on their mating flight. The males live only a short time afterwards and as soon as the queens land, they bite or break off the wings they have finished using. Sometimes, they accomplish this by rubbing against weeds or pebbles, sometimes they bite off the wings with their jaws, at other times pull them off with their legs. For the rest of their lives, most of the queens will be voluntary prisoners beneath the ground.

They begin this subterranean existence by digging a little chamber in the soil, or in rotting wood, according to the species. Some tropical ants even build nests of leaves, sewing them together with silken threads. This is accomplished by a curious example of insect child labor. The larvae of these ants secrete a silk-like adhesive. Some of the insects hold the leaves together with legs and jaws while other workers pass the larvae back and forth like living shuttles to bind the leaves together.

Most of the ants we know, make their nests in the ground. After the queens have torn away their wings and dug out a chamber, they begin laying eggs. Out of these hatch soft, translucent, legless grubs. They are shaped like crook-necked gourds. Among the relatives of the ant—the wasps and bees—the young have fixed cradles or cells. But ant babies are moved about, washed, and, as every boy knows, rushed from the underground chambers to a place of safety when the nest is disturbed.

The first grubs that hatch from the eggs are fed with the saliva of the queen. For weeks and even months, the queen is not able to obtain food. She is too busy laying eggs and caring for the grubs. As a hibernating bear lives on its fat, she lives by digesting the tissues of the now-useless wing muscles. Tests have shown that queens can go without food for the greater part of a year and that even workers can live for almost nine months without food.

In other ways, ants can endure astonishing hardships. Members of one species have been revived after being under water for twenty-seven hours; another after being submerged seventy hours; and a third after being without air for eight days! This probably explains how ants nesting in the bed of a dry stream are able to live through sudden floods and freshets. Even more amazing is the vitality of injured ants. In one laboratory, a beheaded ant remained alive for nineteen days and, in another, a worker lived forty-one days after its head was severed from its body. It even continued to walk up until within two days of its death!

Because the first grubs that hatch out receive less food than those which come later, they are usually smaller than the average. As the colony grows, the job of caring for the young is turned over to the workers. Some larvae are equipped with spines and ridges at the base of the jaws. By rubbing them together they produce a shrill sound which, like the crying of a baby, attracts the attention of the nurses that wash and feed them. In return for their care, the nurses get a fatty secretion which the grubs exude and which the ants relish greatly as food.

As soon as the grubs are full grown, they spin little cocoons for themselves. When you buy "ant eggs" for goldfish or canaries, these cocoons are what you get. In the Black Forest, in Germany, collecting ant cocoons used to be a regular occupation. Millions of the "eggs" were shipped to all parts of the world.

It is within these tiny silken shells that the grubs change into adult ants. Sometimes, they have to be helped from the cocoons by the nurses who bite holes in the little prisons and help the weak inmates out. Then, like babies, the newborn insects are washed, brushed and fed.

It may take years before a colony becomes well established. Sometimes the queen is killed by fungus in damp soil. But, ordinarily, she is soon able to turn the care of the young over to the workers and to devote herself to laying eggs. This she continues to do year after year. Unlike honey bees, the ant queen feels no hostility toward younger queens. Sometimes, the latter return to the home colony after the mating flight, and add their eggs to those of the original queen, thus swelling the population of the insect city. . . . .

The habit of feeding one another with food which has been swallowed and stored in a "social stomach" is a characteristic of the ants. Most of the food they eat, instead of going directly to their stomachs, is retained in a sort of crop from which they can bring drops to feed other members of the colony. This process is called regurgitation.

Once, a scientist made a test to see how widely a given bit of food would be distributed throughout an ant nest. He dyed some honey bright blue. When an ant swallowed some of the liquid, the blue showed through the sides of its abdomen. When it gave drops to another ant which solicited food, that ant's abdomen also became blue. In the course of time, dozens of ants in the nest were going around with blue showing through the thin walls of their stomachs. All had been fed with regurgitated honey from the original feeding.

Bees live on nectar and pollen, some beetles eat only carrion, termites rarely consume anything but wood. But the ants can live on a wide variety of things. They eat meat, seeds, vegetable matter, honeydew; they are both carnivorous and vegetarian. This has helped them survive. They not only hunt afield for their food but produce it close at hand. Two of the most remarkable examples of "ant husbandry" are the activities of the harvester ants and the leaf-cutting ants.

I. DIFFERENT WAYS OF USING THIS MATERIAL AS A LISTENING
EXERCISE
A. *Reading for Comprehension.* After reading this material
   aloud, hand out these ten comprehension questions.
   1. There are three and one-half million species of ants.
      (*Yes   No*)
   2. What two adjectives (descriptive words) describe a good
      swarming day for ants?
   3. Which type of ant has no wings?
   4. Our northern ants build nests of leaves. (*Yes   No*)
   5. The first ant grubs are fed with _____.
   6. The ant queen eats all the time the grubs are hatching.
      (*Yes   No*)
   7. The last grubs hatched out are smaller than the first.
      (*Yes   No*)
   8. What commercial use is made of ant eggs?
   9. The reason why ants first store their food in a "social
      stomach" is for self-feeding. (*Yes   No*)
   10. Ants feed only on vegetable matter. (*Yes   No*)
B. *Getting Vocabulary Meanings from Listening.* After finishing the reading of the article, read aloud these sentences
   once each, leaving a short writing time between each one.
   1. In the sentence "Certain weather conditions stimulate
      the ants to make their mating flights," what does *stimu-
      late* mean?
   2. In this sentence what does *voluntary* mean? "For the
      rest of their lives, most of the queens will be voluntary
      prisoners."
   3. "They begin this subterranean existence by digging a
      little chamber in the soil." In this sentence what does
      subterranean mean?
   4. In what way is a queen ant like a hibernating bear?
   5. In this sentence is the meaning of the word *hostility*
      love or hate? "Unlike honey bees, the ant queen feels no
      hostility toward younger queens."
   6. Another name for ant eggs is _____.
   7. Does *shrill* as used in this sentence mean high or low?
      "By rubbing them together they [the larvae] produce a
      shrill sound which, like the crying of a baby, attracts
      the attention of the nurses."
   8. What is the meaning of *solicited* in the clause, "to an-
      other ant which solicited food"?

9. In this article which is the meaning of *regurgitation:* "casting up as a cow casts up a cud" or "shooting up like a fountain"?

10. "Termites rarely consume anything but wood." What is the meaning of *consume* here?

C. *Using This Material from a Note-Taking Point of View.* After the article is read aloud, pass out sheets of mimeographed questions.

1. What was the title of this article?

2. Give in one sentence what the writer used as his central idea.

3–7. Name five ways in which the author said ants resemble humans.

8. What proof did the writer give that ants swarm in great numbers?

9. Name two proofs given by the author that ants can endure astonishing hardships.

10. Which of these three words or phrases describe the writer's attitude toward ants: loathing, lukewarm feeling, admiration?

D. *Writing a Summary after Listening*

1. One type of follow-up procedure

Directions: This is a listening lesson. When I have finished reading the article, be ready to write a summary of what you have heard. Listen especially for the ways in which ants are like people. Take no notes; just listen. After the reading is finished, hand each person a sheet containing this outline:

> I. Ways in which ants resemble humans
> A. Ants go to war.
> B. They keep cattle and milk them.
> C. Some ants plant gardens and gather crops like farmers.
> D. Others have servants and slaves to wait on them.
> E. Ants keep pets and domesticate other insects.
> F. Some ants live in great cities.
> G. For insects, ants are long-lived.

Choose any topic sentence given in the outline and develop it into a paragraph with all the details you can remember.

2. Another follow-up procedure

Directions: This is a listening lesson, but you may take any notes you wish, especially noting the ways in which ants behave like humans, since that is the central idea of this article. After I have finished reading this article entitled "The Ants," be ready to use your notes to write a summary of the article.

II. A LISTENING EXERCISE BASED ON A STORY

This story was written for you by Jerry, a sixth grader from Wisconsin, telling about the first time he drove a truck at the age of six. Jerry has called his story "Truck Ride." (Turn to "Truck Ride," page 286 in Chapter Eight of this book and read it aloud.)

Directions: Now I am going to read some sentences about this story. You'll have to listen carefully because I'm going to read each sentence only once. Some of the sentences are true, some are false, and some aren't mentioned at all in the story. Fold the paper on your desk into three equal columns. (Wait here, but give directions only once.) On the left-hand side of the paper close to the edge, number from 1 to 10 down the page. (Wait.) Then write TRUE at the top of the first column, FALSE at the top of the second, and NOT MENTIONED (spell) at the top of the third. After I finish reading each sentence, put an X in the column that tells whether the statement is true, false, or not mentioned in the story. Are you ready to begin?

1. This is a story about an accident that didn't quite happen.
2. This is a story that happened to a boy when he was in the sixth grade.
3. Jerry asked his sister to play house with him.
4. The sister had yellow curls and blue eyes.
5. The uncle left the motor running.
6. Jerry said to his sister, "I'll take off the brake and we'll go for a ride."
7. Jerry tried every knob and lever he could see, but he could not stop the car.
8. The car was headed toward a fence post.
9. The uncle jumped into the car and stopped it just before it struck the pole.
10. Jerry and his sister were properly punished by their parents for their naughtiness.

III. Listening to Learn How to Play a Game

The name of this game is "Describit." Any number can play, and the object of the game is to show skill and speed in thinking of adjectives to describe nouns.

Two players have charge of the game. The first player has a pack of 26 cards, each marked with a different letter of the alphabet. He places these cards face down on a table and mixes them thoroughly with his hand. He then draws out any one card announcing its letter in a clear voice. If he has drawn "C," for instance, the adjective named will begin with the letter "C." The second player then calls out any one of the three kinds of nouns: person, place, or thing. Let's say that he chooses "person." As soon as the second player has spoken, any player in the group may call out an adjective beginning with "C" modifying a person beginning with a "C." Such answers as "careful child," "clumsy cat," "clever coyote," or "curious colt" are possible. The first person with an acceptable adjective and noun gets the card. The player with the most cards wins, and the game is over when all cards are gone.

All these suggestions and those in the Cupboard of Ideas following this chapter (page 126) are merely possible exercises for a student's determining, quasi-scientifically, two things:

1. Whether he is a good listener
2. How much (if any) he is improving in his listening habits

But never for a moment imagine that such cut and dried exercises as these will ever alone change a child's listening habits. They are mere gauges to show him how he rates as a listener. As Sandburg says, only a "rich wanting" [4] changes people. Children will change their listening habits for the same reasons they are willing to practice for interminable hours to improve their baseball or tennis skills—they have a burning desire to do so. Only a "rich wanting" truly changes habits. This is why I so strongly stress the interest angle in the teaching of all language arts.

Interest is one of the few motivations for learning left to the elementary teacher. Gone is much parental pressure; gone in many schools is the fear of nonpromotion; gone is much of the public disapproval of poor English habits; and almost gone is the staying after school. This is why some children continue to be nonlearners. They simply are not interested in what the schools teach. We

[4] From *The People, Yes,* by Carl Sandburg, copyright, 1936, by Harcourt, Brace and Company, Inc.

must somehow learn to gear educational opportunity to intellectual and potential interest. But motivation for learning must never
come from the schools alone. Both parents and teachers must engender interest and pride in children to learn; the schools can never
do it without the help of the home. Interest in improving our listening habits, experimenting to see how we rate as listeners, action to
get one's score up to par or beyond it—these are the three steps to
listening improvement whether at home or at school.

What Can We Do to Improve Listening Scores?

Homes and schools together:
1. Must decide on common procedures.
2. Must, in so far as possible, make work meaningful by including children in the planning.
3. Must start the teaching of listening skills as early as possible
in a child's life and consistently work at them.
4. Must interest a child in improving his own scores.

We Listen to Directions

A large percentage of children's listening time is spent in listening to directions: lesson assignments, arithmetic processes, fire drills,
scientific formulas, how to proceed on an excursion, how to play
games, how to act in assembly, what to buy on the way home from
school, how to find a new friend's house, how to deliver a note for
your mother, how to prepare baby's formula, how to diaper the
baby when mother is gone, what to report to the principal, how to
fill out questionnaires, how to take an achievement or mental test,
how to arrange a book display, how to study. Get your school children interested in keeping track of how much of their day is spent
in listening to directions. As one fourth grader remarked wearily,
"All my 'day hours' are filled with *how-to's* and I like to do *I-want-
to's.*"

Children look forward to the time when they will be free of
directions only to find that adult life is full of still other kinds:
taking directions for exercises or processes over the radio; listening
to recipes for baking and cooking; directions on how to raise children (from both experts and relatives), where to meet your husband or wife, how to get to a certain spot on the map; directions

given by the boss in the office. Truly this is a direction-filled world; therefore impress upon children that since they never can escape directions, they had better learn to listen to them. The smart chap doesn't have to have directions repeated; he listens and gets ahead. Modern children can be impressed with the idea that in the space age we're going to have to operate faster and with more dispatch than we have been doing. The man who doesn't follow directions in a space age will be dead before he realizes what has happened. Rockets move fast. High-powered machines take high-powered minds to run them. Point out for youth the difference between the danger of a stalled car, a stalled plane, and a stalled space machine. We are rapidly moving into an age of machinery that can almost think; men will have to think faster to keep ahead of them. Get the children to make a real game of getting directions the first time. Begin at home and in kindergarten and never lapse along the way up through the grades. The trouble with following directions arises from their being so poorly given.

These ideas may help you parents and teachers to become better givers of directions:

Directions at home and at school. Parents and teachers must get into the habit of giving directions only once. If it is necessary to repeat occasionally, let a child do the repeating.

These precautions will guarantee better listening habits:

1. Have the attention of your audience before giving directions. Talking into confusion means repeating. Inform children that directions will be given but once—and mean it.

2. Speak in a clear voice at a normal rate.

3. Never give more directions at once than children of that age can assimilate.

4. Be sure that you yourself are clear on the process you are attempting to explain.

Do you remember the spot in *Alice in Wonderland* where Alice says, "I'm afraid I can't put it more clearly, for I can't understand it myself to begin with." In the wonderland in which we live today Alice's words are doubly true. Work out instructions for playing a game, for instance, ahead of the time you must explain it to a group. One of the hardest directions in the world to make clear is to explain in the simplest terms how to play a game. I worked on the one on page 101 for hours until I got it even as clear as it is. Try getting your children to make up original games with simple directions for playing; it's the best kind of writing discipline.

5. Start children with simple directions, gradually increasing the complications.

This idea of starting with simple directions makes me think of the chuckly old story of the young man who was lost on a back road in Alabama, and who asked an old farmer sitting on a fence the way to Montgomery. The farmer looked down the road, scratched his head, and gave a complicated set of directions.

About thirty minutes later, after following the farmer's directions carefully, the young man could hardly believe his eyes when he came upon the farmer at the very same spot. Thoroughly exasperated, he pulled up and shouted: "Look here, you act as though you expected to see me again. What's the big idea?"

"Waal, young feller," the farmer drawled, "I didn't aim to waste my time explainin' how you get to Montgomery till I found out if you could follow simple directions."

6. Help the child to see a complete picture of what he is going to do or make before he begins. Never give directions blindly. Illustrations that clarify directions:

I am going to show you how to find the Old North Church from the museum.

This game I am going to teach you will test your ability to use homonyms.

First we will fold this paper to make a three-cornered hat.

This beautiful valentine I am showing you is easy to make. Listen carefully to the directions.

Imagination in the use of direction-giving helps the directed to visualize the whole before he begins each part; an intelligent worker can proceed faster and better if he knows his goal ahead of time. Too many teachers work toward a picture in their own minds instead of helping each person to see his own picture in his own mind.

7. Put enough word pictures into your directions so that the other fellow can reach back into his experience for help. "Mix the clay to the consistency of sour cream." "Boil the sugar until it threads from the spoon." "Try to mix the blue of an October sky."

What young cook would not understand how to handle cookie dough from these picturesque directions by Edith Benedict Hawes?

ADVICE TO A YOUNG COOK [5]

Handle cookie dough as gently as you would a baby kitten;
Sift flour over the board and rolling pin—no deeper than the first
    snow flurry.
Hold the rolling pin more up than down; barely let it touch;
And when the dough is as thin as an oak leaf,
Cut the cookies as carefully as you'd lay a pattern on expensive silk,
For cookie dough rolled twice is tough.
Pop them into the oven, but don't start anything else—
They'll be done before you turn around.
When you put in the last pan, turn off heat, the last pan is so apt
    to burn.
Lift the cookies carefully onto the rack;
You hear the sound of feet that follow noses.
You are glad your brothers like your cookies—
They were made to eat. But save the heart-shaped one for Mother.

Recipe books give amounts beautifully but so often forget the directions that skilled cooks know only from experience. Even in the field of direction-giving, it makes for clarity to use the imaginative touch. The best I have ever heard came from Helen A. Ryan by way of "Life in These United States" in *The Reader's Digest:*

When my son, a Marine staff sergeant, was home on leave, he was quite unexpectedly left in charge of his three-month-old niece for an afternoon. All went well at first; then a crisis arose and the sergeant put in a frantic call to his uncle, who took care of the problem in man-to-man fashion.

"First," he said, "place the diaper in the position of a baseball diamond, with you at bat. Fold second base over home plate. Place baby on pitcher's mound. Then pin first base and third base to home plate."

It worked.[6]

We must always give directions in word pictures the listeners can understand.

Listening to place directions. Getting directions straight as to how to get from one point to another depends upon the listener as much as on the director. The man who asks his questions intelligently tends to get more intelligent answers. If possible, ask your questions

[5] By permission of the author and *The Christian Science Monitor.*
[6] By permission of the author, Helen A. Ryan, and *The Reader's Digest.*

of a policeman or a filling-station attendant. Direction-giving is their business.

1. Find out where you are now—on the corner of what streets.

2. Find out the general direction of the address you are seeking and face in that direction. (This is important.)

3. Ask the director to use the terms *right* or *left,* instead of *east, west,* and so on.

4. Ask him to approximate the number of blocks or miles before turns and if possible to name the streets and number of the highways on which turns are to be made.

5. Ask for landmarks or distinguishing buildings for turns. ("Turn right at the post office two blocks down." "Turn left two blocks past the park.")

6. Repeat the directions carefully, perhaps even jotting down such helps as L2, R3, for the blocks and turns if the directions are complicated.

Schools in cities or near cities would do well to have city maps in the children's hands and often have a listening lesson such as this: "You are on the corner of 8th and King Streets and wish to go to 821 Carroll. Trace the easiest route and write it down."

Another day have the children work in pairs, one giving directions and the other listening, then tracing his way on the map. Children love to send for maps of New York or Chicago and note the pattern of the main arterials. They enjoy finding the location on the map of places they long to visit and point them out to each other. Keep a large map of your own community hanging on the wall, and use it in direction-giving whenever you can.

Oh, how much better we'd make connections,
If we knew how to listen to directions.

We Listen to Report to Others

This type of listening is one of the most important listening skills. Show your children what poor reporters they are by keeping scores on such incident tests as these:

1. Read aloud a detailed description of an automobile accident. Let the children pretend to be bystanders who saw the accident happen. Let each write or tell exactly what happened. After reading the items, select the widely divergent reports and read them to the

class. Most children are appalled at their inability to report an action correctly.

2. After something exciting such as a fight, an accident, a game or a performance has happened on the playground, ask everyone who witnessed it to write what he saw. The reporting may be more surprising than the initial performance.

3. Ask your class to listen to a television performance in the evening and the next morning choose four as reporters. While one reporter explains exactly what happened on the program, the other reporters remain in the hall out of earshot. As soon as a reporter is finished with his story, let the next come in with his report on the same program. After the four have reported, let the class judge the accuracy of the reporting of each.

4. Ask a small group to prepare a short skit full of melodramatic action such as this:

Mary, feeling hungry, wanders downstairs in the middle of the night for a snack and, hearing a noise in the dining room, finds a burglar preparing to take off with the sterling silver. Mary engages the man in conversation and finds out that he has a son her age. She impresses on him how bad the son would feel if he would discover his father's source of income, and after fixing some hot chocolate and a sandwich for the would-be thief, the man goes home without the silver. [This scene may be further complicated by the arrival of Mary's father.]

Swear the cast to secrecy until the performance; then after the skit is over, ask several people to pretend to be Mary telling the story to her family at the breakfast table. Some groups may wish to add more players and act out another scene. For an assignment, you might ask the listeners to write in a pretend letter exactly what happened in that midnight scene.

5. By means of a diagram on the board, a person describes an accident or an odd occurrence he witnessed over the week end. Let one or two listeners try to retell the child's tale, leaving out none of the details the speaker mentioned. If they are given as they happen, these reports will not occur often enough for children to tire of this reporting technique.

6. In sight of the whole class let a pupil perform five quite unrelated actions: (*a*) stand in the middle of the floor and whistle three short blasts; (*b*) go over to the window and write with his finger on the pane; (*c*) go to his desk and frantically search for something; (*d*) stop to straighten his tie (hair, sweater) ; (*e*) laugh

excitedly and tiptoe out of the room. See how many people can list his actions in sequence.

The skill of listening to report is needed in conversation, story-telling, news reporting, and accident reporting, in courts of law, and in general truth telling. Children love to improve their scores in this listening area.

We Listen to Learn

Listening to learn starts in the home and is further strengthened at school. But many people lose most of this potential learning because they do not know how to sieve out essentials from nonessentials as they listen.

After listening to an interesting nature talk over the radio at home, have a little game with your children to see who can remember the most facts about the subject with which to regale father later around the dinner table. (He'll be thrilled, no doubt.) Teach conversational manners here, and see that you observe them yourself. When the children are older, listen to lectures together and, pencil and pad in hand, learn to pick out the main points and the unfamiliar words. Never appear to have planned home-listening activities. Let them seem to be spontaneous and just for fun; otherwise children may resent them as being too much like school.

When interesting guests are entertained in the home, plan with the children to listen to what is said and the next day have a family "post-mortem" of the facts and opinions gathered during the evening. Children often spot inconsistencies faster than their parents.

At school, the listening program is not a casual one as it usually is at home. School-listening lessons are as carefully planned as a bride's first dinner party.

In preparing listening-to-learn lessons, teachers should keep these points in mind:

1. Match the material to your children's interests and ability to understand.

2. If background material is needed to understand the lessons, provide it. If the children are going to see a sound film on Antarctica, find that continent on the map ahead of time, and let the pupils make conjectures from their known geographic concepts as to the type of life there.

3. If it seems best to do so, give pupils several topics to listen for. These topics or questions should broaden as the children grow in listening ability.

4. Begin simple note-taking from listening in fourth grade and gradually raise the requirements.

As a variation from *your* reading orally to children who are listening to learn, get your friends who are excellent oral readers to make tape recordings of their readings of interesting informational material, poetry, or plays. This will give children experience they need with listening to a wide variety of voices, inflections, and tempos.

5. Exchange tape recordings of children's reports and discussions with other schools and other classes, and use them in listening lessons.

6. In listening to lecture material, teach children to listen first for the title, then the main idea of the lecture. In the material on ants, the main idea is how ants are like human beings. The central idea is named or hinted at in the title and usually stated early after the warm-up or introductory part.

Help the young listener to listen for key words and expressions, such as "I want to give you the reasons why . . ." "I will explain how . . ." "In summary . . ." "In conclusion . . ." Go back to the "ant" article on page 95, and find the key words and expressions used by this author.

7. Listen often for the topic sentences of single paragraphs read aloud or played from tape.

8. Begin note-taking with a single paragraph of informational material read aloud with definite directions for listening, and gradually increase the dosage.

9. Invite as many visitors in to talk to your class as seems wise: travelers from foreign lands and other states; men and women in industry from your area; older boys and girls from your own schools who have read widely on a subject, who have recently made a trip, or who have an unusual hobby. Then let the children take notes on the lectures.

When note-taking is a new skill, take notes along with the class, then mimeograph the notes or put them on the board so that the children can grow in this skill. Be content if the top two-thirds or even one-half of the class become good note-takers; some children who can excel in other areas can never achieve this skill.

Listening to learn, with or without note-taking, is one of a modern citizen's most useful skills. It should be taught consistently and regularly and with an eye to need. Note-taking must become a commonplace before high school.

Listening to radio and educational television programs. Listening to a program "cold" without preparing the listeners for it is to lose half the program.

No two teachers get ready for a program in the same way. A nature, science, or geographical program may be prepared by:

1. Guessing the nature of the program from the title.

2. Finding out what the children already know about the subject, listing the statements they think are true, and finding out how many of them are actually false.

3. Reading poetry on the subject.

4. Reading stories that pertain to the subject.

5. Playing map detective.

6. Teaching new vocabulary that is sure to be used.

7. Looking at pictures.

8. Listing questions the children hope the program will answer.

9. Giving the children definite questions to listen for.

10. Presenting and working with mechanical skills needed after the broadcast.

In short, the preparation for a program is to prepare the minds of the listeners for seeding. The directions included in the program will, of course, determine the after-broadcast procedures. These may include:

1. A gathering of ideas suggested in the broadcast for creative work

2. A summary of facts in many different forms

    a) Written summaries

    b) Material put into letters

    c) Pictured summaries

    d) The summary in creative story form

    e) Material put into a radio diary

    f) Facts dramatized or creative episodes worked out from the broadcast

    g) New ideas sparked by the program discussed

3. Further reference reading done by those interested

4. Definite questions that arose from the broadcast and that were assigned for research

5. Facts used to build an original radio program (Be sure to use the manual for a radio program if one is obtainable. But always think beyond and above the manual if you can, and adapt it to your group.)

We Listen to Analyze

In this day of mass communication, when we so seldom know much about the speaker, listening to analyze is doubly important. Schools must help children visualize the man behind the voice. Teach the children from sixth grade on to seek to find the beliefs behind the words.

Especially if you strongly liked or disliked a speaker, analyze why. Was it his voice? Was it his manner? Was it what he said?

Violent liking or disliking usually points out that the speaker has stirred you emotionally. At that point learn to say to yourself, "Just what did he say that I can think about?" and often you will find that a strongly emotional speaker has left nothing with you but feelings.

A friend of mine, who could speak no German, went to a meeting one night at which Hitler gave a speech during the early days of his rise to power. He reported that so persuasive and powerful was Hitler's voice that despite the fact that he caught little of what was being said, he left the meeting enthusiastic and full of hope for Germany's future. Indeed, we must show our children how to look behind the voice and find the speaker—what he thinks and what he stands for.

The shyster lawyer who explained to a young barrister how to win a case knew a great deal about the psychology of the audience: "If your evidence will stand by itself, proceed quietly and with dignity; if your case is shaky, slyly poke fun at your opponent and incite the jurors to laugh at his points, but if your side has practically no leg to stand on, become powerfully melodramatic and pound the table like the very devil."

If children can learn to find the gold in a speech and to discard the baser metal, we shall have done them a great service in helping them to see through propaganda. (See Cupboard of Ideas, page 131, for techniques.)

There are many opportunities for analysis in the daily program of a modern school: analyzing arithmetic story problems for steps in solving (a fine exercise in critical thinking) ; listening to taped class discussions and reports and determining what was actually said; analyzing playground situations by having them dramatized before a school council; examining evidence to determine subsequent procedure; gifted children's re-enacting political scenes that are then evaluated by the class; gifted children's analyzing the news (sports, fashions) ; analyzing a science problem, separating fact from opinion; determining a writer's bias by reading several of his articles. Be sure to set children looking for strong points, not flaws.

A child in the intermediate grades who perpetually doubts is in a sorry state. The attitude of analysis must not be begun too early in the elementary school. A certain level of maturity is needed before children are ready to look for flaws. Wait until children see life whole before you teach them to take life apart. Young children need faith more than they need doubt. Analyzing arithmetic problems and school reports, yes, but analyzing speeches, no. It is this element of timing as much as anything that will keep us from having machine teachers. When to introduce a skill to a child is almost as important as the skill itself.

We Listen for Pleasure

When they get interested in the teaching of listening skills, many teachers forget that listening for sheer pleasure is one of the most useful of all listening skills. A person who never listens to exquisite music, who is never carried along by the sheer pleasure of the spoken word in poem or play or story, or who has not spent an afternoon in a hammock between trees listening to nature's wonderful monotone, as Shakespeare says in *The Merchant of Venice,* "is fit for treasons, stratagems and spoils."

Listening for pleasure begins at home. Children are not born with a love of listening to fine things; this is a learned skill. We learn to love the best by associating with the best. How lucky our generation is to be able with little cost to hear so many fine things! He who is used to associating with the high will eventually be uncomfortable with the low. Remember that always.

Every school day, however crowded, has a few minutes' time in which to "listen lovely" as a second grader put it. Music sometimes while we paint and write, soft music on some days during library reading, background music during the reading aloud of a mighty poem or a moving story—these are the things that rest our souls and help us to be discontented with wandering in wastelands of the spirit.

Van Dyke reminded the last generation, "Don't forget the best." Balance tension with relaxation if you would be whole. (What a wonderful word *whole* is!) Yet most groups of people, old or young, do not listen well either to music or to reading. As Oscar Wilde says in *The Importance of Being Earnest,* "You see, if one plays good music, people don't listen, and if one plays bad music, people don't talk." We must begin these listening associations in childhood.

Probably by far the most crucial problems of today's home listening, both for pleasure and for profit, are the problems presented by television viewing.

Is listening at your house a pleasure? How shall the problem of differing tastes for television programs be settled for a family? Which programs are inimical to a child's wholesome growth? Which are innocuous but interesting to children? Which programs are interesting to the whole family? I believe that the areas of choice I discussed in Chapter Three on thinking pertain here. If your children can listen unbridled to any program they choose at any hour of the day or night, then you parents had better take a sober look at the condition into which your home has fallen. After looking, you had better quietly but persistently take steps to change that condition.

But giving bossy directions even to one's children does not change their attitudes about television, and changing behavior without changing attitudes promotes greater subsequent misbehavior.

Parents should study children's programs at home together and with the school or community group of parents. If mothers and fathers would meet with the parents of children with whom their children associate, talk over television programs together, even study them together and decide as a group on some common procedures, their children's chorus of "all the other kids listen to that one" would be stilled—until they think up a new rejoinder, that is. *Parents' Magazine* and other popular publications rate children's television programs. Groups of parents and teachers could be of mutual help to one another in doing their own evaluating and discussing magazine ratings. (Whenever I used to tell my father that everybody in school but me had a "certain kind of pencil," he always said wryly, "Name five." If I could name five, I got the pencil —but I seldom could.)

It is not wise, however, to judge programs children love by adult standards. It may be you, not your child, that has hardening of the arteries of taste. Programs interesting to children are usually interesting to parents, but not always. One can never decide for another person what is interesting to him. The parents' job is not to determine a child's television tastes, but to improve them and to actually forbid a few programs.

However, this forbidding will only whet a youngster's determination to see a program unless the veto of that program comes as a result of a family discussion. (All television rules for a home should be the result of parent-child discussion.) —

Supplementary to parents' deciding on programs suitable for children is the appointing of a group of intelligent youngsters to evaluate programs they consider wise listening. Children usually live up to the standards expected of them. If they believe that adults value their opinions, they take care to be worthy, and their opinions tend to be respected by their contemporaries as well as by adults.

In disagreements about television concerning only the children, allow the children to attempt the first compromise procedures. If, on the other hand, the television set *must* be placed in the room where guests are entertained, to avoid scowling looks and offensive manners in front of guests, decide ahead of time how to take care of the situation. Remember that parents as well as children have rights; it is insanity to let children get all the windfalls. Children learn consideration for others by living in a considerate home, but learn to be thoughtless from parents who allow themselves to become door mats. Yes, children as well as parents have rights, and procedures affecting both must be determined together. If television is nothing but a source of trouble at home, better put a "Temporarily Out of Patience" sign on it, freezing its sounds and sights for a week until the members of the family learn to respect each other's rights.

Viewing television programs can be the best kind of family listening pleasure if it is worked out by all the members for all of the members.

We Listen to Conversation

Intelligent listening to conversation is another listening skill learned first at home—one of the most needed of the social skills. "The girl with the patient eardrum is the girl who first nabs a husband," declared George Jean Nathan. The best speakers are often only the best listeners. The listening part of a conversation is answering with the heart the questions of the mind: it is the communication that shows the profoundest respect. We must teach children to listen intelligently in order that they can carry on conversation intelligently.

In listening to conversations, we must make children aware of these listening skills:

1. Give the person speaking, your undivided attention. Unless it is necessary to look disinterested in order to stop a bore, look at the speaker as if you were hanging on his every word—even if you're planning how to get more allowance out of your father at the time. Children must learn early that they cannot always act or look as they feel; people who do are often not socially acceptable because they are not kind.

2. Don't be a cut-in listener, waiting breathlessly for a chance to put in your two-cents' worth. However, if you are unlucky enough to have a nonstop speaker present in the group, you may have to use some strategy to stop him—temporarily.

3. Try to bring out quiet people by the right kind of questions: "What do you think about that, Donald?" "What is your opinion, Mary?" "You've just come back from a trip to Yellowstone, Glen. What part of your trip did you enjoy most?" "You were telling me a wonderful story about your family's adventure in Colorado yesterday, John. Tell it to the class, will you?"

The secret of being a good listener is to be thoughtful of other people, to be more anxious to learn than to tell; all true social skills begin in our attitudes toward other people.

What can we do to help thoughtless children to *take part in,* rather than *take over,* a conversation? Since most children who have this annoying habit are only so excited about living that their words fairly spill out, we must help them to restrain their output of words without squelching their exuberance. I have found that ignoring the child does not help this situation much, but a quiet talking-over with the child does help. (How blessed children are about guidance if they only know we like them; if we make them see without censure; and if we talk to them alone. (All of child guidance is in that one sentence.)

"What can we talk about to grownups?" children often wonder. "We never know what to say to them." If children only realized it, many adults feel the same way about conversation with children. The answer to both questions is the same: Bring out the other fellow and be a listener. Try to find out ahead of time what the other person's interests are, and get him started talking about them. Adults love to talk about their hobbies, their trips, and their sports interests, and so do children. Television programs and common interests in pets make good topics of conversation, the listener watching carefully to note when the conversational ball needs picking up: "And then what happened?" "Weren't you afraid?" "What do you think of the Braves' chances for this season?" Help children to know how to pass the ball in the conversational game.

4. Teach intermediate children how a listener can steer a conversation away from the rapids of violent controversy and dissension into calmer waters. When a conversation tends to become too heated, the hostess tactfully suggests a new subject, or a wit relieves the tension with a remark that makes everybody laugh.

Abraham Lincoln was a master hand at clearing the air with clever remarks. Once when defending a poor man in a damage suit against a more successful one, Lincoln found that the defendant had torn his Sunday trousers in the accident. At the psychological moment, Lincoln pointed out that because of the end in view, he thought the man should be awarded damages, and the jury got so good a laugh that the case was settled in the defendant's favor.

The listener to a conversation is the one who learns and who has time to think. What wit was it who said, "The only time we can't learn anything is when we have our mouths open, talking"?

We Listen to the Power of Spoken Words

Although this heading is actually included in "We listen for pleasure," it goes far beyond that title. Listening to the power of spoken words, while definitely a pleasure, is at the same time an inspiration, a depth bomb, and a stirrer of sluggish souls. Many people who find music an elixir are deaf to the power of poetry and proud prose read magnificently.

Truly listening to reading aloud is the king of spirit sports. For what other listening sings as it says and says as it sings? What other form of listening enters into the blood stream and changes our very thoughts and ambitions, causing us to outgrow the rooms of old desires and compelling us to seek new dwelling places? What other aesthetic experience speaks even more clearly to the mind than to the senses?

One of the best ways to handle classics, which were discarded in the thirties because they were too hard for the average child to read, is to read them aloud to children—read them beautifully so that the sound as well as the sense of the words inspires. Great prose as well as fine poetry was meant to be read aloud; the two not only gain in the sharing but combine the music of the words with the power of their meaning.

I have a feeling that schools are at the threshold of a new day in reading aloud—not the silly "barbershop" reading around the class of yesterday, but teams of outstanding reading choirs or solo readers presenting material above the reading, but not the understanding, level of the class—Charles Laughton style.[7]

The reason why youngsters in the elementary school so often fail to discover their reading voices is that there is actually so little use made of them in school.

Think of the powerful influence the ideas in classics, both old and modern, could have on these golden-voiced youth whose hobby is reading aloud to their classes, to the children of other grades, and to groups of townspeople.

When will school systems ever get smart enough to hire teachers with varying abilities and interests? One a silver-tongued reader, one a vocal musician, another a band enthusiast, one whose interests is puppetry, another outstanding in creative dramatics or art, one or two expert in getting children to think, one whose hobby is choral reading, another whose interests lie in semantics, and possibly one dedicated to folk or interpretive dancing. What a well-rounded education that school could give its children during their elementary years of training! Think of the on-going effects of each teacher's enthusiasm, of how the children would take interests and skills acquired in one room on to another and into their postschool lives.

If the level of our television and radio programs is to rise, we must encourage in our schools the study and use of skills used in the entertainment world. Reading choirs, readings of plays, humorous programs, script writing for homemade radio and television programs—these must be studied and performed by talented children for critical listeners. [Children must make use in school of the gifts they may later give to the world.] Talent, like the ancient god, is renewed every time it touches the earth of practical use.

And what, pray, you ask, has all this to do with listening?

Have you caught the vision here of whole roomfuls of children listening to live programs provided by their own gifted classmates? Truly if listening skills are taught only through devices warmed up to provide tests for improving listening abilities, how unlike real life they will be. In real life no one gets us ready to listen; we figuratively bend our ears because we are interested in hearing. When training

---

[7] See *Tell Me a Story* by Charles Laughton (McGraw, 1957).

in real experiences begins in the classroom, we already have the listening problem half solved. Listening to the power of words could transform our church schools, our church services, our family gatherings around the fireplace or the dining table, and our schools.

Just one enthusiastic teacher in a building can get the whole school excited about Laughton reading and verse choirs. Almost any fire can be set with enthusiasm.

TEACHER

He taught; he died with this regret—
"Oh, for the fires I might have set!
Only mechanics was I skilled for.
Oh, for the depths I might have drilled **for.**"
They buried him with scanty tears,
And knew not he'd been dead for years.

We Listen to Create

Listening in order to create is the highest form of listening skill. Such listening goes out and beyond someone else's directions, yet builds its foundation on them. It is listening tailor-made to each individual's ability to think for himself, yet to create on someone else's suggestion, a much-needed skill in the space age.

Radio programs, such as Wisconsin's own "Let's Draw" and "Let's Write," are listening-to-create programs; they build launching platforms for each student's rocket ideas. The majority of children are capable of creating, but all except a few need help in getting launched; the ideas are there, but usually lie dormant unless stimulated from outside.

Listening-to-create programs are of even more importance to teachers than to children. A creative program over radio or television once each week is only the starting of creative habits of thought. Unless the teacher seizes on the techniques of creativity, utilized by and demonstrated in the programs and uses the same techniques in other situations, little of permanent worth is accomplished by the programs.

The steps of a listening-to-create lesson are the same for any medium: drawing, painting, working out designs, making murals, construction work in any medium, soap carving, clay modeling, story writing, poetry writing, creating music or a dance. Let us pretend to tape a listening-to-create program from "Let's Write," analyzing each step as we go along and realizing, as we go, how each could just as well have stimulated a project in any other artistic medium than writing.

Title: "I Hear America Singing"

Step 1. *Introduction:* Tying the idea to each child's experience.

Each of us has our own personal theme song, whether we know it or not. Our faces sing a sad or happy tune. Our feelings come dancing or dragging out from our hearts; our emotions bubble and form on our lips. Always and always we are consciously or unconsciously playing our tunes to the world; and those who can read the notes of the music of people are aware of our private tunes.

Some days we purr like cats "with an enclosed and private sound" as the poet Rosalie Moore says in "Catalog." On other days we are out of tune and our gears grind, and we make far more discord than melody.

Walt Whitman, one of the most joyful and enthusiastic of American poets, loved to listen to the music of American people at their work. He was good at listening to the "private ditties of no tune" as Keats called them, which is just a poet's way of saying he liked to listen with his eyes to the theme songs in people's hearts. Whitman's "I Hear America Singing" is a lovely poem. Notice that he writes without rhyme. Listen!

(Here read the poem on page 86.)

What are these "varied carols" the poet heard with his eyes? Some day your heart will sing in the rhythm of life's work. It is the song of the workers we are going to listen to and write today. But before you can write the songs of others, you must understand the songs your own heart sings now.

Just the sun shining on you or the twitch of a fish on your line may start that inside music going.

Sometime when something happens at home that makes you know how much you love and appreciate your parents, that inner song comes right out in words as it did to fourth-grade Jill at Christmas time when she wrote:

DEAR MOTHER,

We are having a Talking Christmas Tree in our room. Now if you don't know what a talking Christmas Tree is, it's a tree with wishes instead of presents.

I know that you would like an automatic washer to get your clothes clean. Now I know that you still get our clothes clean without one. Am I ever glad I have a mother and an old washer.

LOVE,
JILL

P.S. Merry Christmas and a Happy New Year.

How Jill's mother's heart must have sung after that letter; it was so warm and appreciative.

Sometimes after school you get another song in your heart when you hear your mother singing your little sister to sleep. There wells up within you, as you listen, a song of love and helpfulness and the safety of home and parents. Maybe the lullaby was as old as time; perhaps it was a lovely new one, but it is the voice not the tune that is important.

Inner singing comes not only from scenes at home but from the challenge and ecstasy of sports. Some of you wrote wonderful chants after the January "Swoops and Oops" program. First, listen to this inside song of Dale's. It is exceptionally full of real verve and fast music.

SAILING ON A SLEIGH

Put a sail on a sleigh
On a windy day
And away you'll go like loose hay;
Swoopen and loopen up hill and down
Over the snowbanks and all around.
Some say it's not fun
But I say it is.
Oh! Oh! Here I go again.
Whiz! Whiz! Whiz!

Step 2. *Writing Stimulation and Assignment:* By now I think you have the feeling of what we mean by inner singing and are ready to talk about today's writing. Together we're going to listen to the songs of the various workmen of America—the airplane pilot, the railroad engineer, the nurse, the physician. We're going to choose our favorite one; we're going to watch him at work awhile and write into a poem what he is feeling and thinking. Unless it rhymes naturally, let the lines come out today as they will, in unrhymed verse or talking prose. Let the song of your chosen workman tell how he enjoys his work, the thrill he gets out of it, what he sees and thinks about as he works. Perhaps, if you can, you may catch the rhythm of what he is doing. Some of you today may want to pretend that you are already in your chosen job, already experiencing the thrill of it. Which one of these poems, for instance, is answered by a song in your own heart? Listen!

(Read such poems as the following suggestions, varying them according to age and interest:

1. A sky pilot—"Silver Ships" by Mildred Plew Meigs in *Time for Poetry* p. 73
2. A railroad engineer—"The Railroad Cars Are Coming" in *My Poetry Book* p. 395
3. A builder—"Skyscraper Is a City's House" and "Summon the Workers" by Clara Lambert in *My Poetry Book* pp. 400–402
4. A florist—"Florist Shop" by Rachel Field in *Taxis and Toadstools* p. 33
5. A grocer—"Counters" by Elizabeth Coatsworth in *Sung under the Silver Umbrella* p. 53
6. A trucker—"The City and the Trucks" by Dorothy B. Thompson in *Bridled with Rainbows* p. 75)

Step 3. *Final Impetus for Writing*

I hear America singing; the varied carols I hear;

What songs do you hear with the eyes of your ears? Capture the rhythm of your chosen worker and sing his inner song today. Make your words match the song he sings as he works.

Good-by, singers, with eyes in your ears and ears in your eyes!

Step 4. *Illustrative Outgrowths of This Lesson*

I WANT TO BE THE TEACHER

I want to be the teacher.
When I'm the teacher
I'm the boss.
That's what's so much fun.

Get up so early and run, run, run.
Get in school and scold all day.
But I won't want to be that way.

But I guess that's the way I'll have to be.
If they're going to act like they're only three.

Lyn, Grade 4

THE CLAY PLANT

Clang! clang! clang! goes the big machine.
Bang! bang! bang! goes the big machine
  Hum goes the worker who works the big machine.
Oh-hum you hear quite often.
  Dee-dee-dum—clay begins to soften
Buzz-buzz-buzz goes the big saw.
  Scre-e-ech goes the big crane jaw.
Pop-pop-pop goes the boiling water.
  Hum-hum-hum goes the workman's daughter.
Na-na-na goes the working ant.
  Clankety-clank goes the big clay plant.

Patt, Grade 5

THE DENTIST'S SONG

Today he was all thumbs and drill;
I think for sure he was out for the kill.
The nurse ran from here to there;
My mom had me tricked into his lair.

As he worked he sang this song,
"Drill, drill all day long
Here I sing this dentist's song.
In the mirror here I see
One great big cavity
Now I'll have to drill
For sure, but be still."

Kenneth, Grade 6

THE MONKEY PIT

Within the monkey pit
I hear the race cars sputter and spit.

Five hundred horses and that's a fact
Under each hood on that dusty track.

Some of them roar but others quit.
Of all those cars that sputter and spit

The Bluebell is first
And comes in with a burst,

Then into the pit
With a sputter and spit;

Put in a transmission
So it has more friction;

Change the tires
Put in new wires.

That's what happens in a monkey pit
When race cars sputter and spit.

Michael, Grade 7

THE SALESMAN

Hurry, hurry, hurry, says the salesman to his feet.
Try to make a sale before we reach the end of the street.
Knock, knock, knock, goes the salesman on each door.
The salesman's knuckles are getting tired and sore.
Slowly—slowly—slowly—he walks down the street.
Tired and weary are the salesman's feet.

Marie, Grade 7

THAT'S MY LINE

(Tune: "On Wisconsin")

Reading books! Reading books!
Over and down the page,
If you like to do all this, then—
Librarian is your rage.

Numbering and cataloging,
Perhaps put up a sign.
A good librarian I hope to be,
For that's my line.

Help a child! Help a child!
Find a very good book,
In the section of fiction or science
Take a very good look

Fill the card; date it right,
Send him away feeling fine.
A good librarian I hope to be,
For that's my line.

Louise, Grade 8

In order that all children will be able to create this type of listening exercise, it is usually necessary to provide, as in this exercise, a somewhat common background of experience for all listeners. Although all may appear to have the same experience, the one who brings the most experience to the lesson takes the most away. (See Cupboard of Ideas for other exercises in listening-to-create, pages 130–31.)

We Listen for Cues

No chapter on listening would be complete without touching on listening for cues. The unconscious inflections of the human voice speak far more eloquently and truthfully than designed speech. As a new mother of a first baby gradually learns the inflectional meaning of each infant cry, so must we learn to recognize the nuances of meaning in the tones of voice of those around us. Anger, frustration, worry, weariness, hopelessness, sorrow, and joy register their sub-tle message in the voice providing the cues that make for awareness and understanding. Most of us are so wrapped up in ourselves and our own affairs that we fail to recognize the cues to the other fellow's feelings. Awareness is born of the right attitude toward other people coupled with the ability to listen for cues and take note of them. To be a good world or next-door neighbor, to be prosperous without flaunting one's riches, to share without ostentation, to be able to re-ceive help as well as to give help, each comes from a true wholeness of spirit. Such an attitude toward our neighbors can never be taught to our children by precept but by example. But we ourselves must "be still and know" if our children are to grow in a like pattern.

America needs disciplined ears: ears that can bring the wisdom to us that men of other generations and this generation have dis-covered. For in a single lifetime a man can hardly learn firsthand the wisdom he will need for rich living.

America needs disciplined ears: ears that can listen to conver-sation and know how to give wise directions to the tongue and the lips.

America needs disciplined ears: ears that can listen to great music and great thoughts and grow whole again.

America needs disciplined ears: ears that take ideas from the assembly line of life and fashion new and better thoughts and imple-ments of living for themselves and for others.

America needs disciplined ears.

> Watch your ears as to things heard often.
> Watch your ears as to things seldom heard.
> Pick and choose of what comes to your ears.
> Select and sift, believe or disbelieve.
> And on stated occasions, feeling a little high,
> Believe perfectly in the completely unbelievable.[8]

Carl Sandburg

---

[8] From *Complete Poems,* copyright, 1950, by Carl Sandburg. Reprinted by permission of Harcourt, Brace and Company, Inc.

CUPBOARD OF IDEAS   for Chapter Four

We Need Disciplined Ears   ❖ ❖ ❖ ❖ ❖ ❖ ❖ ❖ ❖ ❖ ❖ ❖ ❖ ❖

Primary Shelf

I. Listen to Think

A. Writing simple summaries. After reading an informative article on any subject (bears, for instance), ask the youngsters to copy from the board such a statement as this: "Bears are interesting," then to write as much as they can remember from their listening. The first grade could draw as much information as they can. As an aid to correct spelling, I would have on the board many useful words from the article. "Why I Would Like to Own a Kangaroo" is another good beginning sentence.

B. Writing after character analysis. A good listen-to-think exercise is to read a story about a child with one outstanding characteristic, such as laziness or dishonesty; then have pupils write the answer to this question: "If John lived next to me, why would (or wouldn't) he make a good neighbor?"

C. Thinking after informational material. Read about a visit to a foreign country, after which second and third graders write: "Why I Would (or Wouldn't) Like to Visit Holland (or _____)."

D. Thinking through an arithmetic problem. Use practical arithmetic problems as listening exercises.
Directions: I am going to read a problem in arithmetic aloud to you. After you listen, you are to think through these four steps:

1. What does the problem tell me?
2. What does the problem ask me?
3. What steps must I think to myself in order to get the answer?
4. What is the approximate answer?

Listen: I am reading this problem just once.

Mr. Jones at the grocery across the street sells apples for 5¢ each. How many apples can your mother buy for 25¢? for 50¢?

E. **Listening to solve riddles.** (Kdgn.-Gr. 3) Now we are going to find out if you can guess riddles. Listen carefully to what I read. We have been studying circus animals. Can you name the one I am describing? When you know the answer, do not put up your hand, but when I am finished, write (or draw if the children cannot yet write) the name of the animal I have described.

Read: This animal lives along the river and uses the river for his swimming pool. He is short but very fat and heavy and keeps cool by spending much of his time in the river. His face looks something like a pig's and so does his tail. He has small, popping eyes and small ears and a huge mouth with great teeth. You feel like laughing when you see this animal. He looks as if he needs a girdle on. What animal am I describing? (*hippopotamus*)

F. **Listening for sequence.** Start with one and increase numbers as facility increases.
   1. How sharp are your ears? I am going to read a paragraph with four directions in it. When I have finished, can you do what I ask in the exact order I gave the directions?

   Knock twice on the window nearest the radiator. Then set the doll straighter in the rocking chair. Next pick up the paper by the wastebasket. Last of all eat the peanut hidden under the eraser on the chalk tray.

   2. Listen carefully, then follow these directions in order:

   Write the number 5 on the board. Put a 3 directly below it. Put a + sign in front of the 3. Draw a horizontal line under the numbers and work the example. Test for accuracy. Erase it.

II. *Listen to Follow Directions*

A. **Listening for word meanings.** Listen carefully to see if you can find the words that mean "move" or "go from one place to another" in this paragraph. I shall stop at the end of each sentence to get your answers. As soon as you know the answer, write it.

Jody *lay down* and watched the little insect people *go* about their morning's work. The caterpillar *inched along* like a tank *covering* rough ground. A grand-daddy longlegs awkwardly *covered* the ground on his stilt-like legs. A measuring worm *humped* over the tiny grass hills like a thread *crawling*. A grasshopper *jumped* in great green arcs through the grass as if he were practicing *broad jumps*. Soon funny little black bugs *jiggled* through the grass forest with a clicking sound. A pretty little strange-colored beetle *lumbered* along in front of Jody's nose like a miniature elephant. "Everybody has something to do," Jody thought to himself, "except me; I'm the only lazy one, and I like that."

B. **Listening to the sound of words**
  1. Say the word *whale* softly. How do your lips feel as you begin that word? Now I am going to say a list of words, some of which begin like the word *whale*. Whenever you hear a word that doesn't begin like whale, clap your hands. Listen carefully: whale; which; where; berry; whistle; man; boat.
  2. Say the word *jiggle*. Think of a word that rhymes with jiggle. Yes, *giggle* does rhyme with jiggle. Now think of another word that rhymes with jiggle that means how a little puppy shakes all over with gladness. Yes, *wiggle* (or *wriggle*) is the word. Now let us think of a little rhyme using *jiggle, giggle,* and *wiggle.*

I giggle,
Babies jiggle,
Puppies wiggle.

Choose interesting different sorts of words for this game: tacks, ax, packs; ocean, motion, notion.
  3. (Gr. 2) Let's take a word and see how many funny rhymes we can make with it. Let's take the word *whale.* I'll make the first one. Anyone who is ready may make the second line, and so on.

A funny old whale
Had a tail
That was hit by hail.
He went to jail
That funny old whale!

Let's try the word *bed* now. Think of rhyming words for bed:

I went to bed
And hit my head—
I won't tell what I said
The bump turned red;
Then I dropped dead.

Think of rhyming words for pony, run, snow, rabbit, play, and others.

4. Use a color to describe a thing, like pink sink, blue shoe, red sled, green bean, black sack, yellow fellow, white night, brown gown, orange door hinge. (I don't know any purple unless after we eat grapes, we might burp a purple burple. Excuse it, please; it was just in fun.)
5. Put sounds together (much needed).
   a) Listen carefully; I am thinking of a word that begins like *where* and ends like *hen*. (*when*)
   b) I am thinking of a word that begins like *blink* and ends like *pack*. (*black*)
   c) I am thinking of a compound word; the first part rhymes with *go* and is cold and white; the second part rhymes with *ball*, and we often do when we're skating. What is the word? (*snowfall*)

C. Thinking of the right word for the right meaning
1. I'm thinking of a word or a phrase that describes exactly how you feel when you are angry. (You will get such words as warm, hot, like fighting, like flashes running through you, clenching your fist, like crying, like hitting, and so on.)
2. (Kdgn.-Gr. 1) I am thinking of a long important word for the way Paddy Bear felt when he was caught. It is a good word for the feeling you get when someone sees you at a time when you thought you were alone. (*embarrassed*)

3. I am gathering all the words you can think of for the look on Father Bear's face in this picture (exasperated, angry, frustrated, vexed). (You may give one or two after the children have given all they know.)

III. Listen to Dramatize

A. Dramatizing the action suggested by a paragraph. I am going to read you a short paragraph about an animal in our circus unit. Listen carefully, for when I have finished, I am going to ask somebody to pretend to be the animal and act out what I have read in the exact order that I read it. Will you be the one to get it just right? Listen!

A lion paced slowly back and forth in its cage. Suddenly he stopped stock-still and listened. Then he sniffed the air. Then he gave a low growl and lay down on the floor of his cage.

Begin with one or two sentences and increase the number as the listening efficiency increases.

B. Dramatizing the action suggested by a poem
1. Read aloud "Prince Peter" (Brewton's *Gaily We Parade* p. 142), and have children act out the various conversations that might have happened as the prince visited each animal.
2. Read aloud "The Grasshoppers" by Dorothy Aldis (Brewton's *Under the Tent of the Sky* p. 108), and let the children act it out, adding to the conversation. Because they can talk back to their parents in this poem, they simply love it.
3. Read aloud "If I Were a Little Pig" by Lucy Sprague Mitchell (Geismer and Suter's *Very Young Verses* p. 29). Let the boys pretend to be little pigs getting their dinner at the trough in the way the poem states. Have a girl for a pig mother, suggesting better order and calling out to individual pigs.

IV. Listen to Create (Gr. 3–5)

The following suggested readings are all from Brewton's *Gaily We Parade:*

A. Read "The Pirate Don Durk of Dowdee" by Mildred Plew Meigs (p. 73), and ask the children to make a crayon drawing of what they think the pirate looked like.

B. Read the three-line poem "Chums" by Buson (p. 56). Let those who wish draw the raincoat and umbrella walking and the others write the lively conversation that went on under the umbrella, or the conversation between a blue and a yellow raincoat hung in a school cloakroom.

C. Read "Balloon Man" by Jessica Nelson North (p. 3), and have children draw with crayolas the picture it gives them.

D. Read the chuckly "Grandpa Dropped His Glasses" by LeRoy F. Jackson (p. 38), and choosing the color they might have dropped their mind spectacles into, let children draw a scene they saw through those colored spectacles.

E. Read "Jim at the Corner" by Eleanor Farjeon (p. 75), and ask the children to write any story the old sailor might have told to the children he knew.

F. Read "The New Neighbor" by Rose Fyleman (p. 55), and have children write the questions they'd like to ask of a new neighbor or of anybody they know; or write an adventure they might have with a new neighbor.

G. Read aloud "Penny Problem" by John Farrar (p. 13). Then suggest, "If you had a dollar or a quarter or a dime, tell in a verse or paragraph what you would do with it and why."

H. During a unit on community helpers read these poems:
   1. "Bobby Blue" by John Drinkwater (p. 24)
   2. "The Postman" by Christina Rossetti (p. 25)
   3. "The Dentist" by Rose Fyleman (p. 28)
   4. "The Milkman" by Christopher Morley (p. 29)
   After discussion and exchange of ideas, ask each child to write a poem or paragraph about which community helper he'd like to be and why.

Intermediate and Upper-Grade Shelf

I. Listen to Analyze

A. Analyzing what's wrong with a philosophy
   1. What's wrong with the thinking of this person or animal? Read aloud the story, "Why the Raccoon Wears a Mask," page 289 in Chapter Eight and discuss these questions:

      a) What was Ricky's philosophy about honesty?

      b) How did he rationalize that what he was doing was right? (Explain to the children that *rationalize* means to convince yourself that what you *want* to do is *right* to do; the reason one gives for doing something he knows is not his true reason.)

      c) How did society punish Ricky?

      d) Did it cure him of his wrong ideas? (Be sure to bring out here that no data are given in answer to this question.)

      e) In what other ways might Ricky's wrongdoing have been dealt with?

2. (Gr. 5–8) Read in several sittings John Ruskin's classic "The King of the Golden River," and discuss the difference between the philosophy of Gluck and that of his brothers. What did each philosophy do to and for each one of the brothers? This discussion of philosophy helps clarify children's thinking. They see so much difference between ideals and performance in the adult world that they need to realize that what one truly believes changes his behavior.

3. Read "Portrait by a Neighbor" by Edna St. Vincent Millay (*Gaily We Parade* p. 55). Analyze together what kind of person the neighbor was. Write a little episode that tells how you got acquainted with her and possibly changed your mind about her.

4. Read "Aunt Jane" by Herbert Asquith (*Gaily We Parade* p. 38). Analyze Aunt Jane in the poem. Try to think of all the things that might have made her the kind of person that she is now. Put Aunt Jane into a story, any kind of story, but make her exactly the kind of person the poem says she is.

5. Do the same with "Uncle Andy and I" by LeRoy F. Jackson (*Gaily We Parade* p. 40).

B. **Analyzing oral reports.** There are various approaches to listening to analyze oral reports:

1. To answer questions the speaker has prepared
2. To list the points the speaker made
3. To write a short summary of the points made
4. To determine what made the report interesting or what would have made it more interesting

C. **Analyzing what makes a joke funny.** Turn to Chapter Twelve page 493 and analyze what makes the children's stories in that chapter funny:

1. *Unexpected ending*

Grandmother, coming unexpectedly upon her eight-year-old grandson beating with a large spoon on an overturned dishpan: "Heavens! Is all that noise necessary, Roger?"

"I'm entertaining the baby!"

"Where is the baby?"

"Oh, she's under the dishpan!"

2. *Mispronunciation of a word*

Our maid, who aspires to culture, scorns words of less than three syllables. One morning I heard her tell a telephone caller, "Unfortunately Mrs. G. is decomposed." [1]

3. *Double talk*

The neighborhood dogs were romping together one day when Scottie came along. "Heavens, Scottie, what's wrong with you?" asked little Peke. "You look simply awful!"

"I feel awful. I'm nervous, can't sleep, have no appetite."

"You ought to see a good vet."

"Oh, I've seen them all, and they all say the same thing: 'Nothing wrong organically.' "

"Maybe what you need is to see a good psychiatrist."

"Oh, I couldn't—you see, I'm not allowed on couches!" [2]

II. Listen to Get Directions for Creative Work

A. **To make a hard cover for a loose-leaf book.** I am going to give you streamlined directions for making a hard cover for the horse stories you wrote last week. In art class we will decorate the covers and make a homemade book. We want all the books to look nice so we can display them in the corridor display case. Try to visualize each step in your mind's eye. As I go from step to step, I will wait a short time for you to complete each step.

[1] By permission of the author, Mrs. Helen Gellert, and *The Reader's Digest.*
[2] By permission of the author, J. C. Furnas, and *The Reader's Digest.*

Step 1. Take out your ruler and a pencil and put them on your desk.

Step 2. You will find on your desk two identical pieces of cardboard two inches wider and one inch longer than the paper on which your horse story was written. Lay one piece of cardboard flat on your desk with the narrower end at the bottom toward you.

Step 3. Near the top of the page measure with your ruler one inch from the left-hand side of your cardboard, and place a dot there. Farther down on the page place a similar dot. Now using the dots as guides, draw a vertical line with your ruler the full length of one piece of the cardboard.

Step 4. With your scissors cut along that line. Lay this narrow strip of cardboard close to, but not overlapping, the wider piece from which it was cut so that it looks almost like one piece again.

Step 5. Take the strip of white muslin cloth four inches wide, from your desk, and see that it is exactly as long as the cut strip of cardboard. Clip off any excess length. Now cover this strip of cloth with a thin coating of library paste about the consistency of butter spread on bread. Smooth the paste out with the paste stick until it is even.

Step 6. Join the small piece of your cardboard with the large piece by pasting the cloth flat down over the middle of the cloth following the crease; make a cloth hinge where the two pieces come together.

Step 7. Press the cloth down gently on both the small and large piece of cardboard to ensure that the cloth will stick.

Step 8. Now lay your hinged cover on the stiff back cover and see how the book cover will work. After we get the cover decorated, we'll insert your horse story, punch two holes in the thin strip and lace the book together with these thin buckskin lacings the shoeman at the corner gave us. Some of you will want to finger-paint the cover and bind the corners and the thin strip with a matching solid color. Wallpaper or a small hand-blocked design with some sort of horse motif—horseshoe, stirrup, and the like—would look well, too, with contrasting corners. Some of you will want to draw a single picture and letter your title on plain paper. Be thinking before art class just how you wish to decorate your new book cover.

B. **To create an historical character, a movie or TV character out of a hard-boiled egg.** Have the children bring a hard-boiled egg to school. Show one or two decorated eggs, and read these directions, saying, "Our purpose today is to use hard-boiled eggs as heads, and transform them into historical characters, movie, TV, or book characters."

1. Your first job is to determine which character you are going to choose for a subject. Be sure the character is a distinct personality, one that does not look much like other people; that kind is easiest to draw.

2. Your second task is to decide just how you are going to paint the face and arrange the hair. After you have decided, do your sketching in pencil before you begin the paper construction for the hat. Make your character's hat and clothes true to the time in which your character lived.

3. The next step is to choose the materials. On the first seat of each row are paste and paintboxes, pans and a pitcher of water, cotton, yarn, crepe paper and construction paper as well as pieces of cloth. You may use whatever materials you need to make your character real. A small construction-paper receptacle for holding your egg in place is already on your desk.

C. **To follow first-aid directions.** Find a directive paragraph in the first-aid manual which the children need (how to bandage a sprained ankle; how to apply a tourniquet), and use the following steps in teaching this skill as a listening exercise for the class:

1. First teach the words which the children do not know.

2. Have the children count off by twos for partners and give each pair a long rolled strip of cloth.

3. Read these directions aloud: I am going to read the exact directions of how to bandage a sprained ankle. When I have finished, I shall call out No. 1 or No. 2.

Whichever number is called does the bandaging, and his partner acts as the victim. (In that way both listen.)
4. Read the paragraph and call the number.

D. To fold a nut cup and decorate it. Read directions for folding a nut cup from construction paper; then allow children to decorate the cups as they please.

E. Working together in pairs at the listening game. Have children consult a library book on how to construct one simple thing; copy the directions carefully; then read them aloud to a partner who, in turn, reads his. Each then constructs what the other has directed.

III. Listen to Differentiated Assignments

A. Before you begin to read the story aloud, give these directions: I am reading you a funny, fantastic tale by Dr. Seuss, "The 500 Hats of Bartholomew Cubbins." Listen to the steps in the development of the story, and remember every detail you can. Pay particular attention to how Bartholomew acted as he got each new hat.
After-reading directions: Each of you is to work alone in the activity to which you are assigned. As soon as your name is called, listen carefully for your directions.
1. Group A consists of John, Jim, George, and so on (half of the boys). Group A's job is to think of an adventure concerning hats that a modern Bartholomew Cubbins might have, and write that adventure into a story in pencil on theme paper. Do not wait to listen to the directions for the other groups.
2. Group B boys—Bill, Mert, Martin, Roy, and so on (other half of the boys)—pretend to be newspaper reporters, either in the small town where Bartholomew lived or in a nearby big city, and write up a newspaper account of the hat episode for the paper they work for, either a humorous or deadly serious account. (Gifted children who like to write have a "whale" of a time with this type of assignment.)
3. Group C girls (half of the girls) are to pretend that this episode happened to a girl—Barbara Cubbins instead of Bartholomew—and design in water colors the various

girls' hats that might have landed on Barbara's head. Keep your designs under cover so that we'll have dozens of different ones.

    4. Group D girls (the rest of the girls) are to rewrite the story of the 500 hats with Barbara as the girl heroine, changing the story in any way that they like.

Ready. Begin!

B. Read the story poem, "Casey at the Bat," (Cole's *Story Poems, New and Old* p. 197), prefacing the reading with these directions: I am going to read you that old favorite of story poems, "Casey at the Bat" by Ernest Lawrence Thayer. Listen for these things:

    1. How did the townspeople feel about Casey when the game started? when it ended?

    2. Be ready to describe the game play by play.

After-reading assignment: The boys pretend to be sports announcers for the Mudville Radio Station and write the script covering the game. The girls write a letter to a friend away at school describing the game.

C. (Gr. 7–9) Read the ballad, "May Colvin" (Cole's *Story Poems, New and Old* p. 232). *Assignment:* Girls, write what May Colvin wrote in her diary the night she came back home; boys, write the mystery story about the man's body found floating in the river.

D. Read "Richard Cory" by Edwin Arlington Robinson (Cole's *Story Poems, New and Old* p. 162). *Directions:* Paint with water colors or sketch with chalk what you think Richard Cory looked like, or write a sketch of what you think Richard Cory's home life was like.

E. (Gr. 7–9) Read the funny ballad, "The Powerful Eyes O' Jeremy Tait," by Wallace Irwin (Cole's *Story Poems, New and Old* p. 102). Follow with this assignment: Boys, write the story of how Jeremy used his eyes on a whale with extraordinary and terrifying results; girls, tell the story of how Jeremy met a girl named Starin' Sarah, who also had hypnotic eyes and tell what happened.

F. Read "Old Quin Queeribus" by Nancy Byrd Turner (*Gaily We Parade* p. 45). The boys draw cornstalks or the potatoes, and the girls draw the cabbages or lettuce heads with the garden hats. Painting or coloring this picture would be a good time to teach perspective. This would make an effective art lesson for April Fools' Day.

IV. Listen for One-Group Assignments (Gr. 5–9)

The next four suggested poems are in Cole's *Story Poems, New and Old.*

A. Read "Kentucky Belle" by Constance Fenimore Woolson (p. 209). *Assignment:* Perhaps Kentucky Belle had a colt later in Tennessee. Weave into a story how that colt got together with her former owner's son up in Ohio. (Mix paint; see poetry chapter, page 249.)

B. Read the ancient ballad, "Get Up and Bar the Door" (p. 222), and change it into a modern story.

C. Read "The Zebra Dun" (p. 246), and pretend that the handsome stranger played a reciprocal joke on the cowboys on the ranch. Write the story.

D. Read "The Princess and the Gypsies" by Frances Cornford (p. 43). Write a resultant story of what might have happened if the princess had decided not to go back to her home.

The next suggested poems are from *Gaily We Parade.*

E. Read "Potatoes" by Edward Verrall Lucas (p. 4). Write a verse or a paragraph about your favorite food; describe it; tell how it tastes and why you like it.

F. Read "In the Bazaars of Hyderabad" by Sarojini Naidu (p. 8). *Assignment:* Think of the fairs you have attended and write in verse, if you can, what you saw on display there on the grounds: animals, fruits and vegetables, canned goods glowing in glass jars, baked goods, fancy work, clothing, cotton candy, little funny sights and sounds, the merry-go-round, and so on. Try to bring out the smells, the colors, and the sounds of a fair.

G. Read "Old Man Rain" by Madison Cawein (p. 130). Give the children charcoal with which to make their drawings.

H. Read aloud "Tartary" by Walter de la Mare (p. 137). *Directions:* Write about a day in your life if you were a king. (Better mix a little paint here. The resultant writing should give considerable insight into children's hopes and wishes and barren spots.)

I. Read "Three Old Cattlemen" by Monica Shannon (p. 97). Let the children write a tall tale that the old cattlemen told their wives when they got home.

V. Listen to Dramatize

A. Read "When Young Melissa Sweeps" by Nancy Byrd Turner (*Gaily We Parade* p. 43), and have all the girls dance with a pretend broom to an invisible orchestra. (This can get wonderful creativity.)

B. Read aloud "Cat" by Dorothy W. Baruch (*Sung under the Silver Umbrella* p. 64), and have the girls or the boys pretend to be the cat and act out movements suggested by the poem.

C. Read "Shop Windows" by Rose Fyleman (*Under the Tent of the Sky* p. 32), and ask the children to pretend for a minute to be one of the people spoken of, intent on admiring what he loved.

D. Read aloud "Jonathan Bing" by Beatrice Curtis Brown (*Gaily We Parade* p. 138). *Assignment:* Think of another humorous predicament poor old Jonathan might have blundered into, and act it out.

VI. Listen to Remember Details, Sounds, or Clues

A. *Directions:* I am going to read to you a sketch called "The Joys of Baby-Sitting" by Sandra, a seventh grader. The listening directions are simple. Without using your pencil try to remember every type of noise Sandra heard during that evening. As soon as the selection is finished, get out paper and pencil and list as many of the individual noises as you can. Let us see who can win in this memory contest. When I call "Stop," lay your pencils down.

THE JOYS OF BABY-SITTING

I am sitting at the table trying to combine homework and baby-sitting. It is not easy.

The television is blaring, the clock is chiming, and two boys are playing Cowboys and Indians.

"Yah hoo!" The Indian is attacking me.

"Bang!" a galloping cowboy knocks over a chair.

"Wah! hah!"

Oh, no! The assailing chair has fallen on Danny, the baby. I get up to comfort him. Wham! I am on the floor with two yelling boys on top of me.

"Giddap, horsey," they yelled.

After giving them all a ride, I put Danny in bed. Then I settled down to my homework again.

"Hey, we want some pop!" yelled John. So I poured them some pop when "Crash!" broken glass and pop all over the floor. I went to get the broom to sweep it up.

"Ow!"

Yes, Billy had tried to pick up the glass and had cut his finger. After giving first-aid to the little Indian, I went to get him more pop. When I came in with the pop, "Swosh," a pillow narrowly missed my head. That was enough for me.

"Into bed with you!" I said.

"Ah, peace at last," I thought, but not for long.

"Sandra," came from the bedroom, "John hit me."

Finally everything was quiet.

The joys of baby-sitting!

Sandra, Grade 7

NOTE: This exercise may also be done from a record.

B. Read "Old Ellen Sullivan" by Winifred Welles (*Gaily We Parade* p. 44). *Assignment:* Listen for sounds Ellen made in the poem; then think of the working sounds in a modern house and weave them into a poem.

CHAPTER FIVE

Speak—and They Know

One first grader to another: School sure is funny. Our teacher does most of the talking, and we have to keep still unless she lets us talk. I thought every American had freedom of speech!

Second first grader: Maybe it's just for women.

DINNER PARTY [1]

Conversation is a candle in the midst,
Its vivid flame blown fitfully at first
By sudden gusts of laughter, spurts of fun,
The unmalicious malice of sly wit—
Hors d'oeuvre and caviare among old friends.

The candle burns, but now the flame grows steadier,
And in the drawing room, steadiest of all.
Thought deepens, draws together in a glow
Of incandescent unity of hearts.
Premeditated searching of old truths
Checks sudden sallies and the quick aside,
And what is said is center, not who said it,
And the flame stands, pillar-like for strength.

The party's over. The ebbing flame is snuffed.
Goodbyes are said; doors slam and engines start.
And home invites, and the sheet snug under the chin;
And the candle that was a flame now lingers on
In thinnest smoke of retrospective thought,
And little wisps of gratitude and love.

Rosemary Cobham

CLOTHESLINE QUARTET

"Would you like to dance?"
Said my little brother's shirt.

"Don't mind if I do,"
Said my older sister's skirt.

"We'll have a ball,"
Said grandfather's pants.

"It'll be fun for all,"
Said the blue blouse of my aunt's.

Victor Bement, Grade 8

[1] By permission of the author and *The Christian Science Monitor.*

I shall never cease to be thankful that we mortals are born without built-in tape recorders. Think of having to listen every night to what one had said all day; that would truly be a cross past bearing. I never realized how bad it would be to eat one's words until quite a few years ago I was foolish enough to allow a speech I was making to be tape-recorded. When I heard my words coming back at me several hours later, I was sick at heart. So this was how my message sounded when it had left me! I had wanted to give this group a real challenge; I had hoped to share with them my thoughts and findings and dreams for children and schools. These disembodied words coming back at me were surely not mine. They seemed as naked as a sleepwalker in the streets at midnight. For to listen to one's voice is to listen to one's own naked personality, unshielded by self and unaided by bodily gestures.

Speak—and They Know

How much of our true selves comes out in our speech. Those trained in that field can read our biographies in the things we say. They can determine almost invariably which state we come from; they can, with a fair degree of accuracy, guess from what land of Europe our ancestors came and about how many generations ago. We cannot even converse for a short time without giving away the breadth, or dearth, of our education, the depth of our philosophy of life, and our attitude toward other people. The listener to our speech knows whether we are slovenly or whether we have standards; whether we are formal or casual. What the maid said to Peter on the eve of Christ's crucifixion when he tried to deny that he was a follower of the Galilean, "Thy speech betrayeth thee," is still as true in the twentieth century as in 33 A.D. Speak—and they know.

No wonder the English poet-dramatist, Christopher Fry, had one soldier say to his corporal in that wonderful glimpse into modern thinking *A Sleep of Prisoners:*

MEADOWS. Sometimes I think if it wasn't for the words,
    Corporal,
    I should be very given to talking. There's things
    To be said which would surprise us if ever we said them.[2]

Yes—if it were not for the words—!

But it *is* the words. Any psychologist in the business world will tell you that the importance of one's job depends directly on the size and quality of his available vocabulary. An executive hasn't the time to fumble for words; he must think clearly and quickly, and the right words to make his meaning clear must be as readily accessible as the spectacles on his nose.

A man with simple, obvious problems can get along with a simple, obvious vocabulary, but not the person who deals in complexities. He must be as efficient verbally as he is technically. The man with the lazy vocabulary cannot be trusted with the precision job, and the space age is going to be full of such jobs.

Don't for a moment believe that the most important reason for having a rich vocabulary is to get a better job. Quite the contrary! I am one of those die-hard idealists who believe that one must invest himself in life if life is to pay full returns on the investment. Get yourself a rich vocabulary, not for the job it will get you, but for the abundance it will add to your living. The man who can sit on the back steps and enjoy the sunset, knowing the color words that are coming to life before his eyes, is a truly rich man. Flame red trailing its wispy scarves across the sky, changing to crimson—to gold—to crimson—gold, bathed in heliotrope. And all the time that copper-golden ball dripping down over the edges, melting, melting, until it drops down behind the horizon and out of sight, leaving the heavens a bit dazed with their recent glory.

Oh, it's one of the most satisfying feelings in the world to be able to think a sight in words—to be able to say to yourself what you are seeing. But life isn't all a matter of sunsets. Have you ever had a child look up at you with the look of a young fawn getting acquainted with the morning? Have you tried to puzzle out the right word to describe that child's look? "Wonder" is the best word I have arrived at so far, but I believe the word "wondery," which the child coined for the way she imagined a snowflake looked at her, is an even better word (page 31). "It looked at me with wondery," she said, and I like that word she coined.

[2] From *A Sleep of Prisoners* by Christopher Fry. Copyright 1951 by Christopher Fry. Reprinted by permission of Oxford University Press.

I don't believe that most of us realize how much a complete vocabulary enriches our living. True, such vocabulary richness doesn't get us a better job, or not directly, anyway. The boss seldom calls us into the office and says, "John, I'd give anything on earth to have the vocabulary to handle that so-and-so of a Mrs. Black in the way you just did. I've been wanting to kick that woman for years. You just did that very thing in such beautiful words that she fairly genuflected all the way out. You're promoted, John. We need a vocabulary like that in the department of public relations."

No, the right word does not always get us a better job, but it does give us a sense of adequacy which, in turn, engenders power; that sense of adequacy, the feeling that we have on hand enough of whatever we need to carry us through. A homemaker with a well-stocked freezer and a well-filled grocery closet doesn't get panicky in the face of unexpected company. In like manner a person with a mind closet tidily stocked with a rich vocabulary feels adequate; and that sense of adequacy is the sense of power.

Adequacy, not business advancement, is the selling point I would use to interest children in words. Be word-ready; power comes from a mental closet well-stocked with words. Fill up that storehouse of your mind with the garments of flowing speech, garments that swing out at a touch. Keep a rich supply of glowing high-heeled words that your thoughts may be correctly shod for dancing. Have on hand walking-shoe words and verbal oxfords for business use.

How Does One Become Word-Ready?

Do you remember that lovely bit from "Florist Shop" by Rachel Field that points out that what we live with clings to us without our knowing?

> Florists are quiet men and kind
> With a kind of fragrance of the mind.[3]

You know, I think that's what a closetful of colorful words does for us; it colors our personalities and makes us have an aura of our own, unlike that of anyone else. An eighth grader from Wisconsin, Mary Faye, has noticed that colors make her think of her relatives.

[3] From *Taxis and Toadstools*, "Florist Shop," by Rachel Field. Copyright 1926 by Doubleday & Company, Inc.

COLORFUL PEOPLE

Some colors remind me of people. A relative of mine would make an excellent red. She's as bright and peppy as a blazing sunset. Her name, Rosie, even makes you think red.

A cousin of mine reminds me of green. She's as fresh looking as grass in early springtime and she's always trying out new things that she knows nothing about.

Another friend reminds me of pink. She is dainty-looking and has a voice as sweet as pink chantilly lace.

One of my aunts reminds me of black. She is very domineering and when she arrives she looks like an ominous black cloud appearing on the horizon.

Mary Faye, Grade 8

What about it—do you make your relatives *see red, think pink, view blue, sight white,* or are you just another black cloud on their horizon? The words you associate with daily lend their color to your personality. Every child who lives under the influence of an excellent vocabulary is already well on his way to getting an education. Sky-reaching words, like mountains, point those who use them to the sky.

Don't be afraid of sizable words—even little children love them. Let children learn words in the same way Paul Engle says a baby learns touch:

> Touch is learned by letting fingers taste
> Leaf and dog and doll.[4]

Take time to introduce children to interesting new words with the same care you would use to have them meet a cherished friend.

I shall never forget the day I met the word <u>serendipity</u> for the first time through the courtesy of a charming black-eyed friend-of-a-friend from Georgia. The word *serendipity* is drawn from a short story by Horace Walpole and means the little bonuses life deals us that we hadn't counted on—the flower a child brings us because he likes us; the parent who writes that little note of appreciation.

I looked at the word long and savored it. How like life it was: first almost the uneventful word *serene,* with its connotations of gracious days; next then the word *dip,* as all of our days do, eventu-

---

[4] Reprinted from *American Child* by Paul Engle. Copyright 1956 by Paul Engle. Used with the permission of the publishers, The Dial Press, Inc.

ally; then that final flirt of its skirts at the end—*serendipity*—an unlooked-for loveliness in a day, truly a word to warm the heart. I tasted the word carefully on my mental tongue; I said it again and again, being careful to put the heavier accent on the *dip*. Then I began to play with it in light verse, enjoying the swish of the words at the ends of the lines. What I got was not poetry, to be sure, but genuine word fun. And there's nothing better for vocabulary growth than genuine, rollicking word fun.

Serendipity

Today my heart goes hoppety-skippety
I've just had another serendipity;
Those tiny bonuses injected
Into a day all unsuspected.
My eyes grow moist and my nose un-snippety
Whenever I get a serendipity,
That word that Horace Walpole coined,
And that Ogden Nash and I purloined.

I thought I owed a bill to the grocer,
I tried to pay him, but he said, "No, sir."
Did I let the cash burn holes in my pocket?
In a cold bank vault did I cruelly lock it?
Not on your life! My feet went trippety
And I bought me a hat with that serendipity!

One rainy day was enough to tie me
In knots when my only bus went by me,
I hated the rain, but I stepped out in it,
Getting slishier-sloshier every minute.
But a handsome man saw I was drippety,
And he picked me up—that's serendipity!

Oh, serendipities are tiny,
But they make one's days
Awfully gold and shiny.
When life's banana peels go slippety,
Along comes another serendipity.

Oh, the charming serendipities this word has brought me! A high school English teacher sent this lovely poem from *The Christian Science Monitor:*

DIVIDEND OF SERENDIPITY [5]

Serendipity-blest, my child and I
Take the road to We-don't-know-where,
That leads to things never twice the same
Up High-go Hill by a cocklestair.

With nothing promised by Wait-and-See,
My child yet has a frolic face,
Buttercup hair and bluet eyes,
And a hummingbird's grace.

At Meadow-of-music we stop to hear
The larks sing to their mates at home;
And we sing too, wading the drift
Of the white daisies' fragrant foam.

Serendipity-blest, my child and I
Climb High-go Hill by a cocklestair;
But I alone saw the butterfly
Flutter down and nestle in her hair.

Bettie Cassie Liddell

Another acquaintance sent a science advertisement centered around the word. But most interesting of all was this editorial from the February 6 morning edition of *The Des Moines Register:*

DR. VAN ALLEN: SCIENTIST, SERENDIPITIST [6]

Professor James A. Van Allen of the State University of Iowa, whose researches into radiation in space have won him world renown, said in a recent interview that his discovery that there are two vast reservoirs of radiation lying beyond the earth's atmosphere resulted from a project in serendipity.

Serendipity, it happens, is not a term from the lexicon of physics. It is a literary allusion and one that tells a lot about the ways of the pure scientists. The fact that it was used also tells a lot about Dr. Van Allen.

The word Serendipity is drawn from English literature, from a short story by Horace Walpole called "The Princes of Serendip." The princes had a marvelous knack for discovering worth-while things without knowing exactly what they had been looking for.

---

[5] By permission of the author and *The Christian Science Monitor.*
[6] By permission of *The Des Moines (Iowa) Register.*

This, in a nutshell, is what the pure scientists do. They stumble onto phenomena that have always existed and through the use of creative imagination identify them and relate them to other phenomena.

In this same interview, Dr. Van Allen used another literary allusion very appropriately. "When you're out there in space," he said, referring to his research in space radiation, "like the salesman says, 'all you have is a smile and a shoeshine.' " This is a line from Arthur Miller's play, *Death of a Salesman*. It describes well the essential loneliness of the scientist's work.

And not only does Dr. Van Allen call on literature to explain the ways of scientists, he talks like a poet in describing natural phenomena.

In discussing the effects of radiation on the Northern Lights, he said: "Something happens on the sun. It sends out a burst of gases . . . the reservoirs (of radiation) above our earth shake like a bowl of jelly . . . and the radiation droozles out at the end and makes the auroral displays at both our North and South Poles."

The word "droozle" which apparently represents a merging of drizzle and ooze, is just about as expressive as Dr. Van Allen is articulate.

What a great deal that editorial has to say to a teacher about why every child in school with enough intellectual capacity to understand must have a fine background of literature and the stuff of which literature is made—words. Literature, someone has said, "is the spectacles through which we see life." Literature spectacles must not become the exclusive property of the cloistered scholar: the scientist needs them; the businessman needs them; the editorial writer needs them; and what they add to the reader of the morning paper is even more stimulating than the orange juice. Did you notice another quality of that fine editorial? The writer wrote in pictures so that we could see what he means; he coined words, too.

It is time that we realized that word pictures are not the exclusive property of poets. The man who talks and writes in word pictures is smart; he realizes that word pictures help others to see what he means—the reason he spoke in the first place.

Young children have always spoken in picture-packed words. If your two-and-a-half-year-old calls out to you, "Mother, the man with 'cold' is at the door!" don't run for a handkerchief. He is more than likely trying to tell you that the ice-cream man has come. If a five-year-old explains that his leg has ginger ale in it, there's no call for alarm; no doubt his leg has been asleep. Instead of steam shovels, the six-year-old sees dinosaurs eating up the street, and at his first glimpse of a silhouette picture, may exclaim, as one child did, "Whose picture of nobody is that?" Children and poets are perfectly clear as soon as one recognizes their technique; they speak in pictures, Grandma Moses' style.

Folk tales are full of such picturesque expressions: "You're eating mighty high on the hog!" "Spare your breath to cool your porridge." "She'd better sweep her own doorstep first." "The pot calls the kettle black."

Today's conversational primitives, like modern cars and trains, tend to be streamlined, most of them reduced to one hyphenated word: know-how, teen-age, drive-in, take-home pay, grass-roots, fact-finding, sure-fire—a quick picture in every one.

Children's poems are little more than poetic prose, but even their prose is plummy with picture-packed words:

> There she goes
> Like water spurting out of a hose!
>
> My dog is a miniature steam shovel
> For you should see those tiny paws
> Make excavations in our front yard.
> *Karen, Grade 6*
>
> Did you ever look at seeds in the fall?
> Like parachutes, first they unhook,
> Then they drift down like a drop ball.
> *Ray, Grade 6*
>
> The sun is backing through the trees.
> *Lynn, Grade 7*
>
> Here comes the snow in the moonlight glow
> The flakes are like actors in a show.
> *Jan, Grade 5*
>
> Those painted windows of frost.
> *Sue, Grade 6*
>
> He is as green as a vegetable and almost as fresh.
> *Margie, Grade 8*
>
> Her personality shines like a neon sign.
> *Sandra, Grade 5*

Every original phrase posted or pictured in the schoolroom brings at least two or more from the class.

If your children have no feeling as yet for picturesque speech, and you the teacher have no facility in it, use appropriate (or shall I say "appropriated"?) examples from the page entitled "Toward More Picturesque Speech" in *The Reader's Digest* or from samples collected from your own reading. The teachers who are not original must learn to glean from the fields of others without trespassing. Picturesque speech is verbal verse, a child's first form of poetry. We must help him to keep it.

Begin in kindergarten. Help children to discover that writing is just talk written down. This discovery, always a profundity to a child, was dramatically put into words by a little girl, whom Rose Zimmerman Post tells about: "Why," she whispered wide-eyed, "reading is nothing but talk wrote down. That's all it is—just talk wrote down." [7]

A teacher can help children to realize this connection between writing and speaking through tape-recording the children's conversations and individual stories, then printing the more picturesque ones on manuscript charts.

These off-the-record and dictated stories should often adorn the bulletin boards of kindergarten rooms, enticing the children with the promise that this year we can only *tell* stories, but soon we can *write* them for ourselves. Point out how interesting a child's speech is if he talks in pictures. Beginning in the lower grades and continuing throughout the elementary school, stop to appreciate together the choice words or phrases found in your reading aloud. Encourage the children to share with each other the word gems found in their own reading. On bulletin boards top picturesque phrases with illustrative pictures, thus showing graphically that there are picture-written words as well as picture-talked words and word-talking pictures.

Clever salesmen have always said their punch lines in pictures: "In that hat, Madame looks just like a bride!"

"Just a touch of arthritis in those old pipe joints, Ma'am; a bit of elbow grease is all they need. I'll send a joint man to fix them in a jiffy."

"If Sir Walter Raleigh had been wearing this topcoat, sir, the queen would have just had to get wet!"

And when have professional men not brought clarity to their conferences with picturesque speech?

[7] Rose Zimmerman Post, "Reading Geared to Readiness," *School Life*, June, 1953.

"Does it feel as if someone had your heart between the fingers squeezing it—like this? Ah, I thought so."

"In other words, Mrs. Von Eggert, he treats you as if he had just stepped off Plymouth Rock and as if you had just crawled out from under it."

"No, Mr. Timble, I don't think you're sissy for fainting. When that tooth was out, you naturally collapsed like a popped balloon. Better now?"

"Mrs. Spendle, that stock is as unsafe as a president's aide. Better run from it."

Business and the professions are learning much from poets and children about picturesque speech. It is to the conversation what pictured graphs and charts are to the board meeting, a sort of spoken visual aid. In fact, modern advertising is coming to be almost the poetry of the machine age. Like actual poetry it reaches for our hearts and senses, but unlike the muse's gift, advertising has one hand in our pockets as it woos. Doubly dangerous, advertising works its rhythmic racket in a team: picture-packed words with word-packed pictures. Light beers bubble with champagne words, and every desk-bound clerk mentally acquires tweeds and a hunting dog with every pipe he smokes. Advertising substitutes "things" for dreams, selling with petal-soft words each year millions of dollars worth of petal-soft lotions to ladies whose hands are rarely held by any male except her physician. For the first time in history, poetry is actually paying off in dollars and cents.

What business learns to do, schools should have done earlier. Secondary education should not have to be a kind of mental sight-saving of enthusiasms and skills young people should never have lost in the first place. What becomes of a young child's originality between kindergarten and high school?

Each of us is an original, and our speech written or spoken must be ours, not everybody's; must bring our own individual slant to any idea through our own word pictures. If we all wore uniforms, how monotonous! As you read in the Introduction, this book got its name from a Japanese student's bringing a fresh new meaning into an old idea. The term "easy in English" is sheer poetry and capable of as many interpretations as there are readers. Children, like foreigners, because they are not yet set into stereotypes, bring fresh new expressions to our language. Let us help them to become adult speakers and writers who have not lost this picturesque way of presenting new ideas.

A summer school student of mine told me this story of her son when he was a senior in the high school in which she taught. One day she asked her son about a beautiful blonde girl she had noticed in the hall—a Dresden figure of a girl—almost doll-size. "Who is she? Do you know?" she inquired of her son. "I should think you'd want to get acquainted with her—she's so attractive."

"Yes, until she opens her mouth," was the laconic reply and the son walked away with a shrug, leaving his mother somewhat astonished but deeply pleased.

I was reminded, as she told me the story, of this poem from Sydney Harris' astringent pen back in 1957:

POEM IN DISPRAISE OF MODERN YOUNG WOMEN
WHOSE CHARM VANISHES THE MOMENT THEY
OPEN THEIR LOVELY MOUTHS [8]

O goddess garbed by Molyneux, and hatted by Bendel
Why is your favorite adjective the dull laconic "Swell"?

O creature radiant with health, and good looks calorific
Why is your sole superlative the tiresome "Terrific"?

O maiden with the well-groomed hair, who never would look frowsy
Why is your only pejorative the crude and slack-jawed "Lousy"?

O nymph who dreams and plans and schemes for suitors wildly bidding
Why is your conversation piece confined to "You're not kidding"?

O dryad with the starlit eyes for romance ever looking
How can you hope to weave a spell with phrases like "What's cooking"?

O sylph who spends the live-long day rehearsing night's allure
Why must you then dispel the charm by yapping "That's for sure"?

O siren steeped in ancient wiles since Eve first passed the fruit
Think you that Helen launched her ships by simpering "They're so cute"?

L'Envoi

Princess, I plead with you, out of this rut!
Speak proper English, or keep your mouth shut!

[8] By permission of the author and *The Chicago Daily News*.

What about it? Does it pay to try to get Rosie O'Grady to talk like a lady if she isn't one? I've never been sure. George Bernard Shaw intimated in *Pygmalion* and probably against his will in its musical version, *My Fair Lady*, that changing a person's speech changes his inner self. I believe there's a great deal to Shaw's contention; I'm sure of it. We mortals have a tendency to live up to our dress. Why not up to our speech? But what we must not forget is that her unconscious love of Henry Higgins, her new surroundings, and her keen intelligence caused Eliza to change along with her speech patterns. Self-respect often is the child of many strange concomitants. But whether from better speech or from better motivation for changing, the main consideration is that as her speech changed, Eliza Doolittle became a lady! At which end of the training program does one begin to change the speech—at the speech end or the Eliza end? It is important to know, and I for one am not sure.

Of one thing I am sure: that wrong speech patterns can be changed if the motivations are powerful enough and the training period begins early enough and lasts long enough. Only the most intelligent of Elizas with the most powerful of motivations will be able to change if we wait until high school to start the changing; habit is a vice that only a "rich wanting" can break.

How to Change Wrong Speech Patterns?

How can we help children to want to change their poor speech patterns? First, we must bring about the "rich wanting," then retrain the ear so that what seemed wrong now sounds right. Last of all, we must provide plenty of correct speech practice until the habit is as firmly established as a dead-beat relative in the most comfortable armchair in the living room.

I know nothing that will stir up "rich wanting" in a young person like making him aware of his potentialities.

"John, you have the beginning in you of a fine man. I'm sure that you're going to give something to the world. In doing that, you are going to have to feel at home with people who have spoken correct English all their lives. You'll feel at home with anyone you meet if only you can get a few weeds out of your speech.

"Do you suppose, John, that I could help you to pull out those speech weeds so that when you get to your rightful place in the world, you'll feel comfortable there? Nobody but you and me needs to know what we are working on. May I help you?

"Let's begin with your worst weed *youse*. That word probably got into your family, John, from rough days when your ancestors had to work down on the docks with other immigrants. Those sturdy ancestors of yours, John, didn't have time to worry about their speech; they had to think too hard earning enough to eat to worry about how they used the English language. Besides, they worked with people who talked just as they did, so how could they know they spoke incorrectly?

"There is no word *y-o-u-s-e* in the English language. See, I am going to take off that final 'se' and throw it away. Now the word is just plain *you;* 'you fellows,' not 'youse guys'; 'you girls,' not 'youse girls.' 'When are *you* going to have that committee?' not 'When are *youse* going to have it?' See, John, I am going to start you on your getting ready for your future career. I've written Goal I in your notebook! 'John Kalonski is on his way up. From today on he is going to drop *youse* from his speech and say only *you*.'

"Now, John, every time you hear yourself saying *youse,* stop, back up and say *you*. You watch and I'll watch, and every Thursday night we'll hold a short business session and talk over your progress. Is that a bargain?"

Or maybe it's that beautiful child Mary, who not only murders the king's English but hangs it from a conversational limb. I'll get at Mary through her self-dramatization; she always sees herself in one role or another. I'll point out to her that some day she may lose the only man she wants because of her unpleasing speech. Mary is no fool; she'll just see that man shutting the door of his Cadillac and driving away. Yes, Mary's speech problem can probably be attacked "manfully."

That shy, extremely homely child in the sixth grade is a harder problem, the one whose uncouth English makes her appear to be even more unattractive than she actually is. I remember last year when she was in the fifth grade and the class wrote on the topic, "If Dreams Were for Sale, What Would I Buy?" she wrote this bit that fairly turned my heart over, it made me feel so bad:

Changing My Looks

If dreams were for sale I would buy something to change my looks. I want to tell you about it.

When I got my glasses and went to school I always got called names such as "Cross-eyed Annie," "Tugboat Annie," "Slops" and other names. I think I am so ugly because everyone else says I am so ugly. Now do you see why I want to change my looks?

I'm not going to put her first name down—that wouldn't be fair —but that child has a lovely voice, and I'll get at her English through her voice. All her life people will unconsciously be drawn to her lovely voice; she'll have to learn to be worthy of such a voice by speaking flawless English. I know I can raise this girl's standards through any promise of loveliness I can point out to her. She yearns for beauty as dry roots for rain.

Oh, there are so many ways that "rich wanting" can be engendered; there is a way to be found for each child.

However, not one child will change his speech patterns willingly and happily from a teacher or parent's using sarcasm or ridicule with his correction. Calling a child's attention to his mistakes in front of others in a sarcastic way may change speech patterns temporarily but will make permanent character scars. It is hard to forgive those who embarrass us in front of others. In some schoolrooms such a lovely spirit makes its home that children can be helped with speech errors in front of each other without the slightest feeling. The same kind of gentle kidding about mistakes that goes on in a sensitive home can go on in a schoolroom. Where love dwells, rancor cannot easily thrive.

There are a few situations when calling attention to speech errors is always taboo: (*a*) when a child is giving a report (He's usually nervous enough at this point. Never get his mind off his subject and on to himself. It's fatal—to the report, that is.) ; (*b*) when visitors are present (How do you like it when a member of the family corrects you in front of company?) ; (*c*) when a child is in a sullen, tearful mood brought on by personal problems from home or school (Skills taught during an emotional upset simply do not stick. Why bother?) .

How Can We Deal with Speech Errors Successfully?

During the first month with a new group, jot down speech errors on initialed slips and enter at night in a notebook, a page for each pupil. At the month's end give your error report of the whole room, listing the errors most common, with the *number* (not the names) of children who habitually used them. Then get the children interested in such slogans as "All-American Speech," "Save-Our-Speech Campaign," "King-Size Talk" in a drive against their speech errors.

Since our speech habits are as personal as our clothes:

1. We never correct other people's speech errors unless we are asked to and then never in front of others.

2. We never correct an older person's errors.

3. We never ordinarily look or listen for errors. We look for worth in what each person says. (People who are continually looking for flaws eventually see all life through a keyhole.)

4. Incorrect speech is a bad habit like batting a ball the wrong way. To overcome it takes practice, persistence, and skill, but the hard work pays.

After the children's enthusiasms are aroused, work on one misuse at a time. Use posters, tape recordings, homemade television shows, skits, creative dramatics, jokes, businessmen's talks on the subject, individual progress sheets, and parent helps.

If practicable in the community where you teach, enlist the help of the parents in improving the children's speech. English background is something that needs the backing of both home and school. Why not have an evening school to which the parents are invited? Let the children run the show, explaining their errors and why they are wrong.

Perhaps the children can explain some of the activities that they are using at school to improve their English. They might present each parent with a check list of their present English errors for home checking. If this program is presented enthusiastically—and it will be if the children are really interested—the parents, too, may become as excited as the children and work on their own English. We must go after English errors with the same determination to win as we give to school sports and contests. The difference here is that teachers must sell the idea of correct speech to children while sports interests do their own selling. A teacher who knows good salesmanship can get children excited about anything from sarcophagi to the social habits of June bugs. This business of enthusiasm, it seems, isn't transmitted by germs in the air, just by human carriers.

Don't for a moment, teachers, ever confuse incorrect English with slang. Slang is a youth language from which some never recover. There's nothing more pathetic than day before yesterday's slang on wrinkled lips. Slang is today's talk for today's children, and to yesterday's children sounds as strange as men-from-Mars talk.

Eighth-grade "Let's Writer" Jerry has brought this fact to our attention forcefully by having Paul, a Pilgrim youth, meet Ken, a modern teen-ager, and they have a chat. Ken speaks first:

"Hello, what's your name?"

"Are you addressing me, sir?"

"What's all this square talk, daddy-o? And what world did you come from?"

"I beg your pardon? But you're in Salem, Massachusetts, and I am not your daddy."

"What year is this?"

"The year is 1750 if you would like to know."

"Hot diggity and bless Elvis Presley."

"Who, may I ask, is Elvis Presley?"

"You mean to tell me you don't know Elvis? Why, he's a top rock-and-roll singer. We hear him every day."

"Even on Sunday?"

"Of course! And is he cool! Do you dance?"

"Why, yes. I can dance the minuet better than anyone in Salem."

"You guys sure have it rough. Do you go to school?"

"Yes, I go to a school for boys."

"You mean no slick chicks! Boy, you guys are real gone. Well, I've got to take off for outer space. Goodbye."

Slang of this moon-talk variety is intelligible only to the generation that coined it, so is soon gone like fish flies after a humid night on the Mississippi. This mumbo jumbo of youth is not the type of slang that should concern adults. Like braces on the teeth, it is a stage of growing up; it is youth talk, breezy and crisp, giving those who use it the feeling of originality and creation, a feeling badly needed by youth.

Neither must adults be concerned with picturesque slang, which, if it catches the public ear, eventually becomes a part of permanent language. The term "know-how," coined in the field of space missiles, jarred harshly on the ear a few years ago, but today, like the new family that moved into our block last year, is now almost one of us. The expression "you are the most," one of the less vapid of current youth expressions because it has real meaning, may eventually become respectable, but I doubt that it has sufficient appeal. Yet what teacher or parent would not be glad to have any youth say to him, "You are the most!" It's a picture-packed phrase and certainly more meaningful to moderns than the Biblical "You are the apple of my eye," or last generation's picturesque "You're the cream in my coffee."

The only kind of slang that should concern adults is the vulgar variety: "lousy," "swell," "rotten," "gorgeous," "you can say that again," and other expressions that are used to cover so many situations that they are as limp as a reporter after a fire.

There is not a word anywhere as pregnant with meaning as "lousy"; no wonder it has come to be an epithet of deepest scorn. Yet that word is ready for the semantics garbage can because everybody uses it to say everything until it no longer says anything. In its rightful place almost every word ever coined—even vulgarisms— fits like a clerk's shoes on Saturday night—yes, in its right place! It is a discriminating vocabulary, not a properly sterile one, we must sell to our modern youth. And here again, the imaginative approach gives us the cue. The smart teacher studies his children and discovers what they consider smart, then ties his sales job to that point.

Do your junior high students long to be modern and "in-the-know"? How would these captions be to launch your campaign?

Look into a woman's speech before you look into her eyes.

> She opened her eyes and I fell in;
> She opened her mouth and we fell out.

Boy to another boy: Can't you just imagine listening to that English across the breakfast table for the rest of your life?

NOTE: I do not think I'll tarry, Harry,
You're fresher than your vocabulary.
Fresh-out-of-love,
MARY

Boy to life guard: That is why I have to keep on kissing her, sir. I just can't stand her English.

QUERY: What shall I give to my lovely Mary?
My mother suggests a dictionary.

I like Jim for cutting capers
But his English belongs in the funny papers.

One cat to another: She's almost as lean as her vocabulary—and that's lean!

Picture of a beautiful girl:
Dear Emily,
Tell me, is it normal
To wear blue-jean speech
When your costume's formal?
DUMB DORA

A woman's lips should be as fresh as her speech; a man's less so.

Perhaps this couplet says it best:

> A person's career will rarely reach
> Higher than his usual speech.

If we can just get across to young people that there is nothing wrong with slang—in its place. As a three-phrased, full-time vocabulary, slang acts as a hobble to a horse; it keeps one from traveling far. But if you should manage to get away, the minute you open your mouth in the new place, they'll know you have taken your culture with you. "Thy speech betrayeth thee." Nobody, not even a deaf man, wants a companion with a total vocabulary of three phrases: "What's cooking?" "It's lousy," and "You can say that again!" Or "How neat!" "He's a square." "I'm having a ball!"

The person whose speech sparkles with interest and variety tends to make new friends wherever he goes; he brings people toward him like an ice-cream man's bell. In fact, his speech speaks for him more clearly than an article in the newspaper. The minute people hear you speak, they can guess fairly accurately whether they'd like to know you better.

Your phrases may be picture-packed and your answers as correct as an arithmetic answer book, yet if you have nothing interesting to talk about, again you are hobbled.

John Erskine, in an effort to discourage college training from becoming too vocational, wrote this satiric poem that says well what I'm talking about:

MODERN ODE TO A MODERN SCHOOL [9]

> Just after the Board had brought the schools up to date
> To prepare you for your Life Work
> Without teaching you one superfluous thing,
> Jim Reilly presented himself to be educated.
> He wanted to be a bricklayer.
> They taught him to be a perfect bricklayer.
> And nothing more.

[9] By permission of Helen Worden.

He knew so much about bricklaying
That the contractor made him a foreman.
But he knew nothing about being a foreman.
He spoke to the School Board about it,
And they put in a night course
On how to be a foreman
And nothing more.

He became so excellent a foreman
That the contractor made him a partner.
But he knew nothing about figuring costs
Nor about bookkeeping
Nor about real estate,
And he was too proud to go back to night school.
So he hired a tutor
Who taught him these things
And nothing more.

Prospering at last
And meeting other men as prosperous,
Whenever the conversation started, he'd say to himself:
"Just wait till it comes my way—
Then I'll show them!"
But they never mentioned bricklaying
Nor the art of being a foreman
Nor the whole duty of contractors
Nor even real estate.
So Jim never said anything.

What Makes an Interesting Conversationalist?

We must begin early, you know, in order to set any life pattern. And what adult activity, pray, needs overhauling more than conversations? Before we begin, though, perhaps we'd better think through what makes a good conversationalist.

The foremost quality of a good conversationalist is, I believe, *having a variety of interests;* an interesting person always has. And why wouldn't he have? He has used his five senses to take in what's happening, what he's seen and heard and felt all day long. He's watched the faces and actions of his fellow passengers as he rode on the school bus; he's interested in ideas he heard on the radio or from television, in the daily paper, and in school classes. Most people whose sensory intakes are closed to new and challenging ideas, to new situations and people, just aren't interesting.

Secondly, a good conversationalist *is a good listener as well as a good speaker.* Go back to Chapter Four on listening and read the characteristics of a good listener, and you'll remember *why* a good speaker must be a good listener. Listening creates interest, interest triggers thinking, and thinking produces questions or doubts or reminds the speaker of similar experiences to tell the others. There's just no doubt about it; a person can hardly be a clever conversationalist without being a good listener.

The good visitor in a group *is likely to illustrate his points with an apt story.* Such a person has the ability to see quick relationships and from his experience and wide reading to come up with a good illustrative anecdote.

One day in a summer school class in education we were discussing the pro's and con's of grouping when I noticed one student, an older woman with a mobile face, bubbling over with secret laughter.

When I asked her to share her fun with us, she chuckled and said, "Miss Applegate, I know the best story about grouping that happened right here in our state.

"The first day of school, a first-grade teacher friend of mine was lining up the children at noon according to their lunch plans. 'Those who are taking hot lunch form a line at the east door,' she said, 'and those with lunch boxes here at the west.' She noticed one pint-size chap nervously clutching a paper bag and hesitating in the middle of the floor.

" 'What's the matter, Robert?' she questioned gently.

" 'Please, teacher,' he said, 'Where do the bags go?' "

The whole room of older teachers burst into delighted laughter. The person who can round out a situation with a good story is an appreciated member of a group.

A good conversationalist has a fourth quality—*the ability to read clues and to bring out or "pipe down" a member of a group.* This awareness of other people and their needs gives quiet steering power to a person who, though he may actually say little, sees that all the members of the group have a chance to take part.

A fifth and an especially important quality of a good conversationalist is that *he knows when to stop talking.* Getting some people started talking is like uncorking a bottle of sparkling Burgundy, but with this difference—the garrulous one may keep right on talking even after his conversational bottle is drained.

A good conversationalist, then:

1. Has a variety of interests
2. Is a good listener

3. Is likely to illustrate a point with a story or anecdote
4. Has the ability to read clues
5. Knows when to stop talking

How Can Children Acquire These Five Qualities?

We can teach children how to converse by letting them converse. Just to keep talking doesn't make a child a good conversationalist. We all know people who have hardly stopped for breath in seventy years, but still miss on all five points. They are like the teacher who had one year of experience twenty times. Conversing, like any art, must be learned. Just as most children must self-consciously learn the correct position of the feet in executing a dance step, so must most children painstakingly acquire the underlying principles of good conversation by talking.

As Alexander Pope in the eighteenth century said of writing, so in the twentieth century we can say of the art of conversing:

> True ease in writing comes from art, not chance,
> As those move easiest who have learn'd to dance.

We must teach young children how to take part in a social conversation; there are so many ways, but when one's words stick in his throat at a party, it is necessary to attack the problem manfully, but with about as much resultant finesse as a wolf attacks a sheep on a lonely hillside.

I shall never forget an hilarious experience I had in visiting an Indian school at a small mission, where I was seated for lunch at a card table with three ten-year-old boys. I tried every method of creating conversation that I had ever heard of, but not a nibble did I get for my pains. Finally after a number of attempts, all of which fizzled out like wet matches, one little chap blurted out, "How much money do you make?" and suddenly, for perhaps the first time in my life, I was at a complete loss for words.

In helping intermediate children to know how to start social conversations, divide the class into interest groups—five or six to a group—and let each group converse on a topic of interest to them: baseball, favorite ball team, going to a party, girls' gym, fishing, boating, stamp collecting, favorite hobbies, this season's clothes, helping at home, taking care of small brothers and sisters, the new swimming pool, TV programs, favorite books, favorite movies or movie stars. The children will know what they will enjoy talking about. Have a person act as secretary with each group to keep track of the gist of what each speaker said and in the order it was said.

After ten or fifteen minutes, ring a bell and bring the groups back to class to discuss how the conversation went. Such group conversations will usually point up these procedures for keeping the conversational ball rolling:

1. Begin with questions. (Have any of you been fishing lately? Where did you go?)

2. Begin with an adventure that you had last week as you were fishing.

3. Others add their adventures from this or other years of fishing trips.

4. Add an adventure a relative or neighbor had on a fishing trip.

5. A child with awareness tries to bring out another child with a question about what he caught when he went fishing after school yesterday.

6. This usually leads to a discussion of where to catch the best ones and the best bait to use.

After several similar small group discussions and possibly one with the whole class participating, make up together lists of ways by which one may take an active part in informal conversation:

1. Asking questions at the beginning and at intervals
2. Telling an adventure that happened to you
3. Telling adventures that happened to people you know
4. Telling of similar happenings you read about in the paper or magazines or saw in a television show
5. Telling briefly of an exciting book you read on this subject
6. Asking a question to bring out nonparticipants
7. Telling a funny story on the subject being discussed
8. Giving opinions about people and the probable outcome of things
9. Being aware of when the subject should be changed and changing it so gently few people notice you are changing it: a new subject should, if possible, grow out of the old.

A teacher must lead her pupils to become proficient, too, in the art of disagreeing agreeably:

"That's a good point, John, but it's in sharp disagreement with a statement I found in our encyclopedia." (Quote it.)

"That may be true, Roger, but had you thought about this angle?"

"I may be wrong, Mary, but I don't believe that statement is correct. Will you look at your source again, please?"

"That was a good report, Joe, but I'd like to challenge the last statement you made."

"I don't see how that could be true, Alice, it just can't be!" (Explain why.)

"Oh, Dick, I disagree violently with your statement that—."

Jacques Barzun in his penetrating book, *The House of Intellect*, declares that all the red blood has gone from our conversations since good manners dictate that we water down our arguments. If Dr. Barzun had ever been a "hostess" at a dinner party, trying to head off a husband or guest from "blowing his top" on his favorite "sore-toe" subject, he might possibly feel differently. But Dr. Barzun has a point: a discussion without pronounced differences of personality and opinion is about as bland as Jello.

We must remember, though, that these are school children we are dealing with, and perhaps through this training in disagreeing agreeably, we can later head off some violent emotional outbursts that make all the listeners uncomfortable. Violent arguments are for committee rooms, smokers, and club sessions where any listener who wishes to may leave the room. A social dinner party in a modern home is usually confined to too close quarters to allow for fireworks without scorching some of the guests. Bridling our tongues would be good practice for most of us. We must certainly learn to talk informally without a shooting war of words if we are ever going to live together. We must teach children that shouters have no place in social conversations and that heavy arguing is not for dinner parties.

Directed Conversations Give Children Ease in Natural Conversing

Poise and ease are the result of feeling adequate to a situation. The best way to prepare children for ease in social conversations in real life is to give them practice in directed conversations in school.

What are directed conversations? They are conversations as informal as the social type but with a set subject and an arrangement of chairs conducive to informality. The subject matter for a directed conversation varies with the interests of children, of course, but a good general list is found on page 163 of this chapter. The children should often choose the conversational topic a day ahead so that slow thinkers have an equal chance with fast thinkers.

What seating arrangement is used? The five or six children in each group sit in an inner circle facing each other. The audience sits in an outer circle surrounding the inner circle. Use the regular movable desk seats if possible.

How are the small groups chosen? It is better to have the children number from one to five or six and to call those holding the same number one group. In this way all types of children get together. For the first directed conversation some teachers, in order to balance the groups, prefer to do the assigning.

How can children be interested in the idea of a directed conversation? If children are being invited to parties and often feel ill at ease there or if a party at school is imminent, suggest that you are going to help them feel at ease in conversational situations through a game you just heard about. Give the game a name: Talkathon, Talka-round, Conversational Ball Game, Say-Circle, or have a name like Circle Success Contest for the first try. (The name doesn't matter, but having a name seems to.)

How is a topic for a conversation chosen? There are several ways. Write the list on page 163 on the board; let each child choose his five favorite subjects from that list, write them on a slip of paper, and bring them to class. Or have each child list his chief interests, and have a committee compile the results. It is better to have no more than six titles to choose from in final committee; more are too time-consuming. Another possibility is to have a class committee compile the five subjects the children in their crowd like best to talk about.

What happens in the preliminary small group meeting? The children choose the subject of conversation they will discuss the next day.

How do children get ready for the discussion? Together you and the pupils review (or form) a list of criteria for an interesting conversation, mentioning both Do's and Don't's. Explain that such conversations have no leaders and no set form of procedure, but that each member of the group feels responsible for keeping the conversational ball rolling. Review the ways listed on page 164 by which one contributes to a conversation and especially stress the means of transition from one speaker to another. Think through together what constitutes good manners in the conversational art.

Point out to the children that each might work out in his own mind the different ideas he could contribute (if no one else does) to the discussion and suggest that they list a few new vocabulary words they might try.

How long should directed conversations last? From ten to twenty minutes or as long as the children are bringing in fresh material, not just operating conversational treadmills.

How shall directed conversations be evaluated?

A. *By the group.* Ask the children to write or discuss orally both the good and bad points of their group conversation, suggesting what points to work on for the next time. If the group has set up a list of criteria, the conversations should, of course, be checked against the criteria.

B. *By the teacher.* Often you and the group may do the evaluating together. Another time you may do it alone and mimeograph your evaluations. It pays for you to go from group to group, listening carefully to each person's contribution and writing your comments on a slip of paper. On these slips congratulate the child on the new words you noted in his conversation; point out his one or two mistakes in English; praise him for improvement made; and set up goals for next time. These slips, written in a kindly fashion, do much toward improving both children's speech and speaking. All mortals have a tendency to improve if they know that somebody who cares is watching that improvement. School children develop self-respect from being respected by others.

Later conversations are likely to develop out of regular school living or from ideas the children glean from radio, moving pictures, television, or reading. Children of any age have interests to discuss. I once heard a man say that if Robinson Crusoe had been Roberta Crusoe, Friday would have come much earlier in the week; Roberta would have just had to discuss churning goat's milk into butter or some other burning question. Roberta, he said, would have found another woman somewhere, whereas Robinson was glad to be alone to smoke his pipe in peace. (One minute of silence for one's own thoughts at this point.)

Round-Table Discussions Have Been Good since King Arthur

Round-table discussions, so needed in a democracy, are useful from third grade on through adult life. A round-table discussion is a slightly more formal directed conversation about a problem in which the whole group concerned takes part under a chosen or appointed group leader. Such a discussion is not set up so much to answer problems as to air opinions.

Have you trouble on the playground? Why not work it out in a round-table discussion? Are your children up in arms at the way the television viewing is managed at home? Why not a round-the-dining-table discussion? Are your sixth graders glum at the prospect of not being able to play competitive ball with the other city schools? Is your family divided as to where to go for a vacation? Why not use democracy's method of clearing the air—round-table discussions?

A round-table discussion deals with a problem oftener than with a topic, and problems, more than topics, engender emotions. Whenever people are discussing a problem on which they feel strongly, the leader must of necessity be a bit stronger than the arguments presented.

There are two ways of choosing a group leader for round-table discussions in the elementary school. You are usually the leader to begin with until you know your group and their possibilities. Yet sometimes a natural leader in the group is discernible almost from the first day and can take charge of a discussion even better than you can.

It's a wise plan to train the whole class in leadership, since hiding behind a quiet personality may be a boy or girl capable of developing into a fine discussion leader. Some leaders are born; others develop, and still others just aren't easily recognizable until they are actually doing the job.

What are the qualities needed by a strong discussion leader?

1. A discussion leader must have a mind quick enough to know when to change, but strong enough not to be swayed unnecessarily.

2. He must understand people, knowing how to bring out quiet strength and to discourage garrulous weakness.

3. He must possess a sense of timing in order to know when to bring matters to a head and when to let them wear themselves out.

4. A capable discussion leader knows how to move the discussion along without its lagging.

5. He must like people enough to be charitable of their feelings, but have enough fortitude to hurt them if he must.

6. He must know all angles of the subject being discussed and have enough imagination to predict what he doesn't know.

7. It is not necessary that a discussion leader have a sense of humor, but it helps.

Since discussion is democracy's seeking a better way, our children must feel at home with it. Any of these topics could start a round-table discussion:

> What has happened to the fun we used to have on our playground?
>
> What can our class do for the book fair?
>
> How can we help Mr. Smith keep the building looking better?
>
> The principal is sick; what can we do to show him we miss him?
>
> Five neighbors have reported that you children are racing over their lawns. What shall we do about it?

Such homely problems should lead to round-table discussions and sometimes be settled that way under the leadership of you or a trained child, coached in how to manage a group.

But discussion is used not only as a means of seeking better ways; it is also an excellent method of sharing information about a problem or topic.

> What happened to the European peoples who came to America in the early days that makes them different from their forefathers?
>
> What circumstances brought on the conflict that resulted in the Civil War? As you prepare for the discussion, pretend to have lived in 1860; then you'll feel your part.
>
> Why do we have to stock our aquarium carefully?
>
> If we're going to keep this rabbit in our schoolroom for awhile, what must we know about the care and habits of rabbits?
>
> What can we do to make Hawaii and Alaska, our away-from-home states, feel that they belong to the United States family?

These are the questions that make better discussions than mere recitations from a textbook.

What kind of questions and topics allow for good discussion? Questions that have many facets, that are somewhat controversial in nature, that may result in conflicting opinions make the best discussion material. In the field of history, geography, or science topics and questions that take thinking, that are a gathering up of ideas or a working through to conclusions can provide for excellent discussions. In history, the questions that caused the deepest emotions when they were happening tend to engender the best discussions. Warm feelings, not warmed-over facts, make glowing discussion material. If you can help the children to feel their facts, discussions can bring Yesterday into Today or even into Tomorrow. (I suspect that when future families leave for outer space to pioneer on other planets, they will no doubt be motivated by the same reasons that caused our ancestors to have itching feet in the 1600's.)

A good discussion, then, is motivated by interest, powered by wide knowledge, and controlled by imagination and psychology.

Panel Discussions Have Added Advantages

A true panel discussion [10] is carried on precisely like a round table —the same rules, the same type of leader, the same give-and-take without set speeches, nothing different from a round table except the number taking part (usually five or six including the leader). In a panel situation, the members of the audience are just as interested in the discussion as the panel members, but they are not invited to speak until the panel discussion is over.

A panel has much to recommend its use through the intermediate grades and junior high school.

1. It gives children a chance to sit back and watch other children take part; it is hard for a participant to be objective about a discussion of which he is a part.

2. A panel provides variety to discussions. (Children so love a change, and why not give it to them? Education does not have to be "spinach" in order to be good for children. We adults forget that sometimes.)

3. Shy children often do better in a panel than in a group discussion. They have a tendency to get crowded out in the vigorous give-and-take of a round table.

4. The effectiveness of a panel does not depend so heavily upon the skill of the chairman as it does upon the skill of each panel member; this is an added advantage when children are just beginning to practice the ways of democracy.

---

[10] A symposium, which many people confuse with a panel discussion, allows the five or six panel members to give a short introduction to their topic before the interchange between members begins. When a symposium or panel contains only set speeches and no interchange between members, it is not a discussion and must not be so labeled.

Teachers promoting group discussion of any type in the grades must work particularly on these things:

1. Do not *ever* have group discussions in school without adequate *time for* and *means of* preparation; otherwise more sounding off than making sense is demonstrated, and more ignorances than facts are exchanged.

2. See that the children read from many sources before a class discussion. Discussing the material in the text, which is the only material the class has read, is about as exciting as choosing your own Christmas gift, wrapping it beautifully, and unwrapping it under the tree on Christmas morning—alone. A discussion of a problem or a topic is absolutely without merit unless it is an exchange of ideas gleaned not only from a text but from any kind of material obtainable.

3. Teach note-taking from the text, or from any book common to all, before you teach note-taking from reference books. If you teach note-taking as a helpful tool of study *at a time when the children need it,* you will have little trouble teaching this skill to the top two-thirds of the class.

4. Demonstrate to children the various ways by which they can take part in a discussion:

   a) By telling one portion of what they have read (Beware telling all you know the first time round.)

   b) By adding extra points or details to what someone else has said

   c) By asking a question of a designated member or of the whole class

   d) By challenging a statement

   e) By giving original opinions

   f) By backing personal opinions with documented sources

   g) By showing pictures

One way to teach this "how" of discussion to a beginning class is to have them read widely on one phase of an assigned topic, then demonstrate in class how the material would be treated in a discussion class. Beginning teachers sometimes do not show children how to do a skill the first time they use it.

An even better way to teach the discussion method is to invite an upper group to demonstrate a good discussion, having instructed them ahead of time as to the skills you wish *your* class to learn. Follow the demonstration with an analysis after the group have returned to their own classroom. This type of class exchange is challenging and provocative and a real visual and auditory aid to learning.

5. Before the children take part in a discussion, always set up (or renew) a set of criteria by which to judge it, later evaluating the discussion by the same criteria.

6. Let children read and take notes for a week or two before they discuss a topic. No wonder children do not read more widely: either we do not provide a variety of reading material or we give them too little time to do the reading. A discussion is *both* a *sharing of knowledge* and an *airing of opinions.*

7. Before a discussion, give children a language lesson in how to organize notes, and let them have time to *learn* their notes. Teachers who allow children to read their notes during a discussion (except in proving a definite point or exactly quoting a source) are doing them a grave injustice. Allow children an occasional glimpse at their notes, yes; but read them, no. Never allow children to affix a habit the next teacher will have to teach them to unlearn. (Parents might remember this point too, in their home teaching.)

8. Have a "together" planning of the points to be covered before any discussion of any kind takes place. Plan in this session—don't practice. An overplanned discussion is as unbubbly as stale ginger ale; an unplanned one, often a definite waste of time.

9. Have a good discussion in some area once a month. Any method overused destroys interest; any method underused loses learning and hinders growth. Discussion is only one method of exchanging ideas, facts, and opinions.

Reporting Is Another Way of Sharing Information and Ideas

Giving special reports goes on in too many schools year after year without the reports growing any better. When this happens, teachers must take the blame on themselves; there is no one else to blame. Children will do in reporting just about what they are taught or allowed to do.

No wonder children get fidgety listening to special reports. You teachers would certainly run away from hearing them yourselves if only you could! Hearing a "roomful" of reports is often like hearing thirty deadly-dull speeches or sermons one after another.

Once in the early years of my teaching, during an afterschool session with a youngster who had been cutting up during a series of such reports, I looked him straight in the eye and said, "Charley, what did you think of the special reports today?"

The lad, who was as honest as half an apple, looked straight back at me and asked, "Do you want the truth or a 'teacher' answer?"

When I assured him that I wanted the truth, he said, wryly, like a dog snapping at a fly, "They gave me a stomach-ache in the head!" I felt the same way and told him so, and we shook on it.

From that day on, I worked to get better special reports from my school children—and got them.

If you have trouble getting interesting reports from your children, may I share with you what I have tried and seen other teachers try. Let us list our points briefly, elaborating only on those that need more explanation.

Idea exchange on reporting

1. Be sure you are clear as to the purpose behind reporting; purposes change procedures.

   a) Reporting is an excellent way of sharing information without all of the children doing the same reading. This is especially true now that our curriculum is so crowded that much material must be shared in order to be covered.

   b) Reporting is an excellent listening exercise for the audience. The reporter may select his own method for checking how well his audience has listened.

   c) Reporting helps the student to learn the power a correctly used voice has in interesting other students and holding their attention.

   d) It gives the student practice in the gaining of poise and self-confidence.

   e) Reporting is an outstanding skills builder; locating materials, scanning, thorough reading, evaluating, organizing, memorizing, speaking and getting the feel of an audience—these are the skills engendered.

   f) A fifth grader once told me, "The best thing about a report is the good feeling when it's over."

2. In order to hold the attention of the audience, a report must be interesting; the audience-listening ceiling is higher than it used to be. One must be good or he will be turned off mentally.

3. Only a few reports must be given in a single day. Too many become boresome. Except in the case of group reports, it is wise to

have no more than one or two reports scheduled for one day. Seldom schedule the whole room's reporting during a single unit. Every child should have a week's notice before reporting time, and as nearly as possible know just when he is to speak. Delay causes tension and lessens interest.

4. Work to have variety in reports; reporting need not always be straight "telling"; group reporting done in various ways is an excellent method of sharing information when committees have charge of different segments of an outline.

I have seen the following ideas all used during the sharing day of a single unit. In preparation for this particular program, each committee consisted of three persons; there were nine committee reports and two persons with single assignments. The subject happened to be "Hawaii, the Land of Summer," and the children had been working on this unit for three or four weeks.

Group 1 (two boys, one girl) worked out a scene in which travelers just alighting from a ship pictured on a backdrop were met by Hawaiian maids bearing *leis* and warm greetings. The mayor of the city greeted the travelers and bid them welcome. Before they went to their hotel, the travelers were shown a map of the islands posted on an easel. A young guide with a pointer explained the map and gave an interesting map talk. Then a bronzed boy (well doped with his mother's sun-tan lotion, no doubt) was the storyteller who told Hawaii's history from earliest times to now. The boy read what was almost a prose poem that he had written himself. The scene ended with the girl's singing an original Hawaiian song to an old tune, and the travelers went off stage humming the tune and wearing their *leis*.

In this scene, besides a bit of conversation to hold it together, there had been a map talk, a history story, and an original solo, plus a well-planned scene with a few borrowed actors taking nonspeaking parts.

Group 2 (two girls, one boy) showed a homemade movie of the extraordinary sights of Hawaii to guests on the hotel porch. Instead of paragraphs under the pictures, the boy and one girl took turns giving talks about the scenes while the other girl cranked out the movie.

Group 3 (two girls, one boy): The girls were Hawaiian storytellers: one told the story of Father Damien and the leper colony and the other the story of the Goddess Pele. The girls had learned the stories and told them well in soft, musical voices. The male member of this group gave an outstanding book report on *Call It Courage* by Armstrong Sperry, a beautiful tale of a Polynesian boy who feared the sea. He read snatches from the book as illustrations of the writer's style.

Groups 4 and 5 (three boys, three girls) had a round-table discussion on the question "What will Hawaii, the fiftieth state, add to the nation?" The leader was a little red-haired chap with the political ability of a ward boss and a president's aide. (In truth he reminded me of the late Alben W. Barkley, VIP, whom I knew only on television and through the press, but admired greatly.)

Group 6 (two boys, one girl) : Two male reporters had an interview with a girl dressed as an Hawaiian. The three had interviewed an Hawaiian student at our college as to Hawaiian schools, homes, foods, and customs in general, and they did well.

Groups 7 and 8 (four girls, two boys) worked out display boxes of Hawaiian scenes which they explained and presented to the travelers as gifts.

Group 9 (three girls, one boy) sang Hawaiian songs in a quartet and played recorded Hawaiian music as the travelers left for the boat.

Number 29, a girl, was the supervisor and advisor of all the art projects, and Number 30 was a boy who acted as general chairman and emcee of the program.

Except that it was too long, this was as good a sharing day and a demonstration of many ways of reporting as I have ever seen at one time. The parents and a few supervisors were invited, and all of us were really delighted with the program. The children seemed to live their parts, and what was better, had their facts straight.

Besides those just listed, other methods of reporting include television shows ("Keep Talking," "I've Got a Secret," and so on), role-playing, creative dramatics, radio quizzes and talks, panel discussions, talking from a colored frieze, puppet shows, creative stories and poems, talks explaining colored slides, and original skits.

Vary the methods of summarizing and sharing information from unit to unit. If you have straight reporting for the first unit, use a round-table discussion for the second, a television show for the third, a puppet show for the next, role-playing fifth, and so on. The reading in each unit should center around a different facet of spoken communication. Variety in communication is the exciting sizzle in the carbonated drink of daily living. (Or is your school more "boiled water" than fizz?)

5. Have a conference with every child during the week he is doing the reading for his report. Help him to choose a challenging title, get him started on his outline and his note-taking. Help him to select an interesting form for his talk and an intriguing beginning and ending. When he no longer needs help, let the child proceed on his own.
6. Give children plenty of time to organize notes and learn them.
7. Let each person choose the person in the room with whom he would like to practice his report.

Every child must realize that giving a report well is a tremendous responsibility; that he must be prepared to the best of his ability to do it as well as he can; our low standards are showing.

HOBBY LESSON [11]

This boy talks on coins and stamps,
That one dotes on baseball "greats,"
A third reveals the mysteries
Of rods and reels and baits.

But here is an intrepid lad!
"I paint, I like to paint," says he.
He's undismayed, though half his classmates
Grin derisively.

"When I was young," he forges on,
"I loved to color—here's a thing
I did when I began." He holds
It up. "I called it 'Spring.'"

They snort at his crude tree and bird;
The lad continues, "Six years after
I did another 'Spring.'" He holds this up;
There is no laughter.

The maple's real, the robin's true,
The hill is grassed, the river flows—
The child has grown to man's estate
Each boy in that room knows!

[11] By permission of the author and *The Christian Science Monitor*.

. . . .

The speech concluded, fifteen hands
Are waving, eager to be heard—
And eagerly an earnest artist
Speaks the wanted word.

At last they let him sit, but he's
Created such a grand furor
The teacher knows that after class
He'll have to talk much more.

A. S. Flaumenhaft

So many facets are there to the size and accessibility of one's vocabulary: the picturesque quality of his speech; the slang, be it verse or vice; his conversations, social or directed; his discussions whatever form they may take—round-table, panel, or symposium; the reporting that he does alone or in a group; his drama which can assume any one of a half-dozen forms—yet all of these forms of speech reduce themselves to one—the word.

Out of a man's mouth come his power, his possibilities, and his pain. Oh, we who hold the future of children in our hands, how we must consider this truth and act on it. Yet all our words to children will matter little if we have forgotten one word—the Sesame Word.[12]

The Sesame Word will open the door to the minds and hearts of children of any age. Without it there will be little of "rich wanting" in our classrooms or homes. The Sesame Word is a simple word—caring, understanding, love—it doesn't matter which name we give it so long as we have not forgotten it. "Though I speak with the tongues of men and of angels and have not charity, I am become as sounding brass, or a tinkling symbol."

We do not have to tell children that we care about them. We have only to speak and they know.

After enough years and enough suffering together, we may be able to speak, too, to all the peoples of the earth—and they will know, but only if you and I do not forget the Sesame Word.

Even today we can say to the world with Helen Harrington:

[12] This phrase is from the poem, "The Door." by Ryah Tumarkin Goodman.

Across This Air [13]

Distance has no ways
of foiling us. It can raise
no walls, drop
no gorges that will stop
communications between your heart and mine.
We are well practiced for
hurdling mountains who have learned to soar
over differences of mind and mood.
What can confine
us, in river, hill or tree,
who have taken the stiff altitude
of anger, bridged the declivity
of misunderstanding? Let the tide
roll high and wide,
volcano lift its peak
and everywhere
bars be.

Across them, and the ever-widening air,
we shall speak!

[13] By permission of the author and *The Christian Science Monitor.*

CUPBOARD OF IDEAS for Chapter Five

Speak—and They Know ❖ ❖ ❖ ❖ ❖ ❖ ❖ ❖ ❖ ❖ ❖ ❖ ❖ ❖ ❖

These shelves are labeled Primary and Intermediate and Upper-Grade, but you will note that many of the suggestions listed under Primary go beyond the third grade and one Intermediate (VI) may be used also for third grade.

Primary Shelf

I. Getting a Feeling for Words

A. (Kdgn.-Gr. 3) Display many dog pictures that typify such interesting adjectives as playful, annoying, mischievous, dignified, innocent, loving, sad, discouraged, anxious, greedy, thoughtful. Talk about each word as you look at its matching picture. Have children pose with these same expressions.

B. (Kdgn.-Gr. 5) Post pictures of pets at play. Work out in class the action words needed to describe a kitten asleep (cuddled, relaxed, snuggled into a ball); a kitten playing (pounce, chase, bounce, tail, caper, climb, box, eye, pat, spring); a kitten eating (lap, gnaw, crunch); a kitten happy (frolicking, purring, playing, rubbing legs, brushing cheeks); a kitten afraid (shrinking, hiding, cowering, frozen); a kitten dressing (brushing, smoothing, straightening, bathing); the feel of a kitten (silky, satiny, smooth, "rumbly," soft).

In first and second grades keep a book of child's phrases: kitten words, dog words, food words, words with noses (smell words).

C. (Gr. 3–8) Using this sentence "The boy went walking with his dog," gather from the class every verb that delineates the dog's actions: scampered, ran, whirled, reversed, chased, investigated, sauntered, dived, scared, nosed, stopped, froze, sniffed, sailed, pounced, looked, dug, pleaded, barked, snarled, growled, gnawed, protected, pulled, hid, returned, snoozed, caught, teased, retrieved, braced, tugged, and so on. Then ask your class to talk or write about an afternoon's walk with a dog. Leave the words where the children can use them if they wish.

II. Sharing

A. When children are first getting acquainted with the beginning sounds of the letters, have each bring a little paper bag with everything in it he can find beginning in the same way that *bear* and *big* begins—the "B" sound. One little girl had a buckle, button, beer bottle, bag, a little book, a candy bar, birthday card, a dead bug, a bean, a tiny doll bed, a toy bunny, a bubble pipe, a plastic bird, a doll baby, a ball, a little board, a boat, and a piece of Bologna. As she took each thing from the bag, the other children said its name and clapped if the article didn't begin with the "B" sound.

B. Before the children take their bags home, tell them a story about something that was magic—"The Lad Who Went to the North Wind," for instance, from *East o' the Sun and West o' the Moon.* Let each child choose one thing from his bag and pretend that it is magic and tell a story about it. One little girl told a story about a button on her dress that was magic and that she touched when she was scared. One day a dog came along, she said, and was going to bite her, but she touched the button and it went away.

III. Dramatizing (Kdgn.-Gr. 5)

Children learn to dramatize best when they begin with one or two actions or feelings. Let from four to six children perform at one time.

A. After a honey-hunting bear story, pretend to be a bear, hunting honey. Make appropriate remarks.

B. After Pooh Bear's visit to Rabbit's house, act out the pushing and pulling scene when Pooh got stuck.

C. You are a child who sees a beautiful butterfly on the way home; talk and act as you would if you were the child.

D. You have grown-up company at your house. It is your bedtime; your mother tells you to go to bed. You want to stay up. Talk and act as you'd like to; then act as you probably will act.

E. You are a cautious rabbit; you never take any chances. You meet a turtle for the first time. Two children act out what happens and is said.

IV. *Informal Talking* (Gr. 2–7)

Tell a story about somebody who was afraid of something. Start talking about fears. Tell the children one thing you used to be afraid of as a child. Give the details of just how you felt about this fear. Tell how you got over it. Make together a list on the board to help the children remember what they are going to talk about.

> What I'm afraid of
> Why?
> How I feel
> What I imagine when I'm scared
> What I do to fight my fear

Another day you could tell the story of "The Little Rabbit Who Wanted Red Ears" by Carolyn Sherwin Bailey and launch into a discussion of one thing they'd change about themselves if they could.

V. *Talking on a Topic* (Gr. 3–6)

A. Since it is hard for children in these grades to stick to a subject, have chalk boxes filled with review questions from each unit, such as:

1. Name three things that we can do to cooperate with our community helpers.

2. Name four characteristics of desert country.

3. Why is it hard for people of a desert country to act together on troublesome questions such as leasing oil wells and protecting their country from foreign meddling?
4. Why is it hard to set up schools in a country where grazing is the only occupation?
5. What four conditions affect the climate of a country?

B. In another box have good topics for short talks: (Give the whole class five minutes in which to get ready.)
1. Your favorite game and why you like it.
2. Tell about your most exciting day.
3. Tell about the funniest thing you ever saw.
4. If you could do what you want to do for one whole day, tell what you would do and why.
5. What impossible thing would you like to do?

C. Have the children work in pairs. Give each one a short, interesting, informative article to read. (Clippings from *My Weekly Reader* or children's magazines make good ones.) Each person reads his article, makes a few notes to help him remember, then tells the other member of the twosome the news in his article. The second member then repeats the process of the first. When both have finished, each one reads the other's article and grades it Excellent, Good, Fair, or Poor on the information received. (Try to balance the pairs evenly if you can.)

VI. Games

A. **Shades of color.** (Gr. 2–5) Use the following color poems in introducing shades of color; then list as many as the children can think of. I am thinking brown (or blue or green). The shade is yellowish tan and is the color of a lion. What is it? (*tawny*) I am thinking green. It is the green of young willow leaves in the springtime. What is it? (*chartreuse*)

WHICH BLUE?

Blue of wind-swept skies,
Blue of babies' eyes
And blue of delphinium flower;
Aster blue of purplish hue
And deep blue of midnight's hour.
Blue as the lake when the sunbeams make
Gold threads in its shifting sheen;

Turquoise blue taking silver's cue
On an arm that is tanned and lean
There is no name for the blue of flame,
But aqua worn by a maid,
Has a fleeting hint of the water's tint
In lapis lazuli laid,
Deep ocean blue—the Navy's hue,
And hyacinth—springtime's jewel,
While sapphire's gleam is the blue of a dream
In the depths of a sleeping pool.
Light powder blue, royal prouder blue,
Every blue is a different sheen;
So if it's true that you want it blue,
Make sure of the blue you mean.

SEEING RED

There's cherry red and berry red
And red that glints with gold;
There's rosy red and posy red
And red that's deep and old.
There's winy red and shiny red
And red of blood called gory;
There's flag red, too, offsets the blue
That glistens in Old Glory.
There's ruby red, for to be red
A red must catch the light;
There's manger red and danger red
That glares from flares at night.
There's brick red, too, looks well with blue
And red that's full of fire;
Come on and choose which red you'll use;
There's one for every buyer.

B. Synonym substitutes. (Gr. 3–8) I am going to read you a sentence from Emil E. Lier's exciting book, *An Otter's Story:* "Here he found plenty of frogs and <u>crustaceans</u> so dear to an otter's <u>palate</u>. After eating his fill he went back to the main stream and followed it to its <u>headwaters</u>, where the water <u>petered</u> out, disappearing into its underground <u>source</u>." [1] Here write the five underlined words on the board. Have the children race to see who can find the

<hr>

[1] From *An Otter's Story* by Emil E. Liers. Copyright 1953 by The Viking Press, Inc. By permission of the publishers.

meaning (used here) for each word. Be sure correct meanings are given in complete sentences; we teachers have too low standards for definitions. Have a race of this kind often, but let the children find the sentences in their library reading, and be well prepared to teach their words to the class while you stay in the background. Be sure to have the paragraph reread with the synonyms substituted for the words given.

C. **Antonyms paint an opposite picture.** (Play similarly to B.) This is another excerpt from the otter story. Listen: "Then out slid Ottiga rushing off to cavort with Raggles on the dock, while Freddy, the little boy, laughed and squealed at their antics." [2] We learned yesterday that an antonym of a word was its opposite. I am writing four words on the board that I just read from the otter story. Use your dictionaries to locate the best antonyms you can find for these words. (NOTE: Be sure to reread the paragraphs noting how antonyms change meanings.)

Intermediate and Upper-Grade Shelf

I. Learning the Difference between Opinion and Fact

A. (Gr. 6–8) In one chalk box have a number of proverbs or folk sayings such as: "Honesty's the best policy." "The goose hangs high." "He who holdeth his tongue is better than he who taketh a city." In a smaller box have a number for each group of five children in the room.

Each group sends a chairman to the front of the room who pulls out a slip containing a proverb and from the other box a number indicating his group's place on the list of discussions. Those in Group 1 take their places in a half-circle at the front of the room. The leader reads the proverb he has drawn, and the group discusses its probable meaning for today, giving many opinions and applications according to their interpretation of the proverb.

B. (Gr. 4–8) (Follow the same directions as given with A.) Have an "opinion" box containing strips of paper on which such topics as these are written: "What kind of voices do you like best?" "If you had the money, what kind of car or

[2] *Ibid.*

bicycle would you buy and why?" "Discuss why your favorite ball team is your favorite." "I've decided to be a
———— when I grow up." "My idea of luxury is ————."
"I want a college education because . . ."

II. Giving Children a Feeling for Others through Role-Playing

A. **Getting ready for the feast.** You are Pilgrim children, and
your parents have just told you about the Thanksgiving
feast that the colony has decided to have for the Indians.
Assume these roles and play-act the conversation between
these children. Be sure to remain in the character role you
are assuming.
   1. John—in the sixth grade and almost a man, looking
   forward to the Indians' coming
   2. Joshua—a boaster, afraid of the Indians but ashamed to
   show it
   3. Mary—disliking work and thinking of all the work to
   come to get ready for the day
   4. Charity—a little girl, anxious to do the right thing, but
   afraid of the Indians
   5. Truth—full of mischief and hoping something exciting
   will happen that day
   6. Delivered—a roly-poly boy, full of mischief and always
   cracking jokes and always shocking Charity
B. **Runaway slaves.** Be five children who contemplate helping
two runaway slaves they found in the swamp.
   1. Sam—tall, solemn
   2. Harvey—scared
   3. Irv—full of adventure, impractical
   4. Henry—a real abolitionist
   5. Hans—the practical one with ideas
   Assume these roles and plan for ten minutes what you
   are going to talk about and in what order. Then role-play
   before the class the conversation that goes on as these boys
   do their planning in the woods.

III. Giving Children a Feeling for Picturesque Speech

A. (Gr. 5–8) Following are two excerpts from *Black Gold,* a
horse story by Marguerite Henry. The first is the picture

of a horse; the second the picture of a feeling. Mimeograph these and use them at different times. *Directions for first lesson:* How well Marguerite Henry describes Black Gold! Notice the words she uses to picture his looks. Can you almost see him? How would you describe a horse of your own, or one you have ridden? *Directions for second lesson:* This is how Marguerite Henry has given us an excellent picture of a feeling. Think of some deep feeling you have experienced. Try to make it as real as this author made Jaydee's feeling. You need not tell us *why* you felt as you did, just *how* you felt.

1. By the time she was three years old her whole appearance had changed. The wispy look was gone! Now she had developed into a well-formed mare, round and solid as an apple. And her eyes, always beautiful, became so full of health and liquid light that one was stopped by their brilliance. Even the brownness of her coat had taken on a shine like a plain brown boulder made glossy by the water that flows over it.
2. A boy with a streak of meanness in him might have been secretly glad that Black Gold had lost with another jockey aboard. But Jaydee was stunned. He felt like a parent whose child has a big role in a play—a head angel perhaps, at Christmas—and the child not only forgot his lines, but stumbled and fell on the stage and never recovered himself. Deeply hurt and disappointed, Jaydee ran from the track, ran belligerently for the jockey rooms. He wanted to hit something, to punch somebody. "I've got to ride that horse before he's hurt. I've got to!" Swiftly, resolutely, he pulled off his silk, pulled on his shirt, and went out to find Old Man Webb.[3]

B. Read this word picture and think of one of your own; then have a class exchange. Use one subject at a time.

The child looked up at me as helplessly as a baby robin that had fallen out of its nest.

The young woman was as sly as a mother quail trying to lead an intruder away from her young. (When have you watched a person or animal acting sly? Describe what you saw.)

[3] From *Black Gold* by Marguerite Henry. Copyright 1957 by Rand, McNally & Company, publishers.

My dog has a coat the color of rusted steel with two fire-red eyes. (How does your dog or cat look?)

The girl needled me with a look.

After the teacher looked at me, I could feel her glance sticking out through my shoulder blades.

She gave me the radar look. (Looks are eloquent. Describe one you've seen.)

The baby frolicked like a puppy. (Describe the way a human baby or a baby pet plays.)

My father looked as limp as a newspaper that had been out all night. (Describe a tired person's look.)

She went through my pockets like a teacher after a misspelled word. (Can you match this or top this?)

My heart ticked like a Geiger counter. (Describe your heart action under stress.)

C. Make a picturesque phrase to match this picture. Post several pictures of persons, animals, or things that might match picturesque phrases you have found in your reading. Ask the children to think of a phrase to match the picture. After they have written theirs, post under the picture the one you found.

In art class on another day, reverse the process. Make a picture to match the phrases: "As cheerful as a dandelion." "Teeth de-parted in the middle." "Her hair went in all directions at once." "The spaniel looked as if he'd just had a permanent." "The horse might have been Pegasus himself." "His eyes told the secret."

D. *Singing Praises in Better Phrases,* or *Can You Top This Slang?* (Gr. 6–8) Gather from your class every expression they have heard that means, "She's the nicest person I know"; then let the students try to say it better in modern style:

Gathered from the class	Coined by the class
She's tops.	She's in the space place.
She's sky-high.	Perfection—plus.

She's all gold.
She's A-1.
She's top crust.
She's heaven-sent.
She's the cream in my coffee.
She's all wool and a yard wide.
God made her and lost the pattern.
She's 14-carat.
She's "top shelf."

She gives me that ceiling-
feeling.
She comes before "A."
She's in my rocket pocket.
She's steeple people.
She's my high note.
She's outer space.
She's my dessert.[4]

If this creates interest, sometime later try a *Praise Phrase* for the most admired ball player, the best parent, most beloved teacher, and so on.

IV. *Storytelling*

A. People
1. For sharing day following a unit, let several children dress like pioneers and tell original stories around the camp-fire at night.
2. Pretend to be the first scouts back from outer space; exchange stories.
3. Pretend to have been with, or to have been, the first explorers who reached the North or South American continent. Tell of an adventure you had.

B. Animals
1. After having studied the animals native to Africa or Australia, pretend to be the first American to have seen one and tell a friend how you happened to see it and how it looked.
2. Do the same for a purely made-up creature.

V. *Round-Table Discussion*

Choose from a box a subject such as these: "What parents don't understand about teen-agers." "The teachers I like best." "What I can do at home to make it a better place." "The rules that could make bicycle riders safe in this town." "I'd like to know

---

[4] A horse lover said he didn't know one of these, but he knew one for a snooty girl and suggested "chilly filly."

more about manners before I go to high school." (Ask the students to contribute to this box.) Save the topics your group draws for the next day; then discuss them.

VI. *Giving Talks* (Gr. 3–8)

A. Bring to school some materials relating to your hobby; if they fit in naturally, use them in giving your talk. You will be less nervous with something in your hands. Be sure, however, to look at your audience every chance you get and never actually turn your back to them. Work, slightly turned, or better still with the material on a table in front of you.

You may want to use a diagram on the board instead of bringing exhibits. If the design is simple, draw it as you go, telling what you are doing and why as you draw—there must not be long silences in a talk.

If your demonstration is making or constructing something, have parts of it done so that showing how may be done in a few seconds. It is better to demonstrate one hard maneuver and show the half-finished parts of others than to make the whole thing in front of the class and take too much time.

Perhaps you would like to demonstrate how to clean jewelry, how to dry gloves, how to carve a dog from soap. (Show each completed step, actually demonstrating only the hardest part.) Your hobby may be pie-making. Why not demonstrate to the class about what to do with the extra piecrust that hangs over and start crimping the edges? You may want to demonstrate how to play a new game you'd like to introduce to your classmates. Use the board to help you. Don't call the gadgets you play with "whatsits"; show them and call them by their right names. Demonstrate the various plays, too, if they aren't too complicated.

If your hobby is being an amateur magician, don't give away your secrets; just demonstrate a few, acting as if it were as easy as laughing to pick coins out of the air. If you play an instrument, show how it is done, demonstrating each step.

So many interesting things come under the subject of hobbies: card tricks, explaining holds in wrestling, demonstrating movements in boxing; showing how to make a willow whistle, how to construct a fish fly, how to compose a song, how to make something interesting out of a coat hanger; some interesting facts about stamp collecting; your amateur radio activities; how banquets are arranged; how to make a miniature Japanese garden; showing what interesting things can be done with scraps; how to give a dog a bath (just pretending the dog is there, of course).

Remember that every talk needs an *introduction* that interests the class; the *body* of the talk, in which you demonstrate or use a diagram; and a *conclusion* that tells a personal experience that goes with the hobby.

B. Tales at Christmas
  1. Give a demonstration talk on how to wrap and tie a gift handsomely at Christmas time.
  2. Demonstrate the correct way to get a package ready for Christmas mailing.
  3. Show how to make an attractive Christmas ornament.
  4. Pretend to be the city postmaster (after interviewing him), and demonstrate some Do's and Don't's of Christmas mailing.
C. Give talks that guides would give at national or state parks or famous places. (Send for advertising material to make this real.)
D. Pretend to be a famous person and tell exciting things about your life.

Remember: *To prepare your talk carefully*
To organize what you have to say
To use one or two new words
To practice your talk
To give it so clearly that even those in the back seats can hear you

CHAPTER SIX

Reading Is in Good Hands

"Who said Johnny can't read?"
"His parents."
"What made them think that?"
"They read it in a book."

He ate and drank the precious words,
His spirit grew robust;
He knew no more that he was poor,
Nor that his frame was dust.
He danced along the dingy days,
And this bequest of wings
Was but a book. What liberty
A loosened spirit brings! [1]

Emily Dickinson

My Magic Carpet

A book is a magic carpet; it crosses every sea;
It flies above the highest cloud, carrying me.
I look down on skyscrapers, and all the city life
I look down on people's joys, their happiness and strife.
I can see the fluffy clouds, dusting off the sky.
I can see New England herring, brown bread, and Boston pie.
I can see a western rodeo; miles and miles of prairie
Hear the shrieks of witches and ghosts, and everything that's scary.
A book is a magic carpet, it carries me afar;
See the planet Saturn, the moon, and every star.
New and old ways of living; aye, what treasures I gain!
By gathering and storing knowledge, wisdom, from every terrain.
Deep as the earth is the secret, old as the Sphinx; you see,
That a book is a magic carpet that crosses every sea.

Diane Badman, Grade 8

---

[1] From *Selected Poems* by Emily Dickinson. By permission of Little, Brown & Company, publishers.

Some day we may put the "Why Johnny can't read" scare of 1956 into somewhat the same category as the Salem witch hunt of two and a half centuries earlier.

In that year the public, cleverly propagandized by a book of half- and quarter-truths, came to the sudden realization that many of America's elementary school children who should be able to read up to grade level could not, a condition the teachers of America had been struggling with since the first schools were built.

Then the witch hunt began. Educators, stripped of their professional dignity, were tied behind the carts of public opinion and mercilessly flayed by the press and the parents as being the perpetrators of the reading crime. It was like blaming the doctors of a community for an epidemic brought on by the unsanitary conditions allowed by the city fathers within the city limits. It was as if a pronouncement were made that far too many children in the United States have decayed teeth, and the public should suddenly become incensed about a condition which, while true, is infinitely better than it used to be.

Certainly a startling number of children in the United States cannot read up to grade level—that is positively true—but it was equally true in the year 1900 and in all the years between.

What became of the nonreaders and the poor readers of sixty years ago? Many of them dropped out of school into the world of work, and those who, because of parental pressures, were forced to remain in the classroom, were dubbed as stupid, were retained until they were social misfits in their own age groups, becoming under the stigma of nonachievement sullen, neurotic, or ambitious to gain status in some other field.

Few teachers of this era grouped these poor or nonreaders in an effort to teach them; few teachers applied remedial measures; not many tried different methods in an effort to change the status of these poor readers; there were no reading clinics to locate the cause of their disability. The nonreader or poor reader of yesterday was punished, retarded, pushed out of school, but still could not read.

As for poor readers in college—recent research says that from 30 to 40 per cent of today's college freshmen need reading instruction —sixty years ago these young people were not even in college. Except for the shells of schools dedicated to prestige and personality development, colleges of the 1900's were small select groups of real scholars, we are told (a statement that amuses me mightily in the light of some of their graduates I have met) . Since such a small number of the college-age youth went to college at the beginning of the century, the poor readers among them caused little stir outside the ivied walls. And yet we find among slow readers many with high intelligence quotients; we have discovered that there need be practically no nonreaders; that even the stupid can be taught to read up to their capacity levels.

Why, then, are there intelligent children with reading potential who are not reading? How can the schools help every child to read up to his capacity level? It is in an honest attempt to answer these two questions that this chapter is written. However, before we start, there are two facts that must be understood.

1. Reading is not a simple matter of phonics teaching, as Mr. Flesch suggested in *Why Johnny Can't Read*. Rather, even in the hands of an excellent teacher, reading is a complicated, intricate process dependent on many things beyond a teacher's power to change.

2. The majority of children *in the elementary schools* of the United States do read up to their grade level and many far beyond it. If parents had apprised themselves of this fact, the reading scare of 1956 might have been avoided.

Professor William Sheldon, director of the Syracuse University reading laboratory, who reports on the need to teach reading to one-third of college freshmen, believes that the reading instruction is adequate through the elementary school but deficient thereafter.

Is this the time, then, to castigate the reading teachers in the junior and senior high schools? To tell the truth, this is no time for witch hunts of any sort. These are new times with new answers to both old and new problems. In every area of living, earnest men and women are facing the floods of children inundating our schools, and are trying, often without much help from their respective communities, to find ways that will take care of the surging hordes of children of a mobile population that pulls nonreaders into communities that used to be fairly stable. Today's poor reader may have been in four schools during one year. Schools do not always breed poor readers, they often inherit them. But no matter where our children come from, they are America's children and must get the best reading help that can be given them by whoever teaches them, oftentimes in the midst of crowded conditions.

And now let us face the reading situation together.

Today ALL the Children Are in School

Practically all the children of all the people in America sit in our classrooms and face us in the reading class: the intelligent, the average, the slow; the interested, the noninterested; the child emotionally well, the child emotionally sick; the child physically well, the child physically ill; the underfed, the overfed; the overstimulated, the never-stimulated; the book-learner, the muscle-learner, the nonlearner. There they sit—the more than twenty-three million elementary school children in the public schools of the United States —and all of them must become interested in reading whether they want to read or not—a truly challenging situation to teachers, requiring the ingenuity of a devil, the vision of a saint, and the ongoing power of a Mack truck.

The Reading Teacher Must Be an Expert

If reading were learned alike by all children, how easy it would be to train teachers in that one method, and presto—all children would read!

As any mother of several children can report, no two children respond in the same way to the same treatment. To one she needs only to suggest; the second she must strongly coerce; the third she must punish, and with the fourth nothing seems to work, not even after a pitched battle.

Since children learn at school in much the same way that they learn at home, one can readily see that teaching reading *to every child in the room,* far from being a mass process, is an individualistic one and therefore demands high skill and judgment and a great deal of time.

The reading teacher must know not only one method of reading but all methods—plus making up some new ones of his own—in order, like the doctor, to know what to prescribe if the usual prescription doesn't work. Furthermore, the reading teacher must be an expert not only in methodology but in children as well, being conversant with the interests, abilities, attitudes, and backgrounds of every child in his room. That kind of teaching demands a high quality of professional training, a growing knowledge of research, and more time than crowded daily programs of most elementary teachers will allow. If it is determined to get all its children to read (and it should be), America must demand greater professional training of its teachers, give them fewer children to teach, allow them to weed out the curriculum (it was the public who crowded it, you know), not blame them for their children's I.Q.'s, and pay them accordingly. One cannot buy professionals at the ten-cent store, nor can those same professionals do much thinking in the middle of a rat race.

Yet, strangely enough, even overworked teachers with insufficient training and crowded schedules are working like professionals to find the answers to the reading problems of children—and in many cases finding them. Unlike many American laborers, the elementary teachers as a group are spending the major part of their time and energy attempting to improve their product, not their status, a fact that the public fails to recognize until the schools run out of teachers, and certainly fails to appreciate.

Furthermore, parents must realize that in a day when almost every doctor is an expert in one field only, they are expecting their elementary teachers to be reading experts, experts in every other school subject, child guidance experts, public relations specialists —all on a day laborer's wages and often after only a brief professional training. Take away a doctor's long careful years of training and his year or years of graduate work in his specialty, pay him a nonprofessional wage, then publicly deride him because he can't cure *all his patients,* and how long could the public expect to attract the best young people into the medical profession? The teaching profession needs high qualifications and high financial rewards for the same reason that other professions need them. The Johnnys who can't read need true professional help.

Any illness as involved as reading difficulties needs much research, and every child seems to present a different problem, thus making it hard to teach poor readers together in one class. Just as the doctors, in the absence of sufficient research, have always had to grope their way toward diagnosis of disease, so today's teachers must do much experimenting before they can find all the answers to our present reading problems. The vital question in the field of elementary reading today is not how to teach reading—research has taught us that answer—but how we can help John or Joe or Mary with his or her special reading problem. It is the individual aspect of the reading question that is facing overworked teachers in crowded classrooms.

Yes, thank you, they can get their three reading groups into their "bulging-at-the-waistline" daily schedules. But where could even the angels find a spare minute in which to help those five or six children in every classroom, each of whom is a special reading case and cannot be taught en masse? If they even half realized how valiant is the struggle of the elementary teacher to answer that question, the public would be more than a little ashamed of their often unreasonable attitude.

Children Vary Greatly in Beginning Reading

Many intelligent children find learning to read extremely difficult—and it is. Parents know how different were the learning-to-speak habits of their various children, and how little the rate of acquiring those habits affected later speech. The same is true of reading, only more so. Speaking is direct communication, used at first to get needed or wanted things, and is therefore eminently satisfying. Reading is getting ideas from unfamiliar, almost-alike, little squiggles on a page—ideas many children have no special desire to learn the hard way of reading. It is easier to have a parent read or to ask for the information from any nearby adult. There is, of necessity, a wide difference in the speed at which children "catch on" to the reading process in their first year of school. Many a child who is a slow starter in reading, if given enough individual attention, turns out to be one of the best readers. It is no slur on your child that he is a slow starter. If the teacher puts a slow starter in the fast reading group she will be doing both him and you a great disfavor. *Trust* your child with the first-grade teacher. She is usually a wise, understanding woman who knows that beginning readers tend to develop at their own rate despite prayers or threats. As well try to shake a fist at geraniums tardy at blossoming.

Mothers, please do not harry the first-grade teacher if your child is in the third reading group. Take comfort from the mother whose son did not start to talk until he was two years old, but once started could hardly be stopped. Children, like plants, have their own individual rates of developing, a condition their teacher has as little power to control as she has influence over the law of gravity.

Reading groups are elastic groups, and the minute your child shows enough growth to pass him along into the second or first group, the teacher is delighted to do so. But neither parent nor teacher must nag at a child about his slow start at reading, lest he grow confused and build up a block in his mind against reading. You know how you feel if you are a slow starter at dancing or bridge playing! You get such a complex that you don't do even as well as you can. It's that way with the slow starter in reading. He doesn't know why he isn't getting along, but he must not become defeated at six, lest he remain a slow reader all his life.

Truly your first-grade child is in good hands—our primary teaching of reading is the best in the nation—probably due in part to the wide and deep research shared by publishers of primary reading materials.

But, besides the teacher's, reading needs still another pair of hands—the parent's. How can the home help the school to conquer reading difficulties?

Perhaps Your Child Has Shrugamug

What is Shrugamug?

Shrugamug is a disease peculiar to our civilization and our times. It was not shipped into our country from foreign lands; it is a product of our own commercialized, overstimulated age. It seems to stem from several conditions all too prevalent in modern America: overstimulation with its twin virus, spraying attention; confusion in the minds of America's parents and teachers as to their role in child guidance; the absence of the discipline routine tasks build in young people; and the shrugging off of responsibility toward any task that is hard to learn or to which one is averse.

"Reading? What fun is that?"

"We don't like to read and don't intend to do much reading anyway, so why learn?"

"Where will reading get me? I can listen to television and get everything I need!" is the prevailing attitude of our times toward distasteful tasks. Businessmen who hire workmen know exactly what I mean. "Let George do it!" Or "I wasn't paid to do that."

Heaven knows that such an attitude is nothing new. At the end of the last century, Elbert Hubbard complained bitterly about it in a brilliant editorial entitled "A Message to Garcia." Superintendents of factories and schools, however, declare that Shrugamug is growing worse. No wonder children bring this attitude to school with them.

A "Why-should-I?" attitude is a hard one to combat in the reading class. The mother in the home is about the last American worker left without Shrugamug. If she shrugs off her responsibilities, her children will certainly do so.

How can a parent help to combat the spread of this attitudinal virus? If it is not actually in your home, it is in the neighborhood and in the very air our children breathe.

Shrugamug is an extremely contagious disease. Children learn it from their contacts. Homes and schools can successfully combat its insidious advance once they decide together on the most effective methods of fighting it. When have bad habits and influences ever been able to withstand the united efforts of determined parents and dedicated teachers? But how shall we proceed?

The modern parent and teacher must take a new look at their respective roles in child guidance. Afraid to be too dictatorial, we have become too permissive. Lacking sufficient research upon which to rely, we have been afraid to advance. We exchanged a common-sense attitude for a nonsense attitude, and the results have been worse than chaos. *Somebody* has to have the upper hand in a home and a school, and certainly the parents and teachers are better qualified for that role than the youngsters. The adults at home and school have a real responsibility toward building a sense of responsibility into the children.

That task, while just as important today as it was for our parents and grandparents, is infinitely harder to accomplish now than it was a half century ago. In a day when, as someone has put it, everything in the home is operated by a switch but the children, *every member of the family must have his daily chores and be required to do them* or lose privileges or allowance or both. There is a close correlation between the way a child faces his work tasks at home and the way he faces his reading task at school. Many parents are extremely vexed when children must use their play period or their after-school time in which to do the work they failed to do in work time at school.

Yet *any other procedure is full of dynamite.* America was founded on the proposition that those who do not work do not eat. If children who play in work time get the same privileges as those who work, what incentive for work is there? How stupid can we get?

If he would stop to consider how hard it sometimes is to teach the child he is sending to school, the modern parent would regard the primary teacher with awe. A parent can hardly send to first grade a child who has never in his life had any responsibility toward routine tasks, and expect his teacher by some magic to suddenly make him read if he is inclined to shrug it off. Reading work habits have their roots in the home: in daily routine tasks, in responsibility toward work, and in the denial of privileges for nonperformance. Shrugamug is a virus that can be done away with if parents and teachers will work on its prevention. This *can* and *must* be done if America's children will all read. Wrong attitudes toward work are more inimical to learning than low intelligence quotients. In fact, it has been found that the slow child is usually the one with the good work habits.

Let us consider, then, the various component parts of Shrugamug, this new attitudinal disease of our times, beginning with overstimulation.

Overstimulation is the foe of learning, be it in the reading, the social studies, or the mathematics class. When one is overstimulated he finds it hard to focus his attention on any one thing. Use yourself as an example.

Let's imagine that you are going on a trip to New York with your husband—your first trip to that great metropolis. In the desk drawer are tickets to the most popular musical comedy on Broadway; in your mind you envision the dinner you plan to order at the noted restaurant you've seen pictured on television; already you can picture yourself dancing in your husband's arms at that famous night club mentioned so casually in your favorite glamour magazine! In the face of all this joy, you're just downright excited; you find it almost impossible to keep your mind on your work. If you are a housewife you may find yourself "doing" the baby and "feeding" the laundry, or perking the water but forgetting the coffee. If you are a teacher, you forget to notice whether "Lightning Joe" is listening to the seatwork directions or whether "Antsy Nancy" in group three is out of her seat again. Let's face it—you're so overstimulated that you can't keep your mind on your work.

But with you this overstimulation is only a temporary condition. After you get back home from your trip, dead tired but deeply happy, you'll soon get back to normal—more "alive" than ever. For you, overstimulation is a rare condition.

Did you teachers and parents ever stop to realize that hundreds of school children *never get back to normal*—that they are overstimulated from early childhood until adulthood? Three- and four-year-olds in some households watch television from the time it comes on in the morning until they are torn from its arms at a late bedtime. Those young eyes that were meant to survey clear skies and green grass are glued to the flickering kaleidoscope of excitement as program after program rolls by in exciting sequence. The nervous energy that was meant to be used in romping and playing is used on visual intake which is not even first-class "seeing" for youngsters.

Television is not the only culprit; a young child who lives all day on exciting play without a nap or rest period away from other children and who goes to bed late in the evening finds it hard to focus his attention on the quiet business of reading at school. Again look at this idea through your own windows.

Have you noticed after a visit with relatives in another state, how hard it is to get your youngsters down to normal living? You who have trouble with your handful of children at home should have to battle the overstimulation primary teachers encounter before the Christmas holidays, for instance. In many classrooms reading classes have a hard struggle during the month of December; in others, all during the nine or ten school months.

Just the times in which we live are exciting times—the front page of any newspaper is evidence of that. Ordinary living is exciting to children. What is "old hat" to us is an adventure to a boy or girl. But a preschool child must have some quiet periods in that excitement if he is going to be a good candidate for first-grade reading. A mother who visits her child's kindergarten for half a day can see how beautifully a kindergarten teacher balances the children's living into layers: activity with a period of rest; undirected play with directed; a listening time with a talking time. Mothers are too busy for such a controlled day—living at home should never be chopped into segments—but they can see that every preschool child gets adequate rest during the day and at night. It is hard for an overstimulated first grader to keep his mind on his reading.

Overstimulation and inattention have their roots in the home, not the school. It is time parents faced the relationship of overstimulation to facts about school reading problems.

Attitudes toward Work Begin at Home

One of the elements of Shrugamug is the modern child and parents' attitude toward work. It used to be that all children were required to finish the same assigned task in the required time—or else! That procedure stultified the efforts of the brilliant, pandered to the average, and filled the slow child with despair.

What is the difference in today's attitude toward work? Today's teacher knows (or should) the capacity of each child. Her assignments to each level of child (roughly three groups within every class) should be different, but that each child finish his assignment must be expected and be realized. Why?

What is the matter with this generation's workers? Too many of them expect pay for nonperformance or shoddy performance. That attitude begins at home and in the shop and too often is fostered at school. If America is to continue its democratic government, a different attitude toward work must be built into our youth—now. Tasks that are tailor-made for each pupil must be finished and done in accordance with the worker's ability. *But assigned tasks must be finished—or else!*

Please, parents, if the teacher requires your child to finish work outside school hours that he failed to do in work time, *please* do not make objection. Of course, that detention upsets dental appointments and household plans. But a child who gets nothing more than a lukewarm reprimand for nonperformance will, in most cases, grow to be a consistent nonperformer. Work with the schools, parents, in training your child to have an American attitude toward work—not against it. Remember, your own attitude rubs off onto your children.

And, teachers, quit being so permissive. Modernity means fitting the task to the child, not excusing him with a mild reprimand for not finishing his work. The modern is as slippery in evading a task as a street urchin in escaping entanglements. He will wear you out before you wear him down; he is far too "smart" to work if he can get out of it.

I truly wish sometimes that we parents and teachers were half as alert as our children. (Do you suppose we didn't have enough vitamins when we were growing up?) Today we are living with the healthiest group of children—ever!

Shrugamug is by far the most potent reason for poor reading in the schools. However, it did not originate there; it came from home with the children and from the times in which we live. A great many teachers contribute to its spread by not knowing how to combat it. They did not have a course in it in summer school; they did not teach in the fabulous "good old days" when all was as merry as a marriage bell (so we are told).

Providing for Individual Differences in Reading

A. *Grouping Is Being Universally Used*

By far the most common practice in caring for individual differences in reading in the United States is grouping the children within a single room into several reading classes, three being the usual number. This grouping is not done on the basis of intelligence quotients (some of our poor readers are high in intelligence) but on facility in reading—the advanced, the average, and the slow reader.

Our forefathers used to retain children who could not read up to grade, but as soon as research in this matter was conducted, it was found that except in the case of the immature or young child, retention, which put him with people younger than he, often made a child sullen, belligerent, recessive, or maladjusted in other ways. It hardly pays to save a child's reading rate and damn his personality the while. Immature children usually profit by retention, but each child and each case is different. It is dangerous for a school system to have a blanket policy toward retention; in fact, to do so is just plain archaic. Parents will have to learn to trust the schools as they trust their doctors, despite the fact that all people and professions are prone to make occasional mistakes—as are the parents themselves.

There are, of course, some bad points about grouping as there are to any method of dealing with individual differences anywhere in life. Although reading groups are elastic, allowing children to pass from one to the other as they gain or lose power, sensitive children who have to remain in group three all through the elementary grades often get the idea that they cannot improve and settle into a lethargy from which no amount of challenge is able to stir them. There is always a personality danger when grading human beings like cranberries or grapefruit according to excellence, but despite that fact, grouping has done much to improve the reading in the United States.

Grouping, however, has had another bad concomitant, about which little is said, but which is contributing strongly to the reading problems in high school. Because of the time involved and for personality reasons children must not be grouped in all subjects; the children who are grouped in reading in many schools in the United States *are using a common social studies and science book throughout the grade whether a majority of the children can read it or not.* I have visited schoolrooms in which more than a third of the class (sometimes even half) were unable to read the social studies text. In a frantic effort to "cover the material," the teacher has the children read the text aloud to each other, a procedure about as educational as watching a Western on television.

It does little good for a school system to attempt to take care of individual differences in the reading class and to forget all about them in the social studies class where the text is infinitely harder than the reading text. Many a poor reader gives up in third and fourth grades and says to himself, "Oh, what's the use!" because he cannot read in any class but his reading class, the only one graded to his level. Every room should have all subject matter materials graded to the children reading them. But are they? I go into classrooms all over the United States and see everybody in a grade using the same social studies book whether they can read it or not.

Why does not each classroom in the nation have all books that are used graded to the children's reading level? Because that, my dear people, would take more books, and more books would take still more money, and taxpayers who are anxious to have wars fought scientifically are not nearly so anxious to have their children taught scientifically.

Many cities provide Grade A buildings in which Grade A children are taught with Grade C materials by Grade C teachers, a phenomenon truly hard to understand in this scientific age. Yet the unit method of teaching the social studies and science is based on the proposition that each child must study at his own particular level; it is based on the idea that a subject is being studied, not a book. It presupposes that the children in a fifth grade who read at a sixth-grade level and beyond will read supplementary material of that mind-size and those of a third-grade reading level in the same grade will be provided with material on the same subject at a lower reading level. The text for each level is used for directed study while the other groups have other assignments outside their texts. This reading business in the social studies and science classes is a complicated and crucial problem. Those who strongly voice the cry of "more science" had better face the fact that *future scientists* must first be present scientists who are challenged, but not annihilated, by their reading materials in science classes.

Reading is no longer a "hearing" of reading lessons. It is a complicated technical and emotional business guided by a professional teacher who knows not only his business but the children whom he is teaching.

B. The Primary School Is One Answer to the Reading Problem

In order to ensure that children stay in the primary grades until they can read on an intermediate level, a number of cities and villages have inaugurated the primary school. In a primary school setup reading levels, not grades, are used as divisions, and children move from level to level as they are ready. For some it takes four rather than the normal three years to make the desired progress, but since a child is never sure which grade he is in, and since he always moves to another room when he advances, there is no stigma attached to slow learning as there often is in retention or in reading grouping within a room.

However, in the primary school there is still flexible grouping within each room in order to keep groups small. A great deal of attention is paid to individual differences, and group lines are so fluid that a child can meet with any particular class that has help for him.

What happens to the child in the primary school who at the end of even four years of reading is not yet ready for intermediate reading? Those whose I.Q. tests show that they have reached their reading ceiling move to an "Opportunity" or "Special" room, and all others go into a special remedial room where they are given individual reading help.

There are no report cards as such during the years children remain in the primary school, but parent conferences are held at least twice each year, and parents are advised by mail when their child passes to a new reading level.

I have a vast respect for the primary school. I believe that it has few weaknesses and many strengths and does about all that any school system can do for its children. Some cities have used it for years with outstanding results. Like all reading systems, its success depends on the personnel that administers it. But with live, reasonable teachers, I think the primary school answers most children's reading needs. Since most of children's poor reading habits and attitudes are formed in the primary grades, it seems sensible to prevent them before they happen.

I am of the opinion that the Joplin (Missouri) plan of grouping children in the intermediate grades according to their reading achievement has much merit and is a logical next step after the primary school. In that plan children beginning with the upper third grade are together with their own grades or groups in all subjects except reading. During the reading hour all students with the same reading achievement leave their classrooms and have their reading class with other children on their reading level. When changing rooms is not feasible, what is there against dividing children in grades four and five and grades six, seven, and eight by reading ability and maturity alone? Such a division would certainly facilitate the quality of work done in the humanities and science.

Both parents and teachers report favorably on the Joplin plan, which especially challenges bright children and allows teachers to work at needed reading skills, since all the children read at approximately the same level.

The Joplin plan, while it has much to recommend it and many communities are achieving success with it, does have the disadvantage of separating reading from the other school subjects and preventing much integration of school subjects in the grades when integration is necessary. Furthermore, it sorts children into levels as homogeneous grouping of all grades does and has the further disadvantage of moving children from one room to another—always a disintegrating experience to elementary children.

Few systems new to a school work well unless the teachers are enthusiastic about them. Schools contemplating organizing a primary school or the Joplin plan had better send visiting scouts to the cities and towns in their own and nearby states to study the organization and its results. A pair of teachers makes a good team: one interested in accomplishments and the other in children. Always start a new reading project slowly in one or two school buildings with teachers in charge who are enthusiastic about the project. Teacher-prejudice and fear kill more good teaching ideas than meager budgets or old-fashioned administrators ever do.

C. Individualized Reading Is One of the Newest Answers

Although many schools have long been using individualized reading, it is a new idea to the public schools as a whole. It is the current "New" in reading. In fact, one finds an article about it in almost every teachers' magazine and hears it discussed at every state and national meeting.

In seeking to find the answer to the "how" of individual differences in children's reading, the believers in individualized reading have chosen the epitome of methods as far as meeting individual differences is concerned. In individualized reading each child reads at his own rate the library books of his choice, according to his own reading level without any common reading text. Gone, say the enthusiasts of this method, is Shrugamug; gone the feelings of inferiority; gone the lack of challenge to gifted children. Children seem to enjoy reading what they want to read just as adults do. Enthusiastic teachers report new strength in the ability to conquer new words and their meanings. In fact, *excellent reports come from many of the teachers who have tried individualized reading.* However, I am not yet ready to accept individualized reading on even a city-wide scale despite these glowing reports. I learned long ago that almost any method of teaching reading works with most children, provided the teachers believe in it, work at it enthusiastically, compensate for its weaknesses, and successfully sell it to the children they are teaching. I want to be sure that the sparkle here is in the system, not merely in the teacher.

The greatest strength of individualized reading lies, of course, in its individualization: it can answer each child's reading need. Its greatest weaknesses lie in its highly involved organization and its vocabulary teaching. A teacher who is not ready to give her whole self to her job should never begin individualized reading as a substitute for a graded series of readers. Imagine the knowledge the teacher must have about each child and his vocabulary needs. Imagine the number of books she must read before her children do reporting. Imagine the bookkeeping involved. Imagine the time that must be taken in individually checking up on books read. Imagine teaching vocabulary for twenty-five different books instead of one. Yet teachers who believe in this method surmount each of these hurdles and are definitely "sold" on individualized reading. They say they are rewarded for their work by seeing children recover from Shrugamug. As I pointed out to you before, it is not hard work most teachers mind; it is the lack of results in the face of hard work that frustrates them.

After a number of years of observing individualized reading in scattered school systems and talking with the proponents, I have come to the following conclusions, conclusions that are only conclusive in accordance to the evidence now in:

1. A teacher should seldom begin an individualized reading program until he has had enough experience to know children and books very well indeed.

2. Individualized reading must, at first, not be taught on a city-wide scale; it must be carefully experimented with by key teachers who are interested in trying it.

3. In first and second grades and in slow third grades, I would not use individualized reading exclusively, and in first grade not at all for two-thirds of the year. I believe that primary children need that carefully balanced training that a good reading series, even in the hands of an ordinary teacher, can give them. However, with fast and normal readers even in the primary grades, I would certainly believe in supplementing the regular reading program with individualized reading in the spring of the year or in the after-

noon classes, provided that the teachers are interested in doing the prodigious amount of work involved. Children seem to learn best with a variety of experiences.

4. Slow-learning children seem to need a reading text more than fast-learning children.

5. I believe that much more research needs to be done on individualized reading in the hands of ordinary teachers before making up our minds as to its worth on a city-wide basis.

Why don't you start some research going with your own school children? Go to your nearest teachers college or university and spend some time with the *Readers' Guide* and get started on magazine articles. Perhaps a teacher friend could make the bibliography for you at summer school. After you know the system (on paper at least), why not visit a school system that uses it, not only visiting the classes but interviewing the teachers and the parents? But don't even start scouting until you've read and read. A researcher not only knows his business but other researchers' business as well. If you come home from your educational scouting trip with a deep feeling that you can make individualized reading work, try it for a year or two until you find out just what this system does to solve the reading problem. That all teachers have neither the organizational ability nor the planning power to use this method, I am convinced —but one never stays convinced in the face of new evidence. I am heartily for anything and all things that will help children to read.

We teachers must not be so quick to try new educational methods wholesale; education comes in retail lots, and what will sell in one community remains on the shelves of another. But there are in every school system definite research people who can seek out the Promised Land for the Children of Israel who stay at home planting and harvesting the local crops. There should be experimenting in reading going on in every single school building in the United States. The growth that is going on in science must also be developing in reading; the two are inextricably tied. If all of us keep hammering away at this reading problem, who knows but in a few years we may be able to help every child to be a fairly good reader? That this advance shall be the result of any one system, I gravely doubt; I am wary of patent medicines in education or in any other area of living.

Proponents of individualized reading say that it helps children to have more power in word attack, more interest in reading, and better work habits. These will-o'-the-wisps, in themselves, would be enough to beckon any teachers who have been teaching victims of

Shrugamug. However, may I wickedly suggest that if teachers would work as hard and as wisely and as enthusiastically on the system presently used, they might find that an even fairer crop of milk and honey could be had at home.

D. *Homogeneous Grouping Is Gaining More Favor Every Day*

Homogeneous grouping of children, probably the most cold-bloodedly efficient of grouping methods, keeps children within the same range of intelligence together. In this method each group is taught up to its level of capacity, and the teacher, not having to do too much grouping within the group, saves time that he can spend in providing greater challenges to the children. In homogeneous grouping no child is ever embarrassed: the dull are with the slow, the ordinary with the mediocre, and the bright scintillate with the bright. There is no doubt about it—if education were a mere learning of facts and skills, the homogeneous grouping of children would indeed be the answer to efficient learning.

I am always, however, a little concerned when schools tend to become as efficient as factories. Efficiency tends to put ways and means and things before people. The days I am deadly efficient I get my work done, but I undo people. I become a machine: accurate, precise, relentless. I listen to no cries of human hearts; I lift no helping hand to my fellowmen; in short, on my most efficient days I take care only of the things listed on my calendar pad for the day. A machine-like human being is a poor democrat and a poorer educator; he will not be ready to build a brotherhood of man, only a Fascist state.

In America, we are attempting first of all to build more than a state; we are trying to build citizens who can dwell together in peace in a world human beings can enjoy and in which they will grow Godward. Therefore, in America, educational administrators must not think solely of rates of learning and of facts learned; they must consider, as well, what the child learns in the way of attitudes and personality traits along with learning the facts.

I have watched homogeneous grouping and its effect upon personality for some time, and I must truthfully say that I have three grave doubts in my mind against its use *in the elementary school.* It too often gives a feeling of superiority to the highest group; it puts an undue amount of emphasis on intelligence; and it fails to take into account that the high in intelligence are not necessarily high in all branches of learning.

I realize that it is the thinker among us who shall help us to save our democracy. As Edwin Arlington Robinson points out in his poem "Demos," mediocrity can easily smother a country as it can a school system.

> . . . Having all,
> See not the great among you for the small,
> But hear their silence; for the few shall save
> The many, or the many are to fall—[2]

I realize—and reluctantly—that in our efforts to help the slow in our schoolrooms, we have had a tendency to gear our generation to mediocrity. On the other hand, if we breed a generation who consider themselves as supermen, may we not get the sort of result Hitler did with his theory of the superior race? In this day of awakening subjugated peoples all over the world, dare we put too much emphasis on natural endowments in either men or nations? Personally, I would sooner trust ordinary intelligence in a man with right attitudes and beliefs than an unprincipled man with a keen mind. Certainly we have a striking example in the world today of cold-blooded intelligence, from which condition Heaven deliver us. Heads educated at the expense of hearts make only educated monsters—machinemen with answers, but without the wise judgment of a human being who feels and cares.

What is a gifted child? Are only the tops in intelligence worthy? Is it wise for any group of people to consider themselves superior? Intelligence without humility is a truly awful thing. A few teachers can take an ultraintelligent group of elementary children and make them realize not only their potential but their responsibilities and their great lacks—but not many. Any school that uses homogeneous grouping before high school—and even then—had better keep a sensitive ear cocked toward developing attitudes.

When I get worried by some of the directions of our educational efficiency I stop to regain my faith in the world by reading Benét's "The Stricken Average."

> Little of brilliance did they write or say.
> They bore the battle of living, and were gay.
> Little of wealth or fame they left behind.
> They were merely honorable, brave, and kind.[3]

---

[2] From *Collected Poems*, "Demos" by Edwin Arlington Robinson. By permission of The Macmillan Company, publishers.

[3] From *The Stairway of Surprise* by William Rose Benét. By permission of the publishers, Alfred A. Knopf, Inc.

I, along with the forefathers who drafted the Bill of Rights attached to the Constitution, believe that a nation needs more ordinary men than supermen. In a democracy the so-called little men have a tendency to cut down big men enough to size so that they do not get too exalted opinions of themselves.

No, as to the use of homogeneous grouping in grade school, I believe that most children below high school level do not have enough balance as yet to keep a level head in such a rarefied atmosphere. Rather I think, teachers of elementary children must be the wisest money can buy, challenging each child in the room to his best efforts. But that kind of teaching, of course, cannot be done by a mediocre teacher—so there you are.

PEDAGOGY

No, I don't like to sort
My apples that way—
No tree grows just big apples
Else where's the cider and the applesauce?
"It takes all kinds," my grandma-am used to say,
Filling her apron on a winy day—
Oh, well—the proud will season with the weather—
No, I like all my apples in together.

Homogeneous grouping in the high school, if children are divided by subjects, not by I.Q.'s, seems to be fairly successful when in the hands of the best teachers. For many an intelligent child is good in one subject and not in another. When he recognizes that fact, a human will not need often to change the head size of his hat.

As a doctor from Texas once remarked to me, "Miss Applegate, we'll all have to go a right fur piece before we know much about the human heart."

But, for some reason or other, I'm encouraged. I think we're learning.

Grouping within a grade, setting up a primary school where children become proficient readers before the intermediate grades, providing books in the content subjects to fit each reading level, an individualized reading program either to supplant or supplement a series of graded readers, homogeneous grouping throughout a school system in an effort to challenge each mental level—these are all ways and means by which various school systems are meeting the challenge of individual differences. Each system has its good and its bad points and should be carefully studied and experimented with in a small way before it is universally adopted by a school system.

In the final analysis, of course, it is the teacher who makes or breaks a reading system, despite its inherent good or bad points. But it is the school administrator who makes the teachers feel that they are not working alone in a losing fight. A principal is the morale builder for the teachers in his building. He inspires, conspires, yes, and perspires in order to make things go smoothly. Both men and women need appreciation and laughter in order to do their best work. Especially in neighborhoods where there is much moving in and out, the teachers' reading problems are terrific. But they never seem as bad when the principal lends a hand—and an ear.

A wise principal keeps a graph of every pupil's yearly growth in reading, as shown in spring and fall tests, on file in his office. This not only helps a principal to help a teacher but gives him a picture of the reading results in each room. It gives him data to use in parent discussions and, in some cases, points out which teacher needs to be moved to another grade. A school whose principal is a real leader will have in-service training where over coffee or a potluck supper new ideas are reported and discussed. Too many principals live on a diet of cold facts and accumulated statistics. Teachers who have to spend every extra minute filling in forms get mighty droopy ones of their own. There's not much sense in knowing so much about children and doing so little with that knowledge.

Too many educational leaders try to kindle fires with statistics, which though dry enough, goodness knows, start no great movements. But simple enthusiasm in a leader can change a whole town.

I am thinking particularly here of Dr. Michael Scarpitto, who went to Stoneham, Massachusetts, from Joliet, Illinois, and with a reading-for-pleasure plan changed a small New England city from lukewarm about reading to wildly enthusiastic.

The plan that he and his dedicated staff used was simple and direct. From first grade through high school, everyone would read outside of class as many books as interested him. Parents and teachers would record the number of books read by each pupil. Parents of primary children were asked to help their offspring with reading for an hour each evening. The public library did its part purchasing more and more books. In one month from the starting date—November 8, 1957—the 2,800 Stoneham students had borrowed and read more than 14,000 books on their own time. By school closing time in June, the number of books read had zoomed to more than 96,000. Nor did the enthusiasm wane during the summer when 16,000 books were checked out to students.

As can be expected, reading grades of the Stoneham youth went up to a dramatic degree. As they read more, they comprehended more deeply, and grades in history, mathematics, and science took a turn for the better. Many of the so-called troublemakers and "roughnecks" became achievers in school.

But conflagrations of any sort do not sweep through a school system without changing the town. Parents grew so interested in their children's reading that they began to read; consequently the adult membership in the library is rocketing. Churches, newspapers, and municipal agencies fell in line. Dr. Scarpitto and his teachers have started a reading fire with the simple oil of enthusiasm—and all outside of school hours.

We Americans are inclined to make mountains out of molehills. Reading is poor in your town? Well, if it were typhoid, you'd stamp it out, wouldn't you? Any town that wants to improve its reading certainly can. When "the people have a mind to work" and when there is enthusiastic leadership, any bad condition can be improved. Remember that rousing cry in Arthur O'Shaughnessy's "We Are the Music Makers"?

> One man with a dream, at pleasure,
>   Shall go forth and conquer a crown;
> And three with a new song's measure
>   Can trample an empire down.

Yes, and one educator with enthusiasm can arouse a city of indifferent readers and get whole families to read. Enthusiasm for reading, like Shrugamug, comes from home.

A school system that really wants to get better reading can. Any town that can afford a doctor can afford a reading clinician to find out why each child doesn't feel warm toward books. If the condition isn't too bad in your school, there's always an experienced teacher in every building with a knack for diagnosis, who, if she were relieved for half of each day, could diagnose cases and suggest remedies to the regular teachers for follow-up.

To tell the truth, remedial reading is not the main answer to reading improvement any more than medicine is the main answer to health. Poor reading in our day is not so much caused by poor teaching as by wrong attitudes and Shrugamug in general.

Neither do I honestly think we're going to conquer the reading problem wholly by dreary grouping. Every child has interests, and interests jet-propel thought rockets. As soon as he is interested in reading, a child will learn to read. Reading is a complicated business. Teachers already know how to teach reading—but nobody teaches anything to anybody really; it's the mind-set that causes children *not to learn* as well as *to learn*.

As Timberlake says in Robinson's "Matthias at the Door":

> I have found gold, Matthias, where you found gravel,
> And I can't give it to you. I feel and see it,
> But you must find it somehow for yourself.
> It's not negotiable. . . .[4]

We adults must all remember that our children are living in a day of miracles—and marvels, in a day of *doing* instead of *reading*. They don't have to read for thrills as we did; they live with them. No wonder many of them don't see the need to read that we felt. The schools must not make of reading a "bread and butter" thing; the reading idea must be sold to children as any other value is sold to them. If their parents are interested in reading, so will most of them be; if reading is a satisfying experience to a modern child, he works at it; if it means little to him, he shrugs it off.

But interesting our children in more and more reading is not enough; we must see to it that a child's reading tastes grow as he grows and that his reading interests mature with him. A good many middle-aged women, who once had fine minds, still retain their adolescent reading tastes, and far too many keen-minded businessmen know little of the ticker tape that records the heartbeats of awakening nations. The time to broaden reading tastes is while young people are in school, not when life gets too full to start new habits of living and learning.

That is another reason, parents, why we teachers need your hands. Reading tastes start at home, not at school. Children who come from reading homes have a tendency to be readers. More home attitudes rub off on children than parents seemingly are aware of. Surround your children with books that bright minds can grow on. Let your current magazines do more than entertain; let them interest your young people in the world beyond wash lines and grocery lists. If your own life has been too busy with diapers and dishes or scrabbling for food and lodging to have had much time for reading, begin now and grow along with your children. No

---

[4] From *Collected Poems*, "Matthias at the Door" by Edwin Arlington Robinson. By permission of The Macmillan Company, publishers.

student gets as much out of study as the mature student; he brings so much of understanding to the book he reads.

Why not visit the library as a family? A family that reads together has something to talk about around the dining-room table—something to hold them together. Parents can hardly expect children to cultivate a taste for books if they themselves shun everything but the daily paper and one popular magazine.

And, teachers, are you well enough acquainted with the more penetrating books and magazines on the market to know what to hand that gifted child whose tendrils are reaching out for ideas not found in adolescent books? How long has it been since you read a truly fine book, one so challenging that its ideas kept you awake far into the night?

Unless a teacher knows the right book to hand a child who is beginning to reach out for a trellis, what might have been real growth will result only in a vague fumbling.

Oh, men and women—in the classroom and out—let us not blame each other for our sometime failures with youth in the field of reading. Each of us has his part to perform, but together we can certainly do what needs to be done. Neither of us even begins to suspect his own power.

Life is more than food and raiment, and how better prepare for it than by reading the ideas and thoughts of great men of all time? These are days when new mountains are thrusting their peaks up above the sea and when ceilings of air are becoming floors to new worlds. For the man who reads, these changes are not cause for dismay; his mind was prepared for them long before they happened.

Americans must read: read better, read deeper, read wider. There are no nationality lines between books.

Stephen in Grade 7, I believe, has caught the vision of what the world of books is to the world of men. He writes:

TICKET TO ANYWHERE

Almost everyone has a ticket to all places. With it you can go big game hunting in Africa, sightseeing in France, or exploring in Antarctica. You can dive deep under the sea, or fly high into the air. By presenting this ticket you can go anywhere in the world, almost anywhere in the universe, and a number of places that don't even exist. You can go anywhere, do anything, just by showing this ticket which, of course, is your library card.

Stephen, Grade 7

CUPBOARD OF IDEAS for Chapter Six

Reading Is in Good Hands ❖ ❖ ❖ ❖ ❖ ❖ ❖ ❖ ❖ ❖ ❖ ❖ ❖ ❖

Because of the nature of the materials in this particular cupboard, the shelves will be labeled by subjects rather than by grade divisions: Primary, Intermediate, Upper-Grade.

Shelf I. Individualized Reading

A. *Choosing the Books*

One way to ensure that each reader is reading up to capacity is to divide the books to choose from into three reading levels and invite like readers to pick out the book of their choice from their own levels. Many times after the children are used to the procedures in individualized reading, committees from each reading level can do the original choosing of books, thus getting training in responsibility and exercise of judgment.

If you believe that children should read more than one type of material (true adventure, science, biography, fiction) yet wish to lead them into a variety of choices rather than an overdiet of horse stories, for instance, you might use the 3–1 policy: "You choose three books, then I choose one." In this way you can raise the level of a child's reading as well as get him interested in another subject. You might also have a "Surprise" or "Bonus" day when you pick an especially good book you think each child would like as a change from his own choosing. Some teachers believe that since the purpose of individualized reading is to get children to read with facility, children should read only the books teachers choose. Talk this matter over with the teachers in the individualized reading setup that you study. Try various methods of book-choosing in your own school and note the children's reactions to each. The chief reason children give for liking this system is that they can read what they choose. Purpose here makes the difference in policy.

It's fun to have a "book-selling" period every week when discoverers of wonderful books give brief sales talks to the class. In intermediate grades, small carefully chosen book clubs might work together on library visits "discovering" interesting books. Some teachers with librarians' help keep a notebook of books under subject heads, with the reading level of each book marked, thus helping children to locate books that may interest them. You might, one month, for variety try a reading menu with book types as items and call it "A Balanced Reading Menu."

B. Vocabulary Help

Some teachers keep a card for each book on which are listed the key vocabulary words it contains. They try to help the child with the key words before he gets far into the book. More teachers use devices like the following to help children with difficult words either in a vocabulary period or individually.

1. Each child keeps an alphabetized vocabulary list of words he finds in his book that he doesn't know. The most important of these are taught to the whole class.
2. Pages of notebooks are kept by the class under captions such as: Hard Words, Quiet Words, Specific Words for General Words (General: go. Specific: run, stumble, flee, saunter, hurry, hobble, creep, sneak.)
3. For penmanship each child makes a small card for his personal file of the words he has learned to recognize from his "Don't-Know" list. (Parents sometimes help with these.)
4. Some teachers list words from the glossary of the basic reader and work with them in sentences, thus ensuring that children are getting a basic vocabulary.
5. Committees of teachers go through the manuals of several standard series of readers, garnering every idea on phonic

study and vocabulary training and using them in a daily word-study class.

6. Committees gather ideas for word-study games and mimeograph them for each teacher. (Be sure the game is more "word-study" than "game." Many games are too time-consuming to be worth much as a classroom device.)

7. Help students to attack new words for themselves oftener than pronouncing words for them.

8. Stress phonetic families and constantly compare like syllables in the new words the children meet.

C. Ways of Reporting on Books Read

1. For informal reporting either oral or written, let each child use any two of these besides the first.
   a) Name and author of the book, giving the reasons for your liking or disliking it.
   b) What was your favorite character like? (Let him draw or show a picture if he wishes.)
   c) Tell the most exciting or interesting part of the book.
   d) Tell the whole story in a few words. (This item is dynamite. There is no such thing as a few words when children are telling about their favorite books.)
   e) Read an interesting excerpt from the book.
   f) Teach the class the most interesting words this book gave to you.
   g) What have you found out about the author of this book? What other books of his have you read?

2. Creative book reports (written)
   a) Before you read a book with an intriguing title, write the story the title makes you think of; then when you read the book, write the report of the real story and chuckle at the difference. (Sometimes you will feel that you have the better story.)
   b) Write an interview
      (1) Between a character in the book and the author (see page 226)
      (2) Between you and the author (see page 226)
      (3) Between two characters in the book
      (4) Between you and a character in the book
      (5) Between you and a friend about the book

c) Write an entirely different ending to the story.

d) Write another episode as an added small chapter to the book.

e) Write a letter of appreciation to an author you admired asking him questions and sharing thoughts you think he may be interested in. You may even wish to send him a story of yours on the same subject as his.

f) Write your book report in verse (see page 225).

g) You have just finished reading a biography. Pretend you visited the person when he was your age. Tell about the fun you had.

h) Publish a weekly book column for your school newspaper, changing columnists often.

3. Oral reports that are different

a) Each of four or five persons reads a different book by the same author, then arranges a panel discussion covering such questions as: How are these books alike? How different? What are this author's greatest strengths? greatest weaknesses? How do you feel about this author from reading one book? Are you interested in more stories by this author? It would be well for each panelist to sketch or outline his story briefly before the actual discussion in class.

b) Arrange your book report as a television program ("I Have a Secret," for instance). A panel of experts could ask you questions in order to find out what book you are reporting on.

c) Pretend you are your favorite reporter on the radio. Report on a book in such a way that your listeners will want to read the book.

d) Choose a lively scene from a book you and your friends have read and either dramatize it or make a puppet play of it.

e) Have a friend interview you about a book of which you pretend to be the author.

f) Make a hand-rolled movie of a book you have read.

g) Make a radio or television play of your favorite book.

h) Pretend to be a book and tell what you hold within your pages. Advertise yourself a bit.

i) Get together some favorite children's books from your grandmother's day. Have an old-time book fair, each person reading several old-fashioned books. Analyze the

difference between books of their day and yours. Invite a
few grandmothers in to tell about books they used to love.

j) Perhaps a few especially creative children would like to
pretend to be their own children in the year 2000. Have
them compare their current books with those their grandmothers were reading as grade children in 1960. (This
is real fun for gifted children.)

k) Have a school party to which everyone comes dressed as a
book character. Plan a program and give a few prizes.

Shelf II. Teaching the Reading Skills

The teaching of the reading skills most needed in high school,
college, and later living must be begun in the earliest possible grade
and be taught regularly and consistently in social studies, science, or
My Weekly Reader class to all students who need them. Since it is
difficult to teach such skills as scanning, finding the main point and
topic sentence of a paragraph, reducing a paragraph to one sentence, taking notes, summarizing an article, and outlining material
with the fiction stories in our reading texts, it is necessary that the
skill be taught in other subject areas. If you find it hard to find
time in other classes to teach reading skills, transfer the skills
teaching to the reading class, but work with the content subjects
texts; just be sure to teach these skills—in which class doesn't matter. Many young people are being kept out of college because they
do not have the facility with the above skills. Skills teaching must
be taught when needed (in every unit there is a need for at least
one reading skill to be taught). Reading skills must be established
habits before youth reach high school or they will be of little use to
them later.

Get together with other teachers of your building and decide
which skills you are going to stress, and devise lists of interesting
ways to do your skills teaching. Many elementary teachers are
spasmodic in this area of teaching. Newspaper articles make interesting skills material, giving each child an article to match his
reading ability. Some articles from *Time, Newsweek, Reader's Digest, Coronet, Christian Science Monitor,* and *Saturday Evening
Post,* and the like are on the reading level of sixth grade and junior
high school youngsters. Look over discarded magazines for good
articles to use for skills teaching. Sell the idea to children that these
skills will help them into greater understanding of the world they

live in and will do more to help them gain college entrance than prestige and smart clothes. Let your school system be known as one that teaches the skills of reading from the first grade on.

Shelf III. Improving Taste in Reading

A. Offer your city librarian volunteers from a class to act as readers of books she contemplates buying. Get several children to read each book and write a short honest evaluation. Children are better critics of children's books than adults are.
B. Have a classics reading club that gives certificates for reading the prize books that never die, together with those awarded the Newbery and Caldecott medals down through the years.
C. Let your good readers become specialists in the really fine books in any of the various areas: horse stories, other animal stories, science fiction, biography, good books on science, mystery, travel, and advise readers as to good ones to try. A teacher cannot possibly read all the children's books on the market, but the children love to give advice to their contemporaries as to good books. Put some responsibility into the children's hands. They love it.
D. Go back to school and take another course in children's literature as often as you can. This is a field that changes faster than fashions in clothes.

Shelf IV. Examples of Various Types of Book Reports

A. An original story written *after* reading many books in a social studies unit on wool and sheep

WOOLY

Once there was a sheep called Lendy. Lendy was an old Mother sheep. Lendy was very proud for she was going to have a baby lamb. The next day was going to be herding time. This Lendy didn't know. But what was she going to do? If she got the lamb on the way to the ranch the cow boys would think she was sick and they might kill her. What Lendy didn't know was that the cow boys had other lamb coming problems harder than this and they knew what to do. We'll operate on her so that she may have it before tomorrow, said Mac. Just as they left, Lendy had her lamb. You might think that this couldn't be true, I agree. A few days later, Lendy was well again. Then she heard the sheepherders say her lamb was the cutest of all and it would have the best luck, even if it was a black lamb. And this is when the adventure begins.

One day in the middle of July, the sheepherder named Sam woke up with a yell, "Wooly's gone!" At that instant he woke all the sheep and they all went running without stopping for breath. Now there was very much excitement at that moment. Laddie, the dog, went sniffling up the hill. There on the hill was Wooly. Laddie showed his teeth, not at the lamb but at the mountain lion that was in front of him. You may think that the lamb was trapped but he was only trying to get the cat's attention off the bottom of the hill where the sheep were.

Kathy, Grade 3

B. Original stories made from book titles *before* the children had read the book

1.   DANNY DUNN AND THE ANTI-GRAVITY PAINT

Now as it happened Danny Dunn was the best artist in the sixth grade at Dry Gulch Canyon School. The boys preferred to call it the jail-house by the O.K. Corral.

"Now, tomorrow we're going to draw something out of this world," Miss Huckleberry said sternly as she waved her maple stick. (The boys again preferred to call her the spanking stick-happy warden.) "Class dismissed." With that a stampede started for the school door.

"Hi Danny," Jim Backer, who was Danny's friend, shouted.

"What are you so grumpy for? You got out of school on time, didn't you?"

"Yes, but I haven't got any paints and I haven't got any money."

All the way home Danny was thinking about the paints. As he walked he saw something shining in a pile of old leaves. His inquisitive curiosity led him to go see what it was. A narrow long box lay there. On it were printed the words, "Anti-Gravity Paint."

The next day Danny had his paints ready for class. Danny went to his painting which was a space ship. He was sure in for a surprise because, after he was finished, the rocket just started to peel off the paper. Then started to float away! Everybody's face in the schoolhouse turned red. Miss Huckleberry immediately snapped out of the trance she was in.

"Danny, you take your box of tricks and don't let me see them again."

Danny stumbled out of his desk and started hightailing it out of the schoolhouse. He slowed down his pace considerably when he reached the dirt road that led to his home. Then he heard a tiny sobbing sound coming from the same pile of leaves he had found the paints in.

He went over to the pile of leaves and there sat a little man about a foot tall. He had green hair and extremely large feet for a spaceman his size. Danny bent down to get a better look at the odd little man.

"What's the trouble?" Danny asked in an inquisitive tone.

"My name is Mister 001244 and I lost my box of Anti-Gravity Paints (sob). All I have to do to go any place is to paint a picture of a flying saucer and hop in and I'm off (sob). But now that I lost the paints I'll never get back home again."

"Maybe I can fix that." Then he pulled the box of paints out from under his arm. When the little man saw them he jumped with glee. He took the paints and left in place a box of nonanti-gravity paints and I'm sure the little man was very happy with his own box of paints.

Peter, Grade 6

2.   CINNABAR, THE ONE-O'CLOCK FOX

Once upon a time there was a fox named Cinnabar. He was called Cinnabar the one o'clock fox because he always stole chickens at one o'clock. One day a very wise farmer decided he would set a trap for Cinnabar. The farmer worked for three days and nights. Finally he finished. The trap looked like a very plump rooster. Inside the make-believe rooster there was a little motor.

That night at one o'clock Cinnabar came for another one of his bold raids. He saw the rooster and devoured him on the spot. Cinnabar felt a funny movement inside him and off he took.

Now Cinnabar is famous. He has become known as the Foxnik. Every night at one o'clock he still stops at the farmer's yard. The only thing that will bring him down to earth is his love for chickens.

John, Grade 5

3.   A STAR FOR CHRISTI

Christi, who was Mrs. Ghost's only child, wanted more than anything to have a pet star. All the other little ghosts had a star for a pet. But Christi only had a dog, a cat, a canary and a parakeet.

Christi, you see, was not as old as the other little ghosts and couldn't stand the long trip to the milky-way. She could make it to the big dipper and go a little further to the little dipper from where they lived in the turn in the road, just south of the moon.

At night, when Christi looked down on the earth she thought that she could see small stars on the earth. Her mother said they weren't anything but bugs so Christi gave up hoping for a star until she was older.

The next year on Halloween, Mrs. Ghost told Christi she could come along haunting. Usually they haunted New York City, but this year they wanted to haunt Central America.

While they were haunting, Christi noticed some star-like spots of light. She went over to look at them and suddenly shouted with joy! She had found a star! She took it home with her and trained it to follow her. The other pet stars had to be carried. No one ever told her it was a lightning bug. When she was old enough to get a star from the milky-way she got a big one. But she never forgot where she found her first one. So from then on every little ghost has had a pet star even if he or she was one year old.

Walter, Grade 7

4. Another report on the same book

Christy is nine years old. He is very interested in the study of stars. At seven o'clock each night he often goes outside and sits on one of the front steps. He glares at the stars very strangely. His gazing blue eyes make him puzzled and confuse him with questions. He sometimes sits for two hours asking himself who made the stars, what makes stars bright and beautiful, why are there stars and many other questions that he cannot answer.

Christy loves to read and can read very well. But his family is poor and can't afford to buy much. He dreams of the day when he will be rich—rich with books, so he can read and read and read. He wants to learn about the stars that hang above him.

On Christmas Eve, he (like everyone else) was very excited. He couldn't wait till morning when he'd rush out of bed and open his presents. He slept well that night and when morning came, ran out of his room to see what he had gotten for Christmas. He found one large package with his name on that he could scarcely lift. He opened it as swiftly as his fingers would let him. He was struck with surprise as he saw that his dream came true. You read the book and discover his greatest Christmas present he had ever received.

Jean, Grade 8

C. Talking casually about a book

My sister is a reader. She read a book about Robert Fulton. She reads books faster than I. I read Robert Fulton, too. It was good. It took me one week to finish just one book.

It took her two days to finish. She sits all squashed up in the chair reading books all day long.

One thing she liked and I liked was when Robert got sick and his brother, Abe, came and said he was a witch doctor. He had toads, fishheads, garden snakes, and worms. He gave all of them a throw. His mother screamed and ran all over the room. His sisters screamed too. One of his sisters jumped for the hamper and missed. She landed on Robert's bed with a toad on her head.

Then Abe said, "See! Robert's laughing. That means he's well." Abe's mother spanked him and said, "You get all those things out of here, including garden snakes."

"But mom,"

His mother stopped Abe right in the midst of his sentence and said, "No buts."

"All right" said Abe and he took off.

But just the same my sister is a reader.

Sally, Grade 4

D. Book reports in verse

MY BOOK

I've read a book named *The World of Pooh*
In it are Piglet and Eeyore too.

Tigger doesn't know what he eats
And climbing a tree was one of his feats.

And Eeyore, the donkey, is always sad
And when people tell him he often gets "mad."

Many friends and relations has Rabbit
I guess he makes friends his habit.

Edward Bear (commonly known as Pooh)
Makes up little poems especially for you.

Elizabeth, Grade 7

E. Writing a conversation between a character in a book and the author

LET'S WRITE

"Oh, Mr. Twain, it's Tom, me! Tom Sawyer. Will you wait for me please?"

"Why sure, is there anything in particular you wanted to ask me?"

"Frankly yes, Mr. Twain, I'm awful lonesome with just Huck. I wish you would write about another boy my age. Somebody, well, maybe from a different kind of life, or a different part of the country, or even almost the same. Then we could be friends and I wouldn't be lonely and all other people would have another adventure to share with me.'"

"Well, I'll do what I can, Tom, but don't count on it. Say, why not another book about you?"

"Oh no, you told everything about my life that's interesting in the first book."

"Well, here's where I leave the road, Tom, and I'll do what I can about another book. We'll talk about it later. Bye, Tom."

"Good-by, Mr. Twain."

Susan, Grade 6

F. A pretend interview with an author

AN INTERVIEW WITH WALTER FARLEY

"Mr. Farley did you ever have a horse when you were young?" questioned Barbara.

"No, but I had more opportunity than most boys to indulge in my favorite sport of riding because my uncle had a large riding academy, where I spent most of my time," answered Mr. Farley.

"Where do you get your ideas for writing your wonderful books?" asked Barbara.

"I have a farm in Pennsylvania where I have some horses, and by watching and taking care of them, I get my ideas," answered Mr. Farley.

"I especially liked your book *The Black Stallion's Sulky Colt*," commented Barbara. "Do you have a horse named Bonfire like the one you wrote about?"

"Yes, I have a young trotter named Bonfire on my farm."

"Thank you for answering my questions, and I hope you will write some more interesting books about horses," said Barbara.

"I'm sure I will write more books and thank you for coming," Mr. Farley said politely.

Barbara, Grade 7

CHAPTER SEVEN

Children Have *Poems*

School boy: Another poem to write about spring for tomorrow.

School girl: I must hurry home and phone my aunt to come to dinner. She got one published once.

Boy: My aunt teaches math. I'll try the library.

LULLABY FOR A GROWN CHILD [1]

Bring in your horses from the wide wild places,
The lush long pasture of eventful day—
Ranchlands of planning and uplands of vision—
It's time to lead them in along the homeward way.

Strong swift horses of boundless longing,
Fat little ponies of sturdy hope,
Obstinate donkeys of stubborn purpose,
Persuade them all in with carrot or rope.

Day is for running heel-high in clover,
Night is for herding in quiet heart's ease;
Drawn in obedient halter-meek homing
To focus point of disciplined peace.

Bring in your horses, the thoughts that go ranging,
Clearing the future with a single leap;
Bring them, as night falls, back to their stable,
And slip from the saddle, and so into sleep.

Rosemary Cobham

LULLABY OF THE SKY TO THE HILLS

Sleep, ye hills below me
While you have a chance;
Because the deer tomorrow
On your tops will prance.

Hush, ye hills below me
Under your pure white snow;
You need the rest tonight,
For tomorrow you'll have to glow.

Sleep, ye hills below me
While you have the chance.
For tomorrow you'll have to glow,
And the deer will want to prance and dance
Sleep, ye hills below me.

Wendy Kleinheinz, Grade 5

[1] By permission of the author and *The Christian Science Monitor.*

Poetry is what happens when children loosen their spirits and let go with words. A child's poem is simply a word picture of a feeling.

Carol, in fourth grade, sitting at a rigid school desk loosened her spirit one day during a radio program entitled "Sky-Writing" and let loose these five lovely sentences:

Once I saw a heart-shaped cloud. It was as soft as down from a bird. It looked so beautiful when I looked at it. It looked like a flowing dream. I felt like I could reach up in the sky and take it out.

Carol, Grade 4

Is this writing of Carol's poetry? It has no form; it has no rhyme. Would it have been any nearer poetry if Carol had written the five sentences in five lines directly under the other?

Go back and read Carol's bit of writing again. Let your spirit loosen as you read. Do Carol's words make you remember clouds that seemed so close to you that you felt you could reach out and touch them? Do the lines carry you along in a flowing dream of your own?

What makes a piece of writing poetry is, strangely enough, not its form or its rhyme, but what it does to the one who reads it. If a picture, does it help him to see pictures of his own? If a song, does it make his heart sing its own song? If a story, does it start the reader thinking of his own true stories? Poetry wipes time out of experience and makes one smell apple blossoms in the middle of January and feel the coolness of snowflakes in July. Anything that can do all that is as practical as a food freezer in hot weather.

Only a poet can adequately define poetry, and when he does, most people do not know what he means. Eleanor Farjeon undefines poetry by asking questions about it—a truly smart procedure when attempting to define the indefinable.

What is Poetry? Who knows?
Not a rose, but the scent of the rose;
Not the sky, but the light in the sky,
Not the fly, but the gleam of the fly;
Not the sea, but the sound of the sea;
Not myself, but what makes me
See, hear, and feel something that prose
Cannot: and what it is, who knows? [2]

Children do not need poetry defined to them; only adults need definitions. But at some time in your life an inquiring child, more interested in adult answers than in his own questions, may ask you without warning, "What *is* poetry?" and you'll want to be ready.

Poetry is words read like talking, but thought like singing. As you read it aloud, a little tune ticks itself away through the words just as one runs through your head sometimes when you are bicycling or mowing the lawn. Prose walks along in proper sentences, but poetry dances, keeping time to the thought. Some poems are very still as if the dancer were balancing herself on her toes with nobody daring to breathe until she comes down again.

A poem, like an actor, can play many parts. Some poems make us see pictures of places and people as clearly as if we touched them with our hands. Other poems make us smell the sea when we are miles from it, and still other poems help us to taste things we may have tasted only in our minds, and touch things we have not touched for years. Some poems tell stories; others are conversations between things that may have no language; some laugh, some cry, and some do both at once, like an actor or a baby. A poem usually says everything better and in fewer words than we could possibly say it ourselves. Poems are word magic, and we must get acquainted with all the magic we can; magic keeps a shine in the eyes and in the world.

This discourse will enlighten the child very little—children actually learn little about abstract things except by discovery—but it should have tidied your own thinking about poetry, and that's, of course, what I had in mind. The best discourse about poetry I have ever read was written by a Wisconsin child in third grade, not because she was asked to write a poem but because she had something to say.

---

[2] From *Sing for Your Supper* by Eleanor Farjeon. Copyright 1938–1951 by Eleanor Farjeon. Published by J. B. Lippincott Company.

We don't know what the birdies think
How they know what to eat
And how they know what to drink,
But poems know what they think.

We don't know what's in the mind of bees
Why they fly instead of walk
Why they make honey and never make cheese
They seem to know they can't do as they please.

This little poem even knows me
It tells you what I think
I never told him, don't you see
And I'm not even a birdie or a bee.

Jean, Grade 3

What does Jean mean in this poem? I don't know, but I am sure that Jean does. At least she pointed out to her teacher, "Poetry is the mind of my best friends." Jean's teacher didn't know what Jean meant, but remembering her own recent bouts with senior English, countered Farjeon-like, "Why don't you put that idea into a poem?" Jean did. The result is as interesting a piece of children's writing as I have ever seen. The more I read it, the more it says to me. In fact, one line is a real hint as to the meaning: "It tells you what I think." Jean may turn out to be a poet when she grows up, but more than likely she will merely develop into an original-minded woman whose husband will often ponder over what she means.

Many poets lose their poetry with childhood. One of the glorious tasks of the elementary school is to keep the writing door open to young poets. Poetry writing is a soul-satisfying outlet for emotional people of every age. It is a skill worth discovering and developing in children.

In this unsophisticated bit of verse, fifth-grade Paul, too, may be unconsciously telling what verse writing does for him. More than likely Paul is not quite aware of how much he is saying. A child's poem often says for a child what he doesn't realize he is thinking, as third-grade Jean pointed out.

KITE TALES OR TAILS?

My pencil is a rocket,
My pencil works all day,
It soars out of my pocket,
Writing June or May.

A kite soars like my pencil
It soars through the sky
Flying, flying, flying
Flying very high.

Paul, Grade 5

Seventh-grade Mary seems to be more subtle in her poetry writing than Paul. She is identifying herself here with a tree she saw or imagined. Even very young children commonly identify themselves with things: little boys go about "choo-choo-ing" like trains; and tiny ladies, too small for their high-heeled pumps, trip about in borrowed skirts to imaginary teas. This satisfying pastime of dramatizing oneself may be all that Mary is doing here, but I have a feeling that Mary's poem is helping Mary to see what Mary thinks, as third-grade Jean so shrewedly observed about her own verse.

THIN TREE

I'm a tall thin tree
Standing all alone,
With my arms stretched out.

In my dress I have three
Little brown squirrels.
In my hand I have a
Nest of robins.

I'm a tall thin tree
Standing with my friends.

Mary, Grade 7

It could be that Mary is telling Mary in this poem that she is growing mature, and that the baby animals she is holding protectively will be replaced some day with small life of her own. Such delightful contemplations surely go on in the minds of youth, but what business is that of ours? Adults must not read into the poetry of adolescence what may not be there and that which is none of their affair if it is there.

It is only when a poem seems to indicate tender spots or actual distress that an adult should be alerted and then not start probing. Guidance is a Geiger counter for locating, not a pickax for digging out. Whatever Mary's poem means, it is beautiful and Mary would appreciate your saying so, but without questions, please.

This next poem by an eighth-grade boy whose teacher writes that he has never known his father sends an entirely different kind of signal.

SOMEBODIES FATHER

```
Somebodys father is a farmer
   "         "    " " butcher
   "         "    " " baker
   "         "    " " electrition
   "         "    " " contractor
But my father is a father too
   " heaven only knows what work he must do.
```

Does it not seem to you that this particular Geiger counter is showing considerable agitation? This boy's poem gives only one clue, of course, as to what is going on inside, but one clue can alert an interested adult—if there is one.

While you are reading this next poem, also by an eighth-grade boy, try to remember if you can, some of the problems of your own adolescence.

CAST OFF

Have you ever felt alone?
Left out in the world,
Being thrown out on your own
To see what the world will hold?

The feeling of being not wanted
By everyone you see,
You live in a world that's haunted
Like a postage stamp on the sea.
Walking alone in a world unknown
Feeling lonely, frightened and sad,
Walking, walking all alone
With a feeling in you that you've been bad.

Is this how you felt? I can so well remember this "cast off" feeling, this loneliness "like a postage stamp [adrift] on the sea" that this young lad speaks about. I was there with what was left of my family around me, but nobody seemed to sense my feeling of having been abandoned. What a release this poem must have been to this fine boy, and how beautifully he expresses his feelings! What a teacher must have been his that he dared trust her with this evidence of his temporary darkness. What clues to children there are in everything that children write—not full stories—just solitary clues. But even clues help to guide a teacher and a parent to being quietly understanding. Adults are most helpful to adolescents when the "helped" are not aware of the "helping."

As you read this written explosion by sixth-grade Kathy, I can just see you smile.

> Many times I have wished
> For a day of freedom,
> Just one day from these
> Worn down tracks.
>
> Blowing my top off,
> Spitting smoke,
> Guffawing loudly,
> With a tear in my throat.
>
> A tear of hope for a day to come,
> When I can have freedom from
> Busy little people running in and out me,
> Rushing swift as streams on the rugged mountain bed,
> From turning sharp, decisive corners,
> Yes, freedom's on the tracks ahead!

> *Kathy, Grade 6*

No, we won't have to worry about Kathy. She has already learned to rid herself of excess emotion through a mental middleman that acts as *she* feels—in this case, an old-fashioned train. This use of an intermediary makes a "popping off" more exciting and more dramatic. Such identification is just an extended form of the picturesque speech of childhood. When she was little, Kathy might have phrased her frustrations as the boy did who said, "I feel just like foam climbing up in a bottle. You'd better all get out of the way!" Later, as a mother, Kathy may say to her family, "I'm on a rampage; better give me a wide berth today."

So do forms of nervous explosion change from poetry to prose with the years. My thesis is that if the schools keep the explosive Kathys of the world writing poetry, they can develop into more balanced personalities. In fact, I'm sure of it. (Poetic explosions are more satisfying than mere "talk-off's.") Their scope is larger for one thing, and they hurt no one. Besides, after the frustration is written out, one has a word snapshot of his own emotion—and that is a real memento. It's fun to see your late anger lying on a paper completely fizzed out. A poem is just a picture of a feeling, and anybody that has feelings (and who hasn't?) can write out his kind of picture: deeper pictures for deeper people and lesser pictures for lesser. Believe me, we teachers make a good many mistakes about which people are deep and which are shallow. Sometimes a child who seems to be a cup is just a well with a tight lid on. Poetry writing allows a perceptive teacher an occasional look under the lid— but he mustn't stand and stare.

All children do not have violent emotions, and certainly each child meets his problems in his own way: some laugh, some cry, some pout, some retreat, some fight, some deceive, some explode, and the tenderest wither and die. Fifth-grade Mark laughs:

TREASURES

When Mom empties my pockets
At the end of the day,
And lizards and snakes crawl out
She will say,
"Mark, how in the world can
You get so much pleasure,
From those horrid things you
Call your treasures?
Why you have enough here to
Start a zoo!"
"But Mom," I say, "they are useful too
You scream at mice, when all
It takes
To get rid of them is one of my snakes."

Mark, Grade 5

What is a joke to one child is a tragedy to others; and sometimes jokes cover up great tragedies—but not Mark's.

Most children's poems, like these two, one by fifth-grade Jimmie and the other by Janice in the second grade, are neither comedy nor tragedy but simple comments on the wonders of this universe, though not often said as charmingly as these:

MOON QUESTIONS

At night when the moon comes
Shining in my windows, I think
"Does the moon have pretty birds and flowers
As we have on earth?
Wouldn't the moon look glorious
If this was true?"

Jimmie, Grade 5

MY THOUGHT

My thought was that a star fell out of the sky.
It was beautiful.
It was big.
I played with it all day.
I liked it, too.

Janice, Grade 2

Or poems may just be children kicking up their heels and "being calves" with eighth-grade Charlotte:

BEING CALVES

Little wild calves,
Kicking up their heels
Running through the pastures
And running through the fields.

Oh, how wonderful it must be!
To run through the green, green grass,
And it would be like magic,
How quickly the days would pass.

Oh, I couldn't describe it,
There arn't enough words.
Lying in the pastures,
Listening to the birds.

Charlotte, Grade 8

And once or twice a year, or as often as one can realize his fondest dreams, a youth becomes a philosopher and sits back and contemplates himself and his world together.

THE WORLD OF MUSIC

As I stood in the night wind
Apart, adrift from the world,
I was ushered into the exquisite
                world of music.
The dark shadows of the maple
                trees seemed
Formidable, yet the beautiful
                sounds
And tones of the bass clef welcome
                me.
The drooping silhouette of the willow;
The slenderness of its leaves
Gave way to the rippling sound
                of arpeggios.
The majestic pines towering over
                my head in massive shadows;
The slender points and needles
Lifted the scale to higher tones.
As the music rippled and ran on
I heard beautiful tones and chords
As I had never before heard;
And it seemed that as I stood there;
The greatness swelled my heart
                and
Filled it with love for
The wonders of music and its
                Creator.

Marie, Grade 8 [3]

So children meet their problems and their worlds each in his own way. Can we teach all children to channel problems they cannot change, channel them through the creativity of spirit-loosened words?

A child's poem is only a word picture of his feelings or his comments on the world he lives in. Yet what therapy! What loosening of the spirit! Poetry writing helps a child to touch clouds and flow

[3] I get many poems from this girl—all outstanding and contemplative.

along with them in fluid peace. It helps another to put into words the vague feelings about himself that clarifies himself to himself; it writes out his fears and lessens them, and sends smoke signals to the interested adult. Poetry writing brings a child's inside world out into the sun and takes it in again, blessed with ozone and wind fragrance; it fizzes out his corked-up emotions and leaves them flattened and relaxed in black words on white paper; it helps him laugh off his penny problems and buys him a nickel's worth of peace; it gives him a chance to share questions that do not require answers; it allows him to kick up his heels with animals of his own heart-age in sheer delight; it helps him to sit back and look calmly at himself and his world. Nothing so practical has been discovered since the cooking pot.

How Can We Get Children to Write Poetry?

Train Their Ears and Hearts by Reading Poetry to Them

Poetry making, like storms, begins far back—back to the reading-aloud preschool days at home. Children should be given poetry with their pabulum.

Robert Louis Stevenson attributes his love of the glorious music of verse to his Scotch nurse's having read hymns aloud to him before he even knew what the words meant. The lady could not sing, but the lines of the hymns could, and their music helped make a poet of Robert Louis Stevenson.

Poetry is an understanding companion. There is no phase of human experience that poetry has not experienced; no depths it has not plumbed; no heights it has not climbed; no wasteland it has not wandered in. Let it talk to children in their own language every day of every year: poems of laughter, poems of praise, poems that tell stories that leave children spellbound, poems for golden moments around the campfire, poems for "together" moments around the fireplace or the dining table, fast poems, slow poems, and poems that answer questions—poems for every experience of children.

A child inquires of you, "How did the world get to be?" and your tongue cleaves to the roof of your mouth, but James Weldon Johnson's "The Creation" will satisfy that query in any child from five to fifty.

A child asks you, "What is God?" and your creed silences your tongue. Read Emily Dickinson's "I Never Saw a Moor," and children of any age will find help there. Poetry is the friend that has all the answers—answers that satisfy, but do not put the cork to further questioning.

Help Children to Find Out That Poetry Speaks for Them

Children will really begin to enjoy poetry with the discovery that it says for them exactly what they want to say but cannot or dare not. Children who wouldn't think of arguing about bedtime at home delight in hearing and dramatizing Dorothy Aldis' "The Grasshoppers" with that positive "No! No!" My own niece, who loathed going to bed, used to get a real satisfaction in pausing dramatically on the lower stair and saying Edna St. Vincent Millay's perfect protest of all early-to-bedders:

> Was it for this I uttered prayers,
> And sobbed and cursed and kicked the stairs,
> That now, domestic as a plate,
> I should retire at half-past eight? [4]

If the primary teacher, sensing a certain feeling in the room will just say, "Oh, I know a poem that says just what you are feeling. Lay aside your books for a moment and I'll read it to you," children will make friends with poetry early. And what English teacher in junior high is so dead under the fifth rib that he does not read love poems when the season for love has come? That he would fail to read love poems to a class of beginning experimenters in that universal subject would be a failure indeed.

There is on my living-room table an ancient blue glass bottle with a crystal stopper. In the early morning when the sun shines on that bottle, the blue becomes more intense, and the crystal stopper becomes a miniature sun reflecting the light. That is about what poetry does to children; it intensifies their "self" and helps them to radiate a light that is greater than their own.

Read poetry to children. Put poetry into their hearts; then place it in their hands and let it speak to them in their own language. Poetry speaks for the inner life, but few children will discover that truth without a teacher.

[4] By permission of Norma Millay Ellis. From *Collected Poems,* Harper & Brothers. Copyright 1922–1950 by Edna St. Vincent Millay.

Begin Early to Make Them Aware of Imagery

A poem is just an image extended and developed. (See Chapter Two, page 34, and Chapter Five, page 145.) In the beginning stages of poetry writing, children skip from one picture to the other with the facile changing stream of ideas that they have. Note that in seventh-grade Carol's poem snow assumes at least four different images, yet she writes a beautiful poem:

> Snow comes like a butterfly,
> And leaves like a stream.
> Snow comes whirling from the sky,
> And melts like ice-cream.
>
> Snow is like the icing,
> On every birthday cake.
> Snow is like a fairy queen,
> Or maybe a ship's wake.

Carol, Grade 7

Margaret, in sixth grade, sustains her imagery throughout the poem, a sign of growth in poetry writing.

> At night I often like to think
> About the black indelible ink.
> You may not use the ink in the daytime
> Because it is the ink's bedtime.
> The ink in the daytime sheds all its black.
> And then in the nighttime it seems to get it back.

Margaret, Grade 6

Mary, in eighth grade, carries out her image of night as a cat with unusual attention to details. Only a child gifted in poetry does that. Notice that Mary got her idea about "a curious cat" from hearing the T. S. Eliot poem, "Macavity: The Mystery Cat." Children and adults often borrow an idea or a line and make a poem utterly different from the original.

THE CURIOUS NIGHT

> The night is like a curious cat,
> Sending her paws down, plit, plat, plit, plat.
> She drinks the moonlight beam,
> For cream.

All around the house she does creep,
While everyone is fast asleep.
Into the corners quickly leaps
She prowls every corner and room
And all their secrets she keeps.
I think she knows the house better than I
For she sees many things with her bright starry eye.
She crawls right into my closet and takes long looks
At the leather covers of all my picture books.
And when she feels like being gay
Up in the sky she goes to play.
On each soft cloud she puts her feet
They break, then down comes rain or sleet.
So when you think of that
You'll decide night is a curious cat.
Yes, a curious, curious, curious cat
Sending her feet down plit, plat, plit, plat.

Mary, Grade 8

Extend Children's Worlds

In a world in which space has ceased to be a boundary, many children still inhabit worlds smaller than that of Columbus. What a delightful child that Christopher must have been, with a mind that pushed back boundaries and refused to accept the shores of his time. Yet young Columbuses sit in our own classrooms and often annoy us with their doubts and their arguments. We must not forget that the dissenter moves the world.

No-Men

Not the conformist;
Not the sequenter;
Who moves the world
Is the dissenter.

Jesus
Plato
Galileo
Halo-crowned, this shining trio—
Had they accepted the status quo,
Where is the world we moderns know?

Magellan
Columbus
Socrates
Nightingale
Harvey
Hippocrates
No Yes-men,
Guess-men;
No-Men these.

Luther
Loyola
Williams
Edison
The Mayos
in
The field of medicine—
Without their stubborn, tenacious doubt,
What heights our world had been without.

Larry
Jerry
Oliver
Jim
In college what is the chance for him?
We who are the guides and mentors
What do we do to the dissenters?

Oh, Doubt is a mule
With dreams in his eyes;
He stands his ground
Unmoved by cries—
While fat grow the fleas of compromise.

Not the conformist,
Not the sequenter;
Who moves the world
Is the dissenter.

M.A.[5]

We must help children to develop their wings in order that
their worlds may be extended. We must help the oncoming businessmen (like David) to spread out those wings.

[5] Note: Pardon me for putting my own verse in; I'm like the children—I want
to be in, too.

Singing Wheels

Singing wheels whirling round
Beat out a rhythmic pound.
Swirling, buzzing, oh so fast
Gives "grease men" a tiresome task.

Machinery wheels must never stop
Or output won't stay on top.
Rolling on, turning things out
From tanks to poles for catching trout.

This is the land of singing wheels
The main provider of our meals.

David, Grade 7

We can extend children's worlds by extending their experiences and developing their imaginations.

The modern elementary teacher can no more afford to teach the page-by-page textbook method, which is still going on in too many of our schoolrooms under a thinly veiled guise of "project or unit" veneer, than he can avoid using visual aids as textbook extenders.

Of course, he'll use textbooks—there must be some sort of platform to launch idea spaceships from—but the modern teacher must not leave the children on the textbook platform. Textbooks are as much teacher-extenders as children's, and most of them are superb at the job for which they were prepared—guiding their readers to think logically. But a teacher must only *start* with textbooks, not *end* with them. A well-written textbook sends pupils from book lessons to reference books, fiction, pictures, maps, globes, film strips, television, and on excursions into actual first-hand experiences. Yes, sends, too, with definite questions to answer, not only *his* questions or *their* questions but questions and problems to solve, arrived at together.

Many teachers are launching children into space, but without preparation or direction. In a many-dimensional world, we teachers dare not teach one-dimensionally from *a* textbook, nor in a space-wide fashion without guidance. Two teachers can teach side by side from the same curriculum plan book and one give his pupils a world vision and the other never get the children off Main Street.

What does all this have to do with poetry writing? It has everything to do with it. Poetry writing is more a state of mind than a part of the curriculum. Only "loosened spirits" can write verse. If children feel that they are a part of everything they read, if they can identify themselves with heroes living and dead, with space explorers that are and ocean and land explorers that have been, with wizards of test tube and medicine and saints of healing and helpfulness, these children will then write poetry. For a mind's capability to rise above the plains of *Then* and *Now* and survey man's human endeavors from the long view *is* poetry.

Children can understand this loosening of the spirit better than we adults can. They have the faculty of seeing far.

MY BEE FAMILY

I was born in a bee's nest
Way out in space
I lived with the dancing bees
But I never washed my face.

I helped get the honey
I helped tend the young
I even got food
While the bees danced and sung.

I live in a back room
Made out of paper
I bake all the cakes
With spoon and scraper.

Elaine, Grade 6

A WAVE THAT TALKS

As I looked at my desk in school one day
I saw a wave made out of lines.
It seemed to curve and to say,
"I wash the seashore of all man's signs."

As it came in day after day
It kept on washing and washing away.
The signs and lines
Of man's past day.

Kay, Grade 7

Largeness of spirit is the state of mind that brings poetry.

Help Them to See So They Can Say

Seeing large must be brought down to earth with the noticing of details. The "see-er" can be the best "say-er." Begin to notice things together in nursery school and before. The way the sky begins the day and ends it:

Fluffy cotton clouds surrounded an ocean of pink light. Ruby red and lighter red reflected on other larger, prettier clouds. Rays of golden light looked like a beautiful curtain across the evening sky.

Eileen, Grade 7

The colors of the sunlight through the eyelids:

I saw the sunlight
Through my eyelids.
It was yellow-gold at first,
Then orange,
Then a fire-gold I could not stand.

Michael, Grade 1

How smoke looks spiraling from a train:

Smoke! Smoke! Smoke!
Curving and curling in the sky
Twisting and twirling and whirling.
Climbing, climbing, up, up, up
Above the clouds,
Till it is gone.

Karen, Grade 7

How a tornado comes up:

The clouds began to go; the sun came out on the glistening world. Then in from the south came a dark funnel-shaped cloud. We all ran out of the house to see it. Quick as a flash, we ran in again. It was a tornado!

The black cloud let one of its long fingers down right over our bluff where we lived on a farm. All the cloud seemed to turn threateningly. Then the long finger rose as the cloud rose. It passed over. Were we thankful!

Marguerite, Grade 8

How water moves:

> Water crawling through the rocks—I crash and
> tumble over big rocks and make cream-colored foam.

Maewyn, Grade 5

How little chickens look and act:

I love little chickens. They are so cuddly and soft. They look like yellow balls of stuff. Whenever I see little chickens, it makes me think of Spring. They come out from under the brooder on the run at you. This morning when I went to feed them, a rooster crowed outside and a little one stretched up like he was going to crow.

Bette, Grade 4

How a cat looks after a facial:

> Fresh as a pillow in a case
> Because she had washed her face.

Wayne, Grade 7

How a lost dog's eyes look:

> The quietest thing I've ever heard
> Is the word in the eyes of a dog.
> Mournful eyes looking up at you,
> The sorrowful eyes of a lost and wandering dog.

Karen, Grade 5

That scared feeling that comes in a dream:

> My bones were just shrinking little by little
> at the idea.

Vivyn, Grade 6

The best "see-er" can become the best "say-er." The children will furnish the feelings if the teachers will open the eyes of the children to the delights around them.

Have the Weather of Our Schoolroom Right for Creative Work

Since there has been much said in many books about the proper weather for creative writing, may I summarize instead of expanding the idea. Children can write creatively if and when:

1. There is a relaxed, loosened air in the classroom; not a time-tensed atmosphere. The curriculum should not clutter the air; it should clear it for creativity.

2. The teacher sees large so that children are helped to larger vision; the "folk" know that the blind cannot lead the blind.

3. The children know that their creative work is not going to be graded. One can hardly put marks on living experiences or feelings; substitute comments for grades; they are more effective.

4. The teacher never tells a child he *must* write a poem; tell him to say what he has to say *in any form* of writing his thoughts take: a story, a paragraph, a poem, a sketch, a conversation, or a letter. If you discover that his prose is truly poetic, show him how to arrange in verse form what he has written.

5. No child feels he must rhyme; rhymes are word fun, but many children dislike that particular kind of fun. Teach even the rhymers to let their rhyme-resistant lines flow free. (When poetry becomes just some more schoolwork, children are allergic to it.)

6. The children know that the teacher is more interested in what they have to say than in the errors they make; in their own growth than in the rise of the class level.

7. The children are assured that every new idea will receive thoughtful attention, and every fresh vocabulary word used will be genuinely appreciated and adequately praised.

How many times as a child I thought as I looked at the bruised and bloody language paper handed back to me, "If she could only see what I am trying to say; all she ever sees is my mistakes. If she would only once say, 'Mauree, someday you're going to write. Right now your work is full of mistakes but I can help you to mend yourself so that you can get rid of them.'" But she never did—not once.

Help Children to Realize That Poetry Is a Word Bargain

Many practical-minded children who have not lived with poetry think that verse is silly. Explain to them that poetry is the most practical of all writing—you get the most "story" for the least bit of writing—a poem is a word bargain.

As illustration, use this short verse of seventh-grade Norene's, and help these prose-youngsters to discover that even a child can write a whole biography in just four lines. (This minimum activity with maximum results appeals to bargain-hunting children.)

> There is a girl
> With hair like the autumn leaves.
> She has a pretty smile
> And gives it to anyone she sees.

Norene, Grade 7

Let's see if we can find out together what Norene told us about this girl in these four lines:

First of all, what does Norene's friend look like? Yes, she's pleasant, but let's get specific. Hair? Yes, her hair might be red—yes, it will probably have a goldish cast—"hair like the autumn leaves" could have. How do you think it's cut? That's a good suggestion, having it windblown; "hair like the autumn leaves" might be windblown; leaves certainly are.

Do you think Norene knows this girl very well? No? What makes you think that? Yes, she doesn't call her "Mary" or "Pal" as one would a close friend; she just writes "There is a girl." Probably you're right and she's not too close a friend. Do you think her classmates at school like her? What makes you think so? Is there any hint here that she travels with a clique or crowd at school? Yes, I think, too, that the word "anyone" answers that question. Is this girl jolly? Some of you seem to think so and others differ. Give your reasons. Oh, jolly people laugh and pleasant people smile; maybe you have something there. How do you think teachers would feel about this friend of Norene's? What makes you think so?

This sort of analysis with a short poem will help children to realize that a poem is a word-bargain, telling far more between the lines than in them.

For junior high students using Frances Shaw's nine lines of "Who Loves the Rain" to characterize the kind of person the girl wants to marry is much fun and truly revealing to this age group. Boys like to figure out what kind of movie character the "I" of John Masefield's "Sea Fever" would make, and both groups enjoy speculating about the next-door neighbor suggested by Edna St. Vincent Millay's "Portrait by a Neighbor."

Practical-minded young people seem to respect poetry more after one of these "by-guess-and-by-gosh" sessions.

How can we get children ready for verse writing?
1. By reading poetry to them
2. By helping them to discover that poetry can speak for them
3. By making them aware of imagery early
4. By extending their world
5. By helping them to see so they can say
6. By having the mind-weather right
7. By helping them to see that poetry is a word bargain
8. By paint-mixing so that all can write

This last topic and the first are by far the most important of all preparations for the writing of poetry. The reading of poetry develops taste in children—the mixing of paint before writing ensures that all the children will be fired to write.

Help Children to "Mix Paint" before Writing

What do I mean by "mix paint"? In the same way as a painter mixes colors to match the "color picture" in his mind, so you, the teacher, sure that almost every child in the room is interested in the subject at hand, ensure through a stimulation period that all will have ideas to express and words in which to express them. This you do in four steps:

Step 1. Preparing the ground. Since poetry is a product of the emotions, you must ensure that the children *feel* what they are writing. This is done through talking over experiences, reading poetry and stories, allowing music to direct the children's thoughts, or stimulating their imaginations with creative ideas. In your classrooms, you can add other stimuli such as studying units of work, going on hikes or field trips, seeing films, looking at pictures, or listening to travel or experience talks. For a whole class to go into the writing of poetry "cold" without a stimulation period is futile for ordinary children who are not especially gifted writers. The gifted need no lubrication. They are off even before you are ready.

Step 2. Exchanging ideas. Here the creative children share with the uncreative ideas that might make a poem, or suggest the animate things to which the inanimate might be compared. And why not share ideas? Where do the majority of people get their ideas for anything they say and do? From here, from there; from their reading, from pictures they see; from a neighbor's talk, from a meeting they attended. Only a few people are purely original, and one of their purposes in life is to "spark" the less creative. Strangely enough, this middle group which comprises three-fourths of the children in the ordinary classroom often write almost brilliantly after being thus stimulated. This idea-exchange period, however, must not deteriorate into a teacher-dominated period. The creative teacher must hold his own ideas back until the children have contributed and even then contribute sparingly to the exchange. The children usually have ideas enough, but when things bog down a bit, poetry reading or looking at pictures will renew the idea flow.

By the end of this second step all the children will be ready to start writing except the two or three nonwriters in the room. You might as well start these with a first sentence or provide each with a picture starter. It is high time teachers faced facts and recognized that some children are nonwriters, but that each child has some other skill to develop.

"Way back when" we used to create poems in the meter and rhyme scheme of a single adult poem. Now, because many stimulating ideas are exchanged, all children are inspired to write in their own way.

Step 3. Stock-piling specific words. Work toward getting children to suggest specific vocabulary words to replace the general words they usually use. If skating poems are the order of the day, the class may suggest action words such as: *glide, circle, skim* and *wheel;* such feeling words as *exhilaration, winged feet, glow;* such descriptive words as *glass floor, icy rink, numbed feet;* such imaginative phrases as *flaming mittens, rabbit-fur clouds.* Keep a notebook of apt words and phrases children learn from their reading and from the paint-mixing in your classroom.

Two-thirds of the words gathered in one such period will not be used, but there are many carry-overs to other items. Besides there are many rich vocabulary words, spelled right (we hope) on the board for the children if they wish to use them. I am a little suspicious of creative writing situations in which children must use a certain set vocabulary in their writing. Ideas come first, not words; words are only the means by which ideas are made clear.

Step 4. Feeling the rhythm. Help children feel the rhythms that ideas suggest. Take an idea and let the children feel the rhythm it brings to the mind. Let several children demonstrate the rhythm each feels in the idea. Have a drum handy to dramatize some rhythms. Hum others. But, suggests old schoolteacher Me, finger-tapping on the desks is almost noiseless and doesn't excite children so much. Most times say nothing at all about rhythm; let each child express his own.

Use these four steps, then, in preparing children for the writing of poetry:

1. Preparing the ground
2. Exchanging ideas
3. Stock-piling specific words
4. Feeling the rhythm

These steps are practically foolproof and will get creditable writing, either in poetry or prose form, from almost every child in the room, provided, of course, that the subject chosen is one in which children of that age are interested. I have taken dozens of groups of children I had never seen before and by going through these four steps got fine writing. I have seen practice teachers do it even better, and regular classroom teachers do better still, since they knew their children best of all.

What! You haven't time to devote to such lengthy preparation for a writing class! May I answer that I don't believe you have time not to! This type of writing class teaches writing; and each time you use it, the children get more self-reliant. Better two well-conducted classes in creative writing each week than several repetitions of the same mediocrity. *It pays to mix paint before mass creative writing.* Just remember to choose the writing subjects from children's interests instead of your own. As Sandburg says:

> You can never make moon poems
> for people who never see the moon.[6]

What Subjects Bring Poetry from Children?

Whatever children feel strongly about and truly appreciate will make poetry blossom; poetry has to do more with feeling than with fact. But a few subjects are common to all ages of children:

1. *Children like to write about themselves and their thoughts and feelings.* What was on Steve's mind when he wrote this?

> I'm a little leaf
> So dull and ugly and dry
> Oh, how I wish I could be beautiful
> All the other leaves around are so gorgeous
> And I am just an old dried up leaf.

[6] From *The People, Yes* by Carl Sandburg, copyright, 1936, by Harcourt, Brace and Company, Inc.

When children come around
They walk right over me
Just to see who can crumble more.
One day when I was lying there
A little girl came walking near
She picked me up and brought me home
And I am happy now.

Steve, Grade 5

This isn't in verse, but doesn't this fifth grader understand himself and his dual personality well?

He was a funny-looking creature (not me, I mean him). My Whip-Whopper went to town with me. He was hungry, real hungry. He's mean when he's hungry. Whip-Whopper and I went past an outside grocery store. There were apples in front of it. He loved apples, his tongue was hanging out. He grabbed one, but the grocer didn't see him. He grabbed four more, and he kept grabbing. Then, out of a clear blue sky, he got caught. Now I have no Whip-Whopper, just little lonesome myself.

Orval, Grade 5

2. *All children enjoy writing about their pets.* I don't know why, but I want to bow my head reverently when I hear this poem.

My Kitten

I have a little kitten,
Her name is Mitten.
Because she has white paws
And has very sharp claws.

I took her for a walk
And I thought I heard her talk
I thought I heard her say,
"I had kittens yesterday."

Susan, Grade 4 [7]

---

[7] I once published this poem in an article under the wrong name. I mistook the school's name for the child's. Sorry—I just don't want anyone to think I make up the names.

The Countess is a calf:

> The Countess has a bad habit,
> She doesn't like to obey.
> She is a calf, but calves don't act half
> The way she does every day.
> Her coat is brown, and her hoofs are black,
> She takes off the moment you give her some slack.
> She kicks up her heels and runs down the lane,
> If you saw her you'd think she's insane!
> She turns around and comes bouncing back
> And knocks me over from the survivor attack.
> She comes walking up as if to say,
> "You can take me back now, that I've finished my play."

Jean, Grade 8

This is a real he-man dog!

> I have a pet
> Whose name is Bimbo. And oh
> Boy can he go!
> He's as black as coal
> And can wriggle under a rug as good as any mole.
> He grabs a shoe
> And is off like a bullet.
> He runs until he can hardly pull it.
> He chases my little brother
> Around the house
> Like a cat
> Chasing a mouse.
> When they play hide-and-go-seek,
> That dog's off like a streak.
> Then he'll look around a corner
> To take a peek.
> When my brother can't find him,
> He turns around
> And all the time,
> He was right behind him.
> That's my dog, Bimbo!

Stanley, Grade 5

3. *Children beg for a chance to be humorous.* (See Chapter Twelve, page 493.)

4. *Children make poems of action—any kind*. Myron dances with the clothes; in fact, I believe Myron could dance with anything. Myron has rhythm.

CLOTHESLINE BEAT

I'm a big white shirt—white shirt
A-hanging on the clothesline—clothesline.
A big white shirt, minding every
Clothes business but mine—but mine.
I slap and slap and dance, too
An overall kicked me and made
Me blue and made me blue.
I'm a little pair of jeans—a little pair of jeans,
That kicks and kicks and thinks I'm mean.
I'm a long pair of underwear,
Under where you can not see.
I'm a little pair of socks that
Just like to box and box.
You gotta dance with me
Shirt, all right pants, just dance
Dance with me shirt while the
Wind blows on, blows on.
Let the sock, rock, rock, rock
We can waltz, waltz, waltz,
While the wind blows on, blows on.

Myron, Grade 6

Seventh-grade Marjorie ignored the dance; she's a fight fan.

Pow! Sock 'em.
Wow! Knock 'em.
What a bout
Knock him out
Watch him duck
Man! what luck
He got a blow
Back he will go
One with the right
Here's a real fight
It continues all day
Now flat he lay
7–8–9–almost 10
Ooops! He's up again
Hurry up someone win
For soon you'll all be taken in.

Marjorie, Grade 7

And of course action in the snow:

> I like to go sliding,
> I get such a thrill.
> First I go gliding
> And then a big spill
>
> I like to go skating,
> And how I do zoom.
> First I go sailing,
> And then—boom!
>
> I like to go skiing,
> And how I do swoop
> First I go wheeing,
> And then—oop!

Steven, Grade 4

5. *Children enjoy writing of quiet lovely things.* I get the best contributions from programs about deep thoughts and quiet things. In four lines Ruth makes us see this scene with her:

DOWN BY A RIVER

> Quietly at a river
> A mother doe came to see
> If it was safe for a baby fawn
> To come and play with me.

Ruth, Grade 6

Allen almost makes us *see* the silence in his verse:

LEAVES

> They make a carpet on the ground
> And rustle softly as they fall
> Then settle down without a sound
> While the darkness hushes over all.

Allen, Grade 7

Here's Elaine again. Hasn't she an imagination?

NIGHT

I'm never alone especially at night
I look out at the milky way
And see all my friends and all my pets
That I play with throughout the day.

Elaine, Grade 6

Not up to Sandburg's, but mighty good for a fifth-grade poet:

FOG

I like to think of fog as rest
That shuts the day out when it comes
It comes to town on silent feet
And closes out the sun.

Jeffry, Grade 5

6. *Children love to write what their senses tell them.* Suzanne should know: she lay flat on her bed in a steel body cast for months; she has a teacher for the homebound.

WHAT WOULD I DO?

What would I do if I couldn't see?
The little things which mean so much,
A kitten playing in the grass,
With downy fur, I'd love to touch.

What would I do if I couldn't hear?
The sounds that are so dear to me,
The sounds of separate instruments,
Which join to form a symphony.

What would I do if I couldn't feel?
The softness of a piece of cloth
The coolness of a glass of milk
The hot steam from a dish of broth.

What would I do if I couldn't taste?
The foods which trickle down my throat
Angel-food cake with frosting pink
Ice-cream with a chocolate coat.

Without my senses five I fear
I wouldn't live at all
And so because I have them now
My life is just a ball.

Suzanne, Grade 8

Tom's sensual satisfactions are as masculine as Carol's are feminine:

A GAME THAT I LOVE

I like the game of baseball
I like it very well
And the reason why I like it
I'm just about to tell.

I like to grip the dirty bat
I like to smell my sweat-stained glove
I like it when the umpire says
"Hillside has again won!"
But most of all, I like to taste
Cool, clear water when the game is done.

Tom, Grade 8

Carol has written her biography in this one poem.

I love the feeling of mother's furs
Of hands thats full of money,
I love the feeling that you get
When sticking clean fingers in honey.

I love the feeling of a nice, warm bath
Clean bedclothes on my bed,
I love the feeling that you get
With "Shampooey" hair on my head.

I love to touch new dresses
Especially "netty" ones,
I love to touch the letters for me
Whenever the postman comes.

I love the feeling of soft, clean hair
I love the feeling of flowers,
I also love the feeling of books
And to browse around for hours.

Carol, Grade 5

The first-grade child talks off his poetry as casually as his prose. He, too, loves the pleasure of his senses.

> I thought I could smell the sun,
> I buried my nose in the sun-warm grass,
> And smelled a heat smell.
> I thought it was the sun itself,
> But it was just the grass
> Being turned to hay, I guess.

Carol, Grade 1

7. *Anything in nature appeals to children.*

FLOWERS

> On the way to school today
> I saw a yellow flower.
> It was standing in its bed.
> It sang a sweet soft song to me
> And then it hung its head.
>
> On the way to school today
> I saw a small green tree
> It seemed to have little eyes
> Staring up at me.

Janice, Grade 4

ICICLES

> Look at all the icicles,
> Standing in a line
> All ready to march away.
> Hep! three, six, nine.
> First comes the major,
> Then the general, short and fat.
> Six lieutenants looking like
> Napoleon with his hat.
> The bugler blows his horn
> And they're ready to march away.
> But they're fastened to the roof—
> I guess they're here to stay!

Jean, Grade 6

ANIMALS

Around a corner in our house
Peeked a very little mouse.
He stood there looking up at us
As if to say, "People! Oh, shucks!"

He didn't move a tiny muscle
Made no sound; made no rustle
Then he began to squeak and squeak!
And scooted off no more to peek.

Paul, Grade 7

CATS

Cats are meek.
Cats are sleek.

Our cat lived for just one week.
Her tail was thin but furry all over,
Next she had a spat with Rover.

Her skin was torn, her nose was scratched,
I thought she needed a new fur patch.

Ann, Grade 4

RAIN

Rushing! Rushing!
Whirling! Twirling!
Down comes the rain.
Dashing! Crashing!
Running like insane,
As she makes a spring
And rolls on in to the drain!

Under rocks,
Over rocks,
Foaming like milk running
Through a drain.

Rolling! Bowling!
Never stops for rest
But soon it'll settle in a little mud nest!

Marlynn (a boy) , *Grade 6*

BROOKS

The little brook is singing softly
As I sit by its side,
As my toes are dangling in it
They are trying hard to hide.
The little brook then gently laughs
As my toes bob up and down,
I think it would be lots of fun
To sit here all day long.

Patsy, Grade 5

8. *Adolescents, especially, characterize the people they know.* I can't locate this boy's name but he's in sixth grade. Wasn't this outburst wonderful therapy?

MY SISTER

My sister thinks she's quite the stuff,
She thinks she has muscle and plenty rough.
But I guess she's all right, way deep inside,
That is when her mouth isn't open wide.
She reminds me of a chicken strutting around,
And cackling loud, oh, what a sound.
If my sister feels like resting right on the grass,
And I am mowing the lawn, her I must pass.
She wouldn't move out of the way,
She'll just sit there and soak in the day.

No name here either, but this one is truly "terse-verse."

MY PAL

I have a pal whose name is Floppy
When I see him his hair is moppy
His shirt isn't buttoned, his hat not straight
When I go fishing he carries the bait.

Notice how ably a sixth grader takes one characteristic of this man and makes a whole picture.

This fellow, he is big
In a slumpy mood
He slumps up to the table
To eat his breakfast food.

Then after he has eaten
He stretches out to yawn
And when he gets done stretching
It is nearly dawn.

This man is very slow
And his hands are cold
This is so because
This man is very old.

A mature comment on a loved relative. Everything this girl writes is superior.

MY UNCLE

Like a tall, slender tree
Standing straight in the sky
With knots in the wood
And branches arched high.

With hands that are knarled
But as kind as can be
He's sturdy as an oak
Or a lonely pine tree.

Judy, Grade 8

9. *But most of all, children love jets and spaceships and things to come.*

JET

See that streak way up high,
Looks like yarn in the sky.

Jim, Grade 6

Up, up, climbs the jet
Up the ladder of atmosphere
Trying to reach the roof of the sky
Streaking along, stirring the clouds
From deep, deep sleep
Up, up, climbs the jet.

Pat, Grade 7

SKY WRITING

What is it?
A long straight line
It moves into writing!
What does it say?
It's beginning to take form
"Watch for a space ship
Super Delux Thor
It will soar
To moonbeam number four."

Diane, Grade 8

TALE OF THE X-13

The tale of the X-13 I'll tell
The tale of the terrible night
When the X-13 took off from earth
When the moon was glowing a deathly white.
The night was quiet and so were they
As they closed the rocket's hatch.
The flame of the rocket made me think
The flame that should have been green.
It encased the ship in a purple glow,
An unearthly purple gleam
The ship went up and disappeared,
Encased in a purple light,
And vanished forever into the darkness
Into the silent folds of night!

Tim, Grade 5

Which subjects bring poetry to most children? Personally, I know of no subject that will fail to bring poetry from children provided it is an interest of their age level. A child's poem is a talked-out feeling, and only on subjects on which they have feeling will children write effective verse. Fine poems only pop out when they have the push of an emotion behind them. But so facile are children's imaginations that they have feelings on the strangest subjects. No teacher ever has to teach a child to write poetry; it lies in his interests unborn. The teacher is merely the midwife.

On What Basis Should Growth in Verse Writing Be Judged?

1. Is this a good verse for this child? A poem can best be evaluated in terms of the child who wrote it. The weakest poem may mean the strongest effort and the greatest growth.

2. Does the poem sound sincere or does the child seem to be merely trying to write a poem?

3. Did the child get his feeling across to you?

4. Did this child use at least one poetic image (picture phrase) in his poem?

5. Does the sound or rhythm of the verse match the thought? Can you feel the rhythm running through the lines?

6. Does idea or rhyme seem to be more important to the writer?

7. Is this child's vocabulary adequate to his ideas? Are the words specific?

Questions Teachers Have Asked about Children's Poetry

1. *Should grades be put on children's poetry?* Comments are better. In grading any paper, a teacher must ask himself, "What is my purpose in making this assignment?" If your answer here is "To get my children to write poetry," you have answered your own question. Grades on poetry will stop poetry. How would you like your feelings to be graded?

2. *What shall we do with those who can't seem to write verse?* Suggest that they write prose or paint a picture poem.

3. *How shall we proceed when we find a child has handed in a poem he didn't write?* First, ask the question of yourself, "Did I give him a choice, or was my assignment: Write a poem?" He probably cheated for one of four possible reasons: (*a*) he can't write poetry; (*b*) he writes such poor poetry it embarrasses him; (*c*) he detests poetry writing; or (*d*) he meets all problems with cheating.

If the first, give a choice next time; if the second or third, suggest prose. Point out that you would appreciate it if there could be honesty and open-dealing between the two of you; that no one can respect people who hide behind deceits. *Then so proceed later that he can tell you the truth next time.* Usually the fault in a case like this lies in the assignment.

4. *Is the form of a child's poem important?* Not at all (in my opinion) . Only the sense and singing in a child's verse is important. His verse may be rhymed, unrhymed, partly rhymed, and the meter

be "swapped in the middle of the theme." Personally, I do not believe that a child's poem should ever be changed by a teacher unless the child comes to him for advice, and then the child should be helped to help himself. Most children's poems have faulty lines in them; faulty lines belong to childhood; leave them alone. The reason why the poems in this book are as good as they are is that I have thousands of children's poems to choose from, and there are a good many excellent child poets in an entire state. But I usually get as many as twenty-five outstanding ones from a single broadcast. Be content with what the child gives, especially if it matches his growth stage. Poetry is more a gift than an assignment.

Poetry making is magic, a personality extender for whoever attempts it. Fifth-grade Tim knows that it is a way of extending the personality, of helping a person be everything but himself.

THE CLOUD-MAN

Have you seen the cloud-man
Away up in the sky?
He's always looking down at us,
With his large white eye.
Sometimes he's a fairy,
Sometimes he's a cat,
And sometimes he's an elephant,
Or anything like that.
The cloud-man is constantly changing,
Sometimes he is an elf.
Sometimes he's a polar bear,
But he never is himself!

Tim, Grade 5

And seventh-grade Beverly says what poetry does best of all:

I HELPED AMERICA

Working is not too hard
If you think how you are helping America.
If you are working in a store
With clothes to sell
It makes you feel as though you are
Clothing America.

Beverly, Grade 7

Do you, too, want to clothe children's minds with "clothes for a king's son"? Help them, then, to loosen their taut spirits and release the poetry within them.

A POEM IS NOT [8]

A poem is not what you think:
It is not finding, but trembling on the brink
Of finding. It is not the where,
But the road to there.

Edsel Ford

THE UNWRITTEN [9]

In summer I move through sheaves of poems,
O the quiet of poems that have not found words,
So deeply unwritten, so unfarmed loams,
So mute boughs waiting toward singing birds.

In summer's center I move through sheaves
Of ungathered lyrics and unhewn lines,
And all about me the unwritten weaves
Staves for cadenzas and pivots for rhymes.

In brush, in woods, on lane, on lake,
The form of wonder seeks toward speech,
Yet deeper the silence till the first words wake
And move toward their poems, and each toward each.

Adelaide Fitzpatrick

[8] By permission of the author and *The Christian Science Monitor.*
[9] By permission of the author and *The Christian Science Monitor.*

CUPBOARD OF IDEAS   for Chapter Seven

Children Have *Poems* ❖ ❖ ❖ ❖ ❖ ❖ ❖ ❖ ❖ ❖ ❖ ❖ ❖ ❖ ❖

Primary Shelf

I. *Start with Rhythms*

Many poems come naturally out of rhythm and singing about things on the go, such as merry-go-rounds, trains, and cars; having fun on a hike looking for spring; singing as you go to the neighbor's together to see the new kittens. Let somebody start a tune the feet are singing; let the lips hum it and words will come naturally.

II. *Use "Pretends" and Pantomimes*

Be a flower trying to get through the hard ground. How do you feel? What do you say? After a few pantomimes let several children talk out their feelings.

Be a child looking through a toy-store window at Christmas time; a new colt just stretching its legs after birth; a puppy on a sunny day; a kitten playing with leaves; a toddler trying to catch a feather.

Stretch the imagination: A child's mother sent cupcakes as a birthday treat. How does the birthday boy feel? How do the other children feel? How might the cupcakes feel? Pretend to be a new child at school or the visiting rabbit. Tell how you feel. Pantomime? Talking? Be a new stamp starting out on a letter; a mother with a headache when the children are noisy; a lonely child with a new dog.

Begin with actions, pantomime, and creative play; then proceed to words. Poems at first are only "talk-off's" of feelings and actions.

III. *Assume the Feelings of "Reader" Characters*

Be Alice, be Jerry, be Dick, be Jane—then proceed as above.

IV. *Talk Out Your Fears and Wonders and Thoughts*

They are often sheer poetry.

V. *Have Fun with Jingles and Rhymes*

Make them up any time during the day when the occasion arises. Jingles are word-tingles: "Taffy is laughy." "Mary is scary." "We are needing reading." "Rest time is the best time." A campus school first-grade teacher was astonished to have a professor's son sing out to her as he started home, "See you later, Educator." (Prepare to be embarrassed as well as astonished; the publishers would censor some I've heard.) Call word play *jingles* and lovely ideas *poetry.* This will save later misunderstanding.

A. **Making rhymes to tunes.** Circle the room singing a simple song such as "A-Hunting We Will Go," and let your kindergarten youngsters substitute other pairs of rhyming words for "Catch the fox and put him in a box!" (One of the children in a local kindergarten one day sang, "We'll catch a deer and put him in the beer," and not a soul was abashed.)

B. **Jointed rhymes.** Put a small jointed cardboard dog into different positions, and make up rhymes that he might be saying and that the children finish:

> I am a dog; my name is Jack
> I like to lie upon my ———.

I am a dog; my name is Jip;
I'm going with my master on a ————.

See me sit up; see me beg;
See me stand upon one ————.

C. **Rhymes with vocabulary words.** Let your first- and second-grade classes make rhymes with their reading words. (Examples from Grade 2 John B. Cary School, Richmond. Virginia.)

Two little robins up in a tree
They want to fly as you can see.

Cathy Connell

I have a little bear
That goes with me everywhere.
I have a little duck
He gives me good luck.

Alice Marie Winn

D. **New words for old poems.** Make new words to the rhymed chant, "It Is Raining," by Lucy Sprague Mitchell (*Very Young Verses* p. 152). Let the class ask the first question together, then individual children give a two-line answer, all joining again in the poem's refrain. Use it another day as "What would you like to do in the snow?" (or in the sun? or in the spring? or in the fall?) Other poems good for such original chants are found on pages 78, 10, 31, and 163 of *Very Young Verses.*

Intermediate and Upper-Grade Shelf

I. Sensory Poems

A. If your children have never made poetry alone, start out making it together. Begin with the simplest sensory perceptions, "My favorite food," for example, and make us see it and taste it. Do not call on children for lines; let them volunteer. Weave the contributions into a simple "talked-off" poem. Then, ask each child to write about his own favorite food in his own way. Use word sounds, sights, smells, and feelings in similar ways.

B. Ask children to write out their secret fears in a poem.

II. Pets and Poetry

A. Advertise your pet in a poem. Make a list together of points you might want to stress.

B. Listen to your pet talk. What might he have on his mind? Let him write a valentine to you (very revealing).

C. Write a word portrait of your pet. Start out with your pet's actions, and turn the words into a together poem.

D. Let a mother pet give good advice to a baby pet before it goes out into the world.

E. Describe in verse one motion of your pet: how he runs to meet you; how a cat catches a mouse.

F. Write conversations between animals or people or both. You can use such conversation often in your schoolwork: conversations between a child and his pet about the health rules, between two countries as to their problems, about our national parks; a monologue by a native as to why he loves his land; a conversation between a Japanese and an American workman, or conversations between two star lovers.

III. Seasons and Songs

A. "Color pictures" of fall, "feeling pictures" of spring, "action pictures" of winter, "sheer enjoyment pictures" of summer.

B. Write your thoughts in verse as you listen to music.

C. Balance with words a mobile spring has hung in the air.

A blue bird swinging on a bough
Loving the world and telling how
His mate in the birdhouse, with her wings
Keeps the babies warm while he swings and sings.

D. Write a skating poem to the music of "The Skater's Waltz."

E. Write poems of windy weather, loosened ice, or hurrying feet.

F. Instead of a "green thumb," Jack Frost has a white one. Write a short poem describing a scene he made on the window.

IV. Rhyme-a-Stories

Write true stories, hero stories, history tales, current instances of courage into ballads. Occasionally write book reports in verse and change folk tales into poems.

V. Unsung Songs

Try to catch the spirit of one of America's workmen *a la* Walt Whitman's "I Hear America Singing," and write his song. (See Beverly's poem page 264.)

VI. Pretends

A. Pretend you are a tree, a stream, or a cloud telling your story.

B. Be any one of Uncle Sam's treasures (Statue of Liberty, Declaration of Independence, the first flag, and so on), telling what you stand for.

C. Pretend to be a new student and how you feel in this strange place.

D. Pretend you are a student of another race, seeking admission to an integrated school. Pretend to be the pupil of that school. How does each side feel?

E. Pretend you are a southerner the day after Lee surrendered to Grant. Write these feelings into poems.

F. Pretend to be fire, traveling. During fire-prevention week gather from your class descriptive words to show how fire travels: *creeping, climbing, towering, plunging,* and the like. Find several words to rhyme with each and weave them into a descriptive class poem of fire.

VII. Science Poems

A. Write an insect's song in its own rhythm.

B. At the end of a unit on "The Heavens," try to explain the stars, moon, sun in a poem.

C. Personify one member of the weather family and develop the analogy.

D. Tell your thoughts on being the first man to reach the moon or any planet.

E. Write your reactions to one modern miracle.

F. Describe one miniature masterpiece of nature—one small perfect thing.

G. Make up new words for old nursery rhymes, using new scientific ideas.

Bobby Shaftoe's gone to see
What in outer space might be.
He'll come back to me, no doubt
If his spaceship just holds out
Lucky Bobby Shaftoe.
Plucky Bobby Shaftoe.

H. Write the song of a machine, trying to catch the rhythm.

SONG OF THE CRANE

I am a crane
More "reach" than brain.
A mechanical giraffe
I make people laugh.
I bite a big load
From the side of the road
Gnaw, gnaw
Big bites of rocks raw.
Rattle, rattle, rattle
Like weapons in a battle
Gulp! gulp!
That rock's in a pulp
Crunch! munch!
Pebbles for lunch.
I am a crane
More "reach" than brain.

VIII. *History Poems*

A. Interview a history hero via verse.
B. Pretend you were present at any historical event interesting to you. Make your comments in poetry.
C. Assume the personality of any hero of history. Tell your story in verse.

IX. *Rhymed Spelling*

Once a month or so allow children who enjoy rhyming to rhyme the definitions of their spelling words. These are typical:

My diction	Her parents scamper
Causes teacher friction.	Her to pamper.
If you don't placate	A dictionary
You'll have to vacate.	Is wordy very.

Sophisticates in junior high like to picture word meanings on posters. One I saw had a picture of a girl refusing a boy a date which bore the caption:

> Be nonchalant,
> Cool, calm, collected.
> When she says "No"
> And you're rejected,
> If you show it, she'll know it!

X. *A Type Lesson That Will Encourage Poetry Writing*

"My Town!" What a wonderful phrase! There's hardly a more exhilarating feeling on earth than the warm glow one feels when he says, "My Town!"

What makes a town? Is it the population number painted on the sign at the city limits? Is it the number of factories that shriek out the noon hour and quitting time in a shrill voice? Is it the stores? Is it the parks? Is it the people? What does make a town?

Today, take us through your city or town or your community in the country or over your farm. My town! My farm! My city! Help us to see the sights. Get us acquainted with its smells, its great houses, and its hovels. Does your town have a voice? Can you help us to hear it, too?

Before writing time, pretend that you are trying to tell a pen pal about your town. List together some sight, sound, smell, and feeling words you might use to catch the spirit of your town on a night when the stores are open, on a Sunday morning when the church bells call, or at a ball game in the park.

Many interesting lessons may grow out of this program. You can write short paragraphs characterizing the cities or countries you meet in the geography book; catch the spirit of great men and women in poems, make a collection of poems characterizing people and places. Try to capture the spirit of a 4-H meeting you attend or a ball game or a picnic, the feeling of a holiday (Christmas) or your birthday. Good writers are those who catch spirits and change them into words. That is what radio and television do every day.

What is the first thing you do when you get back to your community after you have been away visiting? What do you check on immediately? Whatever it may be, it is a key to your community for you. Write it into a poem or into a poetic paragraph.

Poetry Collections for the Teacher's Desk

*Aldis, Dorothy. *Hello Day*. Putnam, 1959.

Arbuthnot, May Hill. *Time for Poetry*. Scott, Foresman, 1952.

Association for Childhood Education Literature Committeee. *Sung under the Silver Umbrella*. Macmillan, 1935.

*Baruch, Dorothy W. *I Would Like to Be a Pony, and Other Wishes*. Harper, 1959.

Benét, Rosemary and Stephen Vincent. *A Book of Americans*. Rinehart, 1933.

Brewton, John E. *Gaily We Parade*. Macmillan, 1940; *Under the Tent of the Sky*. Macmillan, 1937.

* For primary grades only.

Brewton, John E. and Sara W. *Bridled with Rainbows.* Macmillan, 1949; *Sing a Song of Seasons.* Macmillan, 1955.

*Chute, Marchette G. *Rhymes about the Country.* Macmillan, 1956.

Coatsworth, Elizabeth. *Poems.* Macmillan, 1957.

Cole, William. *Humorous Poetry for Children.* World, 1955.

*DeRegniers, Beatrice Schenk. *Something Special.* Harcourt, Brace, 1958.

*Doane, Pelagie. *A Small Child's Book of Verse.* Oxford University, 1948.

Farjeon, Eleanor. *Eleanor Farjeon's Poems for Children.* Lippincott, 1951.

Ferris, Helen. *Favorite Poems, Old and New.* Doubleday, 1957.

Field, Rachel. *Poems.* Macmillan, 1957.

*Fisher, Aileen. *Runny Days, Sunny Days.* Abelard-Schuman, 1958.

Frost, Robert. *Complete Poems of Robert Frost.* Holt, 1949.

*Gay, Zhenya. *Jingle Jangle.* Viking, 1953.

*Geismer, Barbara P. and Suter, Antoinette B. *Very Young Verses.* Houghton Mifflin, 1945.

Huber, Miriam B. *Story and Verse for Children.* Macmillan, 1955.

Huffard, Grace T. and Others. *My Poetry Book.* Winston, 1934.

*Livingston, Myra Cohn. *Wide Awake and Other Poems.* Harcourt, Brace, 1959.

Miller, Mary Britton. *All Aboard* (*Poems for a Space Age*). Pantheon, 1958.

*Milne, A. A. *Now We Are Six.* Dutton, 1927; *When We Were Very Young.* Dutton, 1924.

Sandburg, Carl. *Complete Poems.* Harcourt, Brace, 1950.

Thompson, Blanche Jennings. *Silver Pennies.* Macmillan, 1925; *More Silver Pennies.* Macmillan, 1938.

*Thompson, Jean McKee. *Poems to Grow On.* Beacon, 1957.

Untermeyer, Louis. *Stars to Steer By.* Harcourt, Brace, 1941. *The Golden Treasury of Poetry.* Golden Press, 1959.

* For primary grades only.

CHAPTER EIGHT

Stories Are Play-Acted

One small boy to another: What's the difference between down-right fibbing and being creative?

Other boy: It's all right if you get caught when you're creative.

THE HATCH [1]

I found myself one day
cracking the shell of sky,
peering into a place
beyond mere universe.

I broke from egg of here
into an otherwhere,
wider than wordly home
I was emerging from.

I breathed, I took a step,
I looked around, and up,
and saw another lining
inside a further sky.

Norma Farber

Once I found a bird's nest with two eggs in it. It was floating on a lake. The nest was in a funny place, I thought. I took the nest and the two eggs home. The next day they hatched. One chick was a very dull black; the other chick was brilliant blue. They were three feet tall when hatched. They were chicks from outer space. They ate moon seeds from the moon, which were in the shell from which they hatched. They looked shiney and glazed.

Ronny Krepot, Grade 5

[1] By permission of the author and *The Christian Science Monitor.*

A story told is a one-man play with bodily gestures as props and each unfolding of the plot a scene. The hands of the teller and the lines of his body unconsciously reinforce the meaning of his words while his eyes hold his audience under a mesmeric spell, and the music of his voice pulls the stops of the emotions as an organist controls a keyboard.

A story written is a one-man show held by a blind man who isn't there to an audience he cannot see. But a written story—really a dramatic play—is not without props. In a story the parts of speech come fully into their own; the nouns characterize the actors as well as furnish the stage, while the adjectives provide the dress and make-up, like the professionals they are. The verbs stalk or skulk across the stage with their adverb dogs at their heels, ready to quarrel, murder, to make love or peace as the script dictates. The conjunctions furnish the continuity; the interjections, the sound effects; prepositions flutter unnoticed in the background introducing subtle phrases into the scenery. In the wings, the stand-in pronouns wait ready to substitute for overworked nouns. When they are introduced as actors in a play, the parts of speech never lose their identity to children.

Nor are the parts of speech the only props in a written story. Punctuation is the play director taking charge of the timing—the long dramatic pauses and the hairbreadth hesitations that make the difference between superb and ordinary acting. Punctuation is of little importance to the meaning of most poetry, but without it a story would be a mumbo jumbo of words huddled together aimlessly like a family in a storm cellar.

Well-chosen parts of speech directed by punctuation marks that know their business are not enough; the length of sentences, too, help to make a story-play a success. The sentences may tense to one word in a dramatic moment of a story or lengthen into a whole paragraph during a soliloquy. The sentences pace the story.

A written story, then, is a play, acted and staged by the words, directed by the punctuation, and timed by the sentences. How can we make these ideas clear to children?

Children have been play-acting since preschool days and in primary school have teacher-pupil planned the steps of every story they dramatized. Getting the steps of a story down in sequential order in third and fourth grade is a natural step in story writing as well as in story acting.

Children's first written stories are not planned, but caught into words as the child thinks them. His writing of stories is like his thinking of stories; it shows little attention to form. But in the last of the primary school and the first of the intermediate grades, when action is the keynote of the children's interests, a story can be translated into a series of actions: what happened first, what happened second, and what happened third. The goals of story writing in the primary grades are release and self-expression—the goals of the creative arts for young children in all areas.

In fourth grade, except with a retarded group, creativity needs the beginning of discipline and form—teachers sometimes forget that life habits begin early. Intermediate children need to learn how to build a story as a carpenter learns how to build a house lest they get themselves into the situation of the young man in depression times.

Being unable to get a job in his own field, this brash youth, in desperation took over the contractor's job in the construction of a small house. After the work had progressed for several weeks, the boy's uncle, a bona fide contractor, happened to come by the site of the new house.

"Uncle John," the young builder said anxiously in low voice to his relative, "when you're building a house, do you begin at the top and build down or at the bottom and build up?"

"Why, at the bottom and build up, of course," was the astonished reply.

The young man cupped his hands and shouted up to his equally greenhorn assistants, "You'd better come on down, boys, we've begun at the wrong end!"

Teachers are beginning at the right end when they allow free expression in the creative arts in the primary school. "How to" build a house and "how to" build a story have no place in a primary room. The first years of school are exploratory years for children in the creative arts. A young child draws pictures and makes up stories and models clay figures for sheer joy. He creates as he sees and feels and discovers the re-creation of creating.

Directing and guiding a child's creativity is a vastly different thing from substituting a teacher's ideas for a child's. In their effort to guide, many intermediate teachers turn off the tap of creativity as expertly as if it were a faucet over the sink. They show how a tree should be painted instead of helping the child to paint better his own idea of how a tree looks to him; they show the child just the right word for his "secret comment" in a poem rather than help him find his own secret comment; they often take away from a child's story the very qualities that made it original.

But even child artists need to learn the laws of proportion and perspective, and child storytellers the laws that control clearness and power in the written and spoken word. "These are the trifles which," said Michelangelo, "make perfection." Behind every work of a genius is discipline and working with the known laws of his particular field. How even more beautiful the Infant in *The Madonna of the Chair* would have been had the artists of that day realized that the proportions of an infant's body are vastly different from those of an adult's. Especially if a child is gifted, he needs to learn the disciplines of the creative arts. Even geniuses must learn to focus.

In story writing three disciplines must be introduced as early as the intermediate grades: the writing of a clear sentence, the construction of a well-built paragraph (both discussed in Chapter Eleven), and the building of a simple story plot, which will be discussed in this chapter.

Before we go into the subject of plot building for a child's story, let me clear up one possible misunderstanding: The three writing disciplines are to be introduced during the intermediate grades, but mark my words, they will not be fully learned there. I doubt that disciplines in any field of endeavor ever come in one year or in three. Writing disciplines come slowly. Children must not be coerced into using them, nor should those be looked down upon who fail to attain them. If 65 per cent of our children would learn to build good sentences, good paragraphs, and good plots before they enter high school, I would personally be more than satisfied. Not all children can learn the disciplines of writing, but children must be exposed to them early if they are ever to become proficient in their use.

With this idea in mind, keep cheerfully at the task of teaching children the writing disciplines, and rejoice greatly at each new inch of progress achieved, but don't break your heart over your failures. Self-disciplines come from great caring, and most youngsters do not care that much about proficiency, and some can't attain it even if they care. The knowledge of how to build plots is more acquired than taught.

Intermediate youngsters love to write stories when story writing is fun; the minute it ceases to be fun, their enthusiasm wanes. If they have to think constantly of techniques of improvement, their stories will grow as limp as grocery store lettuce on Monday morning, and it's absolutely necessary that story writing stays fresh. Accordingly, if he wants children to write and to improve their story writing, a teacher has to "sneak up" on a group of ordinary youngsters. Help fifth-grade children to draw pictures of plots. They'll be more interested if you suggest that a story is a snow hill or stair steps in reverse; you climb up slowly step by step, then go sliding down to a quick conclusion, like this picture of the "Cinderella" plot.

Climax
(hilltop or top of stairs)

She loses her slipper.

STEP 3. The prince falls in love with her.

STEP 2. The godmother gets Cinderella to the ball.

STEP 1. Cinderella helps her sisters get ready for the ball.   Bump

Start plotting plots with a loved folk tale or the most exciting story in the current school reader. I've used "Cinderella" in the drawing, since I am sure it is familiar to all, but for use with children generally, "Cinderella" is a weak story, since it appeals chiefly to girls.

Explain to youngsters that a story climbs up to the climax, but slides quickly down to the conclusion. Notice together the plots of the stories the children like most. From plot-plotting to story writing is an easy step; each step in the plot becomes a scene in a moving picture—a story is just a one-, two-, or three-scene movie show. Don't require intermediate children to draw plots and write steps before they start their stories. When story writing becomes a chore instead of fun, the chance for growth is gone. It's the conception here of what a story is and how it is built that actually helps the child in story writing. Unless he feels that writing the steps will help him, suggest that he *think* his story in steps, in several acts or scenes of an exciting movie or stage play.

How will this concept of a story as a play change a child's story writing?

1. When it is stripped down to actions, a story tends to be more compact and free from nonessential details, thus making the story move.

2. A story thought of as a play is more conversational than narrative; the characters do the talking and acting for the writer.

3. Description used as stage setting takes its proper place in the story; it becomes the background as it should be.

4. One-look picture sentences characterize actors instead of lengthy word photographs.

5. Endings become artistically abrupt.

Until I convinced children over my radio program that a story was a one-, two-, or three-scene play, I got nowhere with story writing, and the stories sent in by the children dragged on like a teachers' meeting. This conception of a story as a play tightened the plots and put conversation into the stories. Of course, the children who were natural story writers got the most help, but the stories of all children showed marked improvement, and strangely enough, the number of stories sent in almost doubled.

Eight Steps to Good Story Writing

Children love to tell stories, but often dislike writing them. You can help them to conquer this aversion by using the eight steps we use on "Let's Write" for all their writing. They will work equally well for you in your classroom.

STEP 1. Choose story areas carefully from children's interests: pets, fun, mischief, interplanetary trips, sports, true stories from home life, stories grandparents tell, daydreams made real, tall tales, stories of how things came to be, hit-or-miss stories (pulling two or three topics out of a box and fashioning them into a tale) , dramatic scenes suggested by storytelling pictures.

STEP 2. Tie story ideas carefully to the child's own experience so that the idea becomes personal to each child. As an idea touches a familiar chord in the child's experience, an idea for a story comes to mind.

STEP 3. Reinforce these ideas with poetry and prose selections so that the child will understand them and experience them vicariously.

STEP 4. Suggest a number of plots so that those who are not self-starters may begin thinking of ideas of their own. In class hold an idea exchange instead of your doing the telling.

STEP 5. Discuss characteristics of the type of tale the children are to write. For example, "tall" tales: Begin as if the story were true; build up the plot until it is too big to believe.

Give your characters self-characterizing names: Big Moo, Scattergood, Johnny Inkslinger.

STEP 6. Suggest fitting vocabulary words the children may wish to use or, better, start their own words perking.

STEP 7. Help them to learn when to finish their stories. Too often, stories are weakened when they go on too long after the "cat is out of the bag."

STEP 8. Show the children how to plan a story as if it were a two- or three-scene play. Let them try to think the idea of each scene into one sentence. For example, (*a*) Jim and Joe decide to frighten their sister Karen. (*b*) They hide behind a stone fence she will pass on her way to a party. (*c*) Jim and Joe get the scare of their lives before Karen comes along. Show the children that, except for conversation, these three ideas will make three paragraphs. Explain that they need to write in the scenery as description and make the characters real by imagery, description, and action.

These eight steps are the same as "paint-mixing" before poetry writing. Except for children gifted in writing, stories do not *just happen;* teacher and class mount the eight stairs together—and there at the top children write and enjoy.

Conversation Makes Stories Talk

Conversations put lightness into solid-paragraph stories as baking powder puts leavening into a cake. What is a story without conversation? It is conversation that makes a story dramatic.

Many children's poems are in conversation form such as this one by fourth-grade Janice.

> Said the cello to the flute,
> "Why do you have to toot?"
> Said the flute to the cello,
> "Why do you have to bellow?"
> Said the cello,
> "I bellow because I'm a cello."
> Said the flute,
> "I toot because I'm a flute."
> So neither knew
> Just what to do.
> The cello that could bellow
> And the flute that could toot.

Janice, Grade 4

And letters? What is a letter or note but a conversation with a person who isn't there? Conversation personalizes children's writing, gives it lightness and zip. Why? Because conversation is the form of writing nearest to talking; and what child doesn't love to talk—if he's interested, that is!

When he writes conversation, a child often writes out his own thoughts and thus we learn about him. Why don't you encourage the writing of conversation in stories and poems you have the children write? Primary children love to "talk-off" a purely conversational story.

Measuring Stick for Written Conversation

1. Does this conversation sound real?
2. Is it compressed enough to be dramatic? Are only the important things said?
3. Does this writing have an original twist?
4. Are the words used appropriate to the occasion?
5. Has the child used specific words instead of general words, especially for the word *said?* (remarked, questioned, laughed, guffawed, admitted)

Ideas for Written Conversations

1. What do your pencil and paper talk about at night?
2. What do your shoes say in the evening after a scout hike? What might Willy Mays's shoes say after a Braves game?
3. What could two ball bats say about the day's game?
4. Write a conversation between two students after a school basketball game.
5. What would the flags of feuding countries say to each other in the museum at night?
6. What might a mammoth and a dinosaur skeleton talk about when all the visitors have left the museum?
7. What might the new star of Alaska or Hawaii, the newest states, say to your own state's star?
8. What might two worn tires say to each other about their owners' driving and safety in general?

Descriptions Are the Scenery of a Story-Play

Description is the scenery of the story-play. Every good storyteller and writer paints his scenery with specific words. Description also puts make-up and costumes on the characters. These are the steps to good descriptive writing:

Step 1. *Catch the mood of a scene and play it up throughout the story:* mystery, joy, sadness, gloom, fear, or suspense. Let it permeate your whole story. Catch the personality flavor of persons and animals described. Dickens' Miss Murdstone was a metallic lady. Do you know an iron man, a clinging-vine wife, a brown-wren of a woman, a nervous weather-vane type? Fifth-grade Weber once spoke of his dog as "the most vibratory dog of all dogdom." Let your character's personality flavor season your whole story.

Step 2. *Select specific words.* The art of writing description lies in being specific. Not "flowers grew on the rocky hillside," but "tiny anemones lifted starry eyes from the crevices of the rocks"; "azure-toned violets thrust their dainty toes downward and held on for dear life." Naming the flower and using the right verb to show how it grows give a distinct picture that general phrases cannot possibly give.

With the right words and ideas, so much less needs to be said. Eighth-grade Lyle has characterized a whole house in four telling lines:

> A flower bed without flowers,
> A lawn without grass,
> A house without people,
> And a window without glass.
>
> *Lyle, Grade 8*

Seventh-grade Carol called her house "the crippled old house in our young block." The right word not only cuts down the amount of writing, but gives us the whole picture first, which can then be followed by details.

We are constantly trying to teach "Let's Writers" to cut down on many adjectives and settle for one or two effective ones, or better still, a word picture. Not "The dirty, broken-down house was covered with cobwebs and dirt," but as Allan said it, "The cobwebs have made a town."

Step 3. _Have trial runs_. Help your children become more effective in writing descriptions by having a short period often in which the children re-create one sight that they have recently seen:

_a_) How the sky looks: It looks like grey feathers just ready to float down. It looks as if it had just been house-cleaned. The sky glowered at us.

_b_) How a boy throws a ball: winds up, hurls, tosses, pitches, jabs the air.

_c_) How a first grader runs across the lawn: frolics, skips, floats, lilts, flutters like a butterfly, dives, skids, thunderbolts.

_d_) The maple on the lawn in autumn: She had put on her red coat. The maple's red signal, "Stop! Look at me!" The tree glowed like a fire in the night.

If short descriptions such as these are kept, they can later be worked into a beautiful class poem.

Steps in Action

Changing the Eight Steps of Story Writing to Escalators

Below are ideas and direct quotations from several types of story broadcasts used on Wisconsin's School of the Air, "Let's Write" program for grades four to eight. Each lesson is followed by several children's stories stimulated by the program.

ASSIGNMENT I: _Write a true story of a time you did something you should not have done._

A. _Psychological tie-up:_ I told the children of a childish sin my sister and I had committed. (Helped establish rapport.)

B. _Planning steps:_ In planning this story about the time you did as you shouldn't, you'll need to remember the three steps to writing a story:

1. What led up to the action you're telling about, or what caused you to step off the straight and narrow path and do what you shouldn't have done?

2. The next step will be the actual doing of the mischief.

3. And finally, how did it all come out?

If you include those three steps in your story—lead up to the action, do the action, and tell what happened as a result—your story just can't fail.

Let's think through your own story—the part that leads up to the action. That paragraph will simply bristle with several of the five senses. You'll want to tell how you felt, what made you finally kick over the traces and do what you should not have done. Yes, in that part of the story you'll want to tell about your thoughts and feelings and your plans, if you actually made any, and perhaps have a bit of conversation, too. If you were angry, use the right words to show just how you felt before you "up and sinned," as the third grader said.

In the second part, the action part of the story, make the story like a play. Take us with you every minute of the plot and make us feel every step of the action with you.

Then in the third or last part, skid to a fast stop and tell us in a hurry how the play came out, or better still, just leave us guessing. But the chief characteristic of the kind of story you are going to write about today is fast movement. Make your story move along and take your readers with you. Conversation will help move your story along.

C. *Using an exciting illustration from a good author:* I read the cow-napping episode from Phil Stong's *Captain Kidd's Cow.*

D. *Typical stories from Assignment I*

Story 1   TRUCK RIDE

One summer day in the morning, my sister wanted to play house. So what does she do? She asks me! So of course I had to play, otherwise she would tell my mother. Just then my dad came from up town. He drove the car in the driveway and got out and let the car run! So my sister gets the bright idea and says let's play in the car. You can be the driver and I'll be the woman. So I agreed. I got in where the steering wheel was and my sister got in the back. We were playing for quite awhile and I just stepped on the gas pedal and the Ford started to move backwards! My legs were strained by the tense moment of the engine starting. My hands were frozen onto the steering wheel! I couldn't move them! By this time, the old Ford was going at quite a speed. My uncle who was going to his home, dropped the rake and started running towards the car. The Ford was heading towards a telephone pole! My uncle was running about as fast as he could. Finally, the tense moment came. My uncle got to the running board and jumped a great leap, opened the door and pushed me aside and put on the brakes. We were just about going to hit the pole. My father came running and put me in the house and I never, never drove a car when any adult wasn't there.

Jerry, Grade 6

Story 2   MY SPANKING'S WORTH

Rocks and glass are flying! One day when I was about five, I went over to grandmother's house. On the way home, I picked up all the rocks I could carry and ran home. Wham! Crack! This was more fun than shooting a B-B gun. One, two, three, four, wham! My, this is fun! All the basement windows out but one. No rock, so I hit that one with my fist. It looked so lonely there alone. All done now. Till dad came—then wow again! What a spanking I got—but really I think I got my "spanking's worth."

Jakie, Grade 4

ASSIGNMENT II: *Write a humorous or magic Just-So story of how an animal or plant got to be.*

A. *Experience tie-up:* I suppose most of you have read a good many Just-So stories. But in case you haven't, I'd better explain that a Just-So story is one that tells how something came to be, "How the Leopard Got His Spots" or "How the Rhinoceros Got His Skin." Maybe you recognize those as titles of *Just So Stories* written by Rudyard Kipling, a very famous teller of tales. Maybe you also know that Kipling spent his boyhood in India. His nurse told him many of the old legends of the people of India, and later he wrote these down and called them *Just So Stories.*

One of Kipling's funniest stories is "The Elephant's Child," in which he explains that the elephant got his trunk because he asked too many questions.

B. *Reading examples of Just-So stories and poems:*
   1. Part of "The Elephant's Child" by Kipling.
   2. Excerpt from Longfellow's "Hiawatha" as to how the man got into the moon and how the rainbow got to be.
   3. "The Elf and the Dormouse," a poem by Oliver Herford (how the umbrella idea was first started).
   Discuss how many of Joel Chandler Harris' "Uncle Remus" stories" are of the Just-So variety—"How the Bear Got a Short Tail," and so on.

C. *Suggesting ideas:* Why do mice have long tails? Why do they like cheese? Why do they have pink ears? Can you think of an answer? Can you make up a Just-So story about mice?

   But mice aren't the only possibilities. There's a whole world of insects, and of animals, and of birds to choose from—yes, and the world's flowers and fruits and trees, too.

How did the grasshopper get his hop? Where did the woodpecker get his red head? the robin his red breast? Why does the pine tree keep its needles all winter? Why are tiger lilies freckled? Where did the zebra get his stripes? Or why does night come? Why do the leaves fall? Why does it snow? Answer a "why" question in your today's Just-So story.

D. *Typical stories from Assignment II*

Story 1   WHY FISH HAVE SCALES

Once upon a time there lived in a stream a fish named Spike. In the days that Spike lived, fish did not have scales. In the forest, the animals lived a very happy life. The mother animals brought their babies to the stream each month to be weighed. They used an old turtle shell for a scale.

Spike wanted to find out how much he weighed. He didn't have a scale, and the turtle shell was on the land where he couldn't reach it.

When he went to sleep that night, he dreamed about having his own scales. When he woke up the next morning, Bully, the frog, asked him how much he weighed. Spike told Bully he didn't know. Bully laughed and made fun of him. Spike swam away and cried. He cried so much that the stream rose a foot on the banks. It flooded them and all of the clerk ants came running out and scolded Spike.

He swam away and came upon a well that had fallen in the stream by accident. The well said to Spike, "I'm Willie Wishing Well. Who are you?"

"I'm Spike," he said soberly.

Willy asked him what was wrong. Spike told him the whole story.

"Drop a penny into me and your wish will come true," he said.

"I haven't a penny," Spike said.

"Oh, you can get your wish free then," said the wishing well.

Spike wished for a thousand scales to show that bully off. He got his wish. All of a sudden, his body was covered with scales.

Willie said he could carry them with him wherever he went. Spike lived happily ever after that. Since then all fish have had scales.

Carol, Grade 6

Story 2   HOW A PIG GOT A CURLY TAIL

One day a pig saw a little girl with curly hair. The little pig liked the curly hair.

A few days later the little pig thought he would like a curly tail. So one day the little girl put a curler in the pig's tail. So that was how the pig got a curly tail.

Kenneth, Grade 3

Story 3   Why the Raccoon Wears a Mask

NOTE: This story, having first been told to a young boy King by his Royal Storyteller, I shall proceed to relate to you in such a manner.

Once upon a time, My Noble King, there lived a raccoon named Ricky, and as at that time raccoons did not have masks, neither did he.

He was always getting into trouble, for you see, O Master every time he went to the farmer's field to get a bit of green corn for his supper, the farmer's watchdog, who always seemed to sleep with one eye open, awakened the farmer who came out with a shotgun, interrupting Ricky's delightful meal.

Ricky was frantic. For according to Dr. Crane he could become emotionally upset if he had such a hectic life. And he certainly did, being continually plagued by Farmer Brown and his horrible dog.

When he was reading the newspaper one evening, he noticed the headlines "Masked Bandits Hold Up Bank." That was all he needed for an inspiration. If people could wear masks to conceal their identity, he could, too. Not that he was stealing. He was only taking his share. Farmer Brown didn't need all that corn.

He bought himself a black mask and decided to try it out that first night. He sneaked into the cornfield and enjoyed a peaceful meal; the first in months. That stupid dog didn't recognize him. It was so frightened that it slunk away to the doghouse to hide.

Ricky was overjoyed, for when he returned again and again and continued to be successful, he thought he would never be bothered again. But he was wrong; for you know, Your Majesty, luck cannot hold out forever. After a few weeks the farmer's dog became suspicious. He became convinced that this was not a creature from another world, bent on destroying all dogdom, but merely an ordinary cornrobber and he let loose with such a frenzy of barking that the farmer (still in his nightshirt) came out to see what was going on.

He found out, but could do nothing about it because he had forgotten his gun. Ricky beat it, fast.

The next night Ricky became caught in a trap the farmer had placed in a cornfield. When the farmer found him there, he was in a very bad state indeed. Ricky was taken to the sheriff; tried and convicted of unarmed robbery and damaging private property. He was sentenced to five years in state's prison.

Getting a prison suit for him was impossible so the warden decided that the only solution was to paint black stripes on him. When he was freed on probation, after taking a solemn oath that he would stay away from the farmer's field, he went to the creek to wash off his "prison suit." He got all the stripes off (after two hours of vigorous scrubbing) except those on his tail. They would not come off.

Also, for some mysterious reason, a mask appeared on his face, perhaps from the god of the animals, to remind him forever of his crime.

So all his descendants from that day to this have inherited his striped tail and mask to brand them forever as criminals in the animal world.

And now, Your Majesty, it is time to retire to your royal bedroom. It's past your bedtime (two minutes to be exact) but if you're a real good King I'll tell you another story tomorrow night.

Diane, Grade 6

ASSIGNMENT III: *Write a "Whopper," a story so outsized no one would possibly believe it.*

A. *Definition and explanation of "whoppers" and tie-up to children's lives:* Chin music, tall tales, whoppers, yarns, fish stories, big ones—it doesn't matter what you call them—everybody loves them and nobody believes them. And yet, whoppers aren't lies, for lies are told with the intent to deceive, and whoppers are told with the purpose of making the listeners laugh.

Why, nobody but a small child could possibly believe these tall tales, blown up 'way past normal size, these whoppers that have become part of the folklore of every land.

Perhaps it's because man realizes that most of the things he does are rather "small potatoes" that he dreams up these super-man stunts that get bigger and bigger as the stories go around and the hour gets later.

Tales like those told in our time by the members of the Burlington, Wisconsin, Liars Club may, with time's passing, become real folklore or hero tales. All folk or hero tales started in fun "away back then" and it was their purpose to make people laugh and forget their troubles. Tall tales are really folks laughing at themselves, and folks who can laugh at their troubles eventually conquer them. Today in writing time we're going to write whoppers without an ounce of truth in a carload of them. We're going to let our imaginations soar until we have to cut the line to let them down again. And are we going to have fun! We'll blow up the facts today like bubble gum and probably get limp with laughter before we're through.

Many of our best American whoppers have grown up in times of drought and trouble, told by some old leather-faced spinner of yarns who had to laugh so his troubles couldn't make him cry.

B. *Read the selection from Carl Sandburg at the beginning of Chapter Twelve* (page 494): Well, if we're going to write tall tales, we'd better find out how to write good ones, since who wants to grow tall corn if it isn't a good variety of corn? We might just as well say right now that there's a lot of difference between a silly story and a whopper. A silly story is just silly, but a whopper has a sort of sense running through its nonsense.

Now, let's see if we can discover the sense in the tall-tale type nonsense: First of all a tall tale begins in an ordinary way so as to sound like a true story; then, when the reader has just begun to believe, the story grows with the celerity of Jack's beanstalk; the listener's eyes begin to twinkle and he catches on that he's being "taken for a ride," but he *loves* it.

(Read Dr. Seuss's poem "Marco Comes Late" in the book *Treat Shop*.)

C. *Suggestions for stories:* By this time, you've noticed that a tall tale may be just an exaggeration of an ordinary happening—Marco was late to school and anything could happen—and did. To make a story into a whopper, just see to it that *what happens could not really happen*—and presto! the tale is tall!

Maybe you started out to slide on your sled one night and half-way down the hill you looked up and there coming right out of the sky was the—but whoops—I almost told your story for you, didn't I?

You could hatch a marvelous—and I do mean *marvelous*—story in answer to the ordinary questions you're asked every day: Where have you been? Where did you get that black eye? How come your dress is torn? Perhaps if you tell the tales you'd *like* to tell your mother instead of the truth, but can't—partly because you have a sense of honor, and partly because she wouldn't believe you anyway—you'd have a real whopper for writing time today.

(Discuss how Paul Bunyan, Pecos Bill, and Febold Feboldson stories were constructed.)

But most of you will want to create brand-new heroes in writing time today. The heroes of old tales were outsized and outlandish models of the men and women who actually lived in those times. Real-life loggers working the forests of the American frontier dreamed up their whopping-big hero, Ol' Paul. Then out in the Far West where real-life cowboys lived, Pecos Bill took shape in the imaginations of the people. Now, what sort of heroes might grow out of our times, out of our own modern world? Those are the tall-tale heroes you're going to create today.

Maybe you'll create a "Paul Bunyan" for the world of science, where so much of today's pioneering takes place. But remember, tall-tale heroes must bear *some* resemblance to the real-life people they represent. The real-life heroes of science are the patient men and women who work slowly and carefully in laboratories, searching for cures for polio or cancer, creating new marvels to make our lives better. Real-life science heroes are noted for the good they do, not for hair-raising escapades in spaceships and the fourth dimension. Your tall-tale hero of science should, therefore, work for good.

But maybe you'll create a whopper right out of your own home ground. Maybe your hero will be superman-school teacher who becomes principal of your school and lays low all the evildoers. Maybe you'll give your basketball team an unbeatable, unbelievable, unlikely hero who wins every single game your team plays—and some it doesn't. Or maybe your modern-day hero will be a radio announcer with a voice so big he doesn't need a microphone to be heard all over the state.

Don't think we moderns are too modern to make up whoppers! Why, every day we live among marvels that not even Ol' Paul Bunyan could have invented. So if we put our minds to it, we should be able to write some whoppers that will make the world spin backward and shrink Ol' Paul down to size. Just see if we don't—right now, in writing time.

D. *Typical stories from Assignment III:* I am including here the different types of "whoppers" produced on a number of programs by different names but with some of the same basic build-up as has just been given.

Type 1—April Fool Stories

Story 1   LIBRARY SCARE

At 2:30 Friday afternoon, the 7th grade held its library period. All went well until Betty Brown opened a geography book to see the map. Italy had holes in her boot and Florida was missing. Worst of all, dozing on Oahu, one of the Hawaiian Islands, was a huge bookworm! Betty screamed and ran for sister!

Meanwhile in the history section, Joey Jones's eyes were popping with amazement. Paul Revere's rifle and hat were missing and on the belfry was another bookworm, obviously suffering indigestion.

The library was pretty well vacated now and wasn't used for several days. Only a few books were damaged before the janitor came to the rescue with his spray guns. April Fool!

Candace, Grade 7

Story 2   OUT-OF-THIS-WORLD GAME

It was the annual basketball game for girls. It had started at one o'clock. Our team, the Bowlegs, were playing against the Mophairs. It was a tough game. I was being pushed around quite a bit. One time I landed on a mattress. Springs stuck on my feet. Then you should have seen me make those baskets! I could bounce over the Bowlegs and Mophairs while I had the ball. I just had to give myself a bounce and lift out my hand to make a basket. After a short time the game ended. The score was one trillion to one in our favor. April Fool!

Type 2—Tall Corn Stories (giant-plant whoppers)

Story 1

It all started one summer night when everyone was fast asleep. Everything was silent in the little town of Jacksonville until, suddenly, the earth began to tremble. Huge, white balls were falling everywhere making such a tremendous noise that even the birds in the sky trembled. The people who were sleeping woke with a start, but then passed the strange happening as of a mere earthquake (which was a common happening in those parts). Some of the people were too sleepy-eyed to care until the next morning, even though it was seven o'clock in the morning the houses were still cold and dark for there was no sun shining through the windows of the gay people's homes. Then we heard a furious pounding on the door and when we went to see who it was, it was the town mayor. He had a frightful look on his face. We all stood around him as he gasped out his story ". . . huge plants . . . growing all over . . . crushing houses as they go . . ." he panted, "I don't know what to do, they're growing so fast I can't keep track of them."

We peered out of the window . . . it was true . . . there were huge plants . . . to our horror and amazement there was one growing right beside our home expanding right before our eyes. It was a huge pumpkin-like plant; it grew so rapidly that it wouldn't stop for anything and we knew it wouldn't stop for our home either so we gathered our things and we took them up one of the mountain sides where we watched our home being crushed under the huge plant. I looked over at mom. She had tears in her eyes and Susie was clinging to her with trembling hands.

My heart was throbbing with fear and I felt like sobbing and screaming. I was afraid but I couldn't let it show, it would scare Susie even more. Suddenly I felt someone shake me and calling my name, then I knew I had been dreaming.

Judy, Grade 7

Story 2   SOMETHING UNEXPECTED

One spring day birds were returning from the southland and trees and shrubs were bursting with many a green bud. This gave me the idea to try my luck at gardening.

Because I had heard that people who could grow successful plants had a green thumb, I painted both of mine with some discarded green paint to be twice as sure of my undertaking. Next, I went to a nearby florist shop and purchased a flower seed mixture. Within the next few days I spaded, seeded, and watered my flower garden. Most of the blossoms grew beautifully, but in the middle was an odd brownish, thick stalk. It could be called an "Ugly Duckling."

Every morning it filled me with amazement because it kept growing taller and thicker. Soon the whole neighborhood was well-shaded. Every time it yawned it would send out gentle spring breezes which cooled the whole town.

My green thumbs had really paid off!

David, Grade 7

Story 3

One day I went into the garden. I saw the biggest pumpkin you ever saw. It was as fat as a pig. I was looking for my book. I told mother about it. She said I should bring it in. Mother said she will make pumpkin pie. When she opened it I had a surprise. In it was my book.

Evonne, Grade 3

Type 3—Big Moo: Tall-tale stories (concocting a big cow for the state of Wisconsin)

Story 1   LIZZIE

One morning when the sun was just peeking over the seventeen-story house top, Farmer Alfred Clarence stepped out of the door beaming brightly in his shiny new white suit. He hollered for his super milk cow, Lizzie. Lizzie was as bright as the sun so sometimes he did get rather confused. Lizzie came immediately, making hurricanes in the next three valleys. Lizzie was a Steingern and was just as yellow as a butter ball. She gives chocolate sundaes, cherry and pineapple sundaes and all other kinds of sundaes you can think of. She gives pasteurized, homogenized and chocolate milk. Lizzie gives one kind of milk that no other cow gives. Farmer Alfred Clarence likes her banana splits best of all.

The kind of milk that Lizzie gives that no other cow gives is Butter Brickle. The first time you taste it it tastes something like butter; the next time you taste it, it tastes something like cherries, and it's got kind of a mint taste to it. Its color is lavender. That kind of milk is fifty cents for a fourth of a pint. So not everybody in the world gets to taste it. Farmer Alfred Clarence puts a hose on each of Lizzie's udders and that hose runs right to the factory so he doesn't have to bother hauling it. And the fact is, he doesn't even have to milk Lizzie. He just puts the hose on her udders and she gives. One thing I'll never forget is the day I visited Farmer Alfred Clarence and had those delicious cherry malts that came straight from Lizzie.

Judy, Grade 7

Story 2   ELSINA

One fall afternoon, Huge Hank called Elsina over to him in such a tremendous voice that his neighbor, who lived three miles away, felt his barn tremble and fall to pieces. Elsina came trotting to him.

"Elsina," Huge Hank said, "you have been such a good girl that I thought I would give you something. What would you like?"

"Oh, I would like to have one hundred gallons of strawberry ice cream."

"Well, that's going to be kind of hard to get, but if that's what you want, I'll get you some."

Huge Hank walked over to his friend's house and said, "Do you know how I can get some ice cream for my pet cow, Elsina?"

"What kind of cow is she?"

"Oh, she's a Bernholes," said Huge Hank.

"Well, why can't she make her own ice cream?" asked Huge Hank's friend.

"I never thought of that," Huge Hank said.

So he went back to his house and said to Elsina, "Why can't you make your own ice cream?"

"Why, I have never tried it."

"All you have to do is drink some strawberry milk and I'll put you in the freezer, and when you come out you'll be strawberry ice cream." She did, and when she came out, she was strawberry ice cream. Huge Hank had a treat instead of Elsina.

Christina, Grade 6

ASSIGNMENT IV: *Write an outer-space story.*

A. *Orientation:* Three-two-one-zero-whoosh and into the space beyond the space—those are indeed magic words. "Off into the wild blue yonder! We shall swing on a star. Off to the mountains of the moon."

Do you know that man once looked at the ocean and despaired of ever crossing it? And now the boats of man walk upon the great seas as with seven-league boots. Man once looked upon the air and envied the birds the freedom of their flight; now, man flies the airways in great silver birds of his own making without losing a feather. And now man has turned his eyes upward and onward; past the clouds—past the surrounding blanket of air—past space—to the moon!—to the planets! And where man looks, he eventually goes.

We who have not yet learned to conquer the world within ourselves, we who have not yet learned how to live together as neighbors on the earth are already seeking new worlds to conquer. But that has ever been the story of man's advance: first he discovers things; later he learns how to live with the discoveries he has made. Just now we mortals busy ourselves perfecting rockets and spaceships.

Your great-grandfather would have smiled indulgently had he heard you children discussing spaceships. What one generation considers wild dreaming, the next generation recognizes as a probability, and the third or fourth generation makes possible. The three steps to accomplishment might be classified: (1) Dream the dreams; (2) propose the schemes; (3) lay the beams—and the deed is done.

Well, of one thing about spaceships we can be absolutely sure —they won't be ready for our use today, so we must contrive our own. *Imagination* is the best old spaceship ever contrived to get from the known to the unknown. Imagination is faster than the fastest jet, quicker than the take-off of a rocket. An imagined trip costs less than an ice-cream cone and can go anywhere, any time, any place. Today it will take us to outer space.

B. *Reading of allied material:* Read excerpts about "Space Ship Bifrost" from the book *Farmer in the Sky* by Robert Heinlein.

C. *Writing directions*
   1. Select one part of the spaceship story; the *dream,* the *going,* or the *arrival* and develop it into a story; don't attempt all outer space at once.
   2. Make your story sound plausible. What second quality, other than by not trying to tell it all, does the Space Ship Bifrost's author have? Well, his story is effective largely because it

sounds so plausible; it sounds just as if it were true. If imaginary stories are going to seem real, we must actually feel them as we write. We must see what our space traveler sees; we must think his thoughts; we must hear with his ears; we must worry with his nervous system. A good actor must feel the part he is playing, and a good author must feel the part he is writing.

Climb into the space helmet with your space explorer and let his brain push your pen. Then your story can sound as real as Mr. Heinlein's.

(Read child's space poem here.)

Dialogue or two-person talk lightens a story and makes it more interesting. Put plenty of conversation as well as plenty of feeling into your space stories today.

3. Use new space vocabulary. You may need some special vocabulary, though; new ideas often demand the coinage of new words. You may even want to coin a new word or two for your space story today.

You may need to adopt some new expressions currently used in space stories: the "blast off," for instance, for the take-off of a space ship. You may need *interplanetary* or a *between-planet* trip. You may wish to suppose an *orbital space station* which might be like a little moon circling the earth where spaceships might refuel, and where travelers might talk to the men who send weather reports back home. If you visit the moon, you may wish to adopt the word *lunar* which is taken from the Latin word for moon.

Oh, you're going to need all your descriptive powers today —make us see the moon with your eyes; make us see the men on Mars; make them so real to us that we become almost frightened of them on paper. On the other hand, maybe they aren't frightening; maybe they are more advanced than we are. Maybe they have already learned how to live together in peace—who knows? Be sure to get plenty of color words into your story, the shades of blue of the atmosphere; add *lapis lazuli* and *turquoise* to your vocabulary today, or *opalescent* for that homogenized color of fire and milk.

Describe the stark terrain of the moon with such devastating words as *arid, desolate,* and *raw*. These are space stories, remember; make your action words extra fast. Exchange slow motion words like *went* for rocket words like *pierced, whizzed,* or *split* the air.

The space trip you write about may be one an animal took, may be one a child took in a dream, may be one you yourself plan to take some day; it may be one a pet of yours took quite by accident. Your story may be full of fun or dripping with mystery as a sponge drips water. It may be in letter form, in poetry form, or written as a story.

D. *Typical Stories from Assignment IV*

Story 1   MARS

Ten, nine, eight, seven, six, five, four, three, two, one, zero, blast! We had started. We were off for Mars. I was a bit nervous but I guess we all were. I remember when I was just a little guy, my mother used to scold me for going into other people's yards. It seems kind of funny but I wonder whose yard I'm going into now. Well, we're there. We had landed on Mars. We were in a new world.

I guess I forgot to introduce myself in the excitement. My name's Smoky. I'm a cocker spaniel. My master's the pilot of the ship. His name's Roy and he's 12 years old.

Story 2   PAST ISLAND

Only a few minutes before I test the Bell X-15. I'm in the cockpit with my hand on the starting lever. I feel like a man with a gun to his head. What will happen next? Slowly I pull the lever back. There's a deafening roar. I am forced back with a crushing thrust. Up, up, I watch the altitude meter—8,000 feet, 10,000 feet, then the canopy froze over. Down I went! Then the plane began to get hot. I put back the wing flaps. At 4,000 feet, I jumped. I watched the plane crash! Soon I fell into the ocean.

I struggled for shore. Then a wave crashed me against a rock. I was unconscious when I woke up. I was on an island. I spent the night in a tree. When I looked around all I saw was water. There was a noise behind me. I looked. It was an Allosaurus.

Suddenly I realized that this was a world apart from mine—a world where the past was preserved. I escaped the Allosaurus. For many months, I lived like a cave man.

Then, that happy day—I saw a ship. I shot my flares. It did not even look at me. It went right on past. I finally got home by an oil tanker with a story no one believed.

Rodger, Grade 5

Story 3   My Strange Flight

It was a normal routine flight from San Francisco to New York as always. Nothing seemed strange at the time. You see, I am a pilot for WTA Airlines. We were cruising at approximately 600 mi. per hour when I heard a weird hissing or more of a whirring sound, then I saw a gigantic, dark gray object proceed alongside my plane. I stared unbelievingly at it. It had a long row of barred windows and corridors or cells with dim, blue lights and hanging from the ceiling were humans, hanging by their heels with cut throats, and the blood dripping into buckets. Then the object slackened speed and we pulled ahead of it. Then the plane jarred as if it had been hooked from the back tail. There was a gush of wind like the hatchdoor was being opened from the outside, in mid-air. Then I heard the passengers screaming and yelling. I leaped up from my seat, pulled a pistol from my belt and threw open the door of the cockpit to the passengers quarters. There were wet jelly-like green masses, which would cover a person with itself and then roll out the door and float lightly back to the ship from which it came. I fired all my amo into one of the things and it turned a sickening purple in color. Then lay still on the floor of the plane. Another of the things looked at me with a sort of crimson eye. A radiant beam of red light projected from the eye and struck my hand and gun immediately disintegrating them. It then covered me with itself. I tried to breathe but all I got was a sickening smell which contained no oxygen. I pulled a slip blade knife from my pocket and stabbed it into the object and it uncovered me and lay limp on the floor. Then it and the other one disintegrated into nothing. I piloted the plane back to San Francisco and told the police my story. I am now in the California State Nuthouse.

Ronnie, Grade 8

Measuring the Effectiveness of a Story

1. Was this story a good piece of work for the child who wrote it?
2. Was it written in short dramatic scenes with a background of description?
3. Were the characters real? Did they talk?
4. Did the writing have at least a beginning of style?
5. Were the beginning and ending of the story effective? artistic?
6. Did the vocabulary used enhance the style?
7. Did the writer know how to use the mechanics to help make his story clear to the reader?
8. How does the story make the reader feel?

Once, on a picnic with an attractive young couple, I grew more irritated by the second by the constant attempts of the young woman to make her husband over. After she had kept at him all day like a neat woman after a fly, he turned to her pleasantly and said, like a drop of icing striking cool water, "Honey, why don't you quit trying to improve me, and just appreciate me?"

I often feel that way about children's stories.

Writing a Picture-Telling Story from a Storytelling Picture

Children who have little imagination can get better story results from writing a story from a picture rather than from an idea, since the picture acts as a middleman between reality and fantasy. Since I had not a copy of this former *Saturday Evening Post* cover by Norman Rockwell, I am sketching it with words:

A girl, about ten years old, sits sprawled on a chair in the waiting room of a school principal's office. Her white blouse is awry, her plaid pleated skirt is disordered, her pig-tailed hair is badly in need of a brush—in fact, it is evident that the girl (Let's give her the name of Betts; it's so unsatisfactory living through a crowd of un-identified pronouns.)—yes, it is evident that Betts has just been in a fight. One of her eyes is almost closed by a glorious "shiner" that detracts not at all from the complete satisfaction registered in the lines around her mouth. The girl's whole attitude seems to shout, "I did it and I'm glad!"

Behind the girl, in an inner office, her teacher is consulting with the principal. From studying the faces of the pair, one gathers they are not averse to what the girl has been up to; in fact, they appear to be slightly amused, and one wonders what is going to happen.

Do you remember this particular picture? Children loved it and wove it into stories as varied as their varying personalities.

How Can One Build a Story from a Picture?

By questions that bring out possible plots
1. What is happening here?
2. What happened before the picture?
3. How do you think the story will turn out?

By an exchange of plots suggested by the children
1. A bully teased Betts and she finally turned on him right in school and socked him one in the eye, so he hit her. (This from an an-gelic-looking child who is daily pestered by such a bully)

2. No, I think a big boy was picking on a little boy on the playground, and she tries to stop him and he hits her! (A future do-gooder)

3. No such thing! She'd never look so happy if it wasn't her own score and she was trying to pay off. I think she had a fight with a boy that had been picking on her. She looks really happy! (A future realist or shrewd businessman talking)

4. I don't think she had a fight with a boy! I think another girl took her boy friend and they fought. She got the boy back, but she got a black eye along with him! (This from a future Helen of East Troy)

5. Aw, I don't think she was in a fight at all; she got hit in the eye by a swing! (Another realist)

Ya don't look happy over a swing hittin' ya in the eye! (Realist again)

6. Maybe she's thinking of the insurance settlement her old man will get. (Second realist)

"Well, you've certainly suggested some good plots for a story," the teacher interpolates at the psychological moment, "and in the story you write you may use any one of these or one of a dozen others."

And now back to that third question: How do you think the story will turn out? Will Betts get punished? Will she be forgiven? Let the story slide down the banisters to a quick conclusion.

Impress on the children that the ending to a modern story is swift and as sharply cut off as a business telephone call. Some writers only hint their endings, never actually telling how the story comes out. Get the children interested in noticing story endings and beginnings in the stories they read.

By practicing plot-making with an idea the children suggested

STEP 4. She pops him one in the eye and he pops back.

STEP 3. One day he torments her once too often.

STEP 2. He teases her and embarrasses her until she cries.

STEP 1. Pinky keeps calling Betts "tomboy" because she wants to play ball with the boys.

By having a vocabulary exchange before writing time. Suggest areas in which the children feel they need vocabulary and gather their suggestions in lists on the board, adding a few of your own, if it is necessary.

Other names for a black eye: "shiner," "mouse," "ebony eye," "black patch"

Words for tease: annoy, irritate, pester, tantalize, plague, harry, worry, bait, badger

Substitutes for bully: tormentor, the tease, the menace

Fight words: said hotly, shouted, pushed, tumbled, rolled, a right under the eye, jabbed, thrust raining blows

The look around the girl's mouth and in her one good eye: triumphant, satisfied, exultant

How a person waits for punishment: nervously, expectantly, shifts position of body, fidgets, twitches feet, shrugs

NOTE: Have a dictionary man for each of these vocabulary exchanges, but make it a point of pride not to allow him to contribute until the class ideas are exhausted.

➘ **By studying a chart of possible story beginnings before writing.** Stories may begin with:

1. A conversation
2. A description of the day, the weather, a character, a town, or a building
3. An action
4. The folk tale "Once upon a time . . ."
5. An explanation
6. A question
7. A flashback (end of story given first, then story told from the first)
8. An episode
9. A diary form
10. A letter form
11. A verse or song

It's fun sometimes to pass out a storytelling picture to each group of five. Let each group dramatize the story the picture tells: then in writing time write the story just dramatized.

By helping children to make their stories better

TOPSY

Our neighbor's dog is a fat cat chaser and when a jet zooms over he runs around the yard like he was chasing a cat. He has curly hair and his name is Topsy but we call him Tops for short. He is lazy and likes to lay in the sandbox. He has a nameless cat friend. The neighbor boys have two little ducks and since Tops is a bird dog they had to train him not to chase them because if he did he would eat them all up. *Once they caught him in the act of eating one of the ducks and saved the duck in time.* This dog is black and has long floppy ears and a short stubby tail. When he wags it you can hardly see it. I like to kid the neighbor kids that their dog is a retired bird dog because he doesn't hunt any more.

Jim, Grade 6

Do your children know the difference between a story and a sketch? Jim doesn't. He gives us a fine moving picture of the dog, but what Jim thinks is a story is a sketch; a story presents a dramatic action (that same idea of a story's being a play) , but a sketch presents a picture.

Notice the italicized sentence in the middle of the sketch. That sentence is the seed of a story. If he had developed that story seed to make it the chief subject of his writing, Jim would have written a story, not a sketch—the story of the dog and the ducks.

A story may have many sketches in it, but its main characteristic is one active moment, what led up to that moment, and how that moment turned out. A sketch is a written picture.

Now let's imagine that Jim is writing not a sketch of the dog but the story from that story seed in the center. He will want to follow the three steps in building a plot: (1) What led up to this action? (2) What happened? (3) How did it all turn out? Every good story includes the first two steps and at least a hint or suggestion of the third.

If Jim were writing the story of the dog and the duck, his plot steps might be:

1. Our neighbors' bird dog had a natural interest in ducks; they tried to teach him to let their ducks alone.
2. One day they caught him eating one.
3. What happened?

Carol's story below is no longer than Jim's sketch, but she has added just enough characterization to help us to understand both the situation and the dog. Her story is a short, dramatic episode; yet notice how well she makes us see her dog.

Our dog has the most fitting name of anyone I know. Mischief is always getting into trouble. Yesterday I went skating, leaving Mischief all alone. I forgot to put her in the kitchen so of course she picked the davenport to sleep on. I also forgot to turn off the television. About three-thirty "Lassie" came on. Mischief, hearing the barking and growling, went up to the television to investigate. She's also a very jealous dog so she couldn't stand to see everyone admiring Lassie while she was just standing there. She barked and howled until she saw it was no use, everyone was still admiring Lassie. But that was the last straw when Lassie began eating right in front of her. She just had to stop this, and she did. When I got home the whole television screen was broken and there were little pieces of glass all over. I still say she has a most fitting name.

Carol, Grade 6

A story presents a dramatic action; a sketch presents a picture.

The Fall

On my birthday I got a new pair of roller skates. My mother said she never had roller skates when she was a little girl. So she put on my old ones and I put on my new ones and we went down in the basement and skated across it. I went and sat down on the steps to tighten my skates. When I looked around, my mother was sitting under our wash tubs.

Diane, Grade 5

In this story, Diane did what many of your children do with true stories—she saw every detail of that story so sharply and clearly in her *own* mind that she forgot to make each sentence alive to her readers. When you write a story, remember that the reader must see that story like a movie unrolling before his eyes. Let's reread Diane's story and see how many scenes it naturally falls into; then try to think of a short sentence for each scene.

Now, see if we can think of a sentence that says that whole first scene. We might call it *Diane gets her first roller skates*. But that's all Diane told us about that scene—just that on her birthday she got new skates. There's not much of a scene in that. What might she have told that would have made the scene come to life before our very eyes?

Well, she might have told us about her thoughts and feelings as she put on the skates; practically everybody has excited thoughts and feelings as they try on new things.

If Diane had told us some or all of those things, we wouldn't have had to *guess* about that scene. We'd have watched it being acted and we'd have *known*.

Perhaps we could call the next scene *Diane's mother looks at her skates*. Ah, here's a wonderful chance to inject a bit of conversation into the story; Diane and her mother could talk about the skates.

Conversation puts pep and lightness into any tale, true or make-believe, and makes it seem true.

This conversation could lead us into the third scene, *Diane and her mother skate together in the basement.* With vivid words, Diane could have told us about her mother's faltering steps across the basement floor; she could have made us see her mother as she stumbled and recovered herself.

What have we learned from Diane's story?

1. That it pays many of us to think the scenes of the story into sentences *before we start to write.*
2. That each sentence must be developed into a scene.
3. That either the actors or the writer must describe the actors' feelings.
4. That in a story play the actors must speak.

Did you notice Diane's wonderful ending to this story? That ending surely slid down the banister to a quick stop, and Diane stopped the story when the action stopped.

Diane's story was about a disaster in the basement. David's startling tale happened on the ocean.

ADVENTURE ON THE ANDREA DORIA

I have not had too many thrilling experiences, but just last year I was on the luxury liner, *Andrea Doria,* when it happened. It was foggy that night anyway and then the ship, *Stockholm,* loomed up ahead like a ghost ship! The next thing I knew, I was in the water swimming and the funny part of it was that I couldn't swim.

Getting back to the story, I had been swimming around for about five minutes when one of the boats that the other ship had sent out picked me up. They took the other survivors and me back to the ship where they gave us dry clothes and blankets to keep us warm.

I later learned that the *Andrea Doria* had sunk and had taken fifty people to their death.

David, Grade 7

Not many people live through such an adventure as David's shipwreck was. When a person reads of another's adventure, he really *lives* the adventure as he reads. That puts quite an obligation on the story writer; he must make that story so real to the reader that he lives vicariously what he reads.

David's story makes the reader feel that David has had an exciting adventure. How could David have written his story so that his reader would have felt that he, too, had been on the ill-fated ship?

If the story of the *Andrea Doria* were being made into a moving picture, no doubt two things would be used to set the stage for the tragedy—fog and eerie background music. A story of mystery and impending disaster needs stage scenery and sound effects to get the audience ready for the action. A writer does with words what the movies do with scenery, with background music, and with sound effects.

The writer creates the mind-weather that matches the tragedy he is writing about; sometimes wind, night sounds, or ominous silence may set the mood. In the *Andrea Doria* story, the weather keynote is fog, and the mood is impending doom. Just a few foggy lines are enough to create the weather that is to last throughout the story.

Any kind of a disaster or "scare" story usually begins with mood instead of with action. Mood prepares the reader for what is coming. Mark Twain, the creator of Tom Sawyer, had a knack of scaring his readers along with his hero. In this excerpt, Tom is trying to keep awake so he can go to the graveyard with Huck. Listen!

Everything was dismally still. By and by, out of the stillness, little, scarcely perceptible noises began to emphasize themselves. The ticking of the clock began to bring itself into notice. Old beams began to crack mysteriously. The stairs creaked faintly. Evidently spirits were abroad. A measured, muffled, snore issued from Aunt Polly's chamber. And now the tiresome chirping of a cricket that no human ingenuity could locate, began. Next the ghastly ticking of a death-watch in the wall at the bed's head made Tom shudder—it meant that somebody's days were numbered. Then the howl of a far-off dog rose on the night air, and was answered by a fainter howl from a remoter distance. Tom was in an agony. At last he was satisfied that time had ceased and eternity begun; he began to doze, in spite of himself; the clock chimed eleven, but he did not hear it.[2]

Directly flowing out of mood comes the feelings of the characters. How did David feel as the fog enveloped the ship? How did he feel when the ship struck? What were his thoughts as he found himself swimming when he could not swim? What faraway sounds greeted him from the rescue boat? The reader will never know since David did not tell him.

A writer of a tragedy takes the cover off his feelings and lets the reader see what he saw, hear what he heard, feel what he felt, and think what he thought.

[2] From *The Adventures of Tom Sawyer* (Ch. IX) by Mark Twain. Published by Harper & Brothers.

Youthful story writers usually have very artistic endings to their stories. Notice how dignified and real David's last words are—and yet his story, too, stopped when the action stopped. David's story tells us:

1. *Mood creates the mind-weather of a story.*
2. *Mood helps the reader to get ready for an emotional story.*

When a writer wants to play a trick on a reader, he sometimes uses mood to deceive. This story of Alice's will astonish you, as Alice set out to do, of course.

I woke up about one o'clock this morning at the sound of a terrible storm. I must have had a nightmare because I found myself screaming and heard my mother come into the room. You see, my Dad was on an overnight business trip, and we were alone in the house. All the lights were out so my mother was carrying a flashlight. I think she was afraid too because she came in bed with me. But she jumped right out again screaming, "What's in there? What's in there?"

I couldn't feel anything because I had worn stockings to bed (it was cold that night). But I did feel something moving around and I jumped out, too. We shook off the covers and believe it or not there was a cat and a dog down at the foot of my bed. I thought my mother would faint for sure, so I went downstairs to get a glass of water. As I looked out the window I saw a sight I'll never forget. It was actually raining cats and dogs. That explains the cat and dog in my bed. I guess my Dad never did fix the leak in the roof.

Alice, Grade 6

When we want a humorous effect, we just reverse the process and prepare the reader for the wrong mood.

My mother told me this story about her grandfather. It happened back in the days of the Civil War. Her grandfather was fighting in the famous battle between the *Monitor* and the *Merrimac*. He was on the ship, the *Monitor*.

Once he got too close to a bullet and it tore loose the top half of his ear. The loose part hung down over the rest of his ear for the rest of his life. My mother said she used to sit on his knee and play with his ear.

My great-grandfather also knew Abraham Lincoln personally.

Joan, Grade 5

The reason Joan's story wasn't a better one was my own fault. Most children are three generations away from handed-down history tales, and furthermore, many great-grandparents were not dramatic storytellers in the first place. By the time Joan heard the story, it was pretty well diluted by time and lack of dramatics. But wouldn't that real episode make a truly dramatic story of the "I was there" variety, using plot steps such as these?

1. A child sits on her grandfather's lap and asks him to tell the story of how he almost lost his ear.
2. The grandfather tells her how he felt to be on the first ironclad ship and how the rest of the men felt about it.
3. He explains the battle of the *Monitor* and the *Merrimac,* blow by blow, making the part about the ear very dramatic.
4. The *Monitor* finally wins the battle.
5. The little girl asks the grandfather to tell her about Abraham Lincoln, but he says he will save that story for another time.

Note 1. When a child writes a poor story because he has little interest in the subject, don't pester him with help and with rewriting. Suggest another subject in which he is interested, and allow him to write a new story. And next time use more imagination with the assignment.

Note 2. Pretend history stories usually are more effective than "handed-down-from-three-generations" true stories.

This story takes place in Yellowstone National Park.

We have had supper. Only my little brother is asleep. I am sleeping by myself in a big sleeping bag. Soon I hear a noise as though someone were breathing real hard. Then I hear something tip. I soon come to the conclusion that it is a bear.

My father said he would get up and make him go away but Mom would not let him.

When we got up in the morning there was no bowl of chili that we had left there last night.

Sharon, Grade 5

This is a fine school newspaper article. Show Sharon how she can change it into a good story:

1. By telling it in the first person
2. By putting in all the conversation
3. By telling her feelings when she hears the bear

Note 3. Personal experience sounds more real if it is told in the first person.

Conversation makes a story out of a news item.

I saw Carlsbad Caverns. It was lovely. You went down on zigzaggy trails. It was fun. I saw Grand Canyon, too. But I like Carlsbad Caverns better. It was fun.

———, *Grade 2*

For a second-grade child, how lilting the sentences are and what specific vocabulary she uses. By grade three this fine writer will learn to choose just one phase of a journey in a travel story and develop it into a good story. Children's worst stories are their travel stories; they cover the whole trip in broad sweeps like Cinerama.

Note 4. Do not try to get form from second graders; be thankful for colorful vocabulary and sentence sense.

In third grade teach children to choose the one most exciting part of a journey and make it into a word movie.

My Most Exciting Day

(The most exciting day of my life began as any other August day, the only exception being that the fair was in town. I got up at the usual six o'clock and stumbled around the room getting dressed. I went into the bathroom to get washed up. Which woke me up a bit.)

When I got downstairs, Mom asked me, "What's going on today?" I was really puzzled till it dawned on me: today I was to take my entries to the fair. I gulped down my food in about record-splitting time. Mom excused me from doing the dishes and I rushed out to my main entry's stall: Splotch, in my opinion a blue-ribbon calf. (As a member of the local 4-H Club, I was also entering the following: an aqua plaid cotton skirt, a white blouse with plaid trim, a few baked goods and, as I told you before, Splotch, my calf.)

(Splotch received his name because of the fact that he had white splotches all over; otherwise he was the prettiest brown.) I had been caring for him all summer and he was in good condition. Now all I had to do was touch him up a bit.

Dad took all my entries (and me) to the fairgrounds. He agreed to get Splotch ready while I took the other entries to the exhibition booths. When I returned, bad news awaited me. Dad said that he had been putting Splotch in his stanchion when along came a boyhood friend. In his excitement, he forgot about my calf.

Splotch, being the mischievous calf he was, had "removed himself" from the stanchion. I was horrified when I found out and began a search for him. I searched the fairgrounds but didn't find any signs of him, though I asked at least a million people, it seemed. At last, about twelve o'clock, Dad insisted we go home. After a bit of persuasion, he agreed to let me stay while he went.

I kept up my searching, which had been in vain, until about four o'clock, when I came upon the fact that I had missed a nearby farm. (I had searched and inquired at all the others.) It was nearing six o'clock and I was reaching the bridge, en route to the fairgrounds. (I hadn't found Splotch at that farm, though I had searched for two hours.) Then I thought I was hearing things. I thought I heard a calf bellering and it was. It was Splotch all right and what a sight—bramblers, stickers, burrs completely covering him. It almost made me sick to think of cleaning him up for judging which was to be the next day.

I found Dad, quite by accident, because I thought he was still home. He was about as sick as I was but we sped home, in the truck, to set up work immediately. We must have worked three-fourths of the night.

Early the next day, we took Splotch from a deep slumber to the fairgrounds. When the judging was started, my fingernails were getting less. When the judges called my name, I walked up with my heart going about 3500 B.P.S. (beats per second). When they handed me (rather, us) a blue ribbon, I nearly fainted.

Sally, Grade 7

I was so interested in Sally's calf, and determined it would get the prize, and felt relieved when it did. I am also interested in Sally's story; she conveyed so much of herself to me in the writing. I believe I could help Sally with this story. If I could sit down here with Sally, I'd say to her, "Sally, this story of yours is just like your calf—it won't stay in its corral; it runs away all over the paper. A good story, like a good calf, stays where its title holds it. Your story title is 'My Most Exciting Day.' Now, Sally, why was that day exciting? All because Splotch ran away. Make your story focus; bring the ideas back to the corral of the title; in your story tell just the activities of that day that had to do with your prize calf. Then as you removed the burrs and filth from your calf's glossy coat, remove the extras from this story—everything that doesn't belong to that 'calf' part of the day, pluck off like burrs."

I'd have her discuss the possible removal of the sentences between the parentheses, but I'd have *her,* not me, choose the parts to be taken out. Then I'd show her how to use new transitions to bridge the parts she omitted.

I'd try to get her to see how conversation would lighten her story and make it more interesting as the brush made the calf's coat more glossy; she could talk to her father, to a farmer, and finally to the calf.

I'd do all in my power to groom that story into a winner.

Note 5. If possible, talk to a child through his own interests.

Note 6. A conference should be a real meeting of minds and people. Use the intimacy of a conference to help children who can profit by help. The red pencil may have made Sally stop writing, and she's definitely worth saving.

May I end this chapter on story writing with a story.

There was once a group of dedicated fishermen who fished every weekday when the weather was favorable from a great bridge over the river Time.

One day one of the fishermen said to his companions after an especially unprofitable day, "I am quite discouraged. We have fished this stream for a long time and we used to get so many fish in a day's fishing that our wives had trouble getting the neighbors to accept them. But for a long time now, our catch has dwindled to almost nothing. Do you suppose we have lost our cunning with the rod and reel?" And he sighed.

"I cannot think that is the reason," his more positive companion asserted stoutly. "In fact, I for one think I know much more about the art of fishing than I used to know. I have read every book on angling in the village library and in the state traveling library as well. Furthermore, I have *never* failed even *once* to attend the annual convention of Isaak Walton Nimrods at great cost to myself. No, indeed, I do not feel that I have lost my cunning as a fisherman. I think it's the condition of the fishing grounds that is causing our losses. A half-dozen factories from the neighboring city yearly pour more and more pollution into this river. The fish are so filled with poison that they no longer care for the fancy bait prescribed in the latest manuals." And he gave a few short, angry puffs on his stubby pipe.

A third, more thoughtful companion motioned to the others to rest for a moment on the river's bank.

"I wonder if we aren't looking at our failures from the wrong angle," he said slowly. "What with the increasing numbers of carp in the river, the fish must sharpen their wits considerably in order to keep alive at all. I believe that our losses are due not to pollution or our having lost our cunning but to the fact that the fish have grown more cunning than they used to be."

Just then the fishermen heard a gaily whistled tune and a red-headed lad with a cane pole over his shoulder came up the road, literally loaded down with a sack of fish he had caught.

At the sight of the fishermen, the lad dropped down on the grass, apparently glad to be eased of his load for a moment.

"Where on earth did you catch all those fish?" exclaimed one of the fishermen. "Surely not in this river!"

The boy laughed, as he eyed the fancy equipment of the mature fishermen.

"Because I haven't much in the way of gear," he said ruefully, "I have to be smart in the ways of fish. I know the fish in this river like a book—better than I know schoolbooks," he laughed again. "I know the habits and resting places of every fish in this river. I spend every minute out of school along this river studying fish and it sure pays off. A fellow can't sit on the bridge these days and catch fish."

There was a moment's pause.

"What do you use for bait?" inquired the second fisherman.

"Oh, I use a different kind for every kind of fish," the lad explained, "but always something alive and challenging to the fish and something they aren't looking for. I think fish are getting smarter than they used to be," he continued; "they really ought to be, you know," and here his green eyes twinkled with fun, "our teacher says they're always in schools."

Then leaving half of the contents of his sack of fish on the bank for the less fortunate fishermen, the lad slung his half-empty sack over his shoulder and went whistling down the road.

CUPBOARD OF IDEAS for Chapter Eight

Stories Are Play-Acted ❖ ❖ ❖ ❖ ❖ ❖ ❖ ❖ ❖ ❖ ❖ ❖ ❖ ❖ ❖ ❖ ❖

> Story writing cramps their style;
> They write by inch, but think by mile;
> They positively want to yell—
> What they want to write they just can't spell.

Primary Shelf

I. If's for Oral Stories (Gr. 1–2)

Helpers from another grade act as secretaries for first grade.
Second graders write their own.
A. If you were a circus pony, what adventure might you
   have?
B. If you were a lost dog, what might happen to you?
C. If you were a calf that liked to run away, what might happen to you?
D. If you were a dog that saw a turtle in the road, what might
   happen?

II. Rebus Charts (Advanced Gr. 1)

The children use pictures for words they can't spell. Write
story seeds on chart or board for children to make grow.

A. I am a (picture of boy). My name is Tom. I want a (picture of a bicycle). Tell all about how I got it.

B. I am a (picture of a girl). I wanted a (picture of friend). Tell how I got one.

C. I am a (picture of tulip). I want to push my (picture of leaves) through the ground. Tell about my getting up into the (picture of sun) light.

D. I am a (picture of mother). I have a little (picture of boy). He is naughty. What shall I do?

III. Balloon Stories

They begin little; you must blow them big.
A. I was angry at my mother—I ran away.
B. I had a birthday party.
C. I got a cowboy outfit for my birthday.
D. I am a yellow butterfly. I got scared one day.

IV. Plot Folders

Fold 9 x 12 manila paper like a small book. Put a picture of a cat on one side, a small plot with word list below on the other.

A. I am a kitten named Fluff. Tell the story of how I got chased up into this tree and how I got down again. (Follow with a list of words the child might need: scared, chased, claws, dug, barked, fireman, ladder, afraid, tried, arms, milk.)

B. I am a fireman named Jim. One day there was a big fire. Tell what happened.

C. I am an engineer. I drive a big train. One day my engine could not get up the hill. What happened?

D. I am a monkey named Bimbo. I love to tease my master.

E. I am a baby brother. I got lost one day.

V. Storytelling Pictures

Give a storytelling picture to each two children. Let them make up and write a story together. Pair them carefully for skill.

VI. *Stories of Our Own Pet*

Choose a class mascot, a large picture of which hangs on the wall (donkey, pony, turtle, dog, cat, parrot, rabbit). Every week make up a new adventure for your room pet and print it on a story chart; let a child illustrate it and bind the stories into a huge book with hard covers.

VII. *More Primer Stories*

Make further adventure stories of your primer pair. Put a picture of a new baby on a chart. Tell the children that Alice and Jerry have had a new baby brother. Choose five dramatic children to assume the parts of Alice, Jerry, Baby Sally, Spot, and a neighbor, Sue. Let each one suggest a line he wants to say on the chart:

"We have a new baby."

"What kind is it?"

"A brother. He is very small. He cannot play ball with me."

"My mother is at the hospital. Grandmother has come to stay with us."

"I would rather have had a pony."

"Do you like the baby, Spot?"

"Arf! Arf! I like puppies better."

"I wish I had a brother. I would take good care of him."

After the parts have been said, go back and put the identification in as the children direct you—*said* Alice; *asked* Sue; *said* Jerry, and so on.

If the children suggest "said" for every one, mention others for variety until they see the fun of using different vocabulary words. Soon they will suggest *laughed, answered, shouted,* and the like.

These short "talked" stories allow book children to do what room children do, thus making them real. Bind these stories into a big book.

VIII. *Christmas Books*

At Christmas, let the kindergarten and first grades "talk-off" and illustrate stories which helpers from Grade 3 print for them. They decorate a cover and give to a smaller child for

Christmas. Second- and third-grade children can write their own such stories.

IX. *True Stories*

Kindergarten and first grade tell; second and third grade write.
A. At Grandfather's I had fun.
B. When I was small, I did some funny things.
C. We went on a long trip.
D. Something funny and something small.
E. My pet had a real adventure.

X. *Exciting Stories*

Take advantage of every exciting thing that happens in your room. Make a chart story together and bind the stories into a big book.

Intermediate and Upper-Grade Shelf

I. *Pet Stories*

A. **Add-venture stories with a pet.** $2 + 4 = 1$, or a two-legged child plus a four-legged pet equals one good time.
   1. What were you and your pet doing when the adventure happened? Make us see pictures with you as you walk along; describe animal's actions specifically.
   2. What happened? Describe the action in short, sharp sentences.
   3. Stop the story when the action stops.
B. **A dog's life.** Your pet tells in first person about his life with you from his angle.
   Make this full of feelings—a sort of "bark-off" or "meow-off" of frustrated animal friends. Make this a series of small happenings or one enlarged one.
C. **My horse, of course.** An adventure story with a dream or real horse.
   1. Make us see your horse.
   2. Make us feel your feelings for him.

      3. What happened one day?

      4. How did it all come out?

D. Imaginagerie (imaginary menagerie). Concoct a new animal such as a kangarooster by combining two animals, and make up a story with the new animal as hero or villain.

E. Stories from suggested titles

      1. The Cat That Went to Mars

      2. The Cat That Was a Stowaway

      3. The Cat That Went to America

      4. I Was the Dog in Sputnik

      5. The Calf That Did Not Want to Be a Cow

      6. The Donkey with a Defective Bray

      7. The Dog That Became the Dog Star

      8. The Cat That Went to Oregon

      9. The Cat That Had a Catastrophe

     10. The Kitten with a Complex

     11. How the Bird Got His Song

     12. The Dog Who Got on Television

F. Space animal stories

G. Animals at any great moments in history

II. Ghost or Halloween Stories

A. Create an eerie, apprehensive mood.

B. Build up suspense.

C. Use the five senses.

D. Stop short.

III. Space Stories

A. I Was the First Man to the Moon

B. Rocket in My Pocket

C. I'm the Man in the Moon

D. A Summer in Mars

E. 3–2–1–0 Blast Off

F. Who Is Throwing Those Flying Saucers?

IV. Stories about Me

Biographical episodes: greatest fear; happiest day; most embarrassing moment; proudest moment; greatest wish come true; most momentous moment; a first day at school; when our family moved; an adventure in the country, at the fair, in the city.

V. *Adventures in Imaginary Situations*

    A. Discuss what adventures you might have in this situation.
    B. Imagine how it would feel to be there.
    C. Work much with vocabulary.
    D. Tell of an imaginary adventure.
       1. If you were a kite
       2. If you were very small and had wings
       3. If you were Crusoe on an island
       4. If you were rocket-wrecked or plane-wrecked
       5. If you were diving underseas
       6. If you were rich
       7. If you could invent an unusual thing
          a) Think of something you hate to do.
          b) What might you invent to get rid of the situation?
          c) Tell how it all turned out.

VI. *Stories That Come to You as You Listen to Music*

Let the mind relax and your subconscious will bring stories to you. (Play several different kinds of music for different tempos of people.)

VII. *Sing-a-Stories*

Write ballads or rhymed tales of heroes, or heroic happenings from now or long ago.

VIII. *Other Ideas*

See Chapter Nine, page 355, for history and science story ideas and Chapter Twelve, page 517, for ideas for humorous stories.

Practical Writing Needs Wings

Teacher's wife (looking up from reading Chapter Nine): Remember when you're writing that letter to the Board today, pretend you are the fellow you're writing to.

Irate teacher: I should call myself such names!

When I was a beggarly boy
    And lived in a cellar damp,
I had not a friend nor a toy,
    But I had Aladdin's lamp;
When I could not sleep for the cold,
    I had fire enough in my brain,
And builded, with roofs of gold,
    My beautiful castles in Spain!

James Russell Lowell

YOU CAN'T FORGET

Sure I saw a field of gold,
A sky of silk.
I saw a valley of grass
As green as Irish lace itself.
I saw a mountain of gold,
An ocean of gold!
Everything possible.
But best of all I saw peace.
Of course you cannot get away from it all—
All the bloodshed and torment
We cannot forget the wars,
But we can pray.

Patrick McNally, Grade 5

I wonder what lies inside that picture
That picture on the wall
I wonder if I could enter it
That picture in the hall.

It is starting to get so hazy
Now it's coming back.
But I see a person in the picture
And in his hand a sack.

I seem to be in something queer
Now I hear a call
Then I snapped when I knew where I was
In the picture on the wall.

Again it's getting hazy
And again it's coming back.
I am still standing in the hall
And in my hand a sack.

Tris Lanti, Grade 6

Practical writing is effective according to whether or not it is wing-tipped with imagination. What do I mean by that statement? Practical writing is one type of sales writing—writing done to interest others in ideas, products, or personalities—and a salesman without imagination is no salesman.

In order to sell, one must feel; that part of salesmanship is elementary. Most of us have, at one time or another, bought things simply because we were fascinated by a salesman's interest in what he was selling. Every house-cleaning time housewives throw away such gadgets, and businessmen try to unload on the public products they should not have bought in the first place. It is only the impractical ideas he bought that a man seems loathe to discard. Many old men and women cherish to their death the outmoded ideas sold them in their youth by an enthusiastic salesman, ideas that may have been wrong to start with. Most of us spend our lives with the results of our ability or inability to buy and to choose.

The salesmanship with which we are bombarded and with which we bombard is terrific; whether one is a merchant, a seller of services, a clergyman, or a teacher, he must be an outstanding salesman of the commodity he is selling. This condition points out three directions in elementary education: We must produce citizens of integrity so that less shoddy stuff will get on the market; we must train youngsters in the art of selling ideas and commodities; we must teach youth how to evaluate before they buy. It is the second idea—the art of salesmanship—with which this chapter is concerned.

Salesmanship starts with feeling, feeling that is rooted in knowledge. In order to fully appreciate a commodity or idea, we must see it under every possible circumstance; we must know its strengths so that we can advertise them; we must be aware of its weaknesses so that we can anticipate what others will say and be ready to answer them.

If our salesmanship is to be direct, our selling task is easier. A direct buyer is more often influenced by a poor salesman who has knowledge and feeling about his product than by a glib talker who lacks those two qualities. But a written sales talk—and that is what an educational book is—is a more difficult method of selling. The words must be three-dimensional; they must engender not only a sales appeal for the product or idea but must convince the prospective buyer of the integrity of the salesman and his knowledge of and feeling for his product. Most people find it hard to get their enthusiasm on paper without its losing zest. It is this skill this chapter is concerned with: written salesmanship—the ability to convey enthusiasms through writing.

At this point imagination enters the picture. To do a good selling job, a writer must get a mental image of the buyer, determine his interests, and anticipate his questions; in short, the seller must imagine he is the buyer and write his sales talk accordingly.

"What will he be like—this reader of mine?" the practical writer must ask himself; then must answer his own question and the probable questions of his unseen reader. A practical writer, unlike a creative one, has a floor of fact and a ceiling of circumstance to circumscribe his writing. He must never depart from the facts, yet he must handle those facts in such an imaginative way that he gives wings to his readers, either kindling desires or questions in their minds or giving them satisfactions.

Since it is written more to inform and to change opinion than to entertain, practical writing must be written so palatably that it will be read. Unimaginative writing fails to stir the reader. The blind man in New York City who was placarded: "Give to the blind," attracted little attention—he was like every blind man. But the sightless man on the next block who solicited money with the imaginative caption: "It is spring and I am blind!" sent hands hurrying into purses for contributions. Practical writing that is imaginative will stand out among the ordinary like a missing front tooth. As each reads that sort of practical writing, he will feel that the message is personal to him. Imagination personalizes practical writing.

Many school children will never write creatively after they leave school. But most adults at some time in their lives will be called upon to do practical writing: news items, advertisements, explanations, business letters, reports of all kinds, summaries, and the like, all of which to be effective must be wing-tipped with imagination. The skills necessary for better living must become second nature to the children in the elementary school. If he can train children to give imaginative treatment to practical writing, each teacher will add greatly to their ability to earn a living.

A good teacher, however, seldom suggests that practical writing be done in isolation; he makes it real through making it a part of genuine or vicarious school living: writing the actual advertisements for school functions, the news items for real school papers, the thank-you letter for the guest who came to speak. Many an elementary teacher substitutes unreality for reality by by-passing live language situations and substituting lessons from language books. The truly helpful language text points out to the teacher the live language situations going to waste in his own schoolroom living and shows him how to make vicarious situations as real and as much fun as possible. The best language texts are those to be used like a recipe book.

Examine the sales ideas in this "Pet for Sale" language lesson, and apply them to other situations.

Writing Effective Advertisements Takes Imagination

(A lesson written *for* and *to* children)

"Pet for sale!" If you were moving away and just had to sell your pet, what sort of advertisement could you write? It takes real skill to write an appealing advertisement.

Although the thought of selling one's pet is usually anathema to the one who owns it, if someone is going to buy your pet, you'll just have to make someone want him—want him *very, very* much. Whenever you're puzzled about what to write in an advertisement, ask yourself this question: *What would I like to hear if I were going to buy this pet, instead of sell him?*

All right, what would you want to hear about your pet if you were buying him instead of selling him? Perhaps the easiest way of thinking of the answer to that question would be to listen to sixth-grade Susan's telling about her dog:

I have a curly-haired cocker spaniel named Duke. He is a very lovable dog. He shows his love by wagging his tail and tries to comfort you when you are ill or crying.

People usually think that dogs are dumb animals but actually I don't think so because when I talk to my dog he sits and looks at me and cocks his head from side to side and perks his ears as though he actually knows what I am talking about. I think the name Cocker Spaniel fits my dog very well because of his cocking of his head, don't you?

My dog actually has a few tricks that he plays on people and animals too. One of the tricks he plays is on squirrels. He waits until they are down on the ground from the tree, then he runs and chases them back up. When they get halfway up the tree, they stop and tease him by brushing their tails against the tree and chatter as though to be laughing at him. When he sees them he gets mad and forgets himself, I guess, because he comes running with a leap and a jump to get up the tree and down goes he.

My dog is a fussy eater; he wants what we eat instead of dog meat. One night for supper we had fish and for supper I brought him some chicken meat which he would not eat. He kept carrying it over to the dirt and burying it. I served it to him on a silver plate and still he would not eat it. Fussy, isn't he?

So I guess you can see why I love my dog Duke. He's the greatest.

Susan, Grade 6

Now let's say you're contemplating buying Susan's dog Duke. What that Susan said about him would make you anxious to buy him?

First of all, I believe Susan's telling of Duke's loving ways and his intelligence would make us want her dog, don't you? And notice, Susan didn't say, "Duke is loving"; these words are too general. Instead, she gave specific instances of how loving Duke is: "He shows his love by wagging his tail and tries to comfort you when you are ill or crying." Instead of just saying, "Duke is an intelligent dog," Susan proves how smart Duke is by telling how he acts when she talks to him. She tells, too, about his tricks; that's a good idea. If you want people to know how intelligent your pet is, tell them about his tricks.

But what did Susan write in her sketch of her dog that it wouldn't be good business to put into an ad?

Yes, you've spotted it; one would never put into an ad that his pet was a fussy eater. If he did, it might prejudice the prospective buyer against him. Later, when the buyer has fallen in love with Duke, it is time enough to give him a few helpful tips about Duke's diet.

So in the advertisement you're going to write, characterize your pet, giving little examples to show the buyer how nice he is. In short, what you'll do is to play up his good qualities and play down his bad ones, telling only his cunning tricks and never mentioning that he chews up any slippers he finds around the house. It's only after the buyer loves the pet that he won't mind even that. Of course, if your pet has a vicious habit, such as dislike of children or biting strangers, it would be only fair to tell the buyer, but not in the advertisement, of course.

Susan did forget one important item in that story of hers. She failed to give us a very clear picture of her pet. She said he was a cocker and curly-haired, but I can't see a picture of him, can you? It's just awfully important when writing an advertisement of a pet to get the buyer to see the pet with the eyes of his imagination before he actually sees him. In order to do that, it will be necessary to write a good word picture or pen portrait of your pet so the buyer can see him in his mind's eyes. If you will do a good job of sketching, someone will surely come to buy.

Let's listen to some written film strips of pets and see if we'd like to buy, shall we? Here's a regular moving picture of Marilon's cat:

My kitten is a soft black ball of fur. When I see him he always reminds me of a dark moonless night with his eyes shining brightly like stars. He is as playful as a butterfly fluttering in the air.

Bette's pup must be a lovable little fellow:

She had freckles on her nose like a little red-headed boy with freckles on his face. Her brown eyes were running over with fun. She is as friendly as the first spring flowers.

"As friendly as the first spring flowers"—isn't that a good comparison? It helps us really see Bette's gentle little dog.

Sandra's picture of Fluff makes us oh-so-anxious to buy her kitten:

My kitten's name is Fluff,
She's as dainty as a muff.
She likes to tackle grasshoppers
Boy! She's caught some great big whoppers.
Her color is a pretty tan,
I play with her whenever I can.

Well, which shall we buy? It's easy to see, isn't it, that a word picture or pencil portrait of your pet will help to sell it? In review, then, we might summarize the first point in our advertisement-writing lesson in rhyme:

> Make the buyer want what you have to sell,
> By singing its praises in picturesque phrases
> Describing it well—
> List all of the good points; play down the minor,
> (Where could one buy a cheaper or finer?)
> In short, just say what you would inquire
> If he were the seller and you the buyer.

Any advertisement is more intriguing if it has a different twist. Can you imagine how eagerly a dog lover would read an advertisement written in the first person as if the dog had written his own ad?

Will some nice person buy me, please? My mistress is moving to California and can't keep me any more.

I believe you'd like owning me. I'm a Cocker Spaniel and quite well-behaved for my age. My fur is the color of golden honey, my eyes are amber brown, and my ears are a lovely shape if I do say so myself.

If you need someone to make you laugh and to keep you company and to love you always, I'm just what you need. Please come to see.

Signed—*Amber*. Phone Ken. 6–9872 after five o'clock.

And just imagine how startling an advertisement written by the dog next door would be.

Will somebody please buy that little golden cocker pup next door? I'm sick of having her around! How can an ugly old mutt of a dog like me get any attention with her next door? It's annoying to have everybody stop and pet her and tell her how cute she is and never even *look* at me.

She's attractive—I'll have to admit that—and she's really smart, for a pup, but this younger generation gets everything too easily.

Her mistress's phone number is Hilltop 61407. Get her off my hands, will you, before I have to go to a psychiatrist?

Signed—*The Bulldog Next Door*

Have the children try writing advertisements for the school paper. Ad-writing is a real challenge. But one lesson on writing an advertisement is not enough. Let the children use the above points in writing about their hobbies. One "sells" his hobby in the same way as he sells his dog.

Ask each child to write about his favorite game, his favorite book, movie actor, or television show. Such writing is only another method of advertising something that belongs to him.

—(The essence of true advertising is to catch the imagination of the people who will read the advertisement.) Advertising often misses the point when it is too blatantly smart.

For years I have been impressed with the quiet effectiveness of the short sketches used by the John Hancock Mutual Life Insurance Company as magazine advertising. This particular one has this caption and copy under a picture of Abraham Lincoln:

He was everybody, grown a little taller . . .

Let's skip all the things you've read about him, all the things you've heard too often or too young. Forget the face on the penny, the speech at Gettysburg. Forget the official things and look at the big thing. What was there about Abraham Lincoln?

He came out of nowhere special. His folks were nobody special. Abe was a smart boy, but not too smart. He told funny stories. He was strong and kind. He'd never try to hurt you, or cheat you, or fool you.

Young Abe worked at odd jobs and read law books at night. Eventually he found his way into local politics. And it was then that people began to know there was something special about Abe Lincoln.

Abe had a habit of growing without changing. So it seemed perfectly natural to find him padding around the White House in his slippers, putting his feet on a chair when he had a deep one to think about. And when the war came that might have torn his country apart, no one doubted what Abe would do. He was a family man. He resolved to keep the American family together.

Abe Lincoln always did what most people would have done, said what they wanted said, thought what they would have thought when they stopped to think about it. He was everybody, grown a little taller—proof of our American faith that greatness comes out of everywhere when it is free to come.[1]

Both teachers and children of the intermediate and upper grades can learn a great deal about the imaginative touch from the reading of fine advertising. What seems to be only hardheaded common sense is usually common sense viewed with the eyes of imagination.

[1] Courtesy of John Hancock Mutual Life Insurance Company.

A teacher who asked the children to write a paragraph on what made Abraham Lincoln great might be surprised at the insight shown by both imaginative and realistic children.

News Writing Takes an Imaginative Approach

From an educator's point of view, there are ten practical reasons why every school should publish a school newspaper. A school newspaper does the following things:

1. Appeals to all children, whether they are imaginative or not.
2. Provides all the children in the classroom with a job.
3. Is live (not book) language work.
4. Makes children feel important.
5. Builds school spirit.
6. Interprets the school to the community and the community to the school.
7. Gives purpose to language classes.
8. Tends to improve spelling.
9. Gives a variety of writing experience.
10. Is democratic living in action.

From the child's point of view, a school newspaper is fun if it is not too teacher-dominated, if he gets a sense of importance from writing it, and if it can be done in schooltime instead of playtime.

The longest-lived school newspaper is the paper that is the least trouble to put out. Our school days are normally fuller than a three-room house at fair time. In a curriculum as crowded as the modern one, something just must be eliminated—and often the school newspaper is the first to go. In reality casting out the school newssheet is like throwing out whole wheat bread and butter from the diet and substituting cold cereal and skimmed milk. A newspaper is the vitamin-filled, stick-to-the-ribs sort of live language lesson that makes writing skills grow brawny.

Teachers tell me that a wall newspaper issued semimonthly by each grade is easy to make because it takes no typing, and forms an excellent basis for a typed newssheet put out once a month for the entire school.

What is a wall newspaper? Fold brown wrapping paper or newsprint over a window stick or piece of lath to form a hanging newssheet about a yard long. Use as many folded sheets as necessary for the news, clipping them together with the stapler. Let the children divide each sheet into two columns on which the items are arranged and pasted by a committee. On one school day each fortnight assign news writing as the language lesson, each person writing at least one news item from home or neighborhood happenings, a letter to the Voice of the School column, or a special feature article to be assigned by the editor.

A group of editors selects the items for each page, another group pastes the sheets in column form on each sheet after proofreaders have scanned the papers for misspelled words and grammatical errors. Some schools organize their wall newspaper by sections: feature articles, local news, school news, sports, interviews, creative writing (original stories and poems), editorial comments, the Voice of the School column, and a joke section.

It usually works well to have an excellent organizer in charge of each committee with the work parceled out so that no one is left with an onerous task to do all alone. The secret of a successful newspaper is to do most of the work in schooltime, to have real "doers" at the heads of committees, and to spread the work throughout the entire student body. The wall newspaper can be hung outside the classroom door for general school reading, and can be handed to any supervisor or parent who comes to call.

As you can readily see, the wall newspaper has several distinct advantages: it takes no typing, it is a real part of school language work, it is easy to assemble, and it can be much larger than a typed newspaper. However, it has one distinct disadvantage: few of the parents get to read it, and a lively well-written newspaper is the best advertisement a schoolroom can have. For this reason, if a few dedicated children of an upper grade can publish an all-school newspaper with articles taken from each room wall newspaper, the results are likely to be good for school spirit. Many small-town newspapers are willing to publish school news if they can be sure of getting it regularly and carefully done. High school typing students will sometimes do the typing for practice.

Primary sheet. Instead of a wall newspaper, a first-grade teacher may prefer to publish a single sheet which the children make together and the teacher types on the primary typewriter. I happened to be in the room when the children were composing this little newssheet. Each line was suggested by a child. The paper is written each Friday morning and read by the afternoon reading classes. Ruth Kellar is the teacher.

EMERSON SCHOOL NEWSPAPER FEBRUARY 20, 1959

Weather

Jack Frost is out today.

School News

Today is Ricky's birthday.
He is 7 today.
A very Happy Birthday to you,
Ricky.

Four Brownies are not here today.

Bonjour enfants! [These children
are learning to speak French.]

John Milne is in Florida.

Maybe we will have 100% this
afternoon.

Home Room News

We made some good puppets
yesterday.

Kathy has some puppet mittens.

Kathy's mother made them.

Nature News

The birds look hungry.

Mary saw a rabbit yesterday.

For the help of those of you who either have never published a
school newspaper or have been unsuccessful in your publications,
these three articles: "What Is News?" "Feature It," and "It's My
Opinion," written directly to the children, may help your school do
a truly good job of writing the school newssheet.

What Is News?

> Mary Sherrity has new shoes;
> Burns's cow has calves by twos
> Joe Ranney fell and got a bruise,
> Bob and Dick took boats on the pond for a cruise;
> There's a red cap found; I wonder whose?
> What's news?
> There's nothing here that I can use!

No wonder this young school newspaper reporter in the rhyme
is in despair—everything happening and as he says, "No news!"
How do you know news when you meet it? Just what is news?

An experienced newspaper reporter will tell us that anything
is news that interests the reader. Of course, we'll fire this question
at him, "What sort of thing are people interested in reading?" Then
no doubt he'll come right back at us with this answer: "People will
read anything that's interestingly written." And here we come to a

little known truth: the appeal of the news many times lies more in the writer than in the event. It is the reporter's handling of the ordinary happenings of the day that makes a paper interesting or uninteresting. But in any community, more than one great big interesting event seldom happens in one week's time.

At school, it's the same: big, exciting stories don't happen every day, but a lot of little things happen. So the reporter must take the little things and make them interesting through the way he writes his stories. Often he can find an extraordinary twist in an ordinary happening that makes his story fun to read. Every reporter must be equipped with a radar imagination so that he can spot the news and dig for it. This ability to ferret out news is known as "a nose for news," but to tell the truth, the nose is not the organ concerned with news gathering. What a reporter needs is sharp eyes and ears and a quick mind. You see, it's only the extraordinary that the untrained reporter thinks is news. But most news appears to be very ordinary indeed, so too many reporters pass it by and wail, "There's nothing to write about! No news!"

I'm sure many reporters would have missed this interesting item I found in a rural school paper:

A Cunning Home Found

While harvesting his corn, Melvin Nelson of Barneveld, Wisconsin, found a tiny nest in the tassel of a cornstalk. It was the nest of a goldfinch. The nest was built of corn silks and thistledown with the tassels sticking out around it. It was later brought to Urness School for the Conservation Corner.

Linda, Grade 7

Suppose we take the list of happenings in that first rhyme by a frustrated reporter and see if we can locate any real news for a school newspaper. The first line says, "Mary Sherrity has new shoes." Well, let's think a minute—everybody in school has new shoes sometime, but there just might be something special about Mary's new shoes. So the reporter goes to the second-grade room and checks to be sure.

This is known as "leg work." Two-thirds of a reporter's time is spent using his legs to hunt out the news. Of course, all that leg work won't always turn up stories; often the news tip turns out to be a dud. A reporter rushes to the source, and he may or may not find a story.

What happens when our reporter interviews Mary. She's a second grader, remember, and rather shy, so he doesn't rush up to her immediately and demand, "Do you have new shoes?" No, he gets to talking with her and leads up to the question he wants to know. And what does he find out? Mary's new shoes are cowgirl shoes sent by her aunt in Montana. Not another girl in school has cowgirl shoes, so the nose of the enterprising reporter twitches with excitement. "This is news," he says to himself and asks Mary all about her new cowgirl shoes: five questions—*what, where, why, when,* and *how.* He already knows *who.* Because he used his legs to get the news and his head to think the news through, the item in the paper may sound something like this:

Little Mary Sherrity of 547 22nd Avenue is all smiles today! She has a new pair of cowgirl boots which her aunt in Montana sent her for her birthday.

Mary says that she hopes to get a cowgirl suit at Christmas time to match her new shoes. The boots, which are made of soft calfskin, are beautifully decorated with scrollwork and fancy stitching. Miss Brown, Mary's teacher, had Mary tell all the children in second grade about her new shoes.

What other facts about a new pair of shoes might make them worthy of a news item in the paper? For one thing, a child might have earned his new shoes all by himself—that would make school newspaper news—*any rare happening is news.* Or last week's newspaper might have reported that a child's shoes had been torn in a bicycle accident with a car. This week's story may follow up the accident story with the story of the shoes the automobile driver had bought the child in the same article that reports her quick recovery from the accident. There is usually more than one story about a happening. *A follow-up story makes good news when more facts are added.*

"But," you inquire," how about a poor child that rarely gets new shoes? Wouldn't his shoes rate a news item—it's a rare event and you said any rare event is news." Yes, I can see why you'd think that. But you'll have to remember that a reporter must learn to use his heart as well as his head, and no reporter on a school newspaper makes news of any event that might possibly make a reader uncomfortable. A child who gets new shoes so rarely as to make news would probably rather avoid the publicity. All right, then, a rare happening and new facts in a follow-up story on last week's item are news.

Now, let's look at the second line of that rhyme: "Burns's cow has calves by twos."

Oh, Jim (let's call our reporter Jim), you surely missed a trick that time, thinking that there's no news in this happening. Not too many cows have twin calves even once, but this cow has evidently had the second pair.

Why, Jim, this is even big headline news. Hurry to interview the farmer and get all the details about the calves. Be sure, too, to get a little information about the farmer. Your article, Jim, might be written this way:

Violet, a purebred Guernsey cow on John Burns's farm, has done it again. She's had her second pair of twin calves.

It's evidently "double or nothing" for Violet since her owner, Mr. Burns, says Violet has never given birth to a single calf. She had a pair of twin calves last year, too.

The calves, a pair of handsome heifers, are miniatures of their mother who kept licking them—evidently so they would look their best for the news reporter.

Ronny Burns, on whose father's farm the calves were born, is a pupil in our sixth grade.

We've had two news stories now, and you've probably begun to notice what part of the story is picked out for the first paragraph or the lead. *What is the lead?* A lead is the whole story in a summary statement. That summary statement is all important, since it must contain all the news "in a nutshell" and must also be interesting enough to hold the attention of a reader.

How is a lead picked out? A reporter thinks through his story and decides what part of it is most interesting. He then starts his news article using that bit in a summary paragraph. In that paragraph, he answers the six questions—*who, when, where, why, what,* and *how.* Perhaps you can remember these six summary items better if you'll learn this verse by Rudyard Kipling, the great newspaper man who wrote the *Just So Stories.*

> I keep six honest serving-men
> (They taught me all I knew)
> Their names are What and Why and When
> And How and Where and Who! [2]

[2] From *Just So Stories* by Rudyard Kipling. Reprinted by permission of The Macmillan Company of Canada, Ltd., Mrs. George Bambridge, and Doubleday & Company, Inc.

Oh, you won't always use all of these serving-men in one article, but a good test is to ask yourself all of them to see if you've answered all the questions the readers would want to know. Let's see now, the first item started out: "Little Mary Sherrity of 547 22nd Avenue is all smiles today! She has a new pair of cowgirl boots which her aunt in Montana sent her for her birthday."

Two types of people will be interested in that news item because of the lead: those who know or have heard of the Sherritys, and the fact that a little girl is happy over an unusual gift. All of us, you know, like to read about children.

Now look at the lead for the calf story: "Violet, a purebred Guernsey cow on John Burns's farm, has done it again. She's had her second pair of twin calves." Have we answered those six questions, *who, what, where, why, when,* and *how?* No, actually we haven't answered the *when* of our news story. We forgot to tell when the calves were born. But we can easily add that information to the first line "had her second pair of twin calves at midnight on Tuesday."

You have probably noticed from the stories written today that the reporter gives no opinions of his own; he merely reports the news. Opinions on news events are printed on the editorial page and in the Voice of the People. We aren't concerned about opinions today —we're reporters, and our job is to report facts.

And now to the next item in the rhyme, "Joe Ranney fell and got a bruise." *Is that news?* Hardly, among boys and girls. We'll have to ask our reporter to interview this Joe about his bruise. If it's a bruise bad enough to keep him from playing in a football game or home from attending school or cause him to use a crutch, then the bruise is news.

Let's talk about another story, one that is just a bit different from the ones we've already discussed. This is an example of a type of news story that is an important part of your school papers. Even the local paper would be happy to print such a story—if it is written well. Everybody likes to know what the different classes are doing.

The French Island school newspaper used as simple a news item as a bird project in one issue. The reporter had to go to the first- and second-grade rooms for this news last winter. Notice how the lead begins with a question.

Have you ever seen a bird climb the trunk of a tree or come down head first? The nuthatch does just this. Grades 1 and 2 are planning a unit on "Our Winter Birds." We want to find out how birds find food and shelter when the weather is stormy. Do they help us by eating harmful insects and seeds of weeds and grasses?

Parents are urged to enjoy this project with the children. Many have already transplanted their Christmas trees in the yard for a winter feeding station. Half an orange scooped out, filled with seeds, and hung from the branches is a good dispenser.

The new film strip machine will help us identify birds later on, and we may borrow records of bird calls from the Public Library. How many birds do *you* know? Mrs. Inga Olson is the teacher of this group of boys and girls.

Joan, in East Troy's *Junior News,* has written an excellent news story about a tiny news event—a dog that was lost for only two hours.

On Friday, November seventeenth, the Mickeets' dog, Lucky, ran away. It was five P.M. when he was lost. However, he came home again all alone two hours later.

Robert Mickeets was taking Lucky for a walk when he got away. Robert had tried to get him but he had scampered away before you could say, "One lost dog."

Father took the car and tried to get him. He chased Lucky in and out the streets. That night at supper no one was very happy. After supper Father went out again and tried to find Lucky. When he came back empty-handed, it sure looked like one lost dog. After awhile a knock came at the door. Mother answered the door, but it was only a lady to see her.

After about ten minutes mother came in and said, "Your dog is hungry." We all rushed to the door to look in Lucky's pen. It looked empty. Then we saw a black and white figure way back in the corner of Lucky's house as if it was hiding. Lucky was back! Later mother told me he had come home alone.

In Joan's news story she followed true newspaper style—gave the whole story in the first paragraph, then retraced her steps and told the whole story again. A true news story is like an inverted pyramid. The most important part of the news story is in the first paragraph. The reason for this is that many hurried readers get no farther than the first paragraph. A good reporter, however, writes his "lead" paragraph so interestingly that the reader just can't help but go on.

Back to our rhyme for one more idea: "Bob and Dick took boats on the pond for a cruise." "What's news in that happening?" you ask Jim. If I were writing about those two boys launching their toy boats on the pond, I'd pretend at first they were real boats. After writing the whole article, I'd give everybody a good laugh by concluding, "Of course, the boats were only toy ones, but Bob and Dick had as much fun as if they were real." That would not be writing it as a straight news story. It would be really what we call a *feature story*. It's real sport to tell a small story as if it were a large one and "let the cat out of the bag" only at the last moment.

There's not a better school newspaper in our state than that published by the Upper Orthopedic School of Madison, Wisconsin. Because such a large number of the children attending this school are polio victims, many of the articles are signed. Here's one signed by Billy!

I don't believe I have ever been as happy as I was the day I came home from school and discovered a (Motorola) TV set at our apartment for me. I knew I was going to get one, but I did not expect it would come so soon. I have been saving my money for it for a year. In fact, I have been the talk of the town for watching my pennies. Long ago I realized the value of money and believed in the old saying, "A penny saved is a penny earned."

I have always been a great radio fan. I kept up with all the world news but I did want a TV set—so I invested my money in one. With the help of some very good adult friends, I got one. I think it is wonderful. I see the people in politics and world affairs while they are speaking. In that way, I remember them better. I see so many wonderful shows, that would probably cost around eighty-five cents, uptown at the theaters. Besides the expense of going to shows, it is a little too hard to get me around. I am not a little guy any more.

I can't think of a single thing bad about TV. However, Miss McKillip can. She says I hurry too much while we are eating our evening meal. She likes to visit while we eat. (You know how women are.) Some of her other complaints are: I keep watching the clock; we cannot get enough algebra done at night; I have "bags" under my eyes; and she can't get her work done because, you see, she likes TV too.

I want to thank those wonderful friends who helped make it possible for me to have a TV set.

Remember to sign the articles in your school paper.

Even though we haven't finished our "start-off rhyme," we'd better think through together what we've learned by now about news.

A news story will hide behind a common-looking exterior unless the reporter hunts it down. After using his legs to find out if the story is really news, the efficient reporter uses its most interesting facet as the lead, writing into his story the answers to our six questions: who, what, when, where, why, and how. Following the lead, the reporter writes the story in detail remembering that a news story must be ready to be cut off at the end of any paragraph to make way for more important items. Up until fifth grade, however, children do not use newspaper style in writing news items and even then, need not so do. Writing style rather than newspaper style is what we are after in the elementary grades.

Remember that even interesting facts can be dull reading if the reporter doesn't write them in an interesting way. It is imagination on the part of the reporter that sees the human interest behind the ordinary happening; news writing is certainly wing-tipped—the writer with the imagination writes the best.

Feature It

What is a feature story? It's a newspaper's "brightener" and "lightener." Feature stories bring us the lighter side of the news, the color, the human interest that make newspaper reading pleasant as well as serious business. Features, like all newspaper stories, report facts, but they are facts that depend for importance on the way they are written. Features report the small news events that are interesting and amusing but seldom of earth-shaking importance. *The number one requirement of a feature story is that it be interesting and unusual.*

What is it that makes a feature story interesting? No *one* thing, of course. Each feature, like each person is interesting for a different reason. Some features are interesting because they're humorous; they make us laugh. You know, everywhere in the world people do funny things every day of the year. And many of those humorous doings find their way into the newspapers as feature stories. Here is an example of a feature story that reports a humorous happening. It's the humor in this story that makes it newsworthy.

I remember clearly the time when our apartment almost caught afire. It was in the morning and Mother and I were still asleep. We smelled smoke coming into the room. We got up and went out into the living room. On the couch lay my brother with six slices of ham in some bread with an unopened coke bottle. We went into the kitchen. There were broken eggs on the floor, the icebox was open and there were things from there on the floor, too. Grillo pads were cooking in a pan—they were supposed to be hamburgers.

Margaret, Grade 4

Some feature stories are helped by names and addresses, but in this story to keep the characters anonymous was real artistry. The antics of small children provide many of the best feature stories. Your little brother or sister usually can provide you with a humorous feature story every week for a school newspaper.

Sad events are just as interesting as the humorous ones. The point to remember is this: (All readers have emotions, and feature stories, most often, appeal to those emotions.) Or to put it differently, news stories are written for the head, but feature stories usually are written for the heart.

Let's think about possible subjects for feature stories. At the top of this list we put people. Probably nothing in the world is quite so interesting to quite so many people as *people*! Famous people, brave people, humorous people, ordinary people—as subjects for features people are "tops."

What a wonderful feature story seventh-grade Sandra wrote about her favorite teacher at school:

When I have a problem that I myself cannot solve, I march right up to my heroine and spill out my troubles. When I'm finished talking to her, my shoulders are broader and my troubles are gone. Her eyes sparkle with understanding, and her personality shines like a neon sign. Everyone loves her; we are attracted to her like bees to honey. When she walks down the school stairs, her long black habit swishes back and forth, her rosary clicking and clacking this way and that. Her long black veil hangs low in the back and encircles her head like a halo. Her smile is as sweet as sugar, and she will always be my own heroine, the classroom Sister.

Sandra, Grade 7

And how about this famous person whom seventh-grade Connie wrote about?

There's a guy sitting down in the third base box, always talking it up. He's a big husky guy usually happy and gay. He always wants his team winning. He is brown almost like an Indian from sitting in the sun. He is always ready to give signals to any of his players. Always saying helping words to some of his players that are at a batting slump or something. But he will always be a friend of his fans in this third base chalking box. He is Charlie Grimm of the Milwaukee Braves.

Connie, Grade 7

Connie doubled the interest of her story by playing a sort of game with her readers—she kept us guessing about the subject of her story until the final line. That's one important difference between a feature story and a news story; a news story must be written according to any pattern that your imagination suggests. A feature may be a poem, a conversation, a riddle, or a story. The form of a feature doesn't matter; it's the way the news is handled that counts. But with any kind of feature, imaginative treatment is the best. Notice how Marshall in junior high seems to make the late Henry Ford real to his readers.

Way back in 1895 when Henry Ford was working on a car, everyone laughed. Henry Ford knew it would work but everybody thought if he made a car that would take the place of a horse—ha! "A miracle!" they said, "A miracle."

So Henry Ford worked and worked. Then one day in 1896 it was here—a new car. He called it a Ford, the first car in America. Henry Ford was proud. He said, "You see, I knew what I was doing. You just wait about ten years. I can see the cars then—so shiny and bright!"

Most readers enjoy features about famous people, people they recognize, people they already know something about. Of course, "famous" may simply mean a person who is well known to your readers. Many of your classmates would fit that description—the captain of your basketball team, the president of your class, the most recent newcomer. Ask questions of people at school and at home, and you'll find plenty of feature stories, all full of interest value.

People are interested in animals as well as in people. For that reason, newspapers carry many animal feature stories. First, help us to see your pet in a quick word picture, as sixth-grade Linda did:

My dog, Butch, is the laziest but cutest cocker spaniel in town. When I throw a stick and say, "Go get it," he looks at me and says, "You mean me?" Then he slowly picks up his long, drooping golden ears and stumbles after it. When he gets back, he's so exhausted he goes to sleep with the simple remark, "Next time get it yourself."

Linda, Grade 6

Some of the very best feature stories are those that relate in some way to major news of the day.

These side lights on a tornado by sixth-grade Judy would provide further interest in a local disaster the readers had read first in the city newspaper.

CLOSE SHAVE

It was a hot, muggy day. The sky was a yellow-green in color and huge gray thunderheads roamed the sky. It was sprinkling a bit, and the wind was coming up. We just happened to have company from California that day.

We all went into the house to watch television and mother started to cook supper on our electric stove. Suddenly the electricity went off. We finally found some candles to give off some light.

Our company thought they had better start for home. We were all settled in bed when a frightening noise was heard at our door. My father got up to see who was there. When he opened the door, in tumbled our company in a panic. When they finally calmed down, Mr. Wozalo said this, "We were not more than down the street when we saw a streetcar split right down the middle."

They told us that all the streets were flooded with torrents of water. The next morning we went out to find one whole side of our garage missing, trees broken, and not more than six blocks from our house a whole shopping center was flattened out.

When I found we had sideswiped a tornado, and it had whipped and torn by at a hundred miles an hour I was very excited, but relieved, too.

Judy, Grade 6

For your own newspaper, you might write a feature story about something that happened backstage just before the class play opened. The feature would appear in the same issue of your newspaper in which the class play's opening night is reported in a regular news story. Or what about the basketball team? Your paper reports all the games, but does it also offer the reader little "behind-the-scenes" stories about the team: how the players train; which player is the tallest; which the shortest; what size shoes the players wear? Put your mind to it and you'll think of dozens of feature stories to write about the basketball team. Think about the news story you wrote last week: is there another story in it, a "behind-the-scenes" story that you might write in feature form this week?

There's another kind of feature story different from all those I've mentioned. This is the feature that gives the reader information—information on how to do things, information on places of interest to visit, or just fascinating facts about many things. For this kind of feature, the reporter must gather facts from reference books and textbooks. For example, Jim wrote this about superstitions involving cats. It's a fine feature story.

There are a lot of superstitions about cats. In Japan, if a man killed a cat, a curse would fall on his family and him for seven generations. The Chinese believed that cats had great wisdom. The devil was often pictured as a black cat. Even today some people believe that a black cat brings bad luck.

Jim's story would be especially suitable for a newspaper published at Halloween time.

But Mary's feature story about cats would be suitable any time of the year. Notice that Mary wrote her feature in verse form.

> The cat is graceful and oh, so proud!
> Its fur is fluffy and soft like a cloud.
> It possesses sharp retractable claws,
> You know there are five on all four paws.
> Three pairs of incisors in each jaw,
> Each one as sharp as a little claw.
> They swallow their food without first chewing,
> Kittens call for dinner with lots of mewing.

These are fascinating facts about cats! But there are other subjects equally good as feature story material. A sixth-grade class I know stumbled onto a wealth of feature story material when they were searching for a name for their class newspaper. They started out by making a list of every newspaper name they'd ever heard. They got quite a list: *Tribune, Star, Sun, Argus, Guardian, Times, Leader, Monitor, News, Globe, Transcript, Record,* and so many others. Their search led them to many interesting bits of history and mythology, facts behind those newspaper names, which they uncovered in dictionaries and reference books.

The word *Argus,* for example, they found went back centuries and centuries to a Greek myth. Jupiter, the king of the Greek gods, had changed a maiden into a young cow. Juno, his queen, was jealous of the girl and set a monster with a hundred eyes to watch her. That many-eyed monster was named Argus. Do you see why Argus is a good name for a newspaper? A newspaper is like a hundred watchful eyes searching out the facts to bring to the people. And do you see why this search for a newspaper name uncovered a wealth of feature story material? The name you chose for your newspaper or the name of your town's paper may have a history. Find out and write up your findings for your readers' information.

Feature stories are usually not dependent on time or place for interest; their sole reason for being read is that they are interesting. Practically any item can become a good feature if we make it interesting; if we make it imaginative; if we make it funny or sad; if we make it true; and if we say it with engaging words.

Never a day does by at any school without material for several feature stories. But it takes imagination on the part of the reporter to see the feature behind the news story. It takes leg work and imagination to be a feature writer.

It's My Opinion

Do you like Language? Why do we have to learn how to talk all over again? We have to learn spelling and arithmetic in order to get a job when we are older. But we aren't going to sit and write all day. I think it's a waste of time learning the opposites and nouns. The same with social studies; we aren't going into the centuries past when we get older; we're going into the future. So why do we have to sit for a half of an hour every day and study the history of some countries thousands of miles away?

Bob, Grade 6

No matter whether you agree with Bob's views or not, his editorial for a school newspaper is a good reminder that it's healthy to have differing opinions. Our country was built on the theory that every man and woman has a right to his own opinion. Back in 1787, when our government was being planned, a lot of leaders thought the common people didn't have judgment enough to rule themselves. They thought George Washington ought to be a king instead of a president. But those who believed in the people worked until government was placed in the hands of the people. All through the history of our country, great men have worked to give the right of a voice in the government to everyone no matter how different or unpopular his opinion may be. And that's a value we must cling to in our free America.

We're going to have a lot of different opinions in this article— opinions you may not agree with. For example, Lorene has an unusual opinion of cats. All you cat lovers will probably get your backs up in true feline style when you hear what she has to say in her article:

MY OPINION OF CATS

I dislike cats because they haven't as much talent as other pets. Dogs can become good watch dogs. A lamb can be the most beautiful pet, if you keep it nice with a ribbon around its neck. Horses are good riding pets. You can teach a dog tricks and a dog is man's best friend. A dog can save you from being hurt, but cats are no good. You can see a glow of mystery in their eyes.

Lorene, Grade 5

This is a good piece of writing; Lorene is a fifth grader and she certainly knows how to write her opinions forcibly and clearly.

What I particularly like, though, about Lorene's article is that she labeled it correctly. She called it "My Opinion of Cats." You know, there is a difference between opinion and fact. A fact about a cat is a statement that is definitely true; for example, cats have tails, cats have four paws, cats like milk. These are all facts about cats.

Here is a quotation from another paper, this one by Janet: "Because of a vertical slit with a pin hole at each end, a cat can see very well in the dark." That statement about cats is a fact. If you say cats are a big nuisance, you are giving an opinion, as Bob did in his paper about studying certain subjects. In a newspaper, articles that give opinion are usually put on a separate page so readers will know they are reading opinion, not fact.

There are several kinds of newspaper articles that give opinions. There is a column written by a columnist. His articles are always signed with his name so you know you are reading the opinion of one man. Every grade or at least every school has at least one person who could write a good, chatty column for the school newspaper. Readers may express their opinions, too, in the "Letters to the Editor" section. Sometimes you can even find opinions expressed in the comic strips of a newspaper. And always you find opinion in a newspaper's editorials, the opinion of the paper's editor or editorial board.

In an editorial you try to state your opinion so well that you can change the opinion of readers who differ with you. Here's an editorial I found in the *Saturday Review* written by 13-year-old David Alexander. Some of you boys will not agree with David's opinion of fishing, but you'll enjoy his different point of view.

Some people like fishing trips. I am not one of these. I do not like the trip to the fishing spot; I do not like sitting still in the boat; I do not like baiting the hook. In fact, the only thing I like about fishing is the smell of fried fish rolled in corn meal coming to me by Mother Natcher's soft breezes.

A fishing trip to me is just a waste of time. Who wants to go on a fishing trip and not catch any fish and be bored for the rest of the afternoon? When one is fishing he could be playing tennis or golf. Then go for a swim in a pool or drink coca cola or pop.

There are some more proofs and one is the distance which must be covered to the fishing spot. If you travel a long distance to get there you will be tired out and might have cramps in your legs. You will wish instead of gazing at scenery for the afternoon you could be watching television and rest your eyes.

The trouble about getting a boat is that it is such a nuisance. You either have to rent a boat or buy one. The rented boat might be unsafe but you can't try it out until you are in it and that is too late. Then, too, the boat that you wanted especially might be out with someone else, so you wait and waste more time waiting. In fact, a fishing trip has more waiting than fishing.

Some people like the long ride to the fishing place and sitting still in a boat. Some people think it is worth the time and money. I think they have a right to their own views, but I want no part of their vacation. Count me out.[3]

Did you notice that in David's editorial he not only said he didn't like fishing but also explained why? In an editorial you must explain why you have your opinion. For example, if you simply say, "I don't like snow," you have expressed an opinion, but you are not going to convince anyone else. To change the opinions of other people, you have to tell why you think your opinion is good. Here's an editorial by Tommy, who is in the fourth grade. Notice how he gives reasons for his opinion.

I want to play tackle football but our school won't let us. But do you know you can get hurt just as easy when you are crossing the street or riding a bike? So why can't we play tackle? It isn't going to hurt the teacher because we're the ones who are playing. Anyway, they have insurance on it. I know why they won't let us play because they are afraid we will get hurt. What do you think?

Tommy, Grade 4

Tommy certainly was upset about the football situation in his school but not too upset to give some of the reasons for his opinion. Don't use an editorial just to complain. Give reasons and facts about your subject. Facts are important in editorials as well as in news stories because it's the facts that prove opinions. After you have

[3] By David Alexander. Courtesy of *Saturday Review*.

stated your opinion and presented your facts, try to offer a solution to the problem you're discussing.

When you write your editorials, try to give them an interesting beginning. In an editorial you should capture the attention of the reader immediately. The following editorial written by Christine in the sixth grade has a very interesting beginning. Notice, too, that near the close of her article she offers some suggestions that might correct the situation she's writing about. That's an important part of an editorial—the suggested solution.

Ways of Peace

"Who's got my sweater?" shouted Mary. "Mother, Susan's got my sweater."

These words may sound ugly and not very pleasant, but do you know that you yourself have probably said those very same words? Do you know that these words may cause a war? Not a big war, but a war. Mary could have asked Susan in a nice way to give back her sweater. We, too, can say and do things in a peaceful way instead of shouting.

Everyone has heard the words, *War* and *Peace,* but does everyone know what war and peace mean? We say and talk about these things, and then we go off and forget them. We're too busy to think about *Good Manners.*

Many accidents occur when Good Manners are forgotten. Maybe Bill was hit with a stone and his eye was taken out. All your classmates were so sorry for him. No one thought it could have been his own fault. No one knew that Bill himself was calling names and throwing stones. One of the stones hit the school building, bounced back and hit Bill in the eye, causing the accident. Remember this, it may teach others, and yourself to use your manners and help make peace. Don't just talk about it; think about it, too. Make your school and home more pleasant to be in.

Christine, Grade 6

Your editorials may take many forms; you may write them in prose, as Christine did, or you may want to write in verse, as this fifth grade of a village school in Wisconsin did:

Where Shall We Play on a Rainy Day?

Where shall we play on a rainy day?
Stay off the front yard the teachers all say.
You are pushed, kicked and shoved all around.
When almost two hundred children all
Want to be on solid ground.

Don't shout on the stairs or run down the hall.
Now just see! You made that little boy bawl!
These commands ring in our ears from morning till night,
What can we do that is really all right?

Some newspapers have a special section in which people can express their opinions in poetry. They also have a special section in which readers can express their opinions in the form of letters.

Billy has written a letter about a problem common to hundreds of you who travel to school by bus. His letter concerns the question, "How shall you act on the school bus?"

As you read Billy's letter, notice that it needs a summary first sentence such as: "The behavior in our school bus is disgraceful," or "If each person who rides the school bus would pretend for a minute that he was the bus driver, conditions on our bus would certainly change." Notice also how Billy persuades you to see his point of view by asking forceful questions.

Some people throw clothes, some keep their feet out in the aisle, some stand up, some hit other people, and some shout. If you were the bus driver, would you like all the noise and have someone get hurt by standing up? Would you like to fall by someone keeping his feet out in the aisle? Would you like to freeze because someone threw your coat out? I have seen almost all of these happen and there are more of them. Watch and see if you can catch anyone doing these things tonight. If we all do that, we will solve these problems.

The purpose of any editorial or letter to the editor is to get people to think, and Billy's letter does just that. Remember, to get other people to think, you'll have to do some thinking yourself. First of all you have to think of a subject for your editorial and then you have to think about your opinion. But you should have more than an opinion before you start writing. You should have facts and a possible solution for your problem. When you have thought all this out, you are ready to decide what form you will use: straight prose editorial, a poem, or a letter.

I'm sure you won't have any trouble thinking of opinions to express, but if you can't think of one right away, take a look at your school or playground. Who is always borrowing pencils or paper? Is there another subject you'd like to be able to study in school? Or is there a subject you would like to do away with? On your playground, do the same people always get the swings or the basketballs? Is there a bully who pushes the little ones around? Theresa's school has a real problem. Perhaps yours has a similar one:

The patrol boys, I think, are letting their work go and are starting to take it easy. The other night I left school a little late. When I got to the corner, the boys were throwing snowballs across the street. These are a few things that bother me. What time are the patrol boys off duty? Can the children pick up snow? If not, why do the patrols do it? The patrol boys are beginning to set a bad example for the little kids.

Theresa, Grade 7

Or is there something you detest doing? Do you simply hate to milk cows; shovel snow; take care of your little brother or sister? Do you hate to be kissed by your relatives? With David, it's practicing his music.

I think practicing is worthwhile to a certain extent, but when it comes to slave labor that's the limit. Siberia is nothing compared to an hour and a half of working your fingers and your lips to the point where you think they are going to fall off. I come home for lunch, practicing . . . after dinner, practicing! I go to bed at night. What do I dream about? Practicing! Books are black and white. What do they remind me of? Practicing! I go to orchestra. What do we get there? Practicing! There's a trumpet at the bottom of every glass of milk I drink. I could be playing football and get everything knocked off. But no, I'm practicing and getting my fingers knocked off.

David, Grade 8

Whatever your opinion is—write it out and you'll feel better. Imagination is the right-hand man of opinion writing. Just imagine you are making your complaint directly to the person who should know, then talk it off—without excitement or abuse.

Perhaps these rhymed directions will help you in writing some opinions:

> Whether at home, on the street, or at school,
> In writing opinions, observe this rule;
> Never make your opponent feel like a fool—
> Don't call him names—though they be true.
> He has the right to opinions as well as you.
> When a person is angry his mind zips up tight,
> And you cannot change him whatever you write.
> Make him see the other fellow's point of view
> And the chances are that before you are through
> He'll see the thing, the way you do!

At least that is my opinion!

Written and Oral Book Reports

We might as well face the fact that teachers dislike ordinary book reports as much as children do. It's the hard work after the fun is over that is the root of this dislike, I believe. And yet, catching and transmitting to others the spirit and story of a book is a skill we need all our lives.

How can we get rid of the tedium of book reports for both teachers and children?

"Will you have your tedium rare or medium?" [4] chortles Ogden Nash. I believe that in report writing we can have tedium rare or not at all.

An imaginative touch to a book report and a variety of ways of reporting can change book reporting from an onerous task to a challenge.

Consider the thinking, the imagining and the real fun involved in giving a report on a book in one of the following ways:

1. Pretend to be a character of the book and tell about the book and the author.

2. Put on a pretend television or radio show in which each speaker does his part to advertise the good qualities of a book (complete with props).

3. Have imaginary interviews with an author or book character. (Here two children work together, with a slower child asking the questions the two have devised, and the gifted child doing the answering.)

4. Have a child interview several children who have read the book, discussing the high lights and their opinions of the book as a whole.

5. Make and show a homemade movie of the story.

6. Have several who have read the book dramatize one of the scenes from the book.

7. Make a series of pictures and use them to explain the book.

8. Several children make a display box or diorama of a scene from a book.

9. Have several children read aloud outstanding passages and descriptions from the book and comment on each passage read.

10. Have a child who is interested in words explain fifteen new words he learned from a book he read, reading the words in context to help explain them. If the child is artistic, he may want to illus-

---

[4] Reprinted by permission of the author, Ogden Nash. Copyright © 1948 by The Curtis Publishing Company.

trate some of the words ahead of time and act out or show commercial pictures of others.

11. Discuss and compare two books on the same subject (horses, for instance) but by different authors.

12. Write one's own story from a book title; then after reading the book, show the class the difference in the two plots.

13. Write a <u>scenario</u> of the story (gifted child).

14. Write a different ending for the story.

15. Two children work together, one sketching portraits of the book characters, the other writing pen portraits.

16. A child writes a first-person account of a scene or chapter in the book, told by the author in third person.

17. Write another chapter or episode for the author's book in keeping with the characters the author has created.

18. Write a letter of appreciation to the author, telling him why you like his book and enclosing the extra episode or short, new chapter that you have written.

19. Write your report as a narrative poem.

20. Write or talk the dramatization for a puppet show based on the book.

There! If you post these suggestions, together with your ideas for imaginative book reports, and ask the children to choose a different one each time, book-report time may be truly exciting.

But should all books be reported on? I wonder . . .

> I love books;
> I need them
> I purr with pleasure
> When I read them,
> But if a teacher said,
> "You'll write reports
> On every book you've read,"
> Indeed,
> I doubt that I would read.

> A good way
> To get a child today
> To hate books
> Is to say,
> "Write a report!"
> No retort—
> Quick decision—
> They just resort
> To television.

Book reports or no book reports? And if reports, what kind of reports? Oh, this reporting business poses as many questions as a three-year-old.

"Use common sense about the number, and imagination about the report" would seem to settle most of the arguments about book reports. I, personally, believe in high standards for the few written and oral reports required, but I would never spoil anything as precious as the love of reading books with too many mechanical checks. Can one measure sunbeams dancing on a window sill?

Would sixth-grade Lynn have written this tribute to books if she had had to report on every one she read? I wonder.

BOOKS

Books take you through mysteries,
Books take you through romance.
Books lead you up through outer space
With just one little glance.

Books take you through the history
Of cave men, long ago.
That's more than one could ever find
In a TV show.

Lynn, Grade 6

One of the best book reports that has come to my attention was this bit of creative writing by fifth-grade Christine:

One day last year I was reading a wonderful book. It was about an orphan boy who lived in Korea. I was sitting in my bedroom on my nice, bouncy bed, by the spic-and-span white curtains at the windows. I had been playing with my dolls. They were all over the floor. Just the day before, I had been sort of pitying myself because I didn't have as many nice things to wear and play with as other kids I know. The book I am reading really opened my eyes to a great lesson: "Be thankful for what you have and don't pity yourself for what you don't have."

I think I was as thankful then for what I have as I have ever been.

Christine, Grade 5

PRACTICAL WRITING IS

Writing is a two-way conversation,
Made possible by winged imagination.
Because the "written to" is seldom near,
It takes imagination to be clear;
One must anticipate his unasked questions
Must be aware of his unmade suggestions
Must talk in conversations; not in platitudes;
Must feel his feelings; sense his coming attitudes;
Must know his type of mind; his hidden ways
Must answer every argument he'd raise.
Yes, writing is a two-way conversation
Made possible by winged imagination.

Creative Imagination Can Be Developed in Children

I. Through Games and Exercises

Creative imagination that starts with facts that are and swings
out on a gossamer thread to facts that may become can be developed
as any other skill is developed—through exercise. Most little children are imaginative, but few are willing to spend all day at the
typewriter as six-year-old Neil did to write a story he had in his
mind. By calling downstairs often for spelling help, this is Neil's
story together with an added note which he typed on the back of
the paper.

THE NIGHT BEFORE NEW YEAR

Once upon a time there was a flying Old Year going to Africa, where
the oil is under the ground and the King of Years lived there. He was the
one who changed the male years into female years. Then the female year
would fly to a cloud between Africa and America. She would go up in the
cloud and rest. She would be there 20 minutes before 12 o'clock. At 10
minutes before 12 o'clock she would have a male New Year. Then the
male would go by people's houses and take a fast look in the windows
and look in the stockings that were hung by the windows. Then he would
look at the note that was in the stocking. After this, he would go back up
to the cloud where he was born. Then at the strict of 12 o'clock he make
every wish that were in the stockings come true.

If you want the New Year to come by your house be sure to go to sleep
before 11:30 o'clock. Happy New Year to you.

NOTE ON BACK: The female year when she gets old the cloud she was in, goes in the ocean then the old female year goes deep under the ocean wear the oil is, and then she takes a long nap and never awakes.

Here's the way the New Year makes your wish, if you ask him to give you a bike he will help you earn it or make it.

Notice how a young child's creating is a lacing together of irrelevant facts and vague impressions gleaned during his short life and put together to form a strange new story of his own. Most young children use plots and ideas similar to those in the tales they have heard read or have listened to over the radio and television.

Parents can have fun with young children playing such imaginative games as "Where am I and what am I doing?" While the parent pretends, the child gets ten guesses: "You're on a rocket going to the moon and you're playing dolls," or "you're sitting out on the lower limb of that tree playing horse," or "you're rocking in the crescent moon, counting stars." Another version of the same game begins with a definite spot such as "You are visiting grandmother on the farm. What are you doing? What fun are you having?" or "We are sliding on a snowy hill with Jimmy and Ned. What happens then?"

Third-grade Carol has this answer for the question: "You're out in the yard watching the birdbath. What is happening?"

> But I think it very funny
> The birdies like their birdbath
> Because the birds brought with them
> Two squirrels and a bunny.

> *Carol, Grade 3*

Fifth-grade Berry made this response to the suggestion: "You are a spring flower with a problem. What happens?"

DOWN OR UP

I am a bulb of a flower and I have a problem. I can't decide which way to go. It will be a miracle if I don't end up upside down in China. If that would happen all my chlorophyll would rush to the top of me or the bottom of me. Anyway the top of me is on the straight side of the world. I'm going to figure it out and take the way I think is right.

Okay! I'm going this way. I sure hope I'm going the right way. There I made it! It is a miracle—my first miracle!

> *Berry, Grade 5*

In school such imaginative exercises as the Pretends listed in the Cupboard of Ideas for Chapter Seven, pages 266 and 270, certainly help to develop the imagination. But such exercises need idea exchanges between classmates before writing time; some children are much less imaginative than others.

Take this idea, for instance, from the poem "If I Had Wings" by Marchette Chute in *Rhymes about the Country*. Talk with the children about some of the places they could go if they were two inches tall and had wings. You may get answers like these: rode on a leaf in a rain pool; had a race with a dragonfly; rode a slippery fish like a bronco. One learns a great deal from listening to or reading what the children wish to do; the timid ones almost always wish to do whatever they would not have the courage to attempt even if they might.

Pamela in fourth grade says:

> I want to drift on a cloud,
> And see the things that don't exist,
> Like a story from fairy tale land,
> As Jack in the Beanstalk,
> Or the Giant so wild,
> Just in Fairy Tale Land.

Pamela, Grade 4

Of course, there is always the puckish sense of humor such as David has:

> If I had wings
> And was two inches tall,
> I'd fly to the cookie jar
> And eat it all.

David, Grade 6

In kite time children have especial fun pretending to be kites that have adventures—getting tangled in trees, talking to clouds, tasting a cloud, getting lost, getting stranded on a bird's nest. After the paint-mixing of words that describe how kites float through the air, you will get from grades three to six some of the most imaginative writings you ever received.

A Kite's Tale

As I went sailing through the sky, a funny feeling went through my paper-made skin. My stick bones seemed out of place. Then I knew what was wrong. My tail was loose. I bent down to tie it and before I even got hold of it, it was scurrying down to earth. I didn't know what to do. In front of me was that horrible looking rain cloud and in back was a telephone pole. I dodged the rain cloud by an inch. I was safe or was I? For in front of me now was a big spruce tree. I tried to escape. Crash! Bang! Rattle! Rattle! Clank! I was sitting in a sparrow's nest. Before I knew what was happening, Mrs. Sparrow was pecking away at me. A squirrel was taking what little stick bones I had left. In a few minutes it was all done. And I was, too. Now I'm spending the rest of my life in Heaven. It sure is peaceful, but I still haven't all of the needles out of my paper-made skin from falling into the spruce tree.

Judy, Grade 6

II. Through Listening to Music

Stories or sketches written while listening to music are usually the most imaginative of all children's writing. Explain to the children to let their minds "sit loose" and let the stories come as the music plays. These are a few of the children's responses to music:

It was a gay day but still the silvery raindrops came tumbling down-down-down. Then the silvery little drops or silver dancing elves and fairies disappeared from sight. As I looked around, I saw a big yellow ball in the sky. I was standing in a pasture of green.

I looked to the sky again. I also saw seven colors—orange, indigo, violet, yellow, red, blue and green. On each color, I saw thousands of those silvery drops standing, crying and waving goodbye. I heard them say very faintly and in a sad voice, "Goodbye, see you another day."

Pamela, Grade 5

I think I'm playing the music, and in some music I think I'm dancing to it. I feel it in my heart. The swaying of the music. It feels so touching, that I like to play music all the time. I wish everyone loved music as I do. I love to dance to music. When I'm alone I make my own music. I love the way the notes go from one to the other. I love to play my records over and over. I sing and dance to the music.

Jennifer, Grade 3

One day a sad little duck was walking along near the shore. The water was icy and the duck hadn't had anything to eat for three days and was starved. A great big snow blizzard was coming and where could he go? He had no home.

After the blizzard I saw the duck lying there. He did not move.

Marlea, Grade 5

Countless years ago, millions of years ago, there lived in a great deep canyon some music that had been trapped inside. Each hundredth year the music would attempt to get out of the canyon by making high pitches to shatter the invisible cover. Normally the music was low—that made it hard. It tried. Up, up, up, it came over the scale seven times! Going higher and higher, then boom, bang, crack, tinkle. The cover broke. The music was free, free! A young boy found the music resting by the edge of the canyon. The music went back to its low tone but now it had a beautiful echo. The boy called it: "The Music of the Canyon!"

Gerald, Grade 5

The music took my mind back to my great-grandfather. It took my mind back to when he was young and handsome. To when he was married to Grandmother. And when he was holding me in his own arms when I was a baby. And I got a kick out of it when he played with me. And I wonder what he was like when he was a boy.

Then I thought about what he was like when he went to school and what kind of books he had. What he had for Christmas and what he had for Thanksgiving. I wonder when his birthday was.

Donnie, Grade 4

III. Through Acting Out Problems in Creative Play and Creative Dramatics

From purely imaginative stories to realistic social problems is a natural step. First have groups of children act out how they would meet one of these situations, then weave their idea into a story, using such common problems as these:

1. You are at a friend's house and accidentally break a cup without your hostess's knowing. What do you do about the accident?

2. You see a woman in a store take something without paying for it. What is your move in the matter?

3. You are with a group of children who decide they are going to pile trash in front of a crippled man's door. What can or should you do about it?

4. For a joke a gang decides to "borrow" a car temporarily. What's your reaction here?

5. A strange youngster, poorly dressed, has just entered your school as a new pupil. How do you react?

Creative play in primary grades, creative dramatics in intermediate grades, and role-playing in junior high school will help children to work out, imaginatively, better answers to their real problems. A teacher with awareness of the children's needs will submit the right suggestions at the right moment.

IV. Through Teaching History Three-Dimensionally

The teacher who can get children to feel that they actually are living the history they are studying has done more toward developing good citizens than he often realizes. Starting with the problems people face today and finding a parallel in past history help children to identify themselves with the past. There is certainly a correlation between moderns getting ready for space travel and pioneers getting ready to go to Oregon and California. Here are several lessons on how to make history real:

A. Covered wagon tales, a creative writing lesson for grades four to eight based on pioneer experiences when going West in covered wagon days.

Assignment: Write in prose or poetry form or in diary form an adventure story you might have experienced on a trip to the Oregon country in pioneer days.

Introduction:

1. Discuss such books as Armstrong Sperry's *Wagons Westward* and Honoré Willsie Morrow's *On to Oregon,* suggesting why the children might enjoy them.

2. Read Arthur Guiterman's rolling musical poem "The Oregon Trail," a real "thriller" of a poem. In between verses talk a bit about what the pioneers went through.

3. Read the description of the western country from *Wagons Westward* and end with the hero's sleeping under the stars.

4. Read the old trapper's tale from *Wagons Westward* about the "putrified forest" (it is so funny). Suggest that the class try humor in their stories if they wish.

Have children exchange ideas:
1. Indian stories
2. Buffalo hunt (Read about Jonathan's buffalo hunt in *Wagons Westward*.)
3. One of the oxen might have a calf.
4. You might find an Indian child in your wagon.
5. You might have a wagon tip over while fording a stream.

How to make the story real:
1. Put in your own feelings and how they affect your horse and the action.
2. Show strong feeling with short, excited sentences.

Summary of writing tips:
1. Write to a real audience.
2. Feel that you are there.

Sample writings from this assignment:

WESTWARD ADVENTURE

I was going to California. I was about halfway there, when we had an Indian attack. We made a circle. They were about to attack us when we got ready. But really it wasn't an attack. They wanted to trade with us. The chief came to me and said, "Ug head," which I thought meant jug head. So I gave him a piece of my mind. Next time when I saw him it was an attack. We circled again and got ready. They circled us and shot arrows at us. The chief was after me the most. I was a pretty bad shot most of the time but a poor shot saved a person. I was coming for the chief and I shot and killed a brave that was just about to kill one of my men. We finally beat the Indians and got to California.

James, Grade 4

AN ORPHAN OF THE WEST

I was walking along side our wagon one day.
When I saw a herd of wild horses eating hay.
Then I saw a colt with his mother lying at his side.
For when he was born, she must have died.
When we came closer they all ran away.
Except for the little one who was eating the hay.

So we took him along to our new home.
And now he is no longer alone.
So now he's here right under my saddle.
And helps me a lot in herding pa's cattle.

Jeff, Grade 6

AFTER A DAY'S TRAVEL

The caterpillar train moved slowly
Its armor of white swayed back and forth
The welcoming smile of the fire
Made the settlers feel at home.

The circle of the wagons had just been made
The pots and kettles are starting to tattle
About the things Ma and Pa hadn't seen
And doubted they'd ever know.

The children are resting their weary bones
Listening to the tales of the old
Telling of the Indian raids
Or the capturing of Black-Eyed Jones.

At the break of day all was at ease
Quiet and still was the unseeable air
Comforting the old and young alike
That were going west, yes, going west.

Diane, Grade 7

COVERED WAGON TALES

I tell you, partner, when I was a whippersnapper like you, we were
on the Oregon trail going to Oregon. Our oxen ran away and there we
sat. I don't know what happened to Ma and Pa but here I am.

Mark, Grade 3

PEOPLE OF THE TRAILS

The rutted roads and dusty trails,
The rumbling wagons and clanking pails,
The mighty rivers, the roaring streams,
The coyote's howl and the cougar's screams.

The lonely nights, the barren days,
The steady rhythm of the wagon's sways:
The endless seas of buffalo herds
The graceful swoop of the vulture birds.

The tough characteristics of the bronzed men
The tough of courageous women, so feminine;
The excited children running to and fro,
Wagons moving slowly moving on the go.

How little you knew of what you did
You opened the West, took off the lid;
I wish you could see the trails that you made
What you did when you worked and when you prayed.

Marie, Grade 8

THE SECRET DIARY OF GRANDMOTHER FOLTZ

June 4, 1847

DEAR DIARY,

As the wheels rolled over the dusty road, I thought of how uncivilized this country is. For a girl like me, one of twelve, it's too adventurous. I hate adventure!

June 5, 1847

DEAR DIARY,

Today wasn't bad, no Indian attacks and we have enough food to feed an Army. And that's unusual! No adventure today. And that's just the way I like it! I guess I'm just lazy.

June 6, 1847

DEAR DIARY,

We went to "Fort Caladryl" today. But I don't know why.

I don't feel so on edge today, I guess it's 'cause Daddy said if we should be attacked, Colonel Grayson of Fort Caladryl would help us. Since we haven't had too much trouble, Colonel Grayson said we should expect some soon!

Oh, I hate all this excitement. I wish I were at home where I could snuggle up in a chair and read a real good book.

[June seventh, eighth, ninth and tenth have gone by and there is no written record for these days. The diary begins again on June eleventh.]

June 11, 1847

DEAR DIARY,

I guess Colonel Grayson was right; we were attacked June 7, and I've been caring for the wounded ever since. That's why I haven't written to you.

After we had left Fort Caladryl, we traveled about five more miles. On the morn of June 7, we were attacked. When I saw those men, although outnumbered, fight for what they wanted and believed in, I realized how selfish I had been. Always grumbling—I'm surprised they didn't drop me off some place and leave me! Oh, I forgot, Dear Diary, today is my thirteenth birthday. I guess I feel different about those things today because I'm so happy. But maybe, Dear Diary, could it possibly be that I'm growing up?

Marylin, Grade 7

A CLOSE SHAVE

This is the day, June 21, 1821, 6:30 A.M. I saddled up my horse, Black Foot, and rode out to join the other group of men. There were three of us. Jim, twenty-one, Buck, fifteen, and me, Bill, thirteen.

We were out for an adventure in hunting the giant "Buffalo." We rode out of the wagon train at 6:45, just as the cool breeze of the morning air hit us. We rode for about fifteen minutes and then heard a rumbling noise. We hurried to an overlooking bluff to see the whole valley swarming with stampeding buffalo. I wouldn't of minded it very much but they were heading for your wagon train.

I gave Black Foot the lead and raced ahead of the tangling mass of fur and reached the train just before they were going to get rolling. I could see the buffalo about three miles away and coming hard. They swarmed over the nolls like water rushing over land. We kicked the train into a dead run and headed for the river about one quarter mile away.

You may of thought we made it in plenty of time but I tell you the side of the herd just missed us by about one hundred feet. As for Jim and Buck had to wait for the herd to pass before setting out to find what they thought was the remains of the wagon train. But instead found a campfire burning brightly and all wagons in a tight circle. The pioneers of the early days had to endure great dangers like that. Some weren't so lucky.

Bob, Grade 8

B. Rhyme-a-story, a lesson on how to write a modern ballad in several ways.

Assignment: Write a story or ballad in rhyme if possible; if not, in rhythmic prose.

Introduction: Begin with a simple rhymed story. The old woman in the nursery rhyme who "went to market her eggs to sell" is an especially good one. Although it's so simple, it is a perfectly rhymed story.

Analyze the plot:

1. It is built around just one exciting episode or happening. Ballads don't wander all over the place; they tell a story about one episode or plot.

2. It has conversation to make it interesting. Some ballads are all questions and answers.

3. It has rhythm; you can tap it out with your finger. Ballads were first sung by wandering minstrels; accordingly, they usually have a marked rhythm or inner tune.

4. It can easily have a chorus added between the stanzas. You can work out one with the students, either a loony-tuney one or one with sense. This one would be a combination of both.

> Oh, tippi down tippi, aye aye;
> She fell asleep on the king's highway.

To illustrate each of the four points use another ballad or storytelling poem. A good ballad with conversation in it would be "The Two Sisters of Binnorie." Explain the ancient marriage customs that so often caused murder in families with several marriageable daughters. This ancient ballad is really a news headline made into a song as calypso so often is, but calypso has far less story than a ballad. Point out how in this story poem the harp made from the dead sister's hair sang and gave the murderer away. A mystical ending was usual to ancient ballads; ballads may have started out true, but as they ripened, the stories grew. Find other examples of mystical lines in old ballads.

A good poem for learning to tap out rhythm is Laura E. Richards' delightful "A Ballad of China," which is a true ballad because it is a story that persists in singing itself.

A good storytelling poem is Aileen Fisher's "The Pirate's Cake" or Ogden Nash's "The Tale of Custard, the Dragon."

Suggestions for ballad subjects:

1. Current happenings: The *Nautilus* sails under polar ice; moon satellites; shots at the moon.
2. History tales that appeal to children: "Old Ironsides," "Paul Revere's Ride," and so on.
3. Stories of ancient heroes and gods
4. Funny situations
5. Folk tales
6. School heroes; heroes of screen and radio
7. Storybook heroes
8. Famous animals

Ballad-making puts reality into fiction and drama into fact. *Sample writings from this assignment:*

FORGOTTEN

(Written about an old house in Mary's home town)

For years and years no one has lived there,
It stands forgotten, unloved, and bare.
The tall, white pillars are all that remain
Of the beauty and love which they ought to proclaim.
The lawn out in front is chocked by weeds,
It smothers the beauty of youth and its deeds.
The house remembers it all quite well,
Also the fact that it housed a belle.
The belle of them all! That was Annette.
It also recalls when the two lovers met.
Annette with her long, soft black hair,
Was the fairest of all that was fair.
She wore a long, flowing white organdy dress;
Made by the seamstress, the aged Bess.
White slippers covered white stockinged feet;
All together she was perfect and sweet.
Her hands were covered with white kid gloves,
As white as the throats of white turtle doves.
The red velvet ribbon around her throat,
Was imported from France on a clipper boat.
With these two young folks it was "love at first sight,"
But Annette was to cry before the coming of night.
As one o'clock, two o'clock, three o'clock came,
The boys got involved in a bad poker game.
Four o'clock, five o'clock, just about six,
Two boys picked up their dueling sticks.
Back to the orchard they marched with teeth set,
They had gone too far with that terrible bet.

Tom, Annette's lover, stood poised with his gun,
The other man stood with his back to the sun.
Then a shot pierced the air and someone fell dead.
Annette ran to Tom and lifted his head.
The funeral was held on the very next day,
And the day after that Annette moved away.
Now, they say on October the twenty-third,
A shot and someone crying may often be heard.

For years and years no one has lived there,
It stands forgotten, unloved, and bare,
The tall white pillars are all that remain,
Of the beauty and love which they ought to proclaim
The lawn out in front is chocked by weeds
It smothers the beauty of youth and its deeds.

Mary, Grade 8

GONE WITH THE SEA

Aboard her old and sea-washed deck
Stood the captain grim and erect.
In the tiny crow's nest
Crouched the guard, taking a rest.

All at once the guard cried
"Enemy ship on starboard side."
All the crew clambered out
To see what the commotion was all about.

Then suddenly the captain said:
"We'll shoot till the crew is stiff and dead.
Then we'll burn her up until
That crow in his nest is burnt to the bill."

The captain said, "Use your fire arrows
We'll burn out the cockeyed sparrows."
But there's one thing the captain didn't know,
He was fighting a famous foe.

It was *Old Ironside,* of course
And also her expert fighting force.
Even before the fight was over
The *Ironside* crew finished that sea rover.

John, Grade 7

Go, Boy, Go!

Go west, boy, and never go slow,
Plow through the mud, the rain and the snow.
Ya gotta, boy, so go, boy, go.

The dust may get you wild,
And the rain may get you mad
But go, boy, go, you can't stop now
Keep up that spirit, boy, and you'll be glad.

To reach the golden sunset
That goes down in the west.
Go, boy, go and don't forget
That the west is always the best!

The Indians may get you scared
But keep on going, boy, keep on going
There are many of men that wouldn't have dared
But keep on going, boy, you ain't scared.

The rumblin' of the squeekin' wheels
And the howl of the wolf
Keep on rollin', boy, keep on rollin'
Keep on walkin' and warin' down those heels.

If you ever get there don't forget
All the things I told ya
About your home and kids
Remember, boy, there will be others commin yet.

Robert, Grade 7

Davey Jones

Davey Jones was a man of old,
Big and strong and very, very bold.
He was a good shot with his double-barrel gun.
But better than that he was lots of fun.

He started out with just one ship
With a single cannon within his grip.
He shot down many an English fleet.
While trying to stand on his own two feet.

Then the English King got very mad
And called Dave Jones a great big cad.
Dave Jones took a ship named "Bore."
And began to attack the English shore.

The King sent out a fleet in the navy.
To try very hard to capture Davey.
Davey fell with a bullet in his chest.
And there he lay in a bloody mess.

The ship suffered a broad side shot,
That made her sink like a great big rock.
That was the end of Davey Jones,
All that is left is his skull and bones.

Kenneth, Grade 6

THE BATTLE OF CONCORD

Over the road the Redcoats marched
They straightened as if they'd been starched,
Over the road so straight and stiff
But Minutemen waited behind a cliff,
The Redcoats were taken completely unaware
And were caught like a fox in a snare,
The Minutemen charged with a furious rage
And cornered the Redcoats like a bird in a cage,
From a Minute's musket a ball was hurled
To be known as the shot heard round the world.

Gary, Grade 7

C. An afternoon with a hero

Assignment: Pretend that you are playing with a hero (real or fictional) when he was your age. Tell of an adventure you had with him.

I am Susan, a Quaker girl, I live next door to Benjamin Franklin.

Ben called to me: "Susan, come out, I wish to talk to thee. Hurry, for it's important."

I ran down in my long Quaker dress. "What is it, Benjamin? What does thee want?"

Ben held a kite in his hand. He motioned for me to follow him to the river. Then he spoke.

"Susan, will thee hold my clothes? I am going to swim in the water. The kite will pull me (at least I think so) in the water."

"Benjamin! Thee must be crazy! A small kite can't pull thee!" I told him. But I was obliged to hold his clothes while he jumped in. Turning on his back, he unraveled the strong cord. Then a puff of wind came and away through the water Benjamin went.

"Benjamin! Thee will catch cold! Come out of the water or I'll—," then Mr. Franklin stopped. His eyes almost popped out of his head, for Ben went right past him! "Benjamin! How could thee?" exclaimed Mr. Franklin. Then he looked horrified for Mrs. Groutch was coming. She spied Ben!

"Benjamin! Swimming around like that! It is outrageous for thee! Oh! Eek! Help me!" Mrs. Groutch thought Ben was sinking as she saw him zooming past her.

"Oh, do something, Mr. Franklin! The wind is angry at your son! Hurry."

"Calm down, madam. You see, it is this way. Ben is experimenting." I explained.

Disgustedly, Mrs. Groutch went home.

"Ben, thee must never do that again," Mr. Franklin told him. And he never did.[5]

Just the Wrights and Me

Did you know there was another fellow
Who helped the Wrights invent a plane that flew like a bird?
Most people won't believe this,
But there were the two of them and I was the third.

Orville and Wilbur furnished the cloth
And I furnished all the wood
It was hard to build the first airplane,
But we did the best we could.

When we completed this machine,
It looked like an oversize box kite.
When the townspeople came to see our plane.
They thought we were crackpots, all right.

[5] This girl took this episode from a storybook and changed and enlarged it into an adventure story.

We were going to fly our plane outside of Kitty Hawk
At a place called Kill Devil Hill.
The guy who was going to fly this plane,
Was surely going to get a thrill!

We had to decide who was going to fly the plane,
Of course, it would have to be the bravest guy.
You'll never guess who was going to fly it,
It was neither of the Wrights, but I.

We started up the engines
And put the motor in high.
There was never a fellow as surprised as I,
When that flying machine took to the sky!

Some people thought it would take geniuses,
To make an airplane fly, you see.
But it didn't take geniuses at all,
It took just the Wrights and me.

Dennis, Grade 8

D. A hero's possession

Assignment: Pretend that you are a possession of one of your heroes, preferably one from history; feel what it might have felt, see what it might have seen, and tell us about it.

THE LIFE OF ME

(Wild Bill Hickok's Gun)

Boy, you should feel sorry for me. I have a headache nearly every day. Bill always feeds me those hard shells with powder inside of them. Then he jumps on his horse, Buckshot, sticking me in that oily holster he keeps me in. Then when he's riding along, I get such a jumping and jolting that I nearly have to throw up those hard shells. But now, here is what is really hard on me. When he spots an outlaw that he's chasing, he pulls me out of the oily holster and then he pulls my leg, and something like an awful explosion goes off inside of me, and nearly blows my insides out. I get a searing pain in my nose, and a lead bullet comes out so fast that you can't see it, and then he pulls my leg again and again. Why, I just about fall apart at the end of the day.

And here are some other experiences. When someone sneaks up on my beloved keeper, and sticks one of my cousins right into his back, they say some harsh words and Bill takes me slowly out of the oily holster and (to my dismay) he throws me to the ground and the other man ties him up. Sometimes I land upside down and I get those awful cramps. Now, here's one more experience before I go. Sometimes when Bill is struggling with a person by a water's edge, I don't see why they always fall in but that's what happens and by the time they're through fighting, I'm nearly drowned. I sure do hope that my twin (Bill's other gun) on the other side has more fun than me.

Raymond, Grade 7

I Was There

The men gathered around the table where I was sitting. They picked me up and dunked me in the ink. Then one by one they signed my friend. Men like good old John with his bold hard writing and Ben Franklin with his reminding remarks. All of them took me and signed my friend. You know who I am; I was the pen they used to sign their names and my friend is the Declaration of Independence.

David, Grade 7

E. Interviewing a hero
Assignment: Have an interview with a dead hero.
Preparation:
1. Each of you prepare for this writing lesson by reading everything you can find about the life of an explorer assigned to you.
2. In class, suggest that each interview his explorer (now a ghost) letting him tell his own tale. Children enjoy doing this writing in pairs.

Francisco Pizarro

I am Francisco Pizarro
Pizarro, the explorer bold;
Pizarro, the heartless and cold;
Whose limits of cruelty are yet untold.

For the life of man I hold endless scorn;
For the many men whose throats I left torn;
I recall this tale of blood and death.

I set out with food and drink, and men who could
    act but didn't think;
For they feared me and so respected my judgment.
And Spanish horses whose worth times ten exceeded
    that of my cowardly men.

Of how I took the powerful Inca prisoner, and
    strangled him before his helpless band;
Of the thousands I ordered heartlessly slain, and
    of whose rule I took merciless reign,
Of whose riches and wealth, I took all;
And of a great civilization I alone, caused to fall.

And now long after when I should relax in death,
    instead I repent,
For these deeds, and the thousands of lives that
    I sent
To an eternal grave.
These deeds I cannot mend and the many lives I
    put to an end;
These many sins have gained revenge.

Bill, Grade 7

MAGELLAN

I, Magellan, the most fearless of men
To sail the ocean blue
Wanted to prove that the world was round.
Columbus had thought so, too.
We found a narrow, stormy strait,
My brawny crew and I.
We never knew what was lying in wait,
Nothing but water to meet the eye.
Monsters, dragons, and whirlpools,
Of which we'd been told,
Turned some of our men to quivering fools.
Through weather that was bitter and cold.
We struggled and hungered and longed for home.
We came to a sea so peaceful and calm
That we thanked the Lord with a joyous psalm.
Back to Spain we brought many spices
For which we received some fabulous prices.
Unfriendly natives took my life
And that was the end of my storm and strife.

We are thankful for his courageous soul
Or this round the world tale would ne'er have been told.

Karen and Charlotte, Grade 7

F. Answering a ghost's questions

Assignment: Answer the ghost of the mother of a hero or heroine you admire. What became of her daughter or son? (This idea originated with the Benéts' poem "Nancy Hanks" and is a technique suggested by May Hill Arbuthnot in "Books for Children.")

CLARA BARTON

As Clara Barton stood by the door
And watched the men go off to war,
She thought:
"Without some help some might die
I will go and soothe and try
To help our men who are off at war,"
So thought:
Clara Barton as she stood by the door.

Paula, Grade 7

EL LIBERATOR

Through the misty twilight, when the flaming topaz sun dipped below the rim of the horizon, I perceived a graceful form gliding down the lane. Strange was the figure's apparel and deathly silent its approach; I voiced my thoughts, "Who are you?" but received no reply.

Then through the gloom a voice asked, "Have you seen my son? Searching for him am I. Traveling the dusty roads since the sun rose on high. You have seen my son perhaps or know of him?"

I replied, quite startled, "Tell me who you are, and what you wish."

"My son a good young man was he. His future was bright and his father and I gave him all, but I never did understand his passion for liberty. He wanted from Spain's good rule to be free. His name Simon Bolivar, lives and haunts my mind." The apparition finished.

"Simon Bolivar? Why, he was the Liberator! Freely he spent his fortune in the cause of freedom and liberty," I exclaimed.

"He is famous and loved by his countrymen?"

"Yes, and Bolivia was named in his honor. Once his enemies tried to kill him, but they were foiled. Simon is known as the George Washington of South America," I exclaimed.

"Known throughout the world?"

"Through most of the countries. Although he died in poverty in 1803, his fame has spread," I related, "and many towns and cities have been named for him."

"My son is famous," the spirit sighed, "although in poverty he died. Now I can go and rest in peace forevermore."

I watched the ghost glide back down the lane with her lacy cloak billowing behind. I turned to go into the house, wondering—wondering.

Clare Ellen, Grade 8

G. You were there

Assignment: You were there when a great event of history took place. Tell your feelings about what is happening.

THE REVOLUTIONARY WAR

Those awful eight years of war;
Wear;
Tear;
Dead;
Alive;
Those awful years in '75;
Hardly a man is now alive;
That remembers that great war;
That lasted two times as many years as four.
First were the battles of Lexington and Concord;
Gun and gun;
Sword and sword
And lots of strong, young men were lost;
In that awful battle of the hills;
That gave everybody chills;
All those things, and many more;
Those were that awful Revolutionary War,
The most awful part was that hard winter at Valley Forge;
Where thousands of picked men scoured
For supplies and wood.
And when Washington saved New Jersey at Trenton and Princeton!
But I'm glad that we are free!

Jackson, Grade 5

THE LIBERTY BELL

Ding, ding, dong,
That makes the song
Of the Liberty Bell
Here's what it tells
The freedom of press
The freedom to dress
The freedom to talk
The freedom to walk.

James, Grade 8

VALLEY FORGE

My name is Pat Brogan and I am a private in the Continental Army. We're in Valley Forge now. Spring is almost here but many brave men will not live to see it come. The British scoundrels are warming themselves by their fires in Philadelphia while we freeze in this forsaken place. But I know we can and will beat the British under the leadership of General Washington.

Nick, Grade 7

WASHINGTON, D.C.

As I stood there
My eyes are dazed
With thoughts of victory
And freedom ablaze.

Lincoln sitting in his chair
Kept a united country
While the South grew strong,
And the North had great despair.

How Washington stood
At Valley Forge,
How brave men fought
Indians at the gorge.

Though Lincoln was great
And Washington, too,
Uncle Sam can be most proud
Of the famous men under the red, white and blue.

V. Through Science Class

Two types of lessons on how to develop creative imagination in science follow:

A. Six-feet low, a lesson in creative writing on insects.

Assignment: Choose an insect to write about in either prose or poetry.

Introduction: A rhymed explanation of insects.

INSECT-ASIDE

An insect's a creature, with make-up fantastic,
It looks to be fashioned of wire and of plastic,
With artistic touches of gorgeous enamels,
And with more lumps and bumps than a mump-humpy camel's.

An insect's six-legged; a spider is not one;
A three-cylindered thorax—each insect has got one.
They have eyes where they need them, which is simply terrific;
Their antennae, if any, are quite scientific.

An insect's achievements in rare engineering
Man, tardily, just now in some fields is nearing;
In spinning and weaving, in the spanning of spaces,
The dew prints his blueprints in impossible places.

An insect's a creature, not noted for beauty,
But no doubt the reason the breed is so snooty
Is that this old dervishy planet has had 'em
Many millions of years ere the advent of Adam.

And since their progenitors date back so far
The complex it gives them is quite D.A.R.

Discuss vocabulary:

1. Read Hilda Conkling's poem "Butterfly Adventure," and discuss the words taken from that poem: iridescent, sapphire blue, opal, winking half-moons of gold.

2. Make lists of color words that could be used in writing about insects: *blue:* turquoise, lapis lazuli, indigo, sapphire; *yellow:* saffron, tawny, golden.

3. Discuss how insects move: slither, dart, skip, caterpillar or jeep along, inch, wiggle, glide, crawl, hurry, scurry, scamper, flit, flitter, skitter.

4. Suggest that children think about the right word for how a butterfly settles on a flower; how a bee's legs look after dusting with gold dust; how a grasshopper makes his way in the grass; how water bugs skedaddle across the pond; how a tobacco worm chews a leaf; how a butterfly emerges from a cocoon.

5. Consider together the sounds insects make: mournful music of cicada; strident, arguing tones of the katydid, and so on. They whirr, buzz, tick, hum, flutter.

Writing suggestions:

1. Pretend insects are people, giving them definite characteristics and having them do what people do: chat, write diaries, play games, have ball games, work, gossip, show a photograph album of illustrious family portraits, tell life stories, have fun, play tricks, sell shoes to a centipede, and so on.

2. Space stories or tales of prehistoric days with insects as heroes.

3. Just-So stories about insects—how these creatures came to be.

Reading suggestions: Read poetry that brings out each of the points—color, origin, and work of a variety of insects.

Sample writings from this assignment:

CATERPILLARS

Caterpillars are squirmy
Light brown and velvety
Caterpillars are fuzzy
Soft as a baby bird.

Jerinne, Grade 5

BUTTERFLY

Butterfly, butterfly, where have you been?
Flying up in the heavens again?
Your coat is made of polished copper,
Oh, that I had such a handsome topper.
You have a little of coral pink,
Run together with little links.
Chinese red, tangerine and burgundy, too,
Midnight, amethyst, and powder blue,
You have a little of everything,
I guess that's why you are the queen.

Patsy, Grade 7

A Wasp Jet

I see a white streak
It must be a jet.
I hear a loud buzz
It's the engine I bet.

Now I see what it is,
It goes by whiz, whiz,
It's a jet-propelled bee
Here he comes, ouch, he stung me.

Dicky, Grade 6

The Honeybee Kingdom

Ta, ta, ta, ta . . . "All right, you guys, rise and shine. The bugler has finished sounding the taps," yelled Sergeant Honeybee.

The tired workers got up and went to breakfast. Then they prepared for take-off. The Sergeant was yelling again. "Fasten your safety belts and check all gear—are you ready?"

"We are ready," they answered.

"Then take off."

Buzz . . . then they go. This is an everyday happening in the bee kingdom. The workers just took off to gather honey. Now the maids awaken their queen and give her breakfast. After this, the queen sits back and relaxes. But not for long because two drones (the male bees) are having a fight. She hurries out to stop the fight, but the guards have already done so.

"Dear me," she sighs, "those drones are so lazy; they won't gather honey, yet they can't keep out of trouble."

The rest of the day passes without much happening until five o'clock comes when the workers come home, tired but happy. One by one, they stand before the queen as she tastes their honey. Then comes the big moment. The queen announces whose honey she likes best. The queen speaks, "The winner is—Isabella." Whoopee!! Then Isabella chose four of her friends to work with her in the honey cannery, instead of gathering honey, and this is considered to be an honor.

After supper, the queen-bee, the drones, and the workers go off to bee-slumberland. The next morning the workers rise and shine and take off to gather honey except Isabella and her crew. They work in the cannery processing the honey. First the impurities are removed, the ingredients added, and then it's ready to be canned and packed. The honey is then taken to the H.W.D. of A. which means the Honeybee Wholesale Dealers of America.

Kathleen, Grade 8

Lightning Bugs

I remember the time when we were outcasts of the insects. Ah, then we were nothing, but now we are called Lightning Bugs. I will tell the story how we were called Lightning Bugs. It happened long, long ago when your great-great-great-great grandfather was living. It happened like this. No one wanted us. We were like giant bats and everybody was afraid of us. They thought we would eat them. We were no help to anyone. One night your great-great-great-great grandfather was floating down over a lamp. He sat on the edge, and he sat there, until finally he jumped off the lamp. He burnt himself! He looked in back of himself. There he saw a flashing light. He looked again. There was his tail blinking on and off! He hurried to tell everyone of his colony to sit on the lamps in town. After everyone was blinking on and off, they went and showed everyone their tails. They helped the owl every night to catch his supper. They helped the worms to see where they were going. Soon the people called them Lightning Bugs.

Ronald, Grade 7

Too Many Feet

A centipede brushed her teeth and combed her hair
But when she got to the shoe store she cried in despair
"Oh, mother," she said, "how many pair?"
The mother said, "I do not care."

They picked and picked and picked out shoes
Until the storekeeper got the blues
And when they strode away down the road
In the store remained no shoes.

Richard, Grade 6

Mr. Firefly

The firefly talks to his wife at night. He talks with his bright lights. His light glows like a little flashlight. It's nice and bright so he can see what's going on at night.

The firefly talks to his friends at night but it's just gossip although it seems all right. Sometimes I see a firefly so bright above the treetops with his built-in flashlight. I see the firefly how brightly he glows. He glows from his head way down to his toes. I think the firefly talks to me, too. I think he says, "Goodnight, little lady."

Helen, Grade 4

B. Weather or not, a creative writing lesson on weather.

Assignment: Personify the weather and write about its actions in prose or verse.

Introduction: Introduce with rhymed explanation of March weather.

> March is just back from a trip
> To the great display rooms of the sky
> Where he has selected again
> From the samples, the weathers to buy.
>
> The salesmen up there must be good
> Some years I am sure they must say,
> "We've never had such snow before,
> And the price—it's a real give-away!
>
> And this rain; it's the purest distilled,
> Every drop is the best H_2O;
> Why not order half-warm and half-chilled?
> The price is just half now, you know."
>
> And the Wind salesmen clutch at their arms,
> And they say, "Oh, such puffs and such poofs!
> We have winds harsh as new fire alarms
> We have winds that can twist off the roofs!"
>
> And the round little men who sell hail
> And the bluff and the gruff
> That sell cloud cotton-fluff
> He visits them all—without fail.
>
> But that March has no starch in his soul
> He has no sales-resistance at all,
> For their jargons of bargains are past his control
> And for all of their lines he will fall.
>
> So for goodness sake, don't be surprised
> And keep questioning each morning whether
> Will it rain? Will it snow? You should certainly know
> March must use all his bargains of weather!

Discussion of personalities weather assumes: Read poems to illustrate—Madison Cawein's "Old Man Rain," May Justus' "Winds A-Blowing," Melville Cane's "Fog, the Magician," Elizabeth Coatsworth's "Winter Rune," Elinor Wylie's "Velvet Shoes," and Rowena Bastin Bennett's "Under the Tent of the Sky."

Vocabulary mix: Fog blankets, envelops, changes, camouflages, blots out, blurs. *Rain* beats, pounds, whines, trickles, knocks, dashes, dances, showers, floods. *Snow* comes softly, drops like down, powders, piles, drifts. *Hail* hammers, flails, bounces, ricochets.

Sample writings from this assignment:

SATIN SNOW

> The snow is as beautiful as swans-down
> Like silks and linens
> Like a queen in her long satin gown
> Who sits around spinning
> The feathery clouds.

Judith, Grade 4

CLOUD SHIPS

The clouds in the sky look like ships to me. There's a destroyer, a battleship, and a cruiser, too. They fire their guns at the enemy. The fire of their guns looks like lightning in the sky. The sound makes the thunder that passes by. The people in the ships start coming down, flooding the hills, the valleys, and cities and town.

Robert, Grade 7

OLD GRANDMA SNOW

> There's Old Grandma Snow as white as white can be,
> Is there anyone so mean and strict as she?
> She blows cold winds about you and covers you with white,
> Until you're cold and shivering when you go home at night,
> You'd better watch out for her, or she'll give you a cold,
> Even though she's little, she's really very bold.

Janet, Grade 5

STORM

Thunder, lightning, soaking rain,
Splashing down on the window pane.
Two gleaming eyes looking out to see,
At the rushing wind in the old oak tree.

Thunder, lightning, noisy sound,
Torrents of rain, pouring down.
Storming, brushing on the roof,
Muddy water on the hoof.

June, Grade 6

THE MAGICIAN

The fog is like a magician.
It makes things disappear.
It makes animals vanish
I think I'll hide in here.

Jon, Grade 4

THE BIG RAIN-CLOUD

The night was dark,
The sky was, too.
And in the Heavens
The lightning flew.

There was a contest,
To see who'd be first
To make that biggest
And best rain-cloud burst.

They tried and tried
And fussed and fussed
But they still didn't get
That big rain-cloud to bust.

Everyone tried it
But all were a flop
Till a lightning bolt bit it
And then it went "pop."

David, Grade 6

SOFT SOUNDS

Soft steps are walking in the snow and snow is falling very softly on the ground. Soft words say soft things. Soft cats walk across the floors.

Charles, Grade 4

HARD ROCK HAIL

Dancing, prancing,
Hail comes to the ground,
It hits like bullets then bounces around.
It crashes and cracks as it hits window panes
The thunder crashes and claps as it does when it rains.

Boom! Boom! It drums with a roar
Rumbling and grumbling we hear by the score.
There the sun comes from behind a hill
Now it has stopped; everything is so still.

Paul, Grade 8

A dancing ballerina whirls through the sky
And sheds her dress,
Well, we think it comes from up high,
Her dress is made from cotton white and lovely
It all comes down beautifully.
Her dress is blown by the wind and starts to fall apart.
It's sheer and soft and it starts
As quietly as it stops
Then she goes away
For another day
As quick as a rabbit hops.

Nancy, Grade 3

FOG

Fog is like a wet, cold and slithering ghost, that creeps over the land with clammy fingers grasping everything that he can reach changing it into a ghostly shape. Its wet cold hands seem to cling to you to make you feel lonesome and alone. All living or moving things on the earth seem to stand still when the misty fog moves in, seeming to hold things with its cold, wet, slimy fingers.

Emil, Grade 8

Imagination Can Be Developed

Yes, imagination, like muscle power, can be developed if a child has even a little imagination to begin with—and more children have than haven't. Nothing can do more to improve practical writing than to give it the imaginative touch; there's no doubt about that. It certainly takes imagination to write to an unseen audience. But the secret of excellent practical writing is to pretend to write to a real person. What will he want to hear? What are his feelings that must be considered?

Wing-tipped writing is really re-creative writing; it endeavors to re-create in the reader the feelings the writer himself feels.

Practical writing, if it is effective, is equipped with the wings of imagination.

> As long as imagination lets our minds fly,
> There is no excuse for practical writing's
> Being dull and dry.

CUPBOARD OF IDEAS for Chapter Nine

Practical Writing Needs Wings   ❖ ❖ ❖ ❖ ❖ ❖ ❖ ❖ ❖ ❖ ❖ ❖

Primary Shelf

I. Writing Out Emotions

A. Angers. When they are angry or disturbed, let second and third graders argue the matter out on paper. First graders and nonwriting second graders can do this with crayola drawings. Answer the questions: What's the matter? Why do you feel as you do? Is something unfair? What can we do about it?

B. Fears. After a discussion of secret fears and the reading of poetry on the subject, ask each child to write or draw his greatest fear. Ask each to describe just how he feels when he is afraid and what he imagines when he is afraid.

II. Writing after Listening

A. After reading an informative article on any subject (birds, for instance), ask the youngsters to copy this statement first: "Birds are interesting," then to write as much as they remember from their listening. First grade could draw as much information as they can. (As an aid to correct spelling, I would have on the board many useful words from the article.) Another good beginning sentence is "Why I would like to own a seal."

B. Have children listen to a story about a child with one out-standing characteristic, such as generous or talkative, then write the answer to this question, "If Betty lived next to me, why would (or wouldn't) she make a good neighbor?"

C. Read about a youngster who lives in another country, after which second and third graders write: "Why I Would (or Wouldn't) Like to Live in India (or Denmark or Panama)."

D. Read the poem about Jonathan Jo by Dorothy Aldis, discussing with the children what makes people interesting. Follow the discussion with a writing lesson expanding this topic sentence: "I know the most interesting person." Explain to children that the first sentence says the "whole thing in a nutshell"; first tell it fast; then tell it slowly, piece by piece. Don't forget in the "paint-mixing" period to get those lists of interesting words on the board.

III. Birthdays

You (or a committee) find out these facts about a birthday child: where and when he was born, where he lives, how many brothers and sisters he has, his favorite toy, food, game, his two greatest wishes, and what he likes best to do at school. Let each write a short biography of the birthday child to show his parents at home. Let the child make a picture of himself by looking in a desk mirror. Put the best biography in a big Biography Book entitled "This is Grade 2," or "All about Us" and use the birthday child's picture as an illustration for his biography.

A fine creative writing lesson following the biography is to pretend the birthday child got his best wish and to tell all about what happened.

IV. Using Words in Sentences

A. Make a list of action words or descriptive words or both, used in any sport or game in which the children are currently interested—playing in the snow, for instance (roll, press, hard, squeeze, throw, make a slide, slick, wade, white snow, delicate flakes), and ask the children to use the words in good sentences. Always stress the mechanics involved before the writing begins.

B. Write an interesting word on the board every day, one that is crisp and new to primary children; let those who can use it in a sentence.

C. At Thanksgiving time, write such words as delicious, savory, tart, and golden-brown on the board; let the fast workers use each correctly about Thanksgiving food.

D. Make folders with pictures of foods and let children learn to spell all the names of foods that make up a Thanksgiving feast.

V. *Writing to Illustrate*

Write paragraphs to illustrate the pictures in a homemade movie.

VI. *Making a Notebook*

Make co-operatively a big class notebook that highlights the unit work you have just studied.

Intermediate and Upper-Grade Shelf

Unit Ideas

A. I am sure that a study of your own state can be enriched tremendously from noting these sixty-three unusual creative suggestions by Arlene Reda.[1]

English Activities for a Unit Study of Wisconsin for Grades 4–8

1. After studying various prominent historical personalities like Professor Stephen Babcock (he gave the Babcock milk test to Wisconsin), Chief Oshkosh, Jean Nicolet, Father Marquette, and Major Richard Bong, compose together some poems on the people. Children who enjoy dramatics can act them out.

2. Some students may wish to compose in their free time poems of an historical person. Without knowing who wrote them, the teacher reads them to the group who guess which character the poem represents. These poems could be brought any time throughout the unit.

---

[1] Mrs. Arlene Reda was a senior in my class "The Creative Writing of Children." She had taught six years in a rural school before returning to college to get her degree.

3. Inventors write their stories of how and why they made their inventions. If they wish, students read them in class.
4. Prominent industrialists write or tell of how they achieved fame.
5. Indians either tell, write, or dramatize their first experiences with white men.
6. Explorers write of their most exciting moment in explorations.
7. Either individually or in groups make lists of sound words during a war.
8. Either individually or in groups compose lists of descriptive words concerning an Indian encampment and Indian costumes.
9. Geographical locations, such as the Wisconsin Dells, tell their formation story either through stories or poems.
10. The capitol building tells its story of how it takes care of the state.
11. The Peshtigo fire tells its angry mood; stress the numerous descriptive words.
12. Pine, hemlock, maple, and various other trees disgustedly converse about the woodsmen. Work out skits or plays from here.
13. The Wisconsin, Flambeau, and Chippewa rivers tell how they beautify the state.
14. The first capital of Wisconsin at Belmont explains in a short paragraph how lonely it feels now that its glory has passed on to Madison.
15. The city of Portage or Green Bay tells in a poem how it got its name.
16. Father Marquette describes his feelings the first time he landed in Wisconsin.
17. Chequamegon National Forest writes a thank-you note to the government expressing thanks for being saved.
18. The Wisconsin River complains to the paper mills of how it is the most overworked river in the world.
19. Milwaukee compares its sounds with those of the forest.
20. The city bird or the country bird sings of its life in a lilting poem.
21. We go on an imaginary trip around Wisconsin with each child adding some fact to the trip.
22. Children in rural areas enjoy tracing the story of milk.
23. The shoe and paper industries have a debate on which is the more important.
24. Lead miners describe their homes in early Wisconsin.
25. Deer hunters and the deer exchange opinions on deer season.
26. Each child represents a leading crop of Wisconsin, pointing out why it is important and backing his views with factual information.
27. After viewing pictures of many farms, have the children write a description of an ideal dairy farm.
28. The children divide into groups, each group representing a nationality of Wisconsin. Dressed in costumes, they tell of their contributions to the state and the areas in which they settled.
29. Make short rhymes on cities, counties, rivers spontaneously in class.

30. Have children who have traveled to beauty spots in the state write descriptions of one scene that appealed to them. Compare the descriptions and note the descriptive words.

31. Wisconsin has many leading sports figures. Have each child pretend to be one and write a ballad, poem, or story about himself. Do this if there are quite a number of sports-minded individuals in the class.

32. The students make up riddles that are puns on county names, similar to the following: If we burn this county in our stove, we'd be minus what county? (*Wood*) What county is the hardest? (*Rock*)

33. Berry pickers have a discussion with a snake in the woods.

34. Compose ballads on state animals, cities, crops, people, and put into a ballad booklet; then send the booklet to other rooms and to the homes of parents.

35. Children bring lists of vocabulary words that they feel are necessary to know. The teacher supplements this with his own list. To know the meanings of the words and to check on the list, use the games called "Word Bee" and "Minister's Cat."[2]

36. Have children write letters to request films on Wisconsin from the state department and other sources.

37. Pupils send for free information from the capitol building and the state department. Upon receipt of the material have others write thank-you notes, telling how much the material helped the class.

38. Letters written to the governor and legislators on various bills give pupils an excellent chance to become more interested in government.

39. Invite old-timers in the community to the school for interviewing. Encourage the pupils to write thank-you notes.

40. To exercise imagination, write stories or poems on what pupils think their community looked like about seventy-five years ago and what it might look like in the future.

41. Write biographies of animals and people.

42. Each pupil keeps a daily diary of life during pioneer days when studying pioneer life.

43. Everyone contributes words that pioneer people used more than we do today. Examples: buckskin, hominy, mush, and so on.

44. Write stories on pioneer pictures that suggest plots.

45. In the upper grades, read informational material beyond the children's reading level, and have them take notes. Follow this with a few oral reports on the material read.

46. Make a list of smell, sound, and scenic words connected with cookhouses in lumber camps. Suggest using these words when writing a story on pioneer days.

47. Pupils act out a discussion between a pine tree and a log cabin.

48. Rural schools that are being abandoned tell their stories of service to the community during the past.

[2] Mauree Applegate, *Helping Children Write,* pp. 144–45.

49. Keep a question box on Wisconsin for pupils who wish to ask questions but are too timid to do so.
50. Write letters to important figures of the day, such as Eddie Matthews; another activity would be to tell of the good job he is doing.
51. Pretend that you are going to enter a Wisconsin college. Write a letter to the registrar asking for a catalogue.
52. Pupils who love the outdoors do a sight and sound tour of the state parks.
53. Individuals keep rhyming word lists on separate interests such as geography and history.
54. Different seasons tell their stories of what they do to the state.
55. A Wisconsin beauty spot or noted place, such as the Old Milton House or Tank Cottage, tells its story.
56. The glacier tells a good story of what it did to Wisconsin.
57. Pupils as a group write radio scripts on Wisconsin history, then act them out.
58. Students who most enjoy drawing cartoons make comic strips on Wisconsin life.
59. Give out sentence starters on phases of life in Wisconsin, and have the pupils write the rest of the paragraph.
60. Compose "tall tales" similar to those of Paul Bunyan and act them out.
61. Make a list of colorful words used in historical stories. Talk these over, bringing out points of why they are colorful and how they can be used in our own speech.
62. Play records of music; then have students write a few lines of what the music makes them think.
63. Write a short summary paragraph upon completion of the unit telling why they liked or disliked the unit study.

B. Different types of school newspapers
   1. Write a historical newspaper for a certain era with advertisements, news, and headlines in line with the times.
   2. Make a Poor Richard's Almanac for this century.
   3. Prepare an April-Fool newspaper with zany articles as well as editorials.
   4. Write editorials that might have been written in Abolition Days, in the days of the opening of Oklahoma, in the Gold-Rush Days.
   5. Put out a school paper dedicated to safer bicycle riding on the streets of your city. Print interviews with important citizens old and young. Youth would earn more respect if they instituted their own reforms.
C. Different methods of review
   1. Put together a radio or television program with speakers, skits, interviews, and so on.

2. Have a committee of gifted children plan a pageant with script as background.

3. Each two children act out an interview with a noted person in the states or countries studied, one posing as the noted person, the other as the interviewer. (In order to heighten the interest in current affairs, let the avid readers often do this type of interviewing; they love it.)

4. Hold a state fair in the school gym with each group having a booth for his state showing through banners and floats, exhibits, songs, skits, and homemade movies what his state is noted for. Small red wagons borrowed from younger children form the basic vehicles for fine floats.

5. Let the whole room go on a "pretend" conducted tour of one or several European countries. Working in committees with pictures and exhibits to show and much information to give, one group could conduct the class through Paris, showing pictures of the noted places; another group could be in charge of the Louvre and show pictures and give talks on the great pictures to be seen there. Another committee could portray a sidewalk cafe; a group of pseudo wine merchants could explain the careful process of wine making to the visitors; a person interested in cathedrals could construct a cardboard model and explain. Such exercises as these give children a reason for study and give them a chance to travel via books.

6. Let upper-grade students preview movies and give introductory talks.

7. Help children to prepare talks to introduce a noted person being interviewed. Even "pretend" interviews help to give children poise.

CHAPTER TEN

Letters Are Self-Stamped

College freshman:

> Mom's always sending me advice.
> Some fellows think, "To heck with it";
> But the feeling that it leaves is nice—
> She always sends a check with it!

A NOTE TO POLITICIANS [1]

Gentlemen, let me remind you that liberty is not
    lost by revolution,
By the sudden appearance of armed men, the parade
    of tanks, machine guns drumming,
And the little flowers of men's regard, made out
    of steel and dynamite,
Blossoming in the streets. All that comes later,
Or not at all. We can do without it. Gentlemen,
It is something else that weakens the freedom
    in us;
A worm in the wood, a little flaw in the flute;
It is this: that we are not sure enough that
    we want it.
It is this: that we give it away like bits of
    an old house,
For something new, a car, or a peck of potatoes.
Liberty, yours and mine, is lost by barter
Before we even begin to know we have lost it;
By trading a little here, and a little there—
For instance, the right to make such things as
    fences,
And to stand and speak as a man, to honor the
    truth,
Or even to do an honest job of work.
We can always get a price for rights like these;
There are always some who will sell if we don't
    want to—
Sell for food, or for spite, or perhaps most often
Just for the sake of being one of the boys,
Brothers by blood, and everyone else stay out of it.

Gentlemen, let me assure you we lose our freedom
When men begin to talk and step like their neighbors,
Even before the guns begin. . . .

Robert Nathan

[1] From *The Green Leaf: The Collected Poems of Robert Nathan* by Robert Nathan. By permission of the publishers, Alfred A. Knopf, Inc.

OUR FREEDOM

Long, long ago our freedom was won
By men who fought at Lexington,
At Valley Forge and Bunker Hill
The fight for freedom continued, until,

In seventeen-hundred and seventy-six,
The spirit which we call Seventy-Six,
Marched in triumph throughout the land
Proclaiming freedom on every hand.

Many had died—and more may perish,
To keep alive this freedom we cherish.

Ralph Knippel, Grade 7

I wouldn't be at all surprised if before we get to the moon, another university professor will come out with a machine that can do our letter writing for us without our assistance. I understand that a professor has already perfected a mechanical teacher from whom, he says, children learn more readily than from a human teacher, as far as correct answers are concerned. I wondered when I heard of this teaching machine if the "tin man without a heart" would notice the symptoms of trouble at home in Mary and compensate for them at school, as Miss Briggs, her teacher, does. Do you suppose a machine would know what to do for Lester when he gets those discouraged spells? (Ah, we foolish, foolish grown-up children playing with our toys and pretending they are real!) I must confess that although I shudder at the idea of human beings without hearts, I am nevertheless intrigued by the idea of a mechanical letter writer. I just don't seem to get letters written, and a letter-writing machine might possibly solve everything. The only thing that worries me a bit is how will the machine know just how to say things to Aunt Agnes, who has so many foibles; I suppose there will possibly be large numbers of buttons to punch in the Foibles Section, but not even a mastermind could possibly have enough buttons for Aunt Agnes.

And love letters! It would be rather embarrassing to have a machine write one's love letters—there's something so unpredictable about love, somehow.

Since a mechanical teacher has already been conceived and built, surely a mechanical letter writer will not be far behind. The small apartment dweller is soon going to be forced to live out and stable his machines in.

In the meantime, the need for more and better paper communication increases as the leisure in which to write them decreases. Are we going to be forced then to resort to other, more expensive means of communication than our time-tried four cents worth? New improvements are being made every day in communications. Even before you read this book, it may possibly be a common thing for friends across the world to see each other as they talk. What a boon that will be for the caller but what a tragedy often to the "callee." Some of the best long-distance conversations one ever has come when one's "glamour is not up to his yammer," as one of my college freshmen so neatly expressed it. A letter can be both written and received without the correct raiment. As a means of communication, long-distance calls are truly wonderful; the live voice of a friend is better at worst than inert words on flat paper. But to talk to a loved one with one's ear listening for that "Your three minutes are up, pul-eze" is a strain on naturalness, that essence of all friendly conversations. To have almost to count one's words as well as to pay dearly for them makes long-distance telephone calling at present a better occasional than a regular means of communication.

What if one had to do all his long-distance communicating by telegram! Most of us would sooner lose our friends than to have to count words in a daily message to them. Imagine trying to convey one's feelings on a cold May morning in terse verse via Morse:

WEATHER CHILLY, NOSE SPILLY, CORRESPONDENCE BILL-EY, WORK WILLY-NILLY, LIFE THRILLY—*Milly*

(Aha! Made it in ten words! But wasted the other five.)

Imagine having to spell all those odd words to a Western Union employee who is not supposed to be a creative speller. (It's easy to see why the job doesn't demand college graduates. Their spelling *is* creative, as I find every time I ask for a batch of papers.)

When it comes right down to what we can afford and to the return on the investment, what is a more satisfactory, pleasurable, economical, natural, and soul-satisfying means of extending communications across the miles than letters and notes? How wonderful to share our joys, exchange ideas, flatten out our anxieties, and express our sympathies—all for a few cents, pouring out the words as naturally as if we were sitting in a patio or living room, talking to friends.

Next to the charming art of conversation in the living room is the more difficult art of conversation via paper in a note or letter. Do you suppose we shall ever be able to fill our pens with a relaxing solution that will unlacquer our thoughts as we write? Our thoughts seem to stiffen as they touch the paper, and what might have been a warm exchange of ideas becomes often as stilted as the first half-hour of a shy boy's conversation on a first date. Perhaps, as Emerson says, we're trying harder to say things better in a letter:

> . . . for in a letter
> We have not better things to say,
> But surely say them better.

Yes, Mr. Emerson, we may say things better in letters from the standpoint of careful English, but without the warmth that spoken words are apt to convey. Our letters must become on-paper visits if they are to fulfill their aim as effective means of communication.

Why can't we be natural in our letter writing? It may be because teachers unconsciously steer young children to word their first letters in the orthodox way. In composite letter writing in the first grade, teachers tend to have things said in the way everybody says them. If it can possibly be arranged, I believe that all first letters should be individually dictated to the teacher, while the class as a whole is engaged in a mind-engrossing activity such as creative work of some sort. Perhaps if children's first letters were individualistic rather than alike, each child's writing might retain his own personality flavor—the only part of letter writing that makes letters worth receiving. Although we teachers want the letter to sound like Johnny, we unconsciously help him to write as all Johnnys write.

Many primary teachers enlist the services of "private secretaries" from a third or fourth grade to take dictation from first graders until, near the close of the year, their first-grade children can write their own letters.

It is better to go back over a child's writing with him than, fearful that he will make a mistake, tell him what to say in the first place. Moreover, I have come to the conclusion that the wrong thing said by a child is often more right than the right thing said by an adult.

For instance, did you ever read a note of condolence half as heart-warming as Donald's?

DEAR MISS UVAAS:
I am sorry that you can't come to teach at school. We are studying hard. I am sorry your mother died. Mrs. Woizeski is very kind to us. I hope you will be back in school soon. I hope you don't feel too bad because when you are sad, I am sad. Well, I guess there is nothing much you can do about it once it happens. Be back soon.

Donald L. Dempsey

Fourth-grade Donald was probably unaware when he wrote it that there is such a thing in the world as a note of condolence. He just wrote as if he were talking. Children need general directions, rather than specific when they are writing notes and letters. For most of the lessons in this chapter on letter writing I have decided to talk directly to the children, not to the teachers, hoping that the teachers will adapt the material to each child's need and stage of development. The last section, of course, is for you the teacher or the student wishing to become a teacher. The lessons follow this order:

  I. With Your Own Stamp—letter writing
 II. Mind Your Manners—thank-you notes
III. Grace Notes—notes of gracious living
 IV. Dear Friend—pen-pal letters
  V. Disagreeing Agreeably—expressing disagreement in a business letter
 VI. My Dear Boss (I Hope)—writing an effective application for a teaching position

I. With Your Own Stamp

(Letter Writing)

Oh, a bottle of ink, a bottle of ink!
What's bottled up in a bottle of ink?

. . . .

More wonderful things than you ever could think
All bottled up in a bottle of ink![2]

[2] By permission of the author, Blanche Jennings Thompson.

When she wrote that verse and called it "Magic," Blanche Jennings Thompson might have been thinking of the magic of letter writing.

"Letter magic!" isn't just an empty phrase. It's time that we moderns recognized magic when we see it. You'd call a thing magic, wouldn't you, that could get you a job, make a friend, or stop a quarrel for you? Of course, but let me tell you—there's more abracadabra in a letter than in Aladdin's magic lamp.

> What is the magic contained in a letter?
> It's something, oh, something that's infinitely better
> Than everyday magic. Friendship and charm;
> Love that will keep wandering children from harm;
> Surcease from worry for ones that we care for—
> These things make magic in letters—and, therefore,
> What wizardry could one conjure that is better
> Than to spend on a friend the few cents for a letter?

Letter magic is that practical kind of magic that you're going to need all your life. It isn't the sudden kind of magic that changes one's life, you know; it's the slow, relaxed magic of everyday living that transmutes the color of one's days from gray to rose. Do you know that the magic of letter writing is so powerful that it has all the explosive qualities of dynamite? In fact, we might even say that a letter is dynamite with a four-cent stamp on.

Let me prove that statement to you! An effective letter can get you a job; a weak letter can lose you a job. A good letter can make you a friend; an angry, thoughtless letter can lose you a friend. A letter that has kept the other fellow in mind can straighten out misunderstandings; a letter you write when you see only your side of a question can plunge two people deeper into misunderstanding.

There's no doubt about it—a letter is dynamite; is explosive. Letters are important because they are a powerful influence. But they are even more important to you because of another reason; the only kind of writing most of you will ever do when you grow up— other than making out the grocery list or writing checks, of course —is the writing of letters and notes.

Bear in mind that because more people than ever will be living and working clear across the world in the next few years, there will be more cause than ever for more letters—better letters. In our world neighborhood, letters take the place of the calls your great-grandparents made to the homes of their neighbors when *world* neighbors were hardly an idea.

Now, if your letter is going to take the place of a personal visit, it must truly represent you.

What is a letter, anyway? To save time, let's seek the answer in a rhyme. Annette Wynne says:

> A letter is a gypsy elf,
> It goes where I would go myself.[3]

Or to say it in another couplet:

> A letter—what is it?
> An on-paper visit.

There, I guess that says it fairly well! A letter is an on-paper visit. What a money-cheap visit a letter is. What other representative of yourself can you send on a personal visit the thousands of miles from ocean to ocean or from Canada to the Gulf of Mexico for a few cents? Truly, a letter is the greatest travel bargain in the world.

> No boats to paddle;
> No highways to tramp on;
> Your letter is *you,*
> With a four-cent stamp on.
> It travels as cheaply as cloud or bird,
> A trip for four cents—
> It's almost absurd!

Our letters *are us,* all right, but an "us" without a face to talk right along with our words. There are no hands to gesture for us and help our words carry our ideas to our listeners. Letters must be done better than talking because letters are one- instead of three-dimensional; letters must talk from a flat surface with no help from facial expression or bodily gestures. Letters must, therefore, be truly excellent writing.

What kinds of good writing belong in a letter? First of all, the good writing that is natural. Your letter must sound like you. Why? Well, a letter is an on-paper visit; and since you're to do the visit-

---

[3] From *For Days and Days,* "A Letter Is a Gypsy Elf" by Annette Wynne. Copyright 1919–1947 by Annette Wynne. Published by J. B. Lippincott Company.

ing, that visit must be stamped with your personality. It must sound like you, talk like you; in short, be a visit from you.

Notice how natural was the letter from fourth-grade Donald (page 394). He wrote it to his teacher whose mother had just died. Donald wasn't trying to say what he thought should be said; he was speaking to his teacher in the same way he would have had he been talking with her instead of writing to her. A letter is first of all an on-paper visit; it sounds like talking.

In order to have your letter sound like you, it's a good idea to pretend that you're really visiting the person you're writing to. Of course, if you're visiting, you wouldn't begin your letter as ten-year-old Tom did:

> Today from camp the ten-year-old
> Inscribed this letter, brief as a bomb:
> "They made us all write home today.
> They do it every Tuesday, Tom." [4]

Not even a ten-year-old in a real visit would tell his hostess that he wouldn't have come to see her if he could have helped it.

Suppose your letter is just one of those friendly, newsy letters that we all are so happy to receive. They're more than just talks; they become something very entertaining if we dramatize things a bit, make little dramas from the short, everyday happenings we write about.

Take for instance this four-line poem story that sixth-grade Gregory wrote at Halloween time. It's wonderfully done—a whole good story condensed into four lines:

> One dark night I met a giant,
> That swung out fierce at me,
> I stood and stared him in the eye,
> And found it was a tree.

Gregory, Grade 6

In a letter, that poem would be fine, but suppose you want to tell the story in prose. We often take, and very happily, a one- or two-sentence happening, a seed story, and blow it up into a clever little drama with a paragraph for each scene. Had Gregory done that, he'd probably have described in the first scene how he felt on that

---

[4] By permission of Edsel Ford and *The Christian Science Monitor.*

Halloween night, trying to whistle, but feeling slightly apprehensive and jumping at shadows. Then just as the scene ends, he sees the tree.

In scene or paragraph two, Gregory would tell all he imagines as he nears the tree. As this second paragraph ends, the tree swings at him.

The third scene or paragraph is short and to the point; no one stops long to tell how silly he feels when his ghost turns out to be a tree; he just blurts it out and stops, and his pencil sounds as if it were laughing a bit at himself.

This business of changing one small happening into a little play with one or two or three short paragraph scenes is the essence of interesting letter writing. Most of us haven't big things happening in our lives, but almost every day some little seed story happens to each of us. Blown up into a few dramatic scenes, it will bring a chuckle or an exclamation of interest to your reader.

I have an example—a fine one—of dramatic writing. Pat, who wrote this, could have written into a letter a single paragraph of how Rusty, his dog, saved Jerry's life. That paragraph would have been interesting, but the whole episode just bristles with questions. How? What? When? So Pat elaborated his seed story into a full-blown dramatic story. How much more his grandmother must have enjoyed the dramatic little group of scenes that form this story of his dog than if he had briefly written, "Today Rusty saved Jerry's life."

Today was a big day for me. My mother was leaving me in charge of my two-year-old brother, Jerry. Of course, my dog, Rusty, was going to help me.

Rusty had come to us as a puppy. Now he was a big, shaggy dog with very bright eyes. When I looked at him, I could just about tell how he felt. When he was sad, the color of his eyes was dull. Most of the time, he was happy and always very helpful. Now I was counting on him to help me.

Mother had left and I was very excited. I was reading to Jerry and he liked it for awhile. Then, as I started to clean up the house, I noticed that Jerry was gone. The door was open and I suddenly realized that he had wandered outside. Rusty knew the danger and followed close behind me.

All of a sudden I heard a terrifying scream. I realized that it was Jerry. I started off at a run with Rusty right behind. Then I saw Jerry. He had fallen off the bridge into the creek in back of our house. Just his tiny head was above water. I reached out my hand but could not touch him. Then, before I realized what had happened, Rusty had jumped in the creek and had Jerry by the collar of his shirt. With a few powerful strokes, he was on the shore. I picked up Jerry and ran to the house. He wasn't hurt but just scared. Rusty had saved his life and he was our hero forever.

Yes, the letter writer who changes a three-line story into dramatic scenes can really write letters. Natural writing—dramatic writing—yes, and now still another kind of writing to make a good letter: a good letter talks to the senses. The use of the right words rolls scenes before the eyes of the reader so he can see what you want him to see: for illustrations, how about these bits of writing from "Let's Writers"? Can you just see these plants of Dinny's?

> Plants . . .
> Tawny, blood red.
> All sizes, too.
> Scarlet, amber
> And sky-tinted blue.

Or Mary's line about pumpkins?

> The pumpkins rested on the soft, golden hay,
> and the silky hair of the corn blew in the soft breeze.

And the right word makes us see eighth-grade Lorraine's dog; her description makes every movement of her dog vivid and alive.

You should see my dog. He's jet black and as fast as the wind. He's happy and pleasant all day long. In the morning before going to school I can see that far away and lonesome look in his eyes, telling me he'd like to come along. Mother is glad dogs don't have to go to school because Happy is very useful around the house. When mom's wash day comes along Happy is right there to help, handing Mother clothes pins or taking care of the baby playing in the yard. When Dad comes home from a hard day of work Happy is already bringing his slippers or running to the front yard to get the evening paper. When Happy does these little things around the house he makes everyone cheerful. I'm glad we own him.

Lorraine, Grade 8

Not only does the right word unroll the right scene before the mind's eye, but also the right word can shake out the right "smell" before the reader's nose. Lo, he has the right "smell" picture of the breakfast table at home or the crisp winter evenings around the fireplace. Don't forget the sound words, too, in your letters. They'll help your reader hear what you hear. There are such good ones! Think of the words you could use for the sounds of snow under boots or ice skates on the frozen river. Use the right words for all the senses.

But one does not have to write of exciting things to be a good writer. A true writer re-creates in words, pictures, and actions that were once lived—or could well be. Luella did this well, as you could, too:

> In the summer, my dad fishes and sometimes my mother, brothers and I go with him. I think it is a lot of fun. The nets are quite long. We get up on top of the boat, and when we see a big fish we yell out "Here comes a big one!"
>
> Sometimes we have people come and see my father fish. They think it is very interesting. Sometimes he gets a lamprey—they are something like an eel—it kills fish by sucking blood out of it. At about noon time we have a little lunch and then my father starts to fish again. In late afternoon, before we go home we might get a little hungry so we have pop and potato chips or something like that. And then the day is just about over, so we get home about four-thirty in the afternoon. That night our beds sure feel good.

Luella's quiet words seem to flow with the water. The most charming letters are often the recreations of ordinary, everyday living.

Sometimes in a letter if you aren't writing to the person who caused it, it's fun to pop off about your favorite irritation. I can just imagine what Stacey would write in a letter about deer hunting, when seeing a deer shot causes her to write this dramatic poem:

> There I watch by my window sill.
> Then I hear a sudden shot,
> And watch him fall.
> "Oh, why, oh, why," I shout and call.
> "You had no reason to shoot at all.
> This is no time to shoot a deer.
> Especially when he is so near.
> Don't you hear?
> You have no reason to shoot a deer."

Stacey, Grade 5

How much her grandmother would enjoy sixth-grade Judy's ironic explosion concerning her particular peeve—unless, of course, it was her grandmother who was causing it.

For as long as I can remember, grownups have said to me, "My, how you have grown." I can't say "Thank you," for I'm not sure it's a compliment. I can't say, "Yes," or "No," since I seldom remember how long it's been since they have seen me. I can't come right out and say, "Yes, a whole inch today," since I don't measure myself daily and I never feel myself growing. I can't disagree for I can just look at a picture or some of the clothes I used to wear, to know that somewhere along the line I really have been growing. I know the remark is well intentioned, but as often as I've heard it, I've never figured out an answer that I dare say out loud. I can't even say, "You have grown, too," even though it might be true. If I did, I'd probably be cut down to pint-size by my father or my mother.

Judy, Grade 6

In writing letters today, try to include some of each of the several kinds of writing we've talked about thus far: natural writing, changing a three-sentence seed story into a three-paragraph story, challenging the senses in order to take your reader right along with you, and perhaps popping off about your pet peeve.

Before we start today's letters, let's do a little more planning together, shall we? Have you ever received a letter from a little child in which he gets his paragraphs all mixed? That's a natural occurrence in a small child's letter, but it can easily be avoided by older writers. Perhaps this two-line rhyme will help you to start:

> Before you start your letter today
> List the things that you plan to say.

That's easy enough, isn't it? All you need is a word or phrase for each item. In a long letter that I have before me, Kathleen is pretending her dog, Honey, is writing to its mother in the Philippines. The letter plan might have been: Pet shop—accident to eye—getting a name—life in Eau Claire—tricks. Yours today might read something like this: basketball game—New Year's Eve party— Christmas at grandmother's—learning to ski. As simple a list as that will sort your letter into the proper paragraphs. As you put down your items, you'll have the person you are writing to in mind. If you were talking with your cousin, face to face, you'd be talking about things that both of you would be interested in. So since a letter is written to one person, you want to keep that person in mind when you are listing your ideas. Today you're going to write actual letters to someone you really want to visit. Then you'll want to tuck your letter into an envelope as soon as it is ready and send it off with your own and Uncle Sam's stamp.

Have you decided in your mind who is going to receive your letter? All right, then, let's talk about a few more tips that will make your on-paper visit the best ever. Here's one—it's a good idea to re-read the last letter from your friend in order to answer any questions he may have put in. Remember how it annoys you when a friend forgets to answer your questions?

Let's say you've made your list of items. How shall we begin?

How to begin? Why, plunge right in!

That is a good way, but there are a few tips that I can give you about that plunge. One is to avoid an opening like this:

I didn't have anything else to do,
So I thought I'd write to you.

Goodness knows, maybe that's true, but we mustn't tell all we know in this world. Now another tip:

Don't begin your letter with an apology—
It will do no good, and it's bad psychology.

Imagine how you'd feel receiving a letter beginning: "Dear Mother, I've been too busy to write you this week" or "Dear Sir: This letter is long past due, but . . . ."

When you begin your letter with such apologies, what you are actually saying is: "Dear Mother, Everything in the world was more important this week than you—so I let you go." Oh, no!

Don't begin your letter with an apology—
It will do no good and it's bad psychology.

Some letter writers like to begin by creating a mood. Through descriptive words, they make their readers get the feeling of a day before they begin their letters.

This bit of writing from an eighth grader might have been setting the mood for a Sunday letter:

Silence thunders throughout the household. Outside the black shroud of night moves slowly away. Lazy bits of cotton float downward—downward. Oh, so silently, so hushed, and gently they land to form a soft, white blanket over all.

Inside the house . . .

There you really begin your letter. The items get checked off your list, one after another punctuated by your own chuckles and giggles probably if it's a friendly, happy letter. Then you're at the end of it. Now how are your brakes? What is a tip for the ending?

Don't suspend it—end it.

That's a good tip. You don't have to say, "Yours till the kitchen sink," or "It's getting late so I must stop." Be smart: Just end it— don't suspend it.

Now it's writing time—letter-writing time. Make your letter sound like you, for:

A letter—what is it?
An on-paper visit!

It bears your very own stamp and is written to a special person. Have you decided on your special person? These are to be real letters, so remember: Develop your seed stories into several dramatic little paragraph scenes; tease the senses of your reader with word pictures; plan your letter; get off to a fast start and come to a fast stop.

II. Mind Your Manners

(Thank-You Notes)

Like the clean, new feeling
Of a fresh-made bed,
Is the feeling after thank-you's
Have just been said.

I don't think there's a more maddening feeling in the world than taking time and spending money to pick out and send a nice present to a person and then never even finding out if he received it, let alone getting a thank-you for it. I always feel like writing an angry note like this one to the person who forgets to say, "Thank you."

Look here, friend, that gift I sent
Was intended as a compliment.
But evidently, it is true
It didn't mean too much to you.

You didn't think it worth a letter.
If you had thanked me, I'd felt better.
It isn't that I wanted banners—
But I did think you'd "mind your manners!"

Of course, I never *send* a note like that—I just *think* it. But the queer thing about this thank-you business is that I *never feel* the same way when *I'm* the one who got the gift and should write the thank-you letter. For some reason or other, it's hard to get around to writing a thank-you letter. I'm too busy, or I haven't the right note paper, or—are you like that, too? Are you like most of us, wanting the rest of the world to mind their manners and feeling about ourselves as Marchette Chute did when she wrote:

Birthdays and Christmas would both be better
If no one expected a "Thank you" letter.[5]

I guess there's just no two ways about it: if we expect to receive presents, we'll just have to discipline ourselves and get right at that writing, and who doesn't just *love* to receive presents? Well, if we expect to receive, we must "mind our manners."

What are manners anyway, and why do we have them? Are manners just a lot of nonsense? I wonder! Thoughtfulness of others is what distinguishes a civilized person from a savage, and we all feel we're rather civilized, even the wildest of us. Manners are just the outward expression of inner thoughtfulness. Moderns don't eat with their hats on, guzzle their soup with sucking noises, wipe their mouths on the backs of their hands, or reach across the table to spear a piece of bread any more, although such manners were customary in the time of King Arthur. If we saw such a shocking display nowadays, we'd wonder where the boor came from. We have our own standards.

For instance, girls "who know" are seldom loud in public places. Your manners quietly or loudly broadcast to the world that you have good taste or bad; that you care what others think of you, or that you don't. This is a good thing to remember—that we are always broadcasting to the world what we're really like. People who never care what others think of them often don't think much of themselves.

---

[5] From *Rhymes about the Country* by Marchette Chute. By permission of The Macmillan Company, publishers.

When they get to be adolescents, boys and girls often get leggy and even awkward; but if their manners are good, they can get through almost anything with little trouble.

So today, let's mind our manners and write thank-you notes for gifts received, but not as yet acknowledged. If you didn't get any presents in the mail, you can thank somebody for a kindness he has done you, or you can practice a thank-you note for the next present you do get. How's that?

Our first rhymed direction for writing a thank-you is easy, yet very necessary:

> Since the note is you a-walking,
> Make it truly sound like talking.

Yes, sir, that letter must represent you, so it will just have to sound like talking. "Dear Grandmother," you could begin. "Since I can't afford an airplane trip, here is my letter to call on you and say 'Hi there, Grams, I want to thank you for that wonderful ball and bat you sent for Christmas!'"

Or maybe it's your cousin in South Dakota you're writing to. "Dear Margaret," your pen might say, "I'm paying you a four-cent visit this morning to thank you for that interesting book you sent me." From there on, just write it the way you would talk it.

> Since the note is you a-walking,
> Make it truly sound like talking.

Now let's plan the contents of the note. What shall we say? We can't, like the little girl, write: "Dear Grandmother, I have always wanted a pincushion for Christmas—but not very much." Nor as my nephew once wrote to his grandmother: "Thank you for the skates. They're nice, but I already had a pair."

No, these two honest approaches will *just not do*. And why not? Can't a person be honest in a thank-you letter? Of course, you can be honest, but you don't have to blurt out all you know. Manners, remember, indicate thoughtfulness of others. How would you feel if you were a grandmother and had made by hand, perhaps with shaky fingers, a pincushion for your granddaughter, and she wrote back that she'd always wanted a pincushion but not very much? How would you feel? Or about the skates! How will the grandmother feel if you tell her you already have skates? You see, we always tell the truth in a letter, but we leave out that part of the truth that would hurt the giver if we told it. What good would it do to hurt the person who thought enough of you to send you a present? That's what you're really thanking the giver for—for thinking enough of you to send you a present at all. He can't read your mind, you know, to find out what you already have.

Truly, about the only way that we can get just exactly what we want is to choose it ourselves. But it's much more fun to get presents than to buy presents, as all of you well know. You know very well, too, that you like almost every present you get—unless, of course, you're a gift-griper.

My father used to tell us when our family sat down to write our Christmas letters together, "No matter how you feel, never put a sword in a letter; kindness is rounded, never sharp and piercing."

So our second point to remember when writing thank-you notes is:

> Remember, you'll always say, "Thank you" better,
> If you pretend *you're* receiving the letter.

That's our second rule, and our third is just as short and concise:

> Even if in your heart you'd like to lose it,
> Describe to the sender just how you'll use it.

What do we mean by that? Let's say that your aunt sent blue beads to you. In your letter, tell her how pretty the beads are going to look with your new blue dress. Or perhaps Uncle Jim has sent his favorite nephew—you—a compass. Explain just how useful it will be to you as a scout.

Suppose you definitely disliked the beads or you already have five pocket compasses. What then shall you say to the loving relative without being dishonest? How would this do for the beads?

DEAR AUNT MABEL,
You certainly know what a girl needs. ["Only not me" you say under your breath but not on the paper.] Those beads will go with any nice blue dress—they're such a delicate color. It was surely nice of you to think of me and I do thank you and hope you had a happy Christmas.
Your loving niece,
Jean

Perhaps it will help you to hear a real letter that a grandmother friend of mine received from her grandson in Indiana:

DEAREST GRANDMOTHER:

It is no fun at home since you went back to Wisconsin. There is nobody here to play games with. Nobody laughs around here when you are gone.

You should have seen our Christmas tree. Daddy and Mother and I trimmed it. It looked like the one we saw down town when you were here, only smaller.

When I found the watch under the tree that you left for me at Christmas, I got so excited that I knocked the Christmas tree over and broke a lot of ornaments. I didn't get scolded because it was Christmas.

I just love the watch. All the kids at school want one too. Thank you, Grandmother, for such a wonderful present.

Come to see us soon as you can.

Your loving grandson,
Bob

Don't forget that there are more things to say thank you for than just gifts. Thank-you's are said to people, too, in real appreciation. Such thank-you notes are the best of all.

Eighth-grade Karen wrote this fine characterization of her father last year. Karen's paragraph isn't in the form of a note, but it comes directly from the heart, and as you read it, imagine how easily Karen could change this material into a note. She'd leave out some of the description, of course; notes of appreciation are brief. They are also sincere and come directly from the heart, just as this does. Notice how beautifully the last line tells about the father's kindness; that is especially good.

My father has straight blonde hair and blue eyes which are deeply set. His voice is very kind but also very gruff and loud. Most often he is dressed in blue overalls and a commonly colored shirt. His deeply set eyes will surely let you know he is a good father to children. Almost anytime he has a little smile on his face. I never did see him with a frown since I can remember him. He is quite short but not very chubby. He is a person with lips that have kind thoughts every minute of the day.

Karen, Grade 8

You can just imagine how happy Karen's father would be to get a note like that! He may not even realize that Karen is as fond of him as she is. Maybe she's never told him.

A grocer recently showed me a letter of appreciation he had received from one of our college students who helped him on Saturdays and after school. The man was so pleased with the letter he showed it to everybody.

In the note, the writer told him how scared she was when she first took the job and the number of mistakes she made. But the grocer hadn't scolded or picked flaws in her; instead he had pointed out each day the way in which she was getting better. She mentioned how kind he had been in cheerfully excusing her from work when college activities compelled her to be absent. She ended by saying she probably never would rate an employer like him again.

I believe that note can help us in deciding what could go into our notes, don't you? After all, we can't say, "Roses are red, violets are blue. Like hot fudge sundaes, I like you." Nowadays, we have to be specific and tailor-make our thank-you messages to the individual.

Notice first that the girl thanked the grocer for his wise understanding of her mistakes, and named, one after the other, his kindnesses. But notice that she acknowledged her own mistakes, too. Many folks expect loud praise for low-grade work. This girl didn't. The grocer had been more than fair; he had given her time to learn and had praised her every effort. Then at the last she had told him how she felt about him as a boss. Summing up the technique in her thank-you letter into a rhyme might read:

> A thank-you note should rate ace-high,
> If you tell him you like him, then point out why.

This sort of note would work fine for a mother, a father, a teacher, a pal—in fact, for almost anybody you'd care to write to.

One last little reminder before we go on to another phase of thank-you writing: the more personal your note, the shorter it is. Deep feeling gets squishy-squashy if we talk too long about it. It's like Sara Teasdale's "falling star—good only to make wishes on and then forever to be gone."

> I saw a star slide down the sky,
> Blinding the north as it went by,
> Too burning and too quick to hold,
> Too lovely to be bought or sold,
> Good only to make wishes on
> And then forever to be gone.[6]

---

[6] From *Collected Poems*, "The Falling Star" by Sara Teasdale. By permission of The Macmillan Company, publishers.

Now for the last rule for thank-you note writing:

> When you've finished your thank-you's, sit and chat,
> Don't say, "Thanks," then grab your hat.

Have you ever had a tiny lad call on you to say "Thank you," one who became so embarrassed that he left abruptly? A letter that says "Hello," "Thanks," and "Good-bye" is like that small child's visit —it came to an end too speedily to be other than embarrassing.

Your thank-you note, then, will be much more fun to receive if you talk a bit before your letter closes. What will you talk about? Oh, almost anything. Perhaps it snowed last night; you can tell of your fun in the snow. Perhaps your dad got a promotion; your relatives will be glad to hear that. Again, pretend you are the person to whom you are talking and ask yourself, "What would I like to hear?"

Let's gather those rhymed rules together before we go on:

> Since the note is you a-walking
> Make it truly sound like talking.
>
> Remember, you'll always say, "Thank you" better
> If you pretend *you're* receiving the letter.
>
> Even if in your heart you'd like to lose it,
> Describe to the sender just how you'll use it!
>
> When you've finished your thank-you's, sit and chat,
> Don't say, "Thanks!" then grab your hat!

There are so many good words you can use today in your notes. There are so many ways to express "Thank you": "I appreciate your gift." "I shall always cherish it." "I am grateful for this wonderful pony." (Who wouldn't be grateful for a pony?) I suspect not a soul will mind if you use a little slang in your letters. You might tell a young relative that her present is the *most*. I doubt whether most grownups who haven't been around children would know what you meant if you told them you'd had a ball, playing with their present. It's always wise to use words the reader knows.

Before we get at those thank-you letters, let's listen to the hilarious tale of the boy who wouldn't say thanks. You may wish to use it as a choral reading:

A young boy there was who was witty and clever.
He laughed and made jokes and was frolicking ever—
He had lots of friends and was brisk as a rabbit,
But he had just the fearfullest, tearfullest habit!
He never said thanks.

(*Faster*)   For the tracks and the racks,
For the trains and the tanks,
For the money collected in large piggy banks,
For tin soldiers that marched
In unbroken ranks,
For ponies with dappled-gray spots on their flanks,
For all kinds of gadgets that turned by their cranks,
For mittens and kittens, some Persian, some Manx,
For a bat signed by Braves and a ball by the Yanks
He wouldn't, just couldn't, or wouldn't say thanks!

So one day his relatives and his close friends
Said to each other, "It's time that this ends!
We're none of us cruel and there's none of us cranks,
But there's nobody living
Who'll just keep on giving
With never a thanks!"

So they bought gallons of ink and they filled up the
          tanks,
And they dunked him and junked him
And paddled with spanks
And left him, all ink-filled
And "think-filled" and blue
And they took back the gifts that they'd given him, too.

(*Fast*)   The tracks and the racks
And the trains and the tanks
And the money collected in large piggy banks
And tin soldiers that marched
In unbroken ranks
And ponies with dappled-gray spots on their flanks
And all kinds of gadgets that turned by their cranks
And mittens and kittens, some Persian, some Manx,
And a bat signed by Braves and a ball by the Yanks
And still this boy wouldn't or didn't say thanks!

I wish I could tell you he changed, but, my dears,
He even got worse through the ensuing years,
And now he's a sergeant who battles with tanks
For soldiers say sergeants just never say thanks
Just never—not ever—no, never, say thanks.

Well, I guess we'd better get at those thank-you notes. The army just *can't* use that many sergeants!

III. Grace Notes

(Notes of Gracious Living)

One of the finest letters of appreciation written by a child that I have ever come across is this one by fourth-grade Dianne. I have the original pencil copy from which the final copy was made.

DEAR GRANDMOTHER,

As I am sitting here looking out the window, looking at all the snow, I think back of all the times we were together this summer. Or should we daydream about last summer together? You let me go on bike rides. You, Grandpa and I went for rides. And when you went baby-sitting, I could go and play with the kids.

You let me go to my Aunt's house and stay awhile. You let me help you with the cookie making, though I ate more dough than I made cookies.

But oh! Would I get disgusted at you because you would say, "Come on Dianne, time for school work" and off went T.V. and downstairs we went to do reading, writing and worst of all, arithmetic.

And now I realize why you made me do school work for an hour or two. It was so I would get a better mark in school.

Today you are on the train going home from California and Arizona back home to Iowa.

Grandma, I may not be the best pine but I am trying to be a good bush like in the poem you sent me.

As always,
Dianne B.

The shortest, unique note of appreciation I ever heard about was received by an aunt in answer to a graduation gift sent to her nephew. She writes:

For his high-school graduation. I sent a check. Several weeks went by without a thank-you note. But when my next bank statement arrived, I found on the back of my canceled check scrawled above his endorsement: "Dear Aunt Virginia—You know how I hate to write, but thanks a lot!" [7]

By far, the longest letter of appreciation ever to come to my attention was sent to Red Schoendienst, ailing second baseman of the Milwaukee Braves. When the seventh-grade children at Maple Dale suburban school heard of his illness, each wrote a letter of appreciation and pasted it on one long scroll, which they sent to their hero.

One can well believe that Mr. Schoendienst had considerable unrolling to do before he found out that his admirers literally measured their admiration for him by the yard.

Most of you children have never seen a letter from a refugee camp. This is the copy of a letter received by the American Red Cross in a Wisconsin city:

DEAR FRIENDS!
On St. Nicholas Day, December 6th, I received your little package for which I want to thank you most sincerely. It was a great surprise for me and has made me very happy. My name is Jurgen Tottewitz and I am 14 years old. On September 18th, 1957, my parents with their four children left the Eastern Zone. We found a welcome in the Federal Republic. The beginning is very difficult for us; but surely we'll be able to work things out again. We have not regretted that we left the Eastern Zone. There are good, kind people everywhere. Much kindness has been shown us. It has made me very happy to find that the children in America also think of us.

Again, many thanks and all good wishes to you.

Jurgen Tottewitz
Sincere Christmas greetings
(Jurgen is pronounced Year-gen)

The return address—Jurgen Tottewitz
Hahn (Oldenburg)
Deutschland
Fluchtlingslager

Deutschland is Germany, Fluchtlingslager a refugee camp.

---

[7] By permission of the author, Virginia S. Pendarvis, and *The Reader's Digest.*

Note writing will show
That you're smart and you know.

Note writing is the outward sign of inner appreciation. To be appreciative is to be happy. Note writing follows few rigid rules; to be correct, a note must fit the circumstances not the form in the etiquette book. Modern rules of behavior are tailored to the circumstances and the individuals involved. When the circumstances call for a warm, informal note, it is good etiquette to write that kind of note. It is seldom good manners to write formal notes to people whose social life is entirely informal. But a cordial note written a few days after a gift is received or a dinner or week-end invitation accepted advertises to your hostess that you not only know the rules of acceptable behavior but care enough about yourself and the people you mingle with to observe them.

We have taken care of thank-you's and notes of appreciation. There are four other types of notes that must be sent.

A. Bread-and-Butter Notes

Young people do not always understand that an overnight visit outside our immediate circle of friends or even a dinner at the home of people with whom we are not accustomed to dine requires a thank-you note. These bread-and-butter notes, as they have come to be called, must be sent within a week after the dinner or the week end.

No one ever needs fear the wording of a note of this sort; he can hardly go wrong if he makes his note an on-paper visit. Perhaps these suggestions may help you to feel comfortable about your thank-you letter.

1. Express appreciation for having been invited. (Even though you may not have actually enjoyed the visit, you can still honestly appreciate having been asked.)

2. Point out the one or two high lights of the week end: the lovely, relaxed spirit of their home, the fun and laughter you had there, the parents' wonderful attitude toward young people, the delicious meals—after dormitory fare or quick-lunch restaurants—the trips on the lake with the boat. If you had no fun, omit this one. In a note you are not on the witness stand to tell the whole truth—just to express appreciation.

3. Comment perhaps on the hostess's hobby—her attractive home, her African violets, her garden, her china collection. Some-

time afterwards you may want to send her a clipping you have found relative to her hobby.

4. Use "sincerely" or "cordially" as a complimentary closing or an unusual one that shows your special feeling such as "an admirer of yours."

5. Once in a while, when the hostess who has entertained you did so as a special courtesy to you, and especially if you are not going to be a regular guest at her home, you may wish to send her a small gift. Never overdo the bread-and-butter gift; make it impersonal: flowers (a few roses are in better taste than many) ; a plant (but not an ostentatious one) ; a white linen handkerchief, or one in *her* color; candy if for the whole family; lovely note paper, white or with a slight touch of color. If you are alert, you will study your hostess and sense what she would like. It's the hostess to whom you send the gift, but the host and hostess or family to whom you direct your appreciation.

A wise public-relations counsel cautions letter writers to delete the pronoun "I" as much as possible. "A week-end thank you note which opens 'had a wonderful time' " he points out, "is not half so captivating as one beginning, 'You are a wonderful hostess.' Both say, 'Thank you,' but, ah, my friends, the second is the one that will get you asked back!" [8]

Never neglect sending a bread-and-butter letter. The omission speaks eloquently of you as a person. The gift is never mandatory; the note is. Children should grow up with note writing; not have notes thrust upon them with adolescence.

B. Notes of Acceptance or Rejection of an Invitation

One of my students calls these the "Uh-huh" and "Uh-uh" notes: yes, I can accept your invitation; no, I can't.

1. If you received the invitation by mail, answer it that way unless there has been a delay in mail delivery.

2. Make your acceptance cordial, your refusal gracious.

3. In a note of acceptance, reiterate the day and the hour of the dinner or party. (Then if there was a mistake, the hostess will know.)

---

[8] From *The Life of the Party* by Bennett Cerf. Copyright, 1956, by Bennett Cerf. Reprinted by permission of the publishers, Hanover House (Doubleday) .

4. In a note of refusal, give the general reason, not the specific: "I have already accepted another invitation," not "I have a date with my boy friend that night."

5. End a refusal with a regret that you cannot attend.

6. If, for any reason, it is wiser not to accept the invitation, see to it that the lady gets a gracious note. Only George Bernard Shaw could get by with the real reason in this case. Only geniuses can afford to be rude and most of them aren't.

C. Notes of Condolence

Since notes of condolence are difficult, these suggestions are made to the teacher to help older students.

The word _condolence_ comes from the Latin word _dolor_ meaning "sorrow."

We write (most of us _don't_ write) notes of condolence when there is a death in a friend's family. Many of us shun writing notes of condolence because we don't know what to say.

Impress upon children that people in their time of sorrow need a warm, friendly note, not a "sad" one. What a friend needs is the assurance that he has friends who care.

Accordingly, in a note of condolence, assure the person that you are thinking of him; suggest some definite help you can offer if you can be of any help. "I'll bring a hot dish over on Tuesday evening for dinner for the family"; "I'll baby-sit for you at _my_ house on Tuesday if you wish." Something definite is better than the general, "If I can do anything, let me know." Tell children to do any little kindness they can do.

Since only the closest friends go calling on a bereaved friend, a note of condolence should be a short, sympathetic call—via the mail. For all but the closest friends, calling by mail is more thoughtful than calling in person.

Tell children that in the case of the aged or chronically ill death is not an occasion for weeping, but a kind of graduation from a hard phase of life to an easier. Even in this circumstance, surviving relatives need friends and will feel lonely and sad.

Whenever a friend of the school dies, or a member of the family of a child in the room, have the children write a nice, friendly note of condolence. (See Donald's letter, page 394, in this chapter.)

D. A Note of Apology

My father used to say that the happiest people in the world are the people who "mend their fences" as they go. "Mending fences for a person," he explained, "means taking care every week of the holes in one's living: the wrongs we have done to others, the untruths we have told. One must report first of all to God, but since God has no hands but ours, we have to mend our own fences." "Never write an apology if you can talk to the person face to face" was the rule at our house, and since we never went very far afield, we youngsters rarely needed to write a note of apology. When it was necessary, it had to be done. However, we never were made to apologize if we weren't sorry. Father told us never to lie in a letter, and keeping one foot on truth and one on honor was a wide spraddle sometimes. I remember once writing to an older woman whom I had offended in some minor way (I can't remember the details) and telling her in the note that I still meant what I said, but that it wasn't good manners to say it, and that I was sorry. She must have been a truly big person because she sent me a nice note afterwards which I cherished for years. Probably because of my own experiences with notes of apology and because I was brought up to "mend my fences," I believe all children need training in this type of writing.

What goes into a note of apology? Again, I don't believe we should put words into children's mouths. Why not make these simple suggestions for notes of this type?

1. Tell why you're writing.
2. Tell how you feel about what you did.
3. Express the hope that the person can forgive you.
4. In a letter of apology, don't crawl; pick up that pen and go at that writing as if you were looking the person directly in the eye.
5. After the note is written, stop worrying; you've mended your fence the best you can; now it's up to the other fellow. And that is that.

Children must be taught that notes are a part of the rules of the living game; just as baseball would be a sorry mess without rules, so would social living.

Almost nobody enjoys writing notes, but the people who observe the amenities of gracious living tend to have friends, while outlaws get tired of going about just with other outlaws. If we're going to enjoy playing the game of living, we'll have to follow a few rules and if we really appreciate people, we'll find it's time well spent because giving is really a part of receiving. Until you've given something in return, you haven't really enjoyed the full pleasure of receiving. The poet Edwin Arlington Robinson shows a real understanding of giving and getting when he speaks of two kinds of gratitude:

> . . . for every gift
> Or sacrifice, there are—or there may be—
> Two kinds of gratitude: the sudden kind
> We feel for what we take, the larger kind
> We feel for what we give . . . . [9]

IV. Dear Friend

(Pen-Pal Letters)

I'm especially excited about this lesson because of Patty's dream. You don't know Patty, of course; she's twelve and has eyes as brown and friendly as a spaniel's. Recently, Patty wrote me about a dream she had, and right away I thought, "I'll share that with the children on Dear Friend Day in the letter chapter of my book."

Don't you just love that expression "Dear Friend Day"? Just to say it gives a good feeling in the heart. You see, "Dear Friend Day" is any day of the year when you write a pen-pal letter to a friend in another state or another country; it's any day when you attempt to get acquainted with faraway neighbors—neighbors sometimes even across the world.

In order to get acquainted with our neighbors, we'll have to call on them, of course. That's easy enough to do if they live on our own street, but a lot harder if they live in Tasmania or in the Union of South Africa.

I guess that's the reason I got so interested in Patty's dream letter —it gave me an idea. But, wait, you'll want to read it. I have a feeling that it will give you an idea, too, of how we can go calling on our faraway neighbors. Patty wrote:

I didn't seem to be asleep in this dream. I was very much awake and for some reason I was awfully excited. It was night, I thought, and summer, and the world looked so bright that I ran outside onto the lawn in my bare feet and in my pajamas. Never have I seen such a moon—it was as

[9] From *Collected Poems*, "Captain Craig" by Edwin Arlington Robinson. By permission of The Macmillan Company, publishers.

golden as honey—it was actually laughing—and so close I could almost have touched it if I had stood on the barn.

Then all at once as I looked up at the sky, I saw the strangest sight! It actually began to rain letters, hundreds of them, thousands of them, each letter letting itself slowly down to earth with a tiny parachute. It was the most astonishing sight I have ever seen—looking up at those letter paratroopers coming down by thousands. And then I saw an even stranger sight. Suddenly without warning our yard and our meadow and our alfalfa field were filled with children, hundreds of children with hands eagerly reaching up toward the letters. And as each caught a letter, I noticed for the time that these children were not our close neighbors—that many of them were from faraway lands and were dressed like the children in the geography book.

As the children opened their letters and read them, there was laughing and shouting and suddenly the children and the letters disappeared from sight like the children in "The Pied Piper of Hamelin," and I was left alone with no one but the moon which seemed to be laughing harder than ever.

Did you get it? *Did* you get an idea of how we can go calling on our faraway neighbors? No, I don't mean by parachute, but wouldn't it be fun if we could go that way? If one bright Saturday morning in February, we said to ourselves, "Well, I guess I'll go see my friend, Ramon, down in Argentina today"? So we'd strap one of our dirigible parachutes onto our belts, press the button marked Argentina, and just as we reached the country near Buenos Aires, pull the rip cord, let our parachute blossom out and land right in a ranch yard where we'd try being a cowboy with Ramon all day. Heigho! Wouldn't that be fun?

Since that's out of the question, why not send a letter paratrooping down to Ramon on a good old mail plane? Why not?

If anything would make a friendly feeling all over the world, it would be for boys and girls to write to unknown friends across the sea. For there's hardly anybody you can really dislike after you get to know him. Have you noticed that?

Let's do just that today. Let's write letters to children in a faraway country and begin them, "Dear Friend." That—as we used to say when we were growing up—should be as much fun as a zebra sliding down a banister and landing in the minister's lap!

What shall we say to our dear friends across the sea? We want this letter to be fun to read and fun to write. Perhaps, first of all, we'd better stop to consider that these children we're writing to are much like us. They feel inside about things much in the same way that we do; they like to play, are not *too* interested in working; they enjoy having fun and they often get disgusted with their parents when they don't get to do as they want to—just as you do.

Take your friend, Ramon from Argentina, for instance. He's really disgusted because his family treats him like a child:

AMBITION [10]

When I am grown an *hombre*
I shall have another *nombre,*
They won't call me "Ramonito" any more;
But they'll call me *"caballero,"*
And I'll wave my wide *sombrero*
At all the señoritas I adore.

I've extravagant ideas:
Butter on all my *tortillas,*
And as much chokecherry jelly as I dare!
I will buy red combs for Mother—
She shall wear them, and no other—
With shiny stones to lie against her hair.

There will not be any, any,
That can use the words so many,
Or make speech so long as mine when I am big;
And for my songs I'll borrow
Uncle Pablo's good *guitarra*—
But now I have to go and feed the pig.

I imagine you've all felt just like that many a time. Children in all lands feel much the same way inside. It's only outside that they're different; that's why going to see them is such fun. Rose Waldo expresses this same idea especially well in eight short lines of verse:

WELCOME [11]

Little new neighbor, have you come to be
A playmate of mine from over the sea?
I'm glad you are here. Oh, won't it be fine
To learn all your games, and I'll teach you mine!

[10] From *The Songs of Marcelino* by Edith J. Agnew.
[11] From *Child Life Magazine.* Copyright 1929, by Rand McNally & Company.

We won't understand all the words that we say,
But I'm sure that we both will know how to play.
So will you come now and swing while I swing,
And we'll sing all the songs that we love to sing.

Yes, your "over-the-sea" friends are just different enough from you to be understood. Take Pedro, for instance, from Spain, in the poem by Mary Austin. What Pedro could teach you and me!

A FELLER I KNOW [12]

His name it is Pedro-Pablo-Ignacio-Juan-
Francesco García y Gabaldon,
But the fellers call him Pete;
His folks belong to the Conquistadores
And he lives at the end of our street.

His father's father's great-grandfather
Was friends with the King of Spain
And his father peddles hot tamales
From here to Acequia-Madre Lane.

And Pete knows every one of the signs
For things that are lucky to do,
A charm to say for things that are lost,
And roots that are good to chew.

Evenings we go to Pedro's house
When there's firelight and rain
To hear of the Indians his grandfather fought
When they first came over from Spain.

And how De Vargas with swords and spurs
Came riding down our street,
And Pedro's mother gives us cakes
That are strange and spicy and sweet.

And we hear of gold that is buried and lost
On ranches they used to own,
And all us fellers think a lot
Of Pedro-Pablo-Ignacio-Juan-
Francesco García y Gabaldon.

[12] From *Children Sing in the Far West* by Mary Austin. By permission of Houghton Mifflin Company, publishers.

No wonder that boy's neighbors called him Pete; he certainly had a long name, hadn't he? But isn't he interesting?

Since the children you're going to write to are something like you, it will be easy enough to decide what to put into the letter. They'll no doubt want to know about you—what you'd like to know about them—the answers to such questions as the English author, Rose Fyleman, put into her short verse:

THE NEW NEIGHBOR [13]

Have you had your tonsils out?
  Do you go to school?
Do you know that there are frogs
  Down by Willow Pool?

Are you good at cricket?
  Have you got a bat?
Do you know the proper way
  To feed a white rat?

Are there any apples
  On your apple tree?
Do you think your mother
  Will ask me in to tea?

Right in this poem, we get a tip about the interests of our "across-the-sea" neighbors: they'll want to hear about the games we like to play. In England it's cricket, as the poem suggested, while in America it's baseball or football or basketball. In your pen-pal letters, you boys could describe just how your favorite ball game is played, perhaps even sketching a baseball diamond with X's to show where the players stand. Then you might ask the boy you're writing to to describe his favorite game; questions help the person you're writing to to get his return letter started.

You girls might be interested in discussing your hobbies with your new "dear friends." They'll indeed be interested in clothes and school and collections of pictures of movie stars, and whatever you enjoy doing most.

I can just imagine how your new dear friends would enjoy hearing about your daydreams and your secret wishes; they have them, too, you know.

[13] From *Gay Go Up* by Rose Fyleman. Copyright 1930 by Doubleday & Company, Inc. Reprinted by permission.

"Let's Writer" Michael may give you an idea of the type of thing you might want to include in your letter to inform your pen pal of your secret desires:

> What would you do on a day of your own?
> I'd go fishing all alone.
> I'd cut a stick, get a hook and some string,
> And throw it in the water with a swing.
> I'd lie down under an old elm tree,
> Put my cap over my head so that I couldn't see.
> About twelve noon, I'd eat my little snack,
> And lean up against the tree with my back.
> And when evening came a crawlin' I'd take my fish and go
> Home so slow, so slow.
> Now what would you do on a day of your own?
> I'd go fishing, all alone.

Do you know what your new friends would rather hear about than any of these ideas—better even than knowing your games and your hobbies and what you like to do best? The first question they'd no doubt ask you if they could actually meet you would be about your home: "What is it like—that place that you live?" You see, writing a letter is only answering people's questions before they ask them.

How easily you will be able to make your new friends see your homes and your families, you who are so used to making pen portraits of your relatives, and writing sketches of your home towns or cities. If you don't put another thing into your letter, be sure to include the answer to your dear friend's directive, "With your pencil, make me see your home, new friend."

"Let's Writer" Joan sketches an evening at her home that would give a faraway child a tip on just what you want to hear about her home when she writes her letter to you:

> During the long, dark evenings in the long, cold months of winter, it is quite natural to find us all in the living room crunching popcorn. Pop snoozing in the rocking chair, waking only when the dish of popcorn is passed to him, and then staying awake only long enough to eat a couple of handfuls. Mom sits near the lamp (and register) darning, patching, or once in awhile reading some book which she has just received from the Book Club.

The rest of us are lined up on the sofa with books, games or something else to keep us occupied. Once in awhile we just sit and act silly and giggle. It is such fun until someone giggles once too often or worse yet the popcorn is gone and it's time for bed.

Joan, Grade 6

There are so many ideas to choose from for your pen-pal letters —a pencil sketch of your home and family, the games you like, the hobbies you enjoy, the dreams and hopes you have! Oh yes, and your pets! What a common point of interest pets would be, since your faraway friend would probably have one of his own about which you could ask him!

Eighth-grade Jeanette will have fun telling her pen pal about her sheep on which she has received so many county and state prizes. Doesn't she make these lambs real? No wonder—they are real lambs.

My bottle lambs are as friendly as can be.
They're always at the door ready to greet me.
They jump over the ewes that are lying on the ground
Whenever they hear someone coming around.

First there was Caesar, a cute little fellow,
Who would jump sky high if he heard a cow bellow.
We found him a mother. And now I must say
That she's taking care of him and all's okay.

Then there was Antony, a gay little Southdown,
That could run like crazy and act like a clown.
He now has a mother for which I am sad
For I hardly ever see him but guess he is glad.

Then there was Cleopatra, or Cleo for short.
When I go near the barn, she gives her retort.
I always bring her bottle when I go into the shed.
She's always very hungry and ready to be fed.

The last one I have was sick a few short days ago.
He was ready to go into the hard ground below.
He had the white muscle disease the Vet said.
He also said I'd better start digging Brutus a bed.

I felt sorry for the poor little lamb
So I fell upon a wonderful plan.
I bottled Brutus for to keep him alive.
And now he can run (Brutus survived) .

Jeanette, Grade 8

Why don't you tell your pen pal about your particular pet? Having a pet in common shortens the getting-acquainted period just as having ice cream to eat does.

By this time I'm sure you know just what you want to write about in your pen-pal letters. You can choose only two or three items to write about, of course, so you'll have to choose as carefully as if you were picking out a new puppy. Perhaps what you'll want to write about can be summarized in one brief sentence. *Include in your letter whatever you'd want your new friend to tell about in his.* Perhaps your teacher can help you gather a list of questions you'd like to ask your friend. Instead of asking questions of him, why not answer his questions ahead of time?

Before you write, perhaps I can help you find a "Dear Friend" to write to. There are sometimes pen-pal lists in *The American Junior Red Cross News.* However, if you wish to send to some country not listed there, the local minister or priest may be able to give you the name of a missionary who has a mission school in the faraway land of your choice. Mexican and South American pen pals can often be located through contacting the Minister of Education in the capital city.

If you are seeking a "Dear Friend" in a European country, contacts can be made through a friend in your community who has relatives or friends in that country. These people can often locate pen pals for school children.

Be sure to proofread and recopy your letters today—one gives his best to his friends.

For goodness' sake, *do* answer every pen-pal letter you receive. Even eleven-year-old Peter Mayor of Hounslow, Middlesex, England, did that, and he got a thousand pen-pal letters in one year from the United States. Perhaps the reason was that both he and his father wrote to a New York paper saying that Peter was sometimes lonely; he had never been out of his home town, and for five years had helped his father run the house during his mother's illness.

Peter has faithfully kept his promise to answer every letter he received, though once he received sixty-eight letters in one day. Patty's dream, you see, almost came true just for that one boy alone.

V. Disagreeing Agreeably

(Expressing Disagreement in a Business Letter)

Today I'm going to help you to say disagreeable things agreeably—a skill as useful as a dinner plate and as necessary to our way of life as a can opener. If you aren't a namby-pamby, you'll often disagree with people, but why put sand under the wheels of life if you can use oil? Anyone can criticize in this world, but it takes a smart person to help the other fellow to improve without breaking down his morale.

A good slogan for today's lesson is "Don't slow your travel with gravel"—the gravel of irritating words, that is.

In writing time today we're going to write a friendly business letter to a television or radio program, a ball team, a school principal, a newspaper, a magazine, or a young people's group. But what are we going to write about? Well, perhaps you'd like a rule changed, an attitude reversed, a policy discontinued; all right, write a friendly business letter suggesting that change.

The idea here is to disagree with the organizations you're writing to so agreeably that they'll agree with you and make the change.

But this disagreeing with folks is a touchy procedure; perhaps it would be well to approach it together. For believe it or not, much of your success in life is going to depend on whether you travel with oil or gravel.

Perhaps the first principle to think about in saying disagreeable things agreeably is, "Don't knock your opponent out before you take him down. Don't close *his* mind before you open *your* mouth."

Suppose, for instance, that you're writing a letter to a newspaper editor, telling him you don't like his paper's policy on teen-agers. What will happen to the editor's mind if you begin your letter like this: "Dear Sir: I think your newspaper is the most stupid in the whole state"?

With that sort of beginning, what have you done to that editor? You've definitely shut his mind before you've had a chance to poke in one single idea, and you might just as well have saved your four-cent stamp; you aren't going to change the policy of that man's paper one iota! You've done nothing but make him angry.

This is the same idea exactly as if you said to a radio actor, "I just hate your program," then followed that statement with several suggestions for improvement. Unless he's an extraordinary person, that actor will say to himself, "Huh—he hates my program, does he?" and he's your enemy before you make a single suggestion.

I saw that technique well demonstrated in a legislative hearing several years ago. A legislative hearing is a meeting open to the public at which citizens can speak for or against important bills before the lawmakers vote on them.

It was a hot day and so many people had come to appear against the bill that the whole assembly room was crowded. One after another fifty people arose to speak against the bill. Without a single exception every speaker intimated that the legislators were a bunch of men entirely too stupid to know a good law when they saw it. Each speaker first insulted the intelligence of the legislators, then proceeded to take three times the amount of time it was fair to take.

I was seated in the assembly room right where I could face the members of the legislative committee. As the men were told how stupid they were, I could almost see the doors of their minds close and their lips lock into thin, negative lines. Then a small plain-looking woman electrified the committee members into interest.

"Gentlemen," she began in a pleasant voice, "you are far too smart to vote for this bill." Unconsciously each man straightened and beamed. Several of them even leaned toward the woman as she explained in a short, concise way why she thought they wouldn't vote for the bill. With these closing words, "I have been thinking ever since this meeting convened. I might just as well have saved myself this trip to Madison. Gentlemen like you will never vote for a bill like this. I feel safe leaving the matter in your capable hands," she sat down.

> ✓The man who calls names before he starts
> Closes the doors of listening hearts.

If we aren't to start calling names at the first of our letters, how shall we start? There's no use telling people what not to do unless we give them some positive advice.

The best way, I believe, to begin critical remarks, either written or oral, is to begin with appreciation. That's all, actually, that the woman in the legislative hearing was doing—she was appreciating the legislators. Appreciation opens doors; abuse closes them.

There's a wonderful example of this appreciative approach in the Bible. The missionary, Paul, was going to Athens, Greece, to try to convert the Athenians to Christianity. On his way into the city, Paul noticed shrines to dozens of gods. One inscription gave

Paul the pointer for his approach; it was the shrine dedicated to the unknown god.

Paul was an excellent psychologist. Accordingly, he began his address to the Athenians, "You men of Athens, I see by the number of shrines on my way into the city that you are very religious. Among those shrines I found one addressed to the unknown god. It is that god, men of Athens, that I have come to tell you about."

The minute you tell anybody that what he believes in, or does, is stupid, you have immediately shut *his* door in *your own* face, and it is you who have been the stupid one.

I am going to read you two letters to a newspaper editor who is always playing up teen-age misdemeanors. As you listen to these letters, pretend you are the editor. Which letter would make you want to change?

To the *Bonneville Times*—

GENTLEMEN:

You are the most prejudiced man against teen-agers that I have ever met with. To read your paper, a person would think that there wasn't one good person from thirteen to twenty in this whole city of twenty-eight thousand. The editorial of last Friday tops everything for misrepresentation. Reading your paper makes me want to do every bad thing you accuse young people of doing. Have you forgotten when you were our age, or is it too long ago for you to remember? Why don't you quit being a square and get really cool for once.

Your Un-Admirer,
Ralph Nicholson

The only thing to do with a smart-alecky letter like that is to copy it on expensive white paper and burn it in the furnace. The person who has been helped is Ralph, not the editor. Write pop-off letters as good therapy for yourself, but never send them. Now for another type of letter:

Mr. John Mortenson
Editor of *Bonneville Times*

DEAR MR. MORTENSON:

We members of the eighth-grade social studies class of Roosevelt Junior High often use your editorials on United States foreign policy as the basis for interesting panel discussions. We like the way you deal with both sides of the questions, especially in your recent discussion of the Arab situation. You always show us that there are two sides to every controversial issue.

But Mr. Mortenson, one thing about your paper troubles us; you seem to be so much against young people, thinking that all of them are bad actors. Frankly, Mr. Mortenson, we know that a few teen-agers in this town are thoughtless and smart-alecky, and some are downright bad, but this group is very small compared to the hundreds who are fairly well behaved. We who admire your fairness in dealing with foreign affairs cannot see why you can't see the two sides to the youth question.

We have a feeling that if we got together we might have more mutual understanding. We're going to have a panel discussion of youth and Bonneville on Friday, November 18, at 1:30 in Rm. 120 Roosevelt Junior High School. Could you possibly be our guest on that day?

We'd like to have you come and we think you'd like us if you knew us. A welcoming committee will meet you at the east door on Adams Street if you can come.

Cordially,

John Kendricks, Class President

112 South 22nd Street

__ But, you ask me, what if John doesn't like anything about the editor? How can he then start his letter with appreciation?

Personally, I don't believe it is sensible to write to anyone who you feel is all wrong. If he's on a radio or television program, turn him off and forget him. Don't stoop to lie to anybody; if you can't see anything at all good in him or his program, you wouldn't change him anyway. Save the stamp and tune in another program.

So far we've had two points in our D.A.—disagreeing agreeably—program:

> The man who calls names before he starts
> Closes the doors to listening hearts.

and

> Appreciation said before
> You criticize will open the door.

Now for the third pointer in disagreeing agreeably:

> Keep impersonal, if you can—
> You're changing the program—not the man!

Haven't you gone to a party at some time or other when you've met a person whose face you longed to punch—a thoroughly disagreeable person?

In a Gilbert and Sullivan light opera, *Princess Ida,* there is a funny lyric entitled "The Disagreeable Man," the man everybody wants to punch, but rarely does:

> If you give me your attention, I will tell you what I am
> I'm a genuine philanthropist, all other kinds are sham.
> Each little fault of temper and each social defect
> In my erring fellow creatures, I endeavor to correct.
> To all their little weaknesses I open people's eyes;
> And little plans to snub the self-sufficient I devise;
> I love my fellow creatures, I do all the good I can,
> Yet everybody says I'm such a disagreeable man!
>   And I can't think why!
>
> I'm sure I'm not ascetic; I'm as pleasant as can be;
> You'll always find me ready with a crushing repartee.
> I've an irritating chuckle, I've a celebrated sneer,
> I've an entertaining snigger, I've a fascinating leer.
> To everybody's prejudice I know a thing or two;
> I can tell a woman's age in half a minute, and I do.
> But although I try to make myself as pleasant as I can,
> Yet everybody says I'm such a disagreeable man!
>   And I can't think why!

Every group has one person in it who tries to take everybody apart, and nobody ever loves him.

But when that kind of person runs an organization and we're writing him a letter to try to change a policy of his, we must forget about his personal qualities and think only of the policy we want changed. After all, we can't expect to run up to a person and say, "Look here, sir, I don't like your face!" then expect him to listen to our suggestions. Only Groucho Marx could get by with that. Do you remember that crack of his? "I never forget a face—but I'm willing to make an exception in your case." [14]

After all, most of us aren't "wits"; and when we want a thing changed, we mustn't begin with the person. Personal remarks are out if we want to disagree agreeably.

We must rarely criticize a person's voice, his face, his laugh, his bald head, or his height or weight; those are personal things he can't help. In your letter stick to the policies and forget the people. A man can't change his nose, but he can change his mind if approached agreeably. In other words:

[14] By permission of Groucho Marx.

> Personal remarks are out of order
> They're rude or closely on that border.

Even personal remarks can be made sometimes to a friendly person if said in a friendly manner.

I got such a chuckle out of a nice little fifth-grade girl who wrote to me last year when I asked my School of the Air radio audience to send evaluations of the program.

This friendly girl wrote me that they'd had a discussion in their room as to whether my chuckle was genuine or put on and if I didn't mind she'd like to know. She worded her letter so nicely that I was glad to answer her question.

If she only knew, I used to get spanked for that chuckle. It's as genuine as a wart on a chin. Even when I was little, it came popping out whenever I got tickled about anything—and sometimes at a point when it was very wrong to laugh; once in church, I remember, and I nearly died of shame.

Few people mind answering the honest questions of children and I certainly didn't.

Now for the final plans for our friendly business letter to any radio or television program, ball team, school, scout organization, club, newspaper, or magazine, whose policy on some point you'd like to change. Maybe you don't like their attitude, their advertising, one of their rules. Remember, if you want to change anybody's ideas, you must disagree agreeably—oil smooths the way better than sand. As Della Adams Leitner says:

> To state one's views with skillful tact
> That will no barb impart
> And disagree agreeably
> Is diplomatic art.[15]

Well, good writing!

> We're foreseeing
> Fine results
> From your disagreeing!

A typical sixth grader reacts courteously to the state superintendent's ideas concerning ten months of school:

---

[15] By permission of the author and *The Christian Science Monitor*.

DEAR MR. WATSON:

I like school a lot. I meet my friends every school day and I meet new friends. I also want to go through high school and college. I like arithmetic, and I want to take up algebra and math.

I like to come to school and I think nine months of school is all right. But I don't think too much of this idea of ten months of school. I'm needed around the farm and I enjoy studying nature. I live next to a river and a woods and I spend a lot of time around them.

So would you please try to avoid the idea of ten months of school. Thank you,

Your friend,
Jeffrey R. H.

A sixth-grade girl states her views clearly:

DEAR SIR:

I like very much the way the city keeps the ice rink open for many children to have fun. But I think there should be more order over there. Someone might get seriously hurt because of some children smarting off. I suggest that you have a policeman over there to check at times. If the children don't mind, I think you should punish them some way . . . like having them stay off the rink for the rest of the season.

I'd appreciate it very much if you did something to make it better for small children who come there to have fun in a decent way.

Sincerely yours,
Lois H.

VI. My Dear Boss—(I Hope)

(Writing an Effective Application for a Teaching Position)

Hiring inexperienced teachers is even more hazardous for a school system than for a teacher. If a first job goes wrong, a teacher can usually move; if a first teacher goes wrong, the children are stuck for a year at least. That is why school superintendents need as many checks as possible on new teachers; they need to get the right system and the right teacher together, a service students should appreciate.

Before hiring, a student's record is meticulously evaluated, his letter of application thoughtfully studied, his interview carefully considered, and the comments of his references weighed for what they say both on and between the lines.

A letter of application speaks for or against the person who wrote it. Therefore, the contents of such a letter must be written and considered carefully.

Your letter, like you, has a personality; unfortunately, not always your own. Your own personality may be warm and joyous; your letter may be as cold as a house-mother's reprimand after a too-late date. Your job is to make your letter tell about you without overstating or understating your case.

Applicants used to copy form letters from a book; today there are so many applicants for every job that a letter must be individual in order to be noticed. The hardest part of writing a letter of application is to make it distinctive without sounding odd. Your letter, therefore, in order to set it apart from other applications, must have an air of "you" about it.

How can you achieve that air? As usual, I am suggesting that you use your imagination to ascertain what this new boss (you hope) will want to know about you. It seems to me that these items would be the minimum essentials in a letter of application:

*1. Name the job you are applying for and tell where you heard about the vacancy.

2. Tell from what institution you are graduating, from what division, when, and with what degree.

3. Tell your marital status and your age if you are a beginning teacher. If you are a widow, it is not necessary to state whether or not you are divorced. This is merely a letter of application, not an inquisition.

*4. Sketch briefly the experiences in your background that may possibly make you a better teacher.

5. Mention your practice teaching, in what grade and in what school.

*6. In a very few sentences tell how you feel about your chosen profession.

7. Suggest that your credentials be sent from the college and give the address of the placement bureau.

8. Ask for an interview, suggesting a definite date and time of day. Give your telephone number and mention enclosing a stamped, self-addressed envelope for the superintendent's use if he finds the time of the interview inconvenient. (This is mandatory.)

*9. Exit gracefully.

Although your whole letter will speak for you, the starred points 1, 4, 6 (1 and 6 especially), and possibly 9 speak the most eloquently. Let us consider Point 1 first.

Point 1. You are meeting your boss ("I" to eye) in this first paragraph; don't fumble. Don't try to impress him; just tell him what you're after and possibly why. Never say, "I would like to make application—" (of course you'd like to or you wouldn't be applying); simply say that you're applying or making application for a particular position. If this is only a nibble at a job and not an application for a definite opening, simply say you are interested in an intermediate (or primary) teaching position in his school system and if he is interested in your application, to send you an application blank. (Always enclose a stamped, self-addressed envelope.) After this different sort of beginning, write the regular letter just as if the superintendent were considering you for a job. Something about this letter may catch his eye; let's hope it isn't the incorrect spelling!

Let that first introduction of you to him be just a bit different from other applications. If you are impressed with his city, say so; if you have always wanted to teach in a town like his, tell him so, but don't "drip"; brush gently only with a thin coating of truth. Insincerity shows up in a letter of application like dyed red hair on a wrinkled old woman.

Point 4. In sketching your background of experience, a superintendent is interested in such items as working one's way through school, summer employment, and positions of responsibility in school clubs, social organizations, and religious groups. However, don't overpower a superintendent with data about too many organizations. Superintendents are much less interested in "Who's Who" than in "Who's going to do a good job of teaching?" What seems to you to be an impressive list may only say to him, "When did this lad (or lass) get any studying done?"

Point 6. In pointing out how you feel about your chosen profession, exercise care. Too much will make you sound like a "ham" actor or a young minister. A young lady who in a sentence or two can tell a superintendent how she has planned all her life to be a school teacher, or a young man who can tell what practice teaching did for him (if it did other than annihilate him) would give any superintendent real joy.

Point 9. How shall one "exit gracefully"? "I shall see you, then, on June 8," or "I am looking forward to June 8," or "Thank you for considering my application."

"Respectfully" or possibly "sincerely" is the preferred complimentary closing for a letter of application.

Standard business form on a good quality typing paper is correct. Be sure to use the proper salutation for a business letter: the man's name, title, and address above Dear Mr. ———: (colon for a formal business salutation) .

Above all things check your letter carefully for clarity and accuracy in spelling and punctuation. Leave nothing to chance. Be sure your letter is correct.

Letters and notes are the backbone of both our family and social life. Scattered families are held together by the warm, loosely-knit ties of letters. Letters make new friends and keep old friends. Letters keep old age from dwelling on the past, and act *in loco parentis* to youth away from home. Letters take the geography out of courtship and bring home to soldiers in faraway places.

Letters and notes bespeak our breeding, yet provide acceptable forebears for those whose family tree must, of necessity, begin with them.

Letters reach across the seas and around the world in friendly handclasp with those whose hearts are like ours but whose history is different.

Because letters and notes comprise most of the writing adults ever do, and since they, next to direct conversations, may well play a major part in bringing about the brotherhood of man, the writing of letters and notes must become a pleasurable habit in childhood.

CUPBOARD OF IDEAS for Chapter Ten

Letters Are Self-Stamped ❖ ❖ ❖ ❖ ❖ ❖ ❖ ❖ ❖ ❖ ❖ ❖ ❖ ❖

Since letters are for everybody, this cupboard will not have shelves marked Primary and Intermediate and Upper-Grade.

I. Learning Correct Letter Form

Keep the proper form of a letter and an addressed envelope in chart size to hang up every time the children write letters. If they are of uniform size, all charts can be hung or stored together compactly in a storage closet.

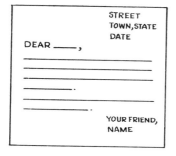
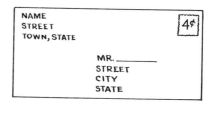

It is the correct form, not the wording, of a letter that should become habitual to children. Correct form begins with those first experiences, not after wrong forms have become set. But in any grade, form is always secondary to content. Stress form before a primary child begins to write, not after he has made the error.

II. Occasions for Letter Writing

Children write letters to Santa Claus, relatives, sick friends, the school board in appreciation of new books or supplies, community helpers, authors of loved books and texts, pen pals in other states and countries, those in charge of making arrangements for trips, sick children in hospitals, to parents inviting them to school functions and in thanks for kindnesses, and to experts who might know answers to elusive questions.

III. Preparation for Letter Writing

A. *Exchanging Ideas*

Before individual letters are written in any grade from first grade on, make a short word or phrase outline of possible news items the children may want to include. Ask third-grade children to start a new paragraph with each new topic.

B. *Gathering Vocabulary*

As they suggest ideas to write about, have children suggest words they might need in their letters. To avoid misspelling, write these words on the board for the children's use. This is especially needed up to grade five.

IV. Letter Writing on Special Days

A. *At Thanksgiving Time*

Each child writes a little note of appreciation to somebody who has been especially nice to him or whom he appreciates greatly. Be sure to include janitors, policemen, groceryman, school principal, Sunday School teacher, minister, and so on.

B. *Valentine Notes*

Fold and decorate plain typewriter paper with hearts for writing notes of appreciation to adults or children on Valentine's Day. Children may enjoy making loving rhymes for relatives, such as:

Dear Grandmother,
We're sending this heart-spangled note to say,
"We wish you'd move closer; you're too far away."

or

This heart doesn't have much lace or such
But it says, "Dear Cousin, I like you much!"

Gathering pairs of rhyming words to get rhymes started is necessary in some classes. Notes of appreciation make hearty valentines.

C. A Talking Christmas Tree

Instead of the usual decorations, allow each child to choose a branch of the Christmas tree, and let him write a special note to each member of his family and as many relatives or friends as he wishes. Make fancy wrapping-paper envelopes for the letters, or use tempera paint to make them gay. Each child hangs his letters on his branch by a silver or gold cord. (Sometimes children make these in the form of tree ornaments.) When school closes, he takes the letters home to hang on the Christmas tree there.

Outline for the contents of a Talking Christmas Tree letter (one idea to each paragraph):

1. Explain the Talking Christmas tree idea.

2. Name and describe the wonderful present you'd buy for this person if you had the money and tell why you'd want to give him such a gift but can't.

3. Wish him a holiday greeting.

Examples of children's letters:

Dear Mother,

We are going to have a talking Christmas tree at school. A talking Christmas tree is a tree with notes in gay envelopes. Each day the tree blossoms more notes. At the end it looks like a tree that is blossoming.

I think you are a wonderful person. You give me loving care when I am sick. You give me things I want.

If I had the money I would buy you a trip to Mexico. But I do not have the money so all I can give you is love, and small things.

With love,

Diane, Grade 5

DEAR SARAH,

I think we're having a wonderful Christmas tree this year. Don't you think so? It helps you know what other people would really like to get you for Christmas. As you figured out I am writing you a Christmas tree note. These notes are fun and I think they are wonderful. I always wondered what other people would really get me for Christmas if they really could get it or afford it and this year I think I might find out.

I'm really writing this note to tell or give you an idea of what I would like to get you for Christmas.

Here are some clues and later on I'll write what it is. It's about twenty inches tall. It has a wardrobe, which includes: four pairs of stockings and shoes, and three dresses. Have you guessed what it is? Well you should have because the clues I have given you have been simple enough. But here is one more clue. It has a braclet, a necklace, and an ankle braclet. Now you must have guessed it. I would give you another clue, but if I did you would know what it was immediately. So I'll just have to lead you slowly up to the big surprise of what I'd get you for Christmas.

First of all you read about it in the paper and from then on your heart was set on getting it. Now if you don't know what it is, I'll have to tell you. (It's the doll you want so badly.) I hope you get it but I haven't that much money and no one else that knows about this will get it for you. But I'll tell you what, let's put our money together and save all we can. So we can buy it pretty soon.

Your friend,

Louise, Grade 6

DADDY,

This year, at school, we are having a Talking Christmas Tree instead of the ordinary kind. Each of us will be assigned a certain branch on the pine. We will write a letter to a person telling them what we would get them for Christmas if we had enough money. We all make as many letters as we want, put them in envelopes, decorate, address them, and hang them on our branch.

When we are finished we will have a pretty tree with colorful envelopes swaying and swinging back and forth.

Now, I think that if I could ever pay for it, I would buy you a bright, new John Deere bailer. It would be very practical and useful. It would look very boastful among the older machines with its shiny coat of green. I know you deserve it, especially for your patience with me.

Merry Christmas

Love, your daughter,

Joan, Grade 8

D. Easter Greeting Cards

Each child writes a short springtime note to a relative or friend enclosing his poem about a modern miracle (see Cupboard of Ideas after poetry chapter, page 269). Easter is the time for miracles. It's fun to enclose poems or paragraphs in notes and letters.

E. A Pen Pal in Every Country and State

From sixth grade on, it's a good idea as the countries of the world are studied to try to have one pen pal in every country to which the children are free to write and in every state of the United States. Since to write to all would take too much letter writing, have each child write to several states only, so that at least in the United States, your room motto could be "Grade 5 Has a Friend in Every State." Each child could practice reading his letter aloud until he could really thrill the class on Read Letter Day,[1] when letters could be read and exchanged.

If a class could arrange to study its own state first, the children would be better able to write to other children about it (effective motivation).

F. Our Alaskan and Hawaiian Neighbors

As an offshoot of the foregoing project, why not shower the children of our new states with letters from American children everywhere? I can think of no better way of making for better understanding. Why not begin with your city or town? Start this in first grade. (Remember that pen-pal letters must be checked more carefully than letters to relatives or to close friends; they could do harm if they were tactless.)

For the sake of variety, children's poems and stories could sometimes be enclosed in pen-pal letters.

G. Taking a Trip "Letter-ally"

When children study the United States, why not have each write once every week or two to his family from the group of states you

[1] Mauree Applegate, *Helping Children Write*, p. 113.

are studying that week, pretending to be at whatever place he liked most? Maybe he's been spending the week at a dude ranch in Colorado; perhaps he's been in the Mormon country around Great Salt Lake; perhaps he's been to a great wheat ranch in Montana or has gone through Carlsbad Caverns in New Mexico. Wherever he's been, he writes from there. He makes his letters real word tours. He describes the country he's been visiting. He might illustrate other pages of the letter notebook with post cards received from those spots or paint water-color pictures of interesting places visited. Finally he binds his letters and pictures into a book and gives it to his mother for Mother's Day.

If each pupil sends for free advertising materials from one or two states of the Union (address requests to the Department of Agriculture and Markets, capital city of each state) , there will be enough material about special spots to make every pupil feel he has actually been there. (Pool the material and keep on file for your room.) Such encyclopedias as *The World Book* have fine material on each state.

It's fun, too, to have a committee for each foreign country studied. The committee members write letters from their chosen country and see which can make the most attractive notebook of letters and pictures.

The outstanding readers can read adult travel books to enhance the study, and outstanding movies can be shown.

H. Letters from Heroes

When history is being studied, once in a while let each child pretend to be his beloved hero, and compose a letter from him to his family at home. If a list of ideas is gathered from the class ahead of time, the letters should be historically correct.

I. Letters from Modern Pioneers

Since all children are interested in and excited about space travel, let them pretend to be pioneers on another planet and write letters home to the earth.

J. Letters from Pioneers

He may pretend to be a pioneer boy or girl going to California or Oregon with a wagon train. Then he writes a letter to the neighbor boy or girl back East.

K. Letter Dictation

Short, well-worded letters dictated by real children to your class not only is a fine spelling exercise, but it gives ideas to uncreative children to use in their own letters.

L. Letters to Alice and Jerry, or to Dick and Jane

Primary children enjoy writing letters to the children in their reading text families and sending the unexpurgated copies to the publishing companies who probably need the chuckles in these competitive days.

M. Room Letters

Some primary teachers write letters on the board each week to their children, praising them for progress in learning and behavior, and suggesting points for improvement. If they are lively and not preachy, the children love them.

N. Personal Notes to Children

Every six weeks a second-grade teacher of my acquaintance writes a personal note to each child in her room along with the report card to the parents. These are copies of several of the notes:

DEAR ALVIN,

I am glad you're getting better in reading. I am so happy your report card is good this time. You're a nice boy to have in a room and I am glad to have you.

Your teacher,

———

DEAR ANN,
Hip! Hip! Horray
You got back today

All of us are sorry
You've been away
With measles.
We've missed you

Your teacher,
————

DEAR BOB,
May I help you a bit extra with your arithmetic at fifteen minutes after 8 each morning? I believe we could both lick it together in that extra time. Will you ask your Mother if you may come early?
Your friend,
————

CHAPTER ELEVEN

Mechanics Safeguard Our Meanings

A principal in an Illinois city sent a third-grade boy to her office to write "P.T.A. Meeting" on her desk pad to remind her to send an announcement to the paper.

He did and spelled it "peteameading."

(Honest! Butshedidenforgedid.)

WIND-BLOWN POEM[1]

My poems are in the wind today
With common noun and preposition,
Where leafy tree and blossomed pink
Use swaying bough for interjection,

And adjectives of new spring greens,
Chartreuse, lime, and avocado,
While verbs and adverbs wistfully play
Their lilting flute and sobbing oboe.

Oh, wind, be gentle, cease and lull,
Blow not your verse beyond my reach.
Poetry is in your path
With nature scanning parts of speech.

Elizabeth Humerickhouse

REPETITION

The petite little dot
Comes after I write down a quick little jot.
We use him a lot.
The petite little dot.
That comes after I write down
A quick little jot.

Georgene Smith, Grade 7

[1] By permission of *The Christian Science Monitor.*

Are Your Brakes Squealing?

M echanics in written work, like taking time to dress in the morning, seem to children a foolish waste of time. When children write, their only idea is to get what they have to say down on the paper and out of their systems. Looking back and over their writing to put in marks that they consider extraneous, anyway, is just too much—after all, they know what they mean, and that's all that is important at the moment. It is a fierce feeling, this fight against doing what we must do, but see no sense in doing; it is the last cry of the individual spirit against regulation and conforming.

We're going to have to approach the restraint of individualism in writing by some other means than we have thus far been using, a restraint that the fierce creative spirit (and that's what children have) will resist less; that's about all we can expect—less resistance, not full conformity. I have found that children resist using the mechanics of writing in reverse proportion to their caring about writing; the more original the writer, the more fierce the resistance. That is why we teachers are being compelled to seek new ways of teaching mechanics. Because the resistance comes in the first place from intense individualism, our method of teaching restraint, if it is to work, must in some way be tied to that same drive.

The fierce desire for self-expression that impels children's writing (if they truly want to write) must be met by the also powerful drive to be clearly understood.

My little half-sister of three, one time, literally shaking with rage because her inadequate vocabulary kept her from getting her meaning about something or other across to me, muttered vehemently, "Oh, you don't know nothin' to a dog!" and marched off in disdain. The essence of that remark is childhood's reaction to dolts who cannot or will not understand its meanings. It is too often we parents and teachers who are the dolts.

In order to get children to submit to the mechanics of writing, we must do two things: (1) introduce mechanics along with the first reading; and (2) prove to children that putting in the right marks is the only way to be sure they will be understood.

As you first-grade teachers print the first sentences on the chart, talk off the reasons why you write as you do. "We always leave a margin at this side of a paper," you point out, "for the thumb and finger to hold the paper; it's a margin and it's the thumb's place like in a winter mitten."

Write on the board: *Run, Sally, run.* Then explain, "Notice when I write this sentence, I do three things: I put a capital letter on the first word to show that a new talking sentence is starting here. We have to put a capital letter so the reader will know how to read it; otherwise he'd read it wrong, all mixed up like scrambled eggs. These little marks—they're commas—that I'm putting before and after Sally mean to rest your breath a short bit before and after her name so she'll notice she's being called. Then at the end I put this little dot; it is called a period, and it's to show that you're finished with that bit of talking.

"Now let's look at how that sentence is written—this capital means that it's the start of fresh talking, those two little commas tell us to rest our breath just a short bit before and after Sally, and the period, this dot, means to stop talking. Now read it just as those marks tell you to read it. Doesn't that sound nice? You'll notice that these same reading traffic signs are in your books, too. They're right there to tell you how to read. Now watch me for a minute. I'm going to rub out that period at the end and put another traffic sign there (!). That's an exclamation or excitement mark. It means that we must read the sentence in an excited way. What might be happening to Sally that might make us want that sentence to sound excited? Yes, maybe there's a big dog coming, or a car when she's out in the street. If we watch those reading traffic signs, we'll all get to be good readers!"

So on the children go, following the traffic signs of the reading road and adding new ones as they meet them. The question mark that tells the reader's voice to stay right up in the air until he gets the answer; the semicolon that means just a longer stop than a comma, and finally, when they begin simple business letters in second or third grade, the colon that acts like a barricade in the road and says, "There's more road on the other side, but stop and look things over before you begin again." When they grow up with the marks of punctuation and realize why they are used, children seem not to resist them so much as they otherwise will. (See the beginning of Chapter Eight on story-writing, page 277, and the Cupboard of Ideas, page 482, for further punctuation help.

Ambrose Bierce in *The Devil's Dictionary,* which H. L. Mencken declares contains some of the most gorgeous witticisms in the English language, suggests that a flyspeck is the prototype of punctuation and that the old literary masters never punctuated their writings at all, but had their wit brightened and their style enhanced by the ministrations of the house fly.

Another source I once read (Heaven knows what!) declared facetiously that the manuscript of the St. James version of the Bible was punctuated by the various kind of jolts the proofreader experienced while riding in a coach over cobblestones and trying to punctuate on the way, an explanation many readers would be willing to concede. As to the reasons for many children's erratic placing of punctuation's dots and dashes, the mystery was partly solved for me one day when a handsome fringe-lashed little angel looked up at me and said, as innocently as Eve the morning after, "I just sprinkle them in where they look pretty," a child's sensible answer (or shall I say a sensible child's answer? I'm never sure which it is.) .

The Parts of Speech Are the Foundation of Grammar

The parts of speech, like the marks of punctuation, must belong to a child's world of experience long before they belong to his world of grammar. Never, never, never introduce the parts of speech to children through definitions. Who can ever define a personality? Parts of speech must become personalities if children are to feel them and know them. The elementary school is a place where definitions are not learned by heart, but are experienced and lived with.

Before junior high school the parts of speech are learned in the same way Paul Engle says a child learns words—through feeling them:

> Now she becomes a world
> Of words: the furious *I,*
> The us like an arm curled
> Over her shoulder, cry
> Of the demanding me,
> The angry yell of you,
> The loving word for we,
> The questioning of who?

> For saying makes things real:
> Ouch! is the cause of pain,
> Wet is the taste of rain,
> Cut is the noun for knife,
> Pig is the pride of squeal,
> Child is the look of life.[2]

When you first introduce a child to a printed word, tell him about it so he will remember it as a distinct personality. He's meeting so many words in first grade that it's hard to remember them all. There's *a, an,* and *the,* for instance, those three words that haven't an ounce of personality in the three of them. They're so nondescript that they melt right into the page. That is, they will unless you personalize them in some way. Why not call them the "towing" words? *A, an,* and *the* are put in front of name words to tow them along just as a towing car tows a wreck along the street; you'll never meet them—ever—without those name words they're towing along. The job of *a, an,* and *the* is always the same, pulling along name words.

A bit later when the situation arises, bring out that *the* will do any kind of towing job, but that *a* and *an* are choosy, *a* refusing to be put directly before a word beginning with a vowel (only consonant towing jobs for *a*) and *an* preferring to be put directly before words beginning with a vowel (not a consonant). Those two words are as balky as a donkey that has its mind made up.

Practice as you go with real things: hold up pictures of apple, monkey, airplane, doll, card, swing, apricot, or ball, and have the children hold up the *a* card or *an* card which they have on their desks. Tell the children that these three words belong to the "article" family and that they're in the towing business—towing is all they do.

Name words or *nouns* (use the two interchangeably) the children meet on the first day of school when every object in the room proudly hears its own printed name: clock, desk, window, book, and even teacher. That would be a good game for the first day, too, learning the names of things. Write the child's name on a card for him and give him the name card of one object in the room to take home, a name he's learned to read on the first day of school. Then as the children get introduced to their first primer pair, Alice and Jerry or Dick and Jane, show the first graders that some names are always dressed up; names of people, names of cities and

[2] Reprinted from *American Child* by Paul Engle. Copyright 1956 by Paul Engle. Used with the permission of the publishers, The Dial Press, Inc.

towns and states and rivers always begin with capital letters, and another stage of the concept of noun has been successfully hurdled.

But the first-grade teacher doesn't stop here. A teacher never leaves an idea with one lesson. On another day she makes long lists of names on the board that take capitals. Then, much later, the question of *honesty* or *truth* comes up, and she writes its name on the board and explains how it's a name, too, but a name you can't *touch* or *see,* one that you just know about in your mind. Children understand even abstract nouns when they meet them in this "accidentally-on-purpose" way in the classroom; it's as natural as getting a drink of water when you're thirsty. The first teaching of nouns in any other way than this meeting-them-as-you-go method is as futile as calling your grandmother "she" until you're ten years old, then one day being introduced to her formally. "Mary Jane, this is your grandmother, your father's mother," they'll say. "You're to call her grandmother from now on." And you probably think to yourself, "Oh, so *she* is grandmother, is she?" but because you've known her as *she* so long, you just keep on calling her "she" because you "feel" about her as "she."

In order to know the parts of speech, we must grow up with them, not meet them suddenly. We teachers so often make things hard for young people to learn.

Verbs are introduced as action words in kindergarten, the time when children are fullest of verbs anyway, and live with them on up to junior high school when they meet the milk-toast or not very respectable "linking" members of the verb family. Those linking verbs have no pep, poor things; there's a whole tribe of them: *was, were, is, seems, looks,* to name a few, and not a handful of get-up-and-go in the whole bunch.

I met Miss Brown, a former college teacher, the other day on a street corner. Miss Brown hasn't even wandered into a grade school for forty years, but her chief topic of conversation is always "The poor children have no phonics," or "The poor dears, they never get any grammar; no wonder they can't spell."

Today it was the grammar routine. "Oh, but Miss Brown," I pointed out archly, "they do have grammar; they live with it from first grade on."

"They do what?" she demanded, looking flabbergasted.

I saw my bus coming so I knew escape was imminent. "There's lots more living with going on in this town than you know about!" I hissed in her ear as I swung up the bus steps.

When I got seated, I giggled to myself. "That's a department you know even less about, Mauree Applegate, than Miss Brown knows about grade school," I thought and then properly led my mind back to listening to bus conversations—a real education.

But to go back to grammar, which we've really never left, I believe in allowing first graders to discover *pronouns* for themselves.

In the first grade after we have finished a together-chart about Mrs. Clarence, our schoolroom rabbit, "Let's look it over," I say to the children, "and see if we've overused any words."

"My goodness," a little sharpie notices, "we've said *she, she, she,* all down the page. That's just too many *she's!*"

"So we have," I answer surprised. "Just what can we do about it?"

This is the psychological moment to help children to discover pronouns, I think to myself. Words like *she* and *he, I* and *me,* and *it,* I explained, are called pronouns because we call them in to help out name words when we need them; they're like baby-sitters. Then I read the chart completely through, using *Mrs. Clarence* all the way through the chart. The children laugh delightedly because, as one curly-head explains, "It sounds all full of knots to have so many Mrs. Clarence's in the story."

"We certainly do need those little what-d'-you-call-'em's," another child points out, "to keep things from sounding awfully funny." I explain the word *pronouns* again and together we make a list on the board of perfectly proper names to call a mother rabbit, who is having a story written about her.

1. Mrs. Clarence (because that's her name)
2. "She" (because that's what she is and we don't want to wear her name out)
3. The rabbit (because that's the animal name like ours is people)
4. This animal (to sound grown up)

So we put the new words in and read our story again, taking time to admire our smooth-sounding sentences. A teacher who makes over a chart herself instead of helping the children to discover their own errors, it seems to me, is missing the point of her job. As for those pronouns—yes, certainly many of the children will forget the word *pronoun* itself, but I'll wager that few will forget the pronoun concept—"substitute for a name word"; pronouns *are* like baby-sitters!

Every part of speech must be presented at the psychological moment in the way that is a part of a child's life at the time. For goodness' sake, don't use the baby-sitter idea if the children aren't familiar with the term; if the teacher doesn't translate the material in the text into a child's vernacular, who is going to do it? Somebody has to translate books into living language!

Adjectives get born in any schoolroom whenever they are needed, and that's soon. Call them technicolor words, winged words, picture words, any word that is meaningful to the children at the time. At the same time call them *adjectives,* too, their proper name, using it interchangeably with more descriptive ways of saying "adjective."

Put one perfect tulip in a vase and try to find the adjectives to describe it: painted, straight, lovely, like a formal dress, red, perfect, proper—yes, and that number *one* is an adjective of counting. Maybe it's not a tulip you're describing, but the wonderful way you all feel today that you're trying to describe. Perhaps it's spring and the earth is stretching itself like a new baby and yawning a soft, almost inaudible sigh. So after the last recess in your third-grade room you go hunting for adjectives and find it isn't very different at all from hunting for wild flowers except you don't get out of your school seats.

Yes, it's a happy feeling we have in our hearts today; yes, it's a warm feeling and a contented feeling; yes, they're all good words, but none of them is the $64,000 word we need. Yes, George, it's a purring feeling—that's almost it. Yes, Betty, it is a singing sensation, an inner singing, a bubbly-feeling. Yes? There you have it, Mark; yes, it's an at-peace feeling that we have in our hearts today, a feeling that "God's in his heaven—All's right with the world." There is nothing quite like seeking that right adjective and finally having it come, settling like a butterfly on our noun and feeling at home so it decides to stay. Adjectives are almost magic words; "they can change an ordinary into a thriller" as second-grade Marcia so aptly said it. Oh, those parts of speech are taught right when they become parts of life along with being parts of speech.

The *adverbs* are useful along with *want*'s and *do*'s: *very, very, very,* with dull old *exceedingly* and *awfully,* that good word that's been used so much for all kinds of jobs it wasn't meant for that it's losing the gold powder off its wings. Yes, and *too,* the word that's blown up into two fat balloon O's, T-O-O, the word that's so full that it will spill over if you don't carry it carefully like a spoonful of water with a rounded top.

Adverbs are indeed useful words; they're the "how" and the "how much," as useful and easy to understand as those *conjunction* joiners that hold pieces of sense together: *and* and *but* and *for;* how carefully they join thoughts and how tightly they hold on. Yet when one doesn't fit just right in a place, how easy it is to put that old safety pin of a semicolon in to take its place. "I went to the movie; Mary Jane went to bed." "I went to the movie, *but* Mary Jane went to bed." "I went to the movie *and* Mary Jane went to bed"; each one of the conjunctions changes the meaning of the sentence ever so slightly. Possibly the easiest one of the speech parts to learn is the *interjections,* bless them! Even all the children recognize them as excitement words: oh! sh! hurray!

Certainly, parts of speech help us to make clear meanings. But we *must* get a feeling for the parts of speech when we're young. It's the same idea exactly as the difference between a young person who learns his table manners young and grows up with them and the young person who acts like a savage until he goes to high school, and then decides he needs new manners as well as new clothes. What you grow up with seems to get built into you and so becomes a real part of your life.

Prepositions used to baffle me—how to get them across to children, I mean. One day while looking at a little branch of blossoms that had blown off an apple tree, I got an idea. Those little prepositional phrases were exactly like branches. The preposition was the growing-on place and the whole branch the phrase. It worked, too; I haven't had any trouble with prepositions since.

The parts of speech—yes, *parts* are what they are—are so basic that we must build them right into our daily living. The first-grade teacher must introduce a few of them. The second-grade teacher must work at them, and each of the intermediate teachers must clinch them again and introduce a few more. In junior high school, where parts of speech are treated more or less formally, what children will have already experienced will fit into the new program like a fat man into a midget car.

It took years for educators in the field of mathematics to learn that children must *experience* their arithmetic before most of them can begin to work problems. Do you suppose we shall ever learn that fact in the field of language arts? It is for a teacher to know when to separate *parts of speech* from *speech*—if they should ever be separated.

COMMON OR PROPER?

The teacher had hammered
Till Marge was well-grammared;
That is, till she dated with Herb,
There was mutual attraction—
That kiss sure had action,—
Was *kiss* then a noun or a verb?

Though she hadn't declined it,
She had a strong mind, it
Was verb, since its object was *her*,
At the time, they were walking,
And not even talking,
So was it a verb—if it were?

Then Marge got to thinking,
"If verb, was it linking?
If a noun, was there really a case?
Was this little caressive,
Proper? common? possessive?"
Here a soft blush stole over her face.

She couldn't forget it,
'Twas a verb, and still yet it
Was a name like a tree or a church,
And since Marge was well-grammared,
As well as enamored,
She went out and did more research.

Shall We Hammer Grammar in the Elementary Grades?

After experimenting with children and youth at every level, I
have come to the firm conviction that in the first six grades of formal
schooling, children need to experience grammar rather than to meet
it in isolated exercises in a book or workbook. Furthermore, unless
children live with the correct grammatical forms, even though they
do not thoroughly understand why those forms are right or wrong,
formal grammar when it is later introduced will usually not have
real meaning in controlling their speaking and writing.

I truly believe, however, that children need a thorough formal
course in grammar in junior high school, and if such a course were
taught by modern methods there, it would be well received by the

top two-thirds of the students in those grades. We are waiting too late, it seems to me, to give children a thorough grounding in the *why* and *how* and *what* of their native language, a subject that is not half as complicated as much of the science with which the majority of junior high youth are conversant. They need such a grounding in their own language in order to enable them to do the kind of high school English work that will prepare them for college entrance and for a study of foreign languages.

A few years ago I "took on" the education of 108 people in freshman communication. It is possible to help college freshmen to do a better job of writing and speaking without their having had any previous formal training in grammar, but such a procedure is extremely time-consuming and time-wasting and, I might add, completely unnecessary.

One young man—and he was by no means a fool—told me that he vaguely remembered having heard of a subject and predicate, but had no idea what they were. He learned. Children in the grades must live with subjects and predicates and their agreements and be able to use them correctly. They must understand and use the parts of speech wisely and well; they must be able to use verb forms correctly, to write interesting sentences, and to know how to develop a paragraph so that it says what they mean it to say. They must be able to safeguard their meaning with correct punctuation.

These along with the ability to speak and write their thoughts with facility and without gross errors, in my opinion, constitute the grammar curriculum for the elementary grades. In these grades children must experience the correct forms of grammar, which in seventh and eighth grades they will meet formally. One cannot let children wait until they are grown up to meet the *why's* of anything they are experiencing.

Certainly teach grammar in the grades, lest incorrect forms become as set as concrete before children even meet the reasons why the forms they use are wrong. But leave *formal* grammar until it cannot choke a child's creativity in speaking and writing. Creativity choked in the grades rarely rises very high later. Even in the grades, I should say especially in the grades, grammatical forms must not be taught as they used to be taught, as isolated lessons in texts and workbooks. Unless grammar makes sense to children, unless it has meaning in their lives, there is little sense in teaching it. You will only choke creative thoughts and phrases with the crabgrass of formality if you do. On the other hand, a garden that has grown wild for eleven years is going to be mighty hard to cultivate. Are

we never going to be able to strike a happy medium in education?
Or is the medium never happy? Frankly, I don't know.

Let's Start with the Trouble Spots

What are the chief trouble spots in usage (both written and oral)
that children of the middle grades must meet early and conquer
before their habits are set?

The *agreement of the subject and predicate* seems to be a chief
offender, yet it can become intelligible to children in grades two
and three. Any normal seven-year-old can see how the subject you're
talking about and the word that tells about it have to be both singular or both plural. He'll understand it better, of course, if he is introduced to it in a game.

Often dramatize sentences in class, sentences about subjects in
the unit you are studying. If you're studying community helpers,
for instance, write a number of both singular and plural subjects
that are studied in the unit on tagboard strips in one place on the
chalk tray: two policemen; four firemen in red hats; a tall handsome milkman; our jolly mailman; many grocers in aprons; a grocer
wearing a broad smile; two polite garbage collectors; the captain
of a shining boat; two sailors with a lonesome look. In another
pile have cards containing singular forms of the verb *to be, is* and
was, and in a third pile the plural forms, *are* and *were.* Call three
children as nearly matched in ability as possible to the front of
the room. The first chooses a subject and reads it, then stands facing
the class and holding the card at waistline height. The second finds
the right verb for that subject, and the third *adds orally* enough
words to make a good sentence. In an ordinary second or third
grade, sentences such as "Four firemen in red hats were climbing
up long ladders dragging a hose" will easily be made. Children get
a real sentence sense from such dramatizations, and one hears far
fewer incorrect expressions such as "they was." Some teachers prefer to play this game with four players; the first picks a simple one-
word subject such as "milkmen"; the second provides an oral description of the subject "carrying a heavy crate"; the third supplies
the verb "were," let's say; and the fourth furnishes more information about the predicate—perhaps "up the stairs." After one group
finishes a sentence, another four are called up to make another
sentence.

Be sure to teach the children that the word *you,* even when singular, takes the plural verb. They remember this better if it is presented in rhyme:

√ The pronoun *you*
Always counts as two.

In the intermediate grades, keep a subject box filled with every known kind of suitable subject words, both singular and plural, written on tagboard cards, and a predicate box with all types of verb cards. In a spare five minutes now and then, call up four children to make sentences, the first and third using cards, the second and fourth providing oral supplements. The most intelligent children soon notice that three kinds of words or groups of words modify or describe subjects, descriptive words that they gradually learn are adjective words, phrases, and clauses.

This same idea of dramatizing grammar or building sentences (whichever you wish to call it) is a wonderful way to teach the marks of punctuation. The animated punctuation marks, holding their symbol cards, take their proper places in the sentence. Even first graders love to act out capital letters and correct endings for sentences the teacher reads or places on the board.

Play-acting is natural to childhood, but seems to be unnatural in many schoolrooms. We must adapt from children their natural ways of learning; their ways work.

Besides needing training in the agreement of subject and verb, children need practice in the *objective and nominative case of pronouns.* They (and too many of their teachers) say, "He gave Mary and *I* a ride"; "Jane and *me* went to the circus." There are two simple ways of attacking this type of error. The more basic way, it seems to me, is to think of *we, she, he,* and *they* as the subject pronouns and *me, us, her, him, them* as the receivers of action or object pronouns. The subject pronouns do things, the receiver or object pronouns get things done to them, or receive things.

I hit the ball. He gave the ball to me.
She was invited to the party. We invited her to the party.
He hit himself with the hammer.
It was she who went. It was I who answered.

That way of looking at the situation seems to clarify it for most children. If the correct practice is kept up in the way suggested on page 155 of Chapter Five, this error can be easily conquered.

The other method of getting at the problem, that of leaving out the noun in the phrase "He gave the candy to (Mary and) me," at first appears to be the easier way of attack, but it actually isn't, since it causes a child to back up his mental car with considerable sputtering before he can decide what to say. This is a device for testing, not for thinking the sentence straight in the first place. Straighten out the thinking that is causing the error rather than concoct a device for testing it if you can. To display the subject and object pronouns on a chart seems to be of help to intermediate children.

A misuse in one or more of the forms of six common verbs (*go, come, sit, set, lie,* and *lay*) is a weak spot in both speaking and writing in many sections of the country. Are these your bugaboos, too? Children have a tendency to say "have went," for "have gone"; "she come" for "she came"; "I'll set here" for "I'll sit here"; "I sit her down hard" for "I set her down hard"; "lay down now" for "lie down now"; and "she laid there for an hour" for "she lay there for an hour."

These are hard errors to break and can actually be explained only by grammar. However, I have found two-thirds of the *lie* and *lay* and *sit* and *set* errors to be easily controlled by this explanation in a modern child's jargon:

Lie, lay, lain are the three forms of a do-it-yourself verb; the "I" in "lie" points out that this is a do-it-yourself verb. *Lay, laid, laid* is not a self-operator, it needs aid; notice the word *aid* is in those two forms. Neither people nor things can use that second verb without help from the outside. Use some objects and have the children say what they seem to be doing. "The book lies on the desk. It lay there yesterday; it has lain there too long." "My purse lies in the drawer. Long it has lain there." Pretend your pencils are people; "Mr. Jack lies here today; he lay there for an hour. He must be tired because he has lain there so long."

Then begin to *lay* things down and let them *lie*. Most children really understand these two verbs when they recognize the real differences between them. Many children were never aware before that *lie* and *lay* were two distinct verbs.

Use the same method of explanation with *sit* and *set,* since those verbs are exactly the same type as the pair *lie* and *lay,* except that they are easier to understand due to *set* never changing its form; it's *set.*

The verbs *come* and *go* can be easily demonstrated with creative dramatics and humorous posters, as can practically any weak spot in usage.

Using the imaginative approach—in this case, dramatization—makes grammar alive and real to children. As long as grammar is a thing, many children see no sense to it. But "language in action" —that's different! Live with grammar in the grades, and in junior high children will greet it as an old friend.

Paragraph Building

Another skill that should be second nature to children before junior high school age is proper paragraphing. Before grade three children's writing is scarcely ever more than a paragraph long, but in grades three and four children begin to think in paragraphs, especially if the teacher steers them in that direction.

A third-grade teacher whom I observed one day had four paragraph boxes that she first used, she told me, in the writing of letters. Whenever letters were being planned, the class made a general outline together on the board of the items they wished to write about. The teacher took the items in the list which came willy-nilly from the children, and wrote them on strips which together the class sorted into the proper boxes. One box usually was marked "School Affairs," the second "Home News," and the third "Fun." Sometimes there was a fourth box, labeled "News about Me." Into each box went all the items under that heading. The class called them *paragraph boxes.* From paragraph boxes to boxed paragraphs seemed to be an easy step and at this point the teacher introduced indenting, a writer's way of telling the reader to steer his mind in a new direction; he's going to read about something new.

At the end of about half the units she teaches in third grade, this teacher writes topic or summary sentences covering what the children have learned and uses them as an oral review.

Each child reaches into a box and draws out a summary sentence. He then develops that topic sentence orally to the best of his ability, the class members adding more details when he has finished. For the sake of variety, sometimes writing instead of oral recitation follows the drawing of slips. Often the teacher does the choosing of slips in order to match the topic to the child's ability. This teacher is careful to include the development of one or more summary sentences in each unit test she gives, since such an exercise is not only a gauge of the facts a child knows but of his ability to organize his knowledge. Such topic sentences as "Indian women in the early days did the work which white men usually did on the pioneer farms," or "Having to move their flocks often, due to lack of rainfall, changes the customs of nomadic people" make excellent exercises that test the children's ability to think and expand ideas. In order to fit the material to the child, a teacher must give an easier topic sentence to the less competent without mentioning that fact before the class. (Children should never be asked to do what they have not the mind power to do.) If enough of this kind of exercise is carried on in the intermediate grades, however, children have little trouble with paragraphing. After all, they shouldn't have— writing a paragraph is just the opposite of outlining; both are a kind of dressing and undressing one's body of facts.

Plan to have fun with paragraph building. On Halloween get committees of children working on different facets of Halloween beliefs (apply the same method to other special days) :

> *Where the Idea of Halloween Came From*
> *Ghosts and Beliefs about Them*
> *Ghost Stories That Still Thrill and Chill*
> *Witches and Their Halloween Habits*
> *Ancient Halloween Customs*
> *Halloween Games*

Let each committee share their findings in any way they choose (see Chapter Five, page 172) on methods of reporting. Then as a written lesson, give each committee member one topic to write for a class booklet to be illustrated by the class artists and left in your room library for a year.

By Grade Five, children should be aware of the different ways by which paragraphs can be developed. This can be begun gradually by noticing together in class how paragraphs are developed in stories in the reading book and in social studies and science texts. After considerable casual noticing, gradually gather the different methods of developing a paragraph and put them on a chart. Different books state paragraph development in different ways, but intermediate children seem to understand the simplest statements best.

1. Piling up details to prove a point.
2. Giving an example.
3. Explaining with a short story.
4. Expanding a definition.
5. Contrasting ideas.

If they discover these types one by one instead of learning them all in one indigestible mass, intermediate children will take them in stride and actually enjoy getting variety into their written papers —they long for variety, you know. However, don't expect more than the top three-fifths of your class to be able to use more than one or two of these methods in their own writing; this is a complicated skill that children gain slowly. Now let us take these paragraph types one at a time and make them intelligible by tying them up to children's experiences.

Piling Up Details to Prove a Point

Some winter day when basketball feeling runs high, take some statement a child makes such as "Our basketball team is likely to win the tournament" and together make a list of reasons *why* they think that statement is true. Then ask the whole class to develop that first sentence (or its opposite) into a paragraph according to their own beliefs. Explain that piling up reasons to prove a point, one after the other, is the most common method of developing a paragraph.

Think of the topics you can use in connection with this type of paragraph: favorite television programs, favorite books, idols of history book and screen, famous ball players of the past and present, the reasons why you'd like to travel to Norway—oh, the possibilities are legion. And don't forget fun—let the humorists of your class stretch out their laughter wings and write funny papers.

Maurine has piled up details to prove she likes winter:

I LIKE WINTER

I like winter when snow gives the flowers a blanket. I like winter when the trees dress up in white gowns and they wear gloves on their long black fingers. I like winter when fairies fly down from heaven. I like winter when houses wear hats and they have icicle hair.

Maurine, Grade 6

Giving an Example

On a pop-off day you might start this one. Let each child state in no uncertain terms a summary statement about his particular pop-off subject.

1. My little brother nearly drives me frantic. One day last week he topped everything he'd done before . . .

2. I have an aunt who broods like a thundercloud over the house. She came Monday . . .

3. I don't understand why my mother will never let the dog in the house. It rained on last Monday and . . . (See pages 400, 401, and 427 for good examples of this type of pop-off.)

Help children to see that this method of giving an example can clarify meanings almost better than any other method.

A number of years ago I read a wonderful newspaper item that I have kept long in my mind because it was such a fine exemplification of this kind of paragraph development. In that item a young Japanese lad said how hard it was for him to understand the concept of democracy when he first heard about it during the American occupation of Japan. He could not understand how such a system could possibly work. One day he was watching some American soldiers having fun on a holiday. One of their games was a three-legged race. "When I watched those two soldiers," the Japanese youth said, "with two of their legs tied together, at first stumbling and falling in their efforts to run as one man, then finally after many attempts, getting the swing of the thing and running together, I said to myself, 'That's what democracy is; men who are used to running alone, finally learning how to run together!' "

Have your children bring from their library reading a sample paragraph developed by giving examples. At this stage of the paragraph development game, do more noticing and gathering than writing.

Explaining with a Short Story

This is the type of "paragraph talking" Abraham Lincoln did. He usually drove home the point he was trying to make with a humorous story. A story is a cut-across-lots way to the clarification of a point. A person can prove this point with a story quicker than in any other way. True stories often provide even better illustrations than commercial ones, since they usually have the ring of truth.

Several summers ago, a group of "workshoppers" and I were sitting around a table together in the school cafeteria drinking coffee. Since most of the group were primary teachers, the talk got around to how meaningless many of the ancient folkways were to modern children.

One first-grade teacher chuckled. "I was reviewing the nursery rhymes last fall," she said, "when one little fellow said to me, 'Miss Johnson, I don't see any sense to that Jack and Jill rhyme at all! It says he went to bed to mend his head with vinegar and brown paper; that just sounds silly to me. What does it mean?' "

The teacher explained to us how she told the boy that people in those days had no bandaids or antiseptics for treating cuts and bruises, but they had lots of vinegar—they made it themselves—and that it would clean out a cut fairly well. She explained that these old-timers made all their cloth by hand, so they rarely tore any of it up to bind cuts. But pioneers always had a big supply of brown paper on hand—everything they got came wrapped in it—and it kept the air and dirt out almost as well as a cloth.

Miss Johnson told us that by the time she finished the explanation, the little questioner's mouth had dropped open with awe at what she knew, and that he exclaimed with admiration, "Gosh, Miss Johnson, did you know Adam and Eve, too?"

I have rarely heard a story that so well illustrates the point being discussed. Make clear that a story need not be funny to be illustrative. In teaching pioneer times to a fourth grade, a child may tell a good yarn his great-grandmother told him about the early days in this country or tell one he read in a book. All of Laura Ingalls Wilder's books are illustrations for such topic sentences as these:

"We had fun at Christmas even without money to buy present."
"When we went a-traveling in those days, it *was* a journey."
"Sometimes we nearly ran out of flour."
"It was the worst when somebody in the family got sick."

Encourage children to use illustrative anecdotes for points they want to bring out, and encourage them to share the stories they find in their library reading. Learning to react to such statements as "That was the happiest day of my life!" "I have never been so scared as I was on last Halloween night" is the start to becoming a good conversationalist.

Expanding a Definition

Being able to expand a definition into a paragraph is a useful skill. Think of the fun your intermediates could have writing a definition of a parent or a hippopotamus or a chair and then expanding it into an explanatory paragraph.

This fun with a definition of a mule may help you to get your students started:

A mule is a strong-minded horse with swiveling ears. In the world of man he would be known as a rugged individualist. When he says, "No," he means it more definitely than any other animal. When a mule makes up his mind, his whole body is affected, especially his legs. They lock into place and refuse to move until they get the "go" signal from the mule's brain, which there is little indication that he has.

If a mule were attending school, he would not get his yesterday's work handed in until tomorrow, and not even the principal could make him stay in after school. A mule has his own principles.

It is necessary that a mule's ears be long and adjustable so that they can swivel around and find out what is wanted of him, so that he will know what *not* to do. We had a mule once that we named "Traffic Signal" because it was so much further between his "stop" and his "go" than between his "go" and his "stop."

A mule is seldom moved by what others think of him; in fact a mule is seldom moved.

Besides its possibilities for fun, this skill is useful in defining and explaining terms, such hard-to-define terms as *democracy* or *freedom* or *education*. It is useful in explaining a new process you've been learning in science, and in making new terms clear generally. Intermediate children probably use it oftenest in explaining games and customs in pen-pal letters.

Contrasting Ideas

It is always easier to make this type of paragraph development clear by contrasting new facts with known facts. This method of expanding paragraphs is used widely in geography books in comparing one country with other countries previously studied. Just as black seems blacker and white whiter when the two are placed side by side, so contrasting ideas make both seem clearer.

This paragraph of seventh-grade Jim's is better because he kept contrasting Pat's abilities with those of lesser fellows:

A Courageous Person

There is a very gifted boy in the 8th grade whose name is Pat Brady. Unlike many very good sports-players who think they are too good to study, Pat ranks as one of the highest in his room. He was living in Milwaukee the past six years after he moved from Chippewa.

Pat captained his St. Monica Team to its second straight championship. He was high scorer for the year (as he is so far with the Royals) but did not brag about it. He will work with the 5th and 6th grade team until they master that play. He is my idea of a courageous person.

Jim, Grade 7

Be sure in your teaching of any form of paragraph development to have each end with a good summary sentence. Seventh-grade Dave has done that after contrasting the work of the various players on a football team:

Football is a celebrated sport, that is played during the fall. It is a rough game. The quarterback, two halfbacks, and a fullback seem to get all the glory, but the ones that could and should receive that glory are the guards and tackles. They open up holes in the line on offense and close them back up on defense. These boys have to be able to take the driving legs of the backfield men who come charging through the line with flaring, digging spikes, but the guards and tackles receive about ten per cent of all football injuries and they leave their marks on many a backfield man. But a bruising lineman in football is usually a gentle person off the field. This is my idea of a true hero.

Dave, Grade 7

About once or twice a year use a storytelling picture as a means of developing paragraphs in story writing. If you will turn back to Chapter Eight, page 300, to recall the details of that picture, we might work out several kinds of paragraphs that usually work well in written stories. Be sure that you are familiar with the picture story before we begin. Notice what variety these three different ways of developing the same idea could give to a story.

A point may be proved by *piling up details:*

Pinky never let Betts alone; he pulled her hair when no one was looking; he slyly tripped her as she walked down the aisle; he baited the other boys until they made insulting remarks to her; he even laid traps for the girl so that she would get in bad with the teacher. Betts often cried in private over Pinky's cruelty, but she loved ball more than she hated teasing so she usually did her crying in private—and kept right on swinging that bat.

A point can be proved with *conversation:*

"Betts! I'll bet you play with the boys because you *like* boys," Pinky tormented one day as Betts was, as usual, the only girl on the team.

"Yah, that's it," another girl-hater shouted, "Betts likes the boys! Betts likes the boys!" and soon the whole team took up the chant. "Betts likes the boys! Betts likes the boys! Betts likes the boys!"

A point may be proved with an *illustrative story:*

It was at a Sunday School picnic that Pinky teased Betts until she cried. The minister was there. Betts' parents were there, and all the people she cared most about were there. At the table, Pinky began badgering Betts right out loud, "Do you know, Reverend Weems," he pointed out—his mouth half full of fried chicken—"Betts is the only girl at our school that plays ball with the boys. All of us fellows call her 'Boy Betts.' She gets sweaty and dirty as the fellows." Betts' ears got red, she choked over her lemonade and ran from the table, her eyes wet.

Instead of always having the story written in full, sometimes divide your class into thirds and let a point be proved in a different way by each of the three groups.

I must warn you teachers on one point here. Paying attention to paragraphing is all very well in short story writing. But don't for a moment be deluded into thinking that you will get good stories from children if you stress the paragraph building instead of the story. When they write a story, children either write it as it comes tumbling out or, thinking too hard about the paragraphing, the muse leaves them, and their story is as dead as a burned-out bulb. Careful story building comes in senior high school and college, not in the grades. The surest way to kill creative writing in the grades is to keep taking it apart and putting it together again; of that I'm sure. "Why, then, take the time in elementary school to study paragraphing at all?" you ask. That's a good question; and this answer is a true one; I've experimented to get it.

Many of the children in your room have quick minds and are facile writers. They will adapt (consciously or unconsciously) much of what you teach them outside the story-writing period. Commend them for this use of new ways, but never destroy creative power with scaffolding—your writing house will only come tumbling down if you do.

Are You Always Yelling about Their Spelling?

STUDYING SPELLING

From letter to letter
From word to word
A stop and a stutter;
A flop and a mutter.

Ralph, Grade 8

The poor spelling of school children has provided more headaches for teachers and more conversations for parents than almost any other topic. That it is a universal subject there is no doubt, for its scope of complaint is country-wide. It is as prevalent at summer school, which abounds with experienced teachers, as in the senior year of college where youth are in the majority. Poor spelling seems to be the one thing colleges can be assured their seniors will take away with them. Unless college graduates mend their spelling habits before they become parents (a statement that businessmen emphatically deny), parents must be as poor spellers as their children and some of their children's teachers. (Is there anyone that I have forgotten to insult at this point? Be sure to let me know if there is; I wish to be fair to everybody!) Oh, yes, I must not neglect here to include myself among the spelling offenders, having often to stop in the midst of a demonstration to ask observers, "Is that word spelled correctly? It doesn't look right." (That one invariably *is* right, but one other one I did not ask about invariably is not.) Perhaps it is because I am myself a contributor to the spelling crime that I am so concerned about the problem. Since we are all involved in one way or another, I believe it would do all of us good to sit down and talk over together the spelling problem and how to overcome it.

I have looked over children's papers continuously from the first year I started teaching school at seventeen, and, to be truthful, I cannot see that children are any worse spellers than they used to be, but poor spellers stay in school longer now than they used to and thus show up more clearly. Let's not fret ourselves with anything as futile as comparing today's spelling with yesterday's. There are absolutely no data for that kind of comparison and even though the subtitle of this book is *An Imaginative Approach to the Teaching of the Language Arts,* this book is not *that* imaginative.

Let's just face it—there are too many poor spellers today among parents, teachers, and children. Since the two of those named are past the help of the schools, what can we do to help children become better spellers?

That's our problem—ours—the schools. Let us face it, ponder it, and, of course, conquer it. What else?

How Can We Help Children to Be Better Spellers?

1. Spelling is an all-day job, yet we've been giving it only a few minutes of our day.

2. Words need teaching far more than they need testing; we seem to have been proceeding on the opposite assumption.

3. We have been helping children with spelling instead of helping them to help themselves.

4. We have not sold modern boys and girls on the fact that spelling is important.

There! Does that list make you feel like the N.E.A. story about the fourth-grader who got home late to lunch?

"I'm sorry to be late, Mother," she apologized as she sat down at the table, "but we've been making a display for a science unit and I had to stay and finish the universe." What about it—do you feel that's your job, too? But this is only spelling, remember, and spelling is easy compared with what most of a teacher's problems are nowadays.

Let's go back and think about that first point a bit.

Spelling is an all-day job, yet we've been giving it only a few minutes of our day.

Spelling is not a quick learning of a list of words for a test; but we've been teaching it as if it were that. Spelling is really not a teaching at all; it is getting acquainted with words, well enough acquainted so that we will have a feeling for those words whenever we meet them. Spelling is a learning of words in the way the poet, Paul Engle, says his little daughter learned them:

> Words were like dogs, to handle, teach and hold,
> Live things all colors, gray or brown or gold,
> That could sit up, say what you wished to say,
> Or bark in stubbornness and run away.[3]

[3] *Ibid.*

You can't teach words like that in ten minutes. If you're going to ask children to get well enough acquainted with words so that they'll know every letter they contain, in the right order—and that's what spelling is—you'll have to make those words alive to children. Together you must hunt in the dictionary and find their root words or stems and become acquainted with the other members of that root family. You'll want to try a prefix and a suffix on the stem and see what effects you can get in several tries. Oh, you just can't become fast friends with a word simply by passing it with the speed of light or by writing it twenty-five times.

Let's take an example of getting acquainted with a word. In a sixth-grade room in which I was supervising practice, a boy came to me for help with the word *belligerent*. We looked it up together in the dictionary and found that it meant warlike. Since its source word was from the Latin *bellum* meaning war, we saw what the word grew from. We found other words from the same stem: *bellicose* with the same meaning; *belligerence,* the noun, meaning that warlike feeling we sometimes get in school when we don't understand things, and *belligerency* meaning warfare. We broke the word into syllables and noticed how simple it was to spell except for that last *e,* and we decided we'd remember that *e* as the doubled-up fist showing in that warlike word.

We also picked out *pugnacious* as a good sensible synonym to use in place of belligerent once in a while. "Say, I'll bet the word pugilist came from that one!" the boy said, his face lighting up.

We talked over how belligerent people acted, how their faces looked, the usual positions their jaws assumed, and the attitudes of their fists. We discussed the nations of the world today that seem to have a belligerent attitude toward us and those we act belligerent toward. We mentioned again that the word ended in the word *rent* not *rant*. We talked about how a belligerent attitude made us feel. Just then the class bell rang. The lad turned to me with a twinkle, "I'll never have a belligerent attitude toward a word again!" he said merrily and was on his way.

Which is more practical: to teach a word and its family thoroughly when a child first meets it so that each subsequent meeting is a short renewal of acquaintance, or never to spend enough time on a word to give it a personality? What do you think?

Science is bringing any number of new words into our language and strangely enough, these words usually come from ancient roots. Three young scientists tackled me one day about the word *astronaut* which they knew, but which they doubted that I did. (Children have lots of fun confronting me with new words, and so do I.) I told the boys I wasn't acquainted with the word but thought I could figure it out. "*Astro* means star, and *naut* in such words as *nautilus* and *aeronaut* means traveler, so I guess that an *astronaut* means a traveler to the stars." The boys almost jumped up and down with excitement, "She's got it!" one of them shouted; "it says in the reading that *astronaut* means 'Star hopper!' " It pays to get children excited enough about words to go after their meanings; that's what a teacher does if spelling is to stick.

What did I mean when I said, "Spelling is an all-day job"? Can you imagine the terrific impact on spelling and reading that would result from on-the-spot teaching of the vocabulary of each school subject whether in elementary or high school? When every teacher teaches the tools of his trade (words) at the psychological moment that they meet them, parents will have to find a new topic of conversation at dinner parties.

To *teach* spelling takes time, and even when teachers feel they have no time to teach it, they must find time or eventually lose more than they have gained.

Words need teaching far more than they need testing; we seem to have been proceeding on the opposite assumption.

The average spelling workbook suggests a pretest on Monday to see whether or not the speller already knows the words (just as if the mere spelling of a word were all you were going to teach him about it) ; a midweek test on Wednesday to see if he's going to be ready for the test on Friday (getting ready to get ready) ; Friday's test to find out whether he was ready; exactly two lists too many, to my mind. Pray tell me this—what with extracurricular activities and special teachers knocking the props out from under our daily plans, when does a teacher teach spelling?

The answer to that one is that he doesn't. What class is pushed into libidinal darkness when time pinches? Spelling! We let the workbook teach it and it does a heroic job. But a workbook can't take the place of a teacher. Words seldom take on personalities without the assistance of a human personality.

Let's gather together the many ways by which we can make a word come alive to a child—that's what teaching is.

To get a word's personality across to a child:
Show pictures of the word, use real objects, draw a chalk sketch. Have it dramatized.

Read a sentence or prose paragraph or short poem in which it is
    used graphically.
Figure its meaning from the context, use the dictionary, figure its
    meaning from similar words, locate its source word.
Tell an anecdote about it.
Think of synonyms for it, get acquainted with its antonyms or its
    opposites.
If it's a homonym, meet its twin.
Make that word a personality.

To get the form of a word into a child's mental picture:
Pronounce it carefully, syllabicate it.
Notice its stem, the prefixes and suffixes.
Notice what happens to the spelling of the stem when a suffix is
    added.
Make different words by adding prefixes and suffixes to its stem.
If it's a phonetic word, list the other members of its phonetic family.
Gather words that rhyme with it.
Note its departures from the rule, if any.
Suggest helpful devices to help him remember its hard spots.
Teach the rule it illustrates if the rule works at least 75 per cent of
    the time.

From these two activity lists, choose the several methods best
suited to teaching the word you have in mind; then, as the children
say, "Go to town!"

In other words, teach a boy to look at a spelling word as thoroughly and as appraisingly as he will later look at a blonde, and
a girl to eye a word as speculatively and as minutely as she will one
day look over each likely male she meets (as if she didn't now!).

Before we go on to the next item, may I elaborate on one point
I made in my list of methods of teaching words—how to help children by means of devices. Devices are crutches for helping to remember the spelling of hard words. Some words are just plain
"cornsarned" to spell; they follow no rules; they change their courses
in the middle of their streams and there seems to be no apparent
reason why they are spelled as they are. "Juice" is such a word, as
Edward Dolch pointed out in a lecture on spelling: "If you will
just keep in mind that folks like *ice* in their *juice*, and that it's always there in the word, keeping it cold, you won't forget it"—and
I never have. To this day, I remember how to spell the word
cemetery from picturing the three little *e*'s in the word as head-
stone. (I always want that last *e* to be an *a*.) I keep the two *n's*

and the one *r* in *questionnaire* straight by remembering that questionnaires are questions 'n a lot of hot air, a device which may not be at all meaningful to you, but says what I think of most of the hundreds I have to fill out. I keep the word *believe* straight because it has a *lie* in the middle of it.

But my most helpful spelling device was the one concocted for myself at the age of ten when I met the word *hydrophobia* in my spelling lesson. That word almost broke my spirit. I just couldn't remember it. Finally, in near panic, I pretended that I had a doll named Hobia, which my dog ran away with, whereupon I chased the dog calling out, "Hy—drop—Hobia!" That device saved me and I have never forgotten the spelling of the word since, though Heaven knows I seldom get a chance to spell the word unless I tell this particular story.

The word *occurred* baffled me for years. One *c* and two *r's* or two *c's* and one *r*—which? I finally almost overcame my problem by concocting this unladylike rhyme:

> Double or nothing in *occurred*
> I'd like to double damn that double-trouble word!

Spelling devices are of much help to imaginative people who have a tendency to picture in their minds every word they spell.

We have been helping children with spelling instead of helping them to help themselves.

Twenty-five years ago when we started more creative writing, we teachers got into the habit of writing the words children asked for on spelling slips which they kept on their desks. This was a splendid idea, but like many splendid ideas in the world of education and elsewhere, we overdid it. The modern teacher, when a primary youngster asks her how to spell a word, helps him to find it for himself.

"How do you spell *discover?*" a first grader asked of his teacher one day when I was sitting near his desk.

"How does that first *dis* part sound?" she asked him, and he figured out the prefix by himself. "I am sure that you had the word *cover* in that story in your reader about covering up with leaves," she reminded him, then showed him how to find the word in his glossary. Needless to say, the children in that first grade are learning to be self-reliant.

Words should be easily accessible to each child in a primary room: cardboard files of words the children often ask for printed on tagboard strips; words from Dolch's list in another file; words from their current unit of interest stuck in a pocket chart; words in several picture dictionaries on the reading table; words on a bulletin board telling a story in conjunction with pictures; words on a chart labeled "Words we learned from television"; words in a stack of picture-name cards for the visual-minded. Words! Words! How successful children feel after tracing down their spelling for themselves!

Make the dictionary a "must" in the intermediate grades. Teach the children to do the first draft of creative writing without paying any attention to spelling, but insist that they correct it in proof-reading with the help of the dictionary.

Some teachers like this method of helping children with the misspelled words on their papers. They keep a four-by-six card for each child, alphabetized under his name. As he looks over the child's paper, the teacher writes the misspelled words (I just had to look up that word *misspelled* again!) on the child's card, but does not underline them on the paper. When the paper is returned, the child must get his card, and as he locates each misspelled word, he writes it correctly above the misspelled one on his paper. The words on the spelling cards are used for the child's Friday list, the day set aside for personal spelling. As both sides of a child's card are filled, he gets another, and at the end of the year there is a complete record of the words he has misspelled. These cards are useful to the child in pointing out his errors, useful to the teacher in planning individual help, and excellent as visual aids in parent conferences.

Help your intermediate children to be real friends with the dictionary. Never teach a spelling lesson without having the dictionary at hand on every desk. Why, you can find out more about words from a dictionary than you can learn about the neighborhood go-ings-on from the invalid next door!

(We have not sold modern boys and girls on the fact that spelling is important.)

Until he feels that spelling is important, the modern child will not do much about it. Can you think of a clever picture or drawing to go with these poster slogans, or better still, can you have your children think of some better slogans?

1. Misspelled words are the black fingernails on a written page.

2. Dere Lulu,
    I luv you madley.

        Even love letters seem absurd
        If you misspell every other word.

3. You may have all other kinds of knowledge,
   But you have to spell, boy, to stay in college.

4. Standards are rising every day!
   Are your spelling standards pointed that way?

5. Misspelling causes yelling!

6. In the space age don't let spelling ground you.

7. The dictionary
   Is important—very!

8. Business men have started to yell,
   "The girls you're sending us can't spell!"

9. Boss's note to his stenographer:
           Dear Miss Brown:
           You *must* get better
           Five misspelled words
           In this one letter!

10. Today: You're hired
    Two weeks later: You're fired!

11. Though you look as smart as a collar ad,
    If your spelling is uncouth
    Folks will dub you as a Goon—
    And that's the honest truth!

12. Short—short—   Met her!
                  Wrote letter!
                  Didn't get her!

13. Your spelling advertises your mental wares
    It's an indication of what's "upstairs."

14. Lazy spelling indicates a lazy mind.

Why not hold a contest for getting the best humorous poster aimed at better spelling results? Humor can sell more ideas than preaching any day. Ask children to depict what their favorite cartoon character might have to say about spelling.

Now the subject of spelling could be linked to outer space. What could young people in a cartoon be saying to one another about spelling and outer space?

Just How Important Is Spelling?

As far as communication is concerned, spelling is of little moment as long as it does not stand in the way of meaning. I get several hundred pieces of writing from intermediate and upper-grade children following my "Let's Write" program each week. Many of the best pieces of writing are spelled the worst.

But I still think spelling is important—important because it is an outward indication of an inward attitude. One's spelling clearly advertises his personal standards to the world. "Look!" a misspelled word says to the reader, "my writer doesn't care enough about doing a good job to look me up in the dictionary—he's careless!"

Yes, that's what poor spelling in the elementary school usually means—carelessness. Poor spelling in high school means more than that; it means lower grades not only in English but in all school subjects with the possible exception of math.

The results of poor spelling habits do not end with a high school diploma. They speak from the letters of application you send to the members of the entrance board of the college of your choice —and you may not get in. They whisper from the pages of the business letter you write for that job you feel you're amply qualified for—and another fellow gets it. Poor spelling stalks one's life as a hunter stalks a deer; it has left its tracks all the way through one's forest of experience. Yes, indeed, spelling *is* important.

But again may I say a grave word of warning for all spotters and chasers after misspelled words. Yes, correct spelling *is* important, but not half as important as vibrant writing. Beware that our demanding of perfect papers from unjelled youth does not drain the life out of their writing, making it good, but good for nothing. Change a child's spelling from pride, not from blood left by the red-marking pencil. The elementary school is a time of learning and living, and its progress is wobbly at best and tied closely to home standards and personal problems. Who can spell when more important things are on one's mind? Who can spell when emotion blots out one's sense like a cloud? A child doesn't usually feel the need for perfection; he has other things to grope for.

It has often been said that writers usually drove their early English teachers wild. I wonder if Paul Engle was a good speller as a boy! One doesn't even think about spelling when he reads these powerful lines he wrote:

> She bit the word off like a chunk of bread
> And spat it in our face.
>
> .   .   .   .
>
> She strokes the day as if it were a dog.[4]

It pays to have patience with children; one is never sure which clam will have the pearl.

Spelling is never as important as writing—never, and writing is never as important as children—never; yet children must have standards. Dear me, we're going to have to consult that happy medium again. Do you suppose she's happy because she's only medium or medium because she's happy?

Teaching Children to Safeguard Their Meanings

You no doubt have noticed that in this chapter and throughout this entire book, I have stressed telling the children to write their first draft of any creative paper without regard either to mechanics or spelling. Attention to such details during the first writing slows the thought flow and sometimes completely stops it. It is important that in the first draft of a paper a child gets onto the paper and out of his mind what he has to say. His second step then is to go back over the paper, step by step, to see whether or not he has safeguarded his meanings with the proper mechanics. The first writing is the joint result of the "paint-mixing" the teacher has done and the ability of the child who is doing the writing. The second step is usually a result of a training that started in the first grade and grew with the child.

A teacher must have so trained children to proofread their papers that they feel positively guilty if they fail to do it. Just looking back over a paper is not enough. Papers must be reread each time with a

---

[4] *Ibid.*

different purpose in mind. Proofreaders who are looking for just any error overlook more than they see.

Have all creative writing papers and major compositions of all sorts (except tests and work-type writing) laid away for a day before they are proofread. Young children tire of their papers as soon as they have finished them. Let them age for a day (both the children and the papers), since after a day away from his paper, a child can feel more objective about what he has written.

Set up, sometime beforehand, an orderly set of purposes for which the child is to reread his paper. (This list is not likely to come all at once; it usually grows slowly over a period of time.) In intermediate grades you'll probably come out with purposes at least faintly resembling these:

Step 1. Rereading for sentence sense

Read your paper to see if the things you said are put into readable sentences that not only make sense but flow as smoothly as fish swimming through the water. Read through each thought carefully putting a capital letter at the first of each sentence and the proper punctuation mark (. ! ?) at the end, according to your meaning. Is there some sentence that makes little sense to you today as you read it? Well, it will probably make less sense to the teacher, since you were the writer, not he. Rework that sentence on a trial scrap of paper until it says what you want it to say. When your sentences are the best you can make them, Step 1 is finished.

Step 2. Rereading for punctuation power

Now go back and read each sentence slowly again. Would a comma or a dash or a semicolon ensure that the teacher will get your meaning better? Have you put quotation marks around the conversation? Has your punctuation pointed out just how you want this paper read? See that it does.

Step 3. Rereading to make general words specific and vague word-pictures clear

Use your mental Geiger counter now to locate your weak word spots. Make every word do all it can to give the teacher real pictures, definite actions, and clear sense.

Step 4. Rereading this time for misspelled words

Even if you get only a faint click with your Geiger counter as you approach a word you aren't sure of, use the dictionary to check it. Every misspelled word you discover before the teacher finds it adds to your grade and to the looks of your paper. A misspelled word sticks out on a paper like a pimple on a nose. Play a game with yourself. Get every single one.

Step 5. Checking the little things

Little things make a big difference in the looks of your paper. The reason why soldiers look so neat is that they are checked for unshined shoes, brushed clothes, dangling buttons, and each tiny detail. Your work is about to be inspected; have all the little things right.

Margin. Put a line ——— in the left-hand corner if you forgot to have one.

Title. Each major word should be capitalized and a space left between the title and the story. Put an X beside the title if it needs attention.

Step 6. Copying your corrected paper in your best handwriting, and good luck to you

It might help the children if you mimeographed these points, together with the written conversation from me to them.

And now may I talk to you teachers for a moment—alone. I believe, teachers, that we have been doing far too much rewriting on children's papers and that the rewriting has changed the children's writing hardly at all, even after all that work on our part. If we do all a child's thinking for him, he doesn't grow, and we only get tired.

Make a child rewrite his paper *after his own checking* not yours, and before you see it for the first time. He'll never learn to proofread his own work if you are willing to do it for him. Except in rare instances, never make a child rewrite a paper the second time. Why? No good comes of it—he just makes the same mistakes again. (Experiment and see.)

When shall a child recopy a paper the second time? Only when he apparently hasn't proofread it at all. But even at this point, use judgment. Always look at a paper with the child in mind. What is excellence? A color to wear: what's good for one is bad for another. Be easier on a child, too, when he's troubled about home conditions. Sometimes children strike back at an unco-operative world with a careless pencil. Keep the child in mind as you correct his paper.

I think it is wise to have pen-pal letters copied a second time. Children will understand that their letters represent their country as well as themselves and will see a reason for the extra work. Since the children of the foreign country may be learning their English from our letters, our children will recognize their added responsibility in writing letters correctly.

If children aren't to copy a teacher's rewriting, how then are they going to improve in their written work? As you read each child's paper, list at the end one or two things he is to work on: sentences and possessives, for example. Then each two weeks have a conference with him on his writing and help him with his problems and mistakes. It is the next paper you hope will show improvement, not this old one. This paper has already served its purpose; it has shown *you and the child* where he is in need of help.

But looking over his paper has served a further purpose; it has pointed out to you, the teacher, the writing needs of the class.

Base your future writing plans on the needs of the children as pointed out by their papers.

Furthermore, looking over children's papers has provided both you and them with a list of words they need to learn how to spell. Keep these on cards for the day each week you reserve for personal spelling. All English teaching should be based on need. Last of all —and perhaps best of all—looking over children's papers and having a conference with each child gives you a chance to report to the child what progress he is making. What wonderful words to hear from a teacher, "Jim, you're improving! Your sentences are so much better. Now, we'll have to work on a better vocabulary!"

What a wonderful thing, too, to be able to say to a girl, "Mary, you're slipping a little. Let's talk it over together so that I can help you. You're worth helping, Mary." Saying a thing is good if it's bad doesn't help a child to grow; but seeing only the bad does more harm than good—too—so . . .

What a delicate operation this attempting to help human beings is anyway. It makes a person feel humble and afraid and, oh, so in need of wisdom from outside one's self. It makes me think of a verse of John G. Holland's with which I grew up:

> These clumsy feet still in the mire,
> Go crushing blossoms without end;
> These hard, well-meaning hands we thrust
> Among the heart strings of a friend.
> The ill-timed truth we might have kept—
> Who knows how harsh it pierced and stung?
> The word we had not sense to say,
> Who knows how grandly it had rung?

Do not spend your precious hours, teacher, only chasing AWOL commas; look for the good in every paper, for lo! what we look for, that we always find.

To teachers everywhere who teach children to safeguard their meanings with the proper mechanics:

> Heart-gladness to you
> For punctuation,
> Moon madness to you
> For exclamation;
> And enough of the quiet
>   commas of praise
> To help you make sense of
> The book of your days.

CUPBOARD OF IDEAS for Chapter Eleven

Mechanics Safeguard Our Meanings ❖ ❖ ❖ ❖ ❖ ❖ ❖ ❖ ❖

> This cupboard is for every grade
> There are no marked shelves—
> Just open the doors, find what you need,
> Then help yourselves!

The Little Stinkers

There are some usages that cause trouble all the way from kindergarten to college. Have you tried these home remedies?

1. *Too* causes too much trouble. Let little children blow up balloons for this one to show that it means *too* much, *too* full, as well as *also*. The two full balloons will stay in their minds as the two *o*'s in *too,* we hope.

2. *In* and *into*. Act this one out, first with pencils for dolls, then with real children. Show that *into* means across the threshold *into* (from outside into inside) the room. Dramatize many sentences to impress the correct use on children. She went *into* the room. She walked *in* the room (up and down *in* it after she got *into* the room in the first place). Goldilocks went *into* the house and *into* many successive rooms, doing much damage *in* each room as she went.

3. *It's—its*. The misuse of these two forms have killed off more teachers than Intelligitis of the Left Spleen. Teach children that *no* pronouns (except indefinite pronouns like *one's, somebody's*) need apostrophes and that *it's* is the contraction of *it is*. Tell chil-

dren to say *it is* when they start to write *it's,* and if it makes sense, to put in an apostrophe before the *s. It's* just cannot show possession.

> When writing "it's"
> Try "it is"; if it fits,
> Put an apostrophe *s*
> And call it quits!

Act this one out and the children will remember it!

4. *Their* and *there.* Which is which? Both of these words begin with *the,* but the one with the *i* in it is possessive; *I* is always possessive. Be sure to teach children that *they're* is the contraction *they are.* They confuse this word with *there.*

5. *Who; Whom. Who* is a subject word; *whom* is an object word. Objects come after verbs and prepositions (in this case, especially *to, for, at,* and *with*). Have each child keep a cardboard of tablet size in his desk, on one side of which *who* is written in large letters, and on the other *whom.* When you have a spare minute, read sentences that call for the use of *who* or *whom.* Substitute *blank* for *who* and *whom* in the sentences you read and ask the children to hold up the right form.

> *Blank* are you?
> To *blank* am I speaking, please?
> It is wise to know *blank* you're talking to.
> She never let him know that she knew *blank* he was.

NOTE: This same cardboard idea works with the conquering of most of these little stinkers, enabling you to see (*who* or *whom*) is doing the thinking.

6. *Those* things or *them* things? Teach a child that *them* is the hem; it comes at the end as a hem does. Never *them things;* just *them.*

7. *Already? Already* is an offender on two counts; children often misspell and put it in the wrong place in the sentence. *Already* has only one *l* and is usually placed just before the verb it modifies, not after. Not "I have done that already," but "I have already done that." Help your children to work on this one; its misuse is not well accepted in speech-conscious groups.

8. *All right!* All right is two words, never one, and unlike "already" has kept all its letters. To be truly all right, it must be spelled two words, two *l's—all right.*

9. *Well* and *good.* I have heard more elementary teachers misuse these two innocent-looking words than you would believe.

Perhaps their misuse is so prevalent because they have two distinctly different meanings.

Neither *well* nor *good* can be misused from a health standpoint because it is permissible to say either *well* or *good* after the linking verb *feel*. To feel *well* means an absence of sickness; to feel *good* means to have a feeling of general well-being. Both *well* and *good* used in regard to health are predicate adjectives used after the linking verb *feel*.

When they use *well* as an adverb to modify a verb, children have a tendency to misuse it. *Good* is rarely an adverb. A person can't do his arithmetic *good*. Neither can he act *good*, nor treat his dog *good*. When one is modifying an action, the correct word to use is *well:* You did your arithmetic *well* today. You play the piano *well*. You treat your dog *well*. A person can *be* good, but not *act* good, for *good* in that first usage is a predicate adjective.

Please work on this one, teachers! It sounds *bad* to say *good* when you mean *well*.

10. *Bad* and *badly*. Almost 95 per cent of the people I listen to misuse these two words: *bad* is practically always an adjective; *badly* is practically always an adverb. A person just can't feel *badly;* he just has to feel *bad,* because *feel* in this case is a linking verb and *bad* is a predicate adjective. An adjective describes nouns and pronouns but never verbs.

The only time a person could legitimately *feel badly* would be to hurt his hand and have to have it bandaged. He therefore couldn't feel the bump on his brother's head as he asked him to do, since with a damaged hand he feels too badly.

A Punctuation Fair

Have you ever held a Punctuation Fair? It's fun and it makes punctuation as real as recess. Each punctuation mark displays its wares in poem, dramatization, dance, or song.

There's the Comma Booth, where one after another the various uses of the comma are demonstrated by groups of children, each of whom holds a word card that together forms a sentence; for example: "At the picnic we had fried chicken, potato salad, baked beans, ice cream and cake."

The Comma Commentator steps forward and calls the comma cards into place in the line; as the words move over, he explains that this usage of the comma is called "comma in a series." He explains why there is often no comma before the *and* in this kind of construction.

For commas in direct address, the cards present a different sentence: "Come here, Sally, come here!" As the comma cards take their correct places, the Comma Commentator comments as to why. Similar sentences are demonstrated for other common uses of commas in punctuation:

1. Between long equal clauses connected by a joiner: "The children were making not a sound, and their mother wondered what they were doing."

2. To separate an appositive from the rest of the sentence: "Our pet rat, a real nuisance, will not stay in his cage."

3. Following the salutation in a friendly letter and after the complimentary close:

Dear Mother,   Affectionately yours,

4. To separate a city from a town, and a day of the month from the year:

Evanston, Illinois   June 4, 1960

5. To make the meaning of a sentence clear: "To save the lemonade from spoiling, the boys put an old umbrella over the stand."

Demonstrate just those comma usages commonly used in your room, and have each word in the sentences written large on tagboard and held in front of each child so it can be easily read by the audience. Choose for the Comma Commentator a self-possessed student with a ready tongue.

A Conundrum

Give the following part to a child who is a born actor and a bit of a clown. The act can be greatly enhanced by having children in question-mark bedecked costumes performing a creative dance at the end of the poem, or singing a question-mark chorus.

There's a mark of punctuation
That is widely used today
If our teachers didn't have it,
Schools could certainly be play!
Mothers use it on our fathers
When they've been out far too late;
Fathers use it on our mothers,
When the bills accumulate.

High school brothers always use it
When they want to take the car;
High school sisters all abuse it
When their spending's gone too far.
Young men use it when they're lovesick
And are wanting to be wed;
God will likely use it plenty
On us all when we are dead.
All the kids in our room use it
When they cannot make their dome work
And must call upon their parents
For a little help with homework.
Judges use it on the people—
Plaintiffs are tried before their court.
Baseball fans all have to use it,
If they're the inquiring sort.
Quiz shows all would fail without it;
Gone would be all interviews,
Pray, what is this punctuation
That so many people use?

ANSWER: *Question Mark*. The actor brings out a big, silvered one from behind his back.

Mr. Kolinsky's Colons

Hawker (in a grandiloquent voice) : Right this way! Right this way, folks. You are about to witness a phenomenal show of Mr. Kolinsky and his talking dots!

Mr. Kolinsky has nothing but this simple device of one dot above another (:) . It's called a colon in honor of its inventor, Mr. Kolinsky. And now for the performance, ladies and gentlemen!

This is colon Magic No. 1.

Mr. Kolinsky places his magic dots right after "Dear Mr. Jones:" in a business letter, like this (puts in the colon instantly, and a business letter appears on the paper—he quickly turns over the chart and the complete letter which was on the other side shows) .

Mr. Kolinsky's first magic is that when the colon is put after the salutation in a business letter, a complete business letter writes itself on the page. How's that for magic?

And now for Magic No. 2.

Mr. Kolinsky makes a statement like this: The reasons why Roosevelt is the best school in this area are the following: (He shows this sentence portion written on a chart) . Here Mr. Kolinsky puts in his magic dots or colon; immediately from wherever they are, those reasons line themselves right up in a row one after the other, correct with commas! See! (Children come rushing out from all sides of the stage with reasons printed on cards and stand in a line after the magic colon.) The reasons *always* line up like this right after Mr. Kolinsky's colon calls for them. See! Have you ever in your life seen anything like that before?

The cleverest magic trick of all is how Mr. Kolinsky's colon can introduce parts of speeches and poems. Notice here's the start of President ———'s speech of the other night, and see—just as I thought, Mr. Kolinsky's magic colon is right there to introduce that speech (shows it on chart) beginning, "The President says: (Copy beginning of the president's latest speech on the chart) ."

(Introduce Mr. Kolinsky here if you wish. Have him dressed to resemble a colon.)

And now, ladies and gentlemen, come right on to the next act in this great punctuation fair!

I'm a Period

(Choric Verse)

Use a deep-voiced lad and his helpers standing behind a screen which allows just their heads to show. If they could know their lines by heart, their arms could be dressed as legs, even to the shoes, and could dangle down from the top of the screen in humpty-dumpty style, giving the speakers a dwarf-like appearance. Each cap could be a large black period cut from construction paper and fastened to a well-fitted headband.

First speaker: (*slow, heavy voice*)	I am a per-i-od, I am a-wer-i-od! I'm nobody's friend I'm always at the end!
Very high voice:	Commas are chummy.
A little less high:	Semicolons gay!
First speaker:	But a period has a myriad Of troubles every day.
Very high voice:	Exclamations effervesce!
Lower:	Commas make suggestions.

Deeper:	Semicolons just sit tight.
High:	Questions ask the questions!
First speaker:	But a period comes at the very last, When the whole parade's gone past!
High:	I'm nothing but a little ball.
Very high:	My nose is out of joint.
Lower:	The only thing I ever do
All helpers together:	Is just come to a point!
First speaker:	Like an old cow's tail,
Very high:	Like the bottom of a pail,
Next highest:	Like the tip end of a sail,
Lower:	Like the ceasing of a gale,
Lowest:	Like the tail end of a whale,
First speaker:	I'm the end of a sentence, Though I've never been in jail.
Low:	I am always at the end.
Lower:	I'm the finalist of final,
First speaker:	Here I sit upon my spinal, And I know I always will. Not a flutter; not a thrill—
All together:	I'm a period.

The Quotation Quiz Is Run by the Quotation Queen

Will you two girls please come forward? What are your names? What grade are you girls in? Now, girls, I'm letting you race each other in writing the proper punctuation of quotations. Each direction counts one for each girl who gets it right. At the end of each part of the contest, I shall ask each girl to read and explain what she has written.

1. Write and punctuate correctly a direct quotation.
2. Write and punctuate an indirect quotation.
3. Use the title of a poem in a sentence.
4. Quote something a noted person said, telling who said it.
5. Write a short conversation between a mother and her little boy or girl, punctuating it correctly.

If two well-matched contestants are chosen and they work at the blackboard where all can see, this is real fun.

Animated Lost and Found

This part of the program about apostrophes is better when worked out by the children themselves in creative dramatics. It will be especially good if a group of imaginative children are put in charge.

Paint a large piece of cardboard backdrop to look like a giant box marked *Lost and Found,* behind which children are hiding and holding the lost articles they represent.

First the school principal comes by, looks into the box, and makes a remark about how forgetful of possessions children are. Throughout the dramatizations, keep playing up the word *possessions* in order to bring out the apostrophe idea later.

Different articles come out of the box bewailing the fact that they are nobody's possessions any more. Then out from the wings rush a number of apostrophes. Their leader explains that they always show possession and gives each article a card to prove it.

Mary's coat   Jim's gym shoes   boys' marbles

The repossessed possessions end up with a happy dance or song or leave stage, each with an apostrophe by the hand in order to show possession later when they find their owner.

An Intrepid Interviewer Interviews Mr. Semicolon

I.I.: So you're a semicolon, sir?

S.C.: Indeed I am—a kind of punctuation "half and half"; half period and half comma. Both halves come from the best families, of course.

I.I.: And with the best qualities of both, I presume, sir?

S.C.: Well, yes, I guess that is partly true; I'm a longer pause than the comma and not nearly so final as the period.

I.I.: Could you explain to the radio audience, sir, just what your job in punctuation is?

S.C.: I'd be glad to. I hire out to "like" clauses usually, and when there's no strong conjunction on hand to join them together, I do the trick.

I.I.: Could you give us an example of what you mean, sir?

S.C.: Indeed, I could! Let's take this sentence from current affairs. "The United States has asked Khrushchev to visit this country, and Russia has asked President Eisenhower to visit that country." Now, you notice, sir, that the joiner in that sentence is *and,* but *and* doesn't sound too well in a sentence of that length. I'll read it so you can see what I mean [reads it stressing *and*]. Now that sentence would sound much better without the *and.* Put a semicolon in and the sentence is improved at once. Hear for yourself, sir [reads again but without the *and*].

I.I.: I see what you mean; a semicolon acts like a safety pin to pin two like clauses together in place of the weak joiner *and*.

S.C.: Exactly!

I.I.: And what is that other job you mentioned, sir?

S.C.: If a writer has used several commas in a sentence and wishes to make a little stronger and longer pause than a comma indicates, he uses a semicolon.

I.I.: To sum up both your jobs, sir, you both fasten parts of sentences together and separate others. Why, you're a regular paradox, I must say.

S.C.: (laughing) Oh, I've been called far worse names than that, sir. I'm being called on more and more to pin clauses together, sir. Sentences are more effective without that weak *and* as a joiner, sir, if I do say it myself.

I.I.: Well, Mr. Semicolon, we've been happy to interview so distinguished a member of the Punctuation Family. Thank you very much.

S.C.: Thank *you*, sir. It's nice getting away from my long sentence for awhile!

Beginning and Ending Song

(Tune: "We Went to the Animal Fair")

The sixth-grade room had a fair
All the punctuations were there.
The question marks were having such larks
Asking just why the bear wasn't bare.
The colons tended the gate;
The periods all were late;
The exclamations enjoyed recreations;
The commas each had a date.

The sixth grade put on a fair
The punctuations were there!
The semicolons were rockin' and rollin'
And all the quotations were rare.
The apostropes put up a tent
Where the Lost and the Found were sent.
You made real concessions to get your possessions.
And wondered just where they went.

The sixth-grade room had a fair
All the friends and the parents were there.
They served some nice punch and suggestions of lunch
And each child had combed his hair.
The children all knew their part
They had learned their speeches by heart.
When the time came to go
The starting was slow
For nobody wanted to start.

If you have a creative grade, have the children make up their own acts for the fair. Children get infinitely more out of creating than from performing someone else's creations. Many uncreative teachers, because they are afraid of creativity themselves, fail to allow the children to try their wings—a real shame!

For the Parts of Speech to hold a fair or put on a television show is a powerful motivation for the learning that must go on long before the show is put on. Did you ever see a mock opera put on by the grammar elements? The one I saw was hilarious. Your gifted children in junior high could write one that would really be good.

Acting Out Sentence Parts

Give out these word cards, one to a person: *subject, verb, object, phrase modifier, adjective.* Then write a sentence across the board leaving a card-long space between each grammatical part, like this: The   fat   boy   hit   his   tormentor   with his fist. The persons holding the right card for each blank holds his card where it belongs. If you pass out cards for every construction, whether it is contained in the sentence or not, there is more judgment exercised. I have tried this method of dramatizing grammar, even with slow children, and they get it. It's a good starter game, too, for teaching simple subjects and predicates.

Dramatizing Parts of Speech

This exercise is played just like the above, but instead of parts of sentences, parts of speech are used. Use "article" as an extra card, making nine cards to hand out at once. If there is more than one of any part of speech used in the sentence, that card-holder uses his card twice.

Presto! Change!

This game is devised for the purpose of learning how to modify meanings.

Write on the board a short, unadorned sentence such as "Mary ran," and have the class see in how many ways they can modify its meaning by adding modifiers to either word.

Subject Modifiers

1. *pretty* (adjective)
2. *with fear* in her heart (adjective phrase)
3. *who was scared of her life* (adjective clause)
4. *panting like a tired dog* (participial phrase)

Verb Modifiers

1. *hard* (adverb)
2. *with flying feet* (adverbial prepositional phrase)
3. *putting all she had into the running* (participial phrase)
4. *as she had been taught to run* (adverbial clause)
5. *to save her life* (infinitive phrase)

This same type of exercise makes subjects and their different make-ups clear. These may all be used as sentence subjects:

Noun	*Dogs* are man's friends.
Pronoun	*They* went away.
Compound subject:	*Dogs and cats* together are too much in a small apartment.
Noun clause:	*What she didn't know* didn't hurt her.
Gerund:	*Dancing* is fun.
Infinitive:	*To water ski* is no sport for me.

Ask the children to write a sentence for each type as you call it out.

Making Grammar Practical

Do a great deal of building of sentences in junior high school. Ask four people to work at the board while the rest of the class work at their seats. After children are well into the study of grammar, give such directions as these:

Make a sentence with a noun subject modified by an adjective phrase and a transitive verb with a gerund for the object.

The girl in the yellow sweater likes skating.

Make a sentence having a compound subject and a linking verb completed by a predicate noun.

Mary and Jane are nice girls.

Now put in an adverb modifying that adjective "nice" (*very* or *not*).

This game works well from card directions, too. Keep a pack of sentences and the card directions on hand.

Don't resist teaching grammar. Have fun with it. You can!

Putting Punctuation to Use

Instead of filling in blanks, give practice in using punctuation marks in real situations as in quotations:

1. Teen-agers write a conversation about any subject they are interested in: sports, dating, and so on.

2. Two dogs talk together about what they have to put up with where they live.

3. A second grader tells his dog that he must eat his vitamins if he ever intends to make it to the moon in a spaceship.

4. A little girl impresses on her doll why she should clean her teeth after every meal. (It's so much more fun to give advice than to take it.)

Let first and second graders use question marks in writing out the questions they wonder about: Christmas, nature, animals, home, school, stories they have read or heard, things they hear or see on television.

Improving Sentence Structure

Long before they know much about clauses, sixth graders and junior high school youth can learn a great deal about sentence structure by experimenting with sentence parts in class together. Do a great deal of work with the reconstruction of poor sentences you saved from last year's papers.

Encourage children to bring examples of sentences beginning with *when, where, as, while, during this time, at the time when,* and point out to the class that such sentences are usually interesting. Frequently find samples of sentences together in class from a favorite story. Suggest that the students read aloud any powerful sentence or paragraph found in their reading and then as a group study its construction.

Often take four such short sentences as these and experiment in class how best to arrange them into one interesting sentence:

> Jim wanted to go fishing.
> He intended to fish from the river bridge.
> He got up early.
> The sun was just getting up when he got there.

These four parts might come out in this form:

> Just as the sun was coming up over the river, Jim sat down to fish from the river bridge.

Experiment with sentence forms in class. Get your children interested in writing more interesting sentences; that's about all a teacher can do in elementary school before his children understand the structure of our written language—just get children interested.

1. Keep a pack of cards on hand on which short sentences are typed.

> Miss Baumeister is my aunt.
> She is a brilliant woman.
> She is the head buyer in a large department store.

2. Keep another pack, similarly numbered, on which the information contained in the first card is written into one good sentence.

> My aunt, Miss Baumeister—a brilliant woman—is the head buyer for a large department store.

3. Type still another version on the back of the second card.

> Miss Baumeister, the head buyer for Tracey's and a brilliant woman, is my aunt.

CHAPTER TWELVE

Laughter Loosens the Spirit

Principal over the intercom: May I have your attention, please. I just read an article by a psychiatrist that suggests that laughter aids learning. I am therefore recommending that all schoolrooms in this building have a seven-minute period for laughter at 2:00 P.M. daily when a double-buzzer will be sounded for that purpose.

That's all!

They have yarns
Of a skyscraper so tall they had to put hinges
On the two top stories to let the moon go by,
Of one corn crop in Missouri when the roots
Went so deep and drew off so much water
The Mississippi riverbed that year was dry,
Of pancakes so thin they had only one side,
Of "a fog so thick we shingled the barn and six feet out on the
fog,"
Of Pecos Pete straddling a cyclone in Texas and riding it to the
west coast where it "rained out under him,"
Of a mountain railroad curve where the engineer in his cab can
touch the caboose and spit in the conductor's eye,
Of the boy who climbed a cornstalk growing so fast he would
have starved to death if they hadn't shot biscuits up to him,
Of the old man's whiskers: "When the wind was with him his whiskers
arrived a day before he did." [1]

Carl Sandburg

Jack Frost was very busy on Wednesday night. He noticed at 11:00 he
had only one pint of frost paint left. It was too late to go back to his island for more paint. What a fix he was in. A wonderful idea hit him. He
stole quietly into a nearby house, took out four eggs, took out an eggbeater
and a bowl. The whites of the eggs made a pretty good paint. The Masons
never found out what happened to those eggs.

Richard, Grade 5

Once I made popcorn at my house. I got the butter, lard, salt and,
of course, the popcorn. When I got out the popcorn, there was a little
kernel named Hot Rod. I poured him into the pot, waited a while for it
to pop but it wouldn't pop. I took off the cover and there he was running
and jumping, holding the seat of his pants. He mumbled and grumbled
his pants were on fire. He yelled at me to turn off the heat. And just as
he was cooling off, he started to pop. He went bop, bop, bing, bing, pop,
pop.

Danny, Grade 6

[1] From *The People, Yes* by Carl Sandburg, copyright, 1936, by Harcourt,
Brace and Company, Inc.

A schoolroom where children feel at home with laughter is likely to be a place where living together is a fine art. Tension and laughter have no compatibility; in fact, where one enters, the other soon takes its leave.

Lilting laughter is a sign of sanity and wholesomeness; of balance and the ability to cope with problems in a positive way.

The titter of tense children, the saw-shrillness of their laughter, the self-conscious loudness of their emotional outbursts are as different from the laughter of relaxed children as kindergarten is from vocational school. Laughter does to children what releasing the tension does for a rubber band—allows it to return to normalcy. Too-long tensions cause the spirits of children to lose their stretch just as rubber bands do.

Since elasticity in meeting his problems must be in every American's built-in kit of habits, school children must grow up with laughter at home and at school. To be normal, humor must be lived, not be artificially induced by gags and wisecracks.

How children long for fun and an atmosphere where laughter dares show its face. An eighth grader recently wrote this adult note to one of her teachers:

DEAR MISS ———,

You have a wonderful and worthwhile way of teaching. I think you give us a gift worth more than words can express. You surely rate highly with me. No one can teach us anything the way you can, and at the same time have fun.

> Your true friend,
> *Pat*

Children are willing to go through much of what to them is mumbo jumbo in order to please a teacher who has time in her daily program for fun. I think it's actually too bad if bottled-up children aren't allowed to pop their spirit corks often enough so that when they are released they don't figuratively hit the ceiling. Little pop-off's are better for growing youngsters than powerful explosions.

This chapter is concerned with writing fun. True, writing fun often causes chuckles to become slightly runny—but how about it —don't you need to be silly yourself sometimes?

Let's begin with word fun in a series of lessons directed to grades four to eight.

I. Fun with Words

Today is just the day to be nutty as a fruit cake, or fruity as a nut cake or in any *condition* you're *wishin'* with or without *supposition* or *nutrition* or *erudition*. You may be a *mathematician,* a *politician,* a *mortician,* a *logician* with or without *ambition* or *recognition.* But simply by turning on your mental *ignition* with or without *contrition* or *intuition* you will be in a *position* to have fun with words.

In writing time you may choose any of these suggested games we're going to play with words today; choose any words that you wish to play with; let your vocabulary and your mind loose and you'll be writing nonsense before you know it. It won't matter at all what form that nonsense takes—word exercises, rhymes, riddles, or hey-diddle-diddle's—anything you like—just so you have fun with words. You won't be thought less of today for being a bit silly. All major poets let themselves go at least once or twice in a while and are just plain silly with word pranks. Harry Behn, one of to-day's major children's poets, certainly kicked up his heels in this one. Notice he put any old kind of endings on these perfectly re-spectable words. You may wish to play this kind of word fun today.

> The things to draw with compasses
> Are suns and moons and circleses
> And rows of humptydumpasses
> Or anything in circuses
> Like hippopotamusseses
> And hoops and camels' humpasses
> And wheels on clownses bussesses
> And fat old elephumpasses.[2]

Some of you have been having the measles and mumps this season and those may turn out to be the words you'll want to put crazy endings on and write about. A. A. Milne, the famous father of Christopher Robin, and next to Lewis Carroll, England's most noted child's poet, did that one time with the word *measles.*

[2] From *The Little Hill,* "Circles" copyright, 1949, by Harry Behn. Reprinted by permission of Harcourt, Brace and Company, Inc.

You'll have to have your teacher read that measles, teazles, wheezles, breezles poem to you from the book *Now We Are Six*.

Is there some word you'd like to bounce around? Why not do it in writing time today? I was looking through the dictionary one day to see what fun I had been missing, and I came across the word *kudu*. The kudu is an African antelope, but I didn't care anything about its meaning; I was just interested in the whoosh of the sounds:

> If you were a kudu,
> My dear, what would you do?
> Try voodoo or hoodoo?
> See red or make blue do?
> If a voodoo would hoodoo
> A poor little kudu
> Whatever would you do
> To help the poor kudu
> To conquer the hoodoo?

Try to say that fast and you'll get more tangled up than a youngster chewing three sticks of bubble gum all at once. Tongue twisters like that are real fun to make. All you need is a few puns.

Here is a fairly new one by Morris Bishop that you may not have heard:

Song of the Pop-Bottlers [3]

> Pop bottles pop-bottles
>   In pop shops;
> The pop-bottles Pop bottles
>   Poor Pop drops.
>
> When Pop drops pop-bottles,
>   Pop-bottles plop!
> Pop-bottle-tops topple!
>   Pop mops slop!
>
> Stop! Pop'll drop bottle!
>   Stop, Pop, stop!
> When Pop bottles pop-bottles,
>   Pop-bottles pop!

[3] Reprinted from *A Bowl of Bishop*. Copyright 1954 by Morris Bishop. Used with permission of the publishers, The Dial Press, Inc.

Why don't some of you use soft-drink trade names and see what you can do to put as much fizz into words as are in these carbonated drinks? It might be fun.

Some poets have taken such puns on words and have woven them into clever poems of some length. Take "The Gnu Wooing" by Burges Johnson, for instance, about a gnu, a type of African antelope, and a spreading evergreen tree called a yew tree. The poem is really clever, but it's so full of puns that you feel when you read it as if you had a mouthful of buzzing bees:

> There was a lovely lady Gnu
> Who browsed beneath a spreading yew.
> Its stately height was her delight;
> A truly cooling shade it threw.
> Upon it little tendrils grew
> Which gave her gentle joy to chew.
> Yet oft she sighed, a-gazing wide,
> And wished she knew another Gnu
> (Some newer Gnu beneath the yew
> To tell her tiny troubles to.)
>
> She lived the idle moments through
> And days in dull succession flew,
> Till one fine eve she ceased to grieve
> A manly stranger met her view.
> He gave a courtly bow or two;
> She coolly looked him through and through:
> Said he: "If guests you would eschew,
> I'll say adieu without ado;
> But let me add I knew your dad;
> I'm on page two, the Gnu's 'Who's Who.' "
> "Forgive," she cried, "the snub I threw!
> I feared you were some parvenu!
> 'Tis my regret we've never met—
> I knew a Gnu who knew of you."
> (This wasn't true—what's that to you?
> The new Gnu knew; she knew he knew.)
>
> "Though there are other trees, 'tis true,"
> Said she, "if you're attracted to
> The yews I use, and choose to chew
> Their yewy dewy tendrils, do!". . .
> The end is easily in view.
> He wed her in a week or two.

> The *Daily Gnus* did quite enthuse,
> And now, if all I hear is true,
> Beneath that yew the glad day through
> There romps a little gnuey new.[4]

I have a book for little tots called *Miranda the Panda Is on the Veranda*. That line kept running in my head and got me started on short, crazy rhymes; maybe it will start you, too.

Milwaukee is the word I started to play with and ended with: "The balky walkie-talkie at the fair in Milwaukee was squawky." It's really easy to make short rhymes like that; first you pick an interesting word and think of three or four words that rhyme with it, and weave them into a verse.

Have you ever tried conversational thrusts in rhyme? They are a sort of a retort discourteous guaranteed to make enemies and alienate friends. For instance, the girl who tells why she doesn't like to dance with a certain boy says, "He doesn't gyrate at my rate," or the boy who thinks his teacher does not appreciate his witticism cracks, "Her sense of humor is only rumor."

Even the janitor might make a rhymed suggestion (do you suppose he'll put it on sandpaper?) :

> Say, kids, it would be really great,
> If you brought in less of the real estate!

Just be sure when you "crack-wise" in rhyme, you don't use poison darts. Nobody really likes a poisoned dart—it's hard to pick out of the heart—and the likability you lose may be your own.

Sometimes you can start rhyming words with a geographical name with a lilt to it. Listen to what fun I had doing rhymes with Pocatello, a city in Idaho:

> I greeted with a hearty hello,
> A mellow fellow from Pocatello.
> A sort of punchinello fellow
> Whose gaudy shirt was red and yellow,
> This merry man, much like Othello,
> Or Santa Claus—shook just like jello.
> When his laugh rang out with a mighty bellow
> I admired this mellow fellow from Pocatello.

Why not open your geography book and find a word in the word list that appeals to you and see what you can do at bouncing it

---

[4] Reprinted from *Bashful Ballads* by Burges Johnson, by permission of Harper & Brothers. Copyright 1911 by Harper & Brothers, copyright 1939 by Burges Johnson.

with rhyme? If you can't think of one-word rhymes, perhaps two together will do it as in this homemade limerick:

> The boy stood as still as a statue,
> And his sister called out, "Frank, is that you?"
> He meowed like a cat,
> So she heaved a brickbat
> And shouted, "Now scat, you old cat you!"

If you don't like verse, you might try taking the letters of the alphabet (in order, of course) and making a sensible sentence out of words beginning with the right letters. This is a fascinating game, guaranteed to keep you awake until all hours. Even though this is one of my best attempts, it certainly doesn't suit me. The only easy thing about this game is that the sentence can begin with *A*.

A bewhiskered cat dove extra fast, grabbing ham in jumbles, knocking ladies, making noise, offending policemen, queering residents, startling townspeople, uncovering victuals, wrecking x-rays, yowling zealously!

Whew! I worked on that sentence. I wish a few of you upper graders would make a try at those fascinating alphabet sentences. Just look at these fine ones that children have worked out:

Andy Bandy, careless Dandy, eats flies, gobbles hornets, imitates jack-rabbits, kills little mice, nets otters, pesters quail, raises snakes, teases unicorns, vicious whales, x-rays young zebras.

Roselyn, Grade 8

Albert Brown caught Danny Ender fighting George Handcock in Jack Karson's Luxury Motel. No one phoned Quincy. Robert Sullivan told Una Veeck. Where's Xavier, young Zone?

Tom, Grade 7

A big circus dog entered, ferociously growling, howling. It just kept little me necessarily occupied! Please, Queenie! Run! Scram! The uninvited visitor was (e)xtracted yowling zealously.

Karen, Grade 8

By the way, have you ever made up Thing-Lings? They are just double rhymes. They're easy and they're fun. First think of the name of something—that's the first step—*squirrel,* for instance;

that's your *Thing*. Now, think of the *Ling,* an adjective to describe the word (how about *girl* or *rural?*) ; a *girl-squirrel* or *rural-squirrel* are your thing-lings.

Let's say you start with *pheasant* as your *thing*—now your *ling* might be *peasant* or *pleasant: peasant-pheasant* or *pleasant-pheasant.* Make as many animal thing-lings as you can. After all, didn't Paul Bunyan have a blue-moo, and hasn't a witch a brat-cat, or is that witch cat story just a sable-fable?

After you get some thing-lings worked out, you might even want to turn them into a verse, plummy with double rhymes as this word-wizard worked out:

> Have you ever seen a peasant-pheasant?
> Have you ever heard a mean shark-bark?
> Has a fat-cat been your pleasant-present?
> Have you ever watched a young lark-park?
> Have you ever owned a legal-beagle?
> Has a chunky-monkey grinned at you?
> Is the horse you have a rapscallion-stallion?
> Then you've truly seen a rhyming zoo!

Perhaps the most fun you can have with thing-lings is to form them into stories in terse-verse. This one coming up is about two who started shooting paper wads in school:

TWO BLUE

> Brassie-lassie
> Mad-lad
> Paper-caper
> Bad-fad.
>
> Preacher-teacher
> Sly-spy
> Principal-Invincible
> Why-try?

And here's a similar type of verse from seventh-grade Barbara:

> Brother boy
> Has toy
> Have shouldn't
> Told couldn't.

Run away
Try play
Is caught
Gets taught
Good lesson
At session
With Mother
Oh, Brother!

Barbara, Grade 7

Rhymed definitions are fun for every age. Even poets try it. One defined his cat as:

A ball of silky fur
Inhabited by purr.[5]

Could you make a rhymed definition of your dog? your baby-sitter? an encyclopedia? a recess?

That old clock is jiving faster than a rock n' roll orchestra—no doubt you're played out, perhaps we should wade-out to a quick fade-out.

Let's see what comes after-laughter. Be sure to play with words today in any way you think is gay. But don't get illusions about your confusions! It's all in fun you know.

Now it's time to write, unless you should happen to feel like sixth-grade Sharon—not funny at all:

Today I'm not funny, not funny a bit!
My ideas aren't funny, I sure admit.

My brains are not working, not working at all,
I think I shall try when I'm more on the ball!

Sharon, Grade 6

If you feel like that, don't bother to be humorous; be deadly serious, for sometimes then you're the funniest of all. Good writing!

---

[5] From *Gaily the Troubadour*, "Contented Kitten" by Arthur Guiterman. Copyright, 1936, by E. P. Dutton & Co., Inc. Reprinted by permission of the publishers.

Some Results of This "Fun with Words" Lesson

A rickety, rackety, rockety man,
Whose name was stickety, stickety Sam,
Decided to rocket a ricket,
Right out of his strawberry thicket,
The rocket got rickets,
And ran out of tickets,
And never got out of the thicket.

Bob, Grade 6

ESOPHAGUS OF A HIPPOPOSAMUS

A baby hippo wouldn't behave
—A baby hippo tried to shave.
I've gotta' description
Of a drugstore prescription,
To heal the esophagus
Of a hippoposamus
I have the medicine
But he won't let us in
To put the medicine
On the esophagus
Of a hippoposamus!

Judy, Grade 8

SING A STORY

Today I got a D D!!
Today I will flee flee!!
For my dad is after me me!!

Annabelle, Grade 8

When Mt. Popocatepetl
Takes to shooting molten metal,
The people in the cities there
Throw their 'taters in the air.
When the 'taters all come down
They're roasted to a golden brown.

For is it not what you've been taught?
Molten metal is very hot.

Tim, Grade 6

Toppers and poppers are almost alike
But toppers are blue and poppers are white.
I like poppers better, because a topper is a horn
The reason why I like poppers,
Is because it's popcorn.

Cynthia, Grade 4

Ahoy! There's the real McCoy
Of a fat little boy
Playing with a skinny little toy.
Ahoy! There's the real McCoy
Of a floating buoy
Ringing a bell and shouting with joy.

Tom, Grade 7

Bysir is a myser kinda guysir,
That eats pieser and says hisir,
Which isn't a liesir, Tysir.

Susan, Grade 8

Mother said,
"Hit sack!
Do not crack back."

Patricia, Grade 7

Bears grow hairs
Bears go to fairs
Bears say, "Where's the bears?"
A bear's fur tairs.
And if it wears
It has to be sewed.

Sandra, Grade 3

Ahoy-boy, have you ever gotten into the rabbit-habit, and ran-like-a-man every time you saw a fat-rat? Have you ever wanted to haunt-a-restaurant and shoot the alligator-waiter? Have you ever entered a mouse-house and found a round-hound eating a fish-dish?"

Judy, Grade 7

I wonder if we will need a translator
When we get to the moon, sooner or later?

Michael, Grade 7

CENTIPEDE

Long and slimy, "Try and find me,"
Said the little centipede

All his million legs a-prancing
Looks like Arthur Murray dancing.

Once I went to a great bazaar
And climbed into a jelly jar.

I love that jell they put on toast,
I really think it is the most.

One man spread me on his toast,
And at once he called the host.

Oh! Why do people fret and yell,
When they see me in a jar of jell?

Ronald, Grade 7

A BEAR

A bare bear bounced for baloney
Over a bar of bamboo with a bang.
While a blind bloodhound blared lonely
And a fat cat screeched as he sang.

Can your bare bear bounce for baloney
Over a bar of bamboo with a bang?
While a blind bloodhound blared lonely,
And a fat cat screeched as he sang?

Richard, Grade 6

Oh, I remember the Alamo,
Where there was a battle so long ago,
If only Jim Bowie and Davy Crockett, too
Would have had a missile rocket or two.
They'd have blown up the Mexicans
With bombs, cannons, and guns.
Oh! Do you remember the Alamo
Where there was a battle so long ago?

Juanita, Grade 7

Have you ever seen a square bear having a mear affair or a plucked duck having a little luck or maybe a blue mouse sitting on a house? Have you ever seen a fake snake swimming in a lake or a horse joining the air force?

Tom, Grade 7

The tile had a crack like a smile
which looked like a crocodile swimming
down the Nile which looked like a
smile in the tile with the crack.

Steve, Grade 6

II. Laughter Looseners

If you are sad
Or feeling bad
As if life had no "juiceners"
Come on—unbuckle—
And oil your chuckle
With Doctor Joy's laugh looseners!

If this were a dinner table instead of a writing lesson, we'd all be sent to bed for overgiggling today. But as long as it's a day for funny papers, we're safe—we can giggle, gaggle, guffaw, chuckle, burst buttons, grin, smile, or chortle!

Today you will be fed Dr. Joy's Laughter Looseners for Logy Listeners in the form of crazy characters, asinine animals, pixilated puns, "vici-verses," silly stories, and loony limericks. So let's get started on those *crazy characters,* created by crazy character creators —for you! As you listen, notice in what way each piece read is funny because today in writing time you'll be Dr. Joy writing a funny caper in a funny paper yourself.

May I present one of the zaniest, "zombiest" characters I ever got from a "Let's Writer," seventh-grade Roger:

HORACE

As I was out walking one day,
I came upon an egg in a field of hay.
I picked it up and found it wasn't as light as a feather,
It was horny and green, but one end was soft like leather.
Then something popped out of the leathery end,
I was stiffened with fright so I couldn't bend.
The thing had ten legs and was about as large as a pup,
I wished it hadn't hatched when I picked it up.
It wasn't unfriendly, nor did it bite or snap;
It just cuddled up in my lap.

I dropped it on the ground and to my dismay
It followed me home all the way.
It walked straight to the trash pile, and with a crunch,
It started gobbling up old metal, munch, munch, munch.
As days went by, he grew big and strong,
And extended about twenty feet long.
He was as strong as a tractor; big as a truck;
And when I climbed on him he wouldn't buck.
He would pull farm machinery with ease,
And I get my work done in a breeze.

He had large, intelligent eyes that could really see,
So I named him Horace, and that suited me.
One day he had bumps on his shoulders that were soft and
    puffy,
And when I touched them he told me to stop tickling him,
    before he got gruffy.

Then he rubbed one of them against a tree,
And a long black thing popped out at me.
Horace said, when seeing my alarm,
"Don't worry, I just grew an arm."
His other arm popped out much the same way,
And got pretty big by the end of the day.
By two days his arms were as thick as my thigh,
I shudder to think of him giving me a black eye.

One day a big ship came down from space,
And the people in it were of the Horace race.
I told them hello, and asked them to stay,
But they had to take dear little Horace home that day.
Horace stood by the window and waved good-bye,
As the ship zipped up through the sky.
Horace said he would be back some day,
So I still look for him in that field of hay.

Roger, Grade 7

Seventh-grade Marcia's character certainly leaves us with an eerie touch. Some of you may want to entertain visitors from outer space today.

I suddenly awoke, I couldn't figure out why.
I looked around the room—on the window sill was a bottle. It looked, yes, it was a pop bottle. But I had no pop for over a week. What was it doing there? Why on my window sill? When and how did it get there? Oh, well, I might as well get some sleep. I turned over and started to put my head on the pillow when all of a sudden a voice said, "Don't go to sleep. Stay up and talk with me."
I looked around and then I saw the bottle was on the chair. Then the bottle started to talk. It talked straight for an hour. I was sure I had met my match at last. Finally I got a question in. "Who are you?"
The bottle told me it could not tell. Just said good-night and disappeared. I still wonder what the bottle really wanted.

Marcia, Grade 7

If you do intend to create a crazy character in writing time, either make your characterization utterly senseless or full of sense in a sly way. You may choose a ball player as your subject, a rocket enthusiast, a teacher, a student—oh, almost any group could contain a fantastic character—and, for a fact, does!

Dr. Joy promises for today's funny drops not only fantastic characters but also *asinine animals*—the word *asinine* means utterly without sense; and the first animal (the insect family of animals) I think of is Paul's "Icicle Worm." Paul is in eighth grade, and his writing is so straightforward that for a half-page he had even me convinced.

Icicle Worm

If you ever visit the North Pole, you will see the funniest insect of all. It is an icicle worm. From a distance it looks light blue in color. When you look closely at it, it is irridiscent. It has a cone-shaped body with myriad eyes projecting from every direction.

All day long it hangs down from a building but at night it drops to the ground. It moves by bouncing on the small end of its cone-shaped body. It bounces toward a block of ice which it devours because it is hungry. It eats in a very greedy fashion. When it eats, the sound is like an ice-crusher. After it has had a meal it goes hopping up and down. At exactly three o'clock in the morning, it jumps back up on the building. He is safe. He can't fall because his cone-shaped body acts like a suction cup.

Paul, Grade 8

Sixth-grade Susie has a Noodley Poodle that instead of apple strudel likes—oh, let's let Susie tell you herself:

I have oodles of poodles and one likes string noodles!
And when he begs he stands still like a peg on his right leg!
And if he doesn't get them, he lets out a bark and sings,
    like a lark.
Most amazing of all, when he parks, he leaves no marks, if
    it is dark.
And sometimes he croons to the tune of a pan being hit by
    a spoon.
He's the craziest loon when he sits on the moon and acts
    like Pat Boone.
But he's a "ton of a hon" to make up for what he's done
And at night he stays in bed and prays, to be forgiven
    for the sins of his days
So you see, I have oodles of poodles, but just one likes
    string noodles!

Susie, Grade 6

Many of you will want to make singing-swinging verse as Susie did to describe your asinine animal. Choose an animal with an odd name and swing its lines into a loony lyric. It helps some rhymesters to sing their rhymings to a homemade tune, like this one about a "collicky" kangaroo. One can't even read it without singing.

THE COLLICKY KANGAROO

The collicky kangaroo
Woke up every one in the zoo;
"Oh, Mother," he cried,
"I've a wild beast inside
And it's tearing me right in two!"

The collicky kangaroo,
Sweat stood on his face like dew,
With each word he uttered
His insides all fluttered,
And his face turned greenery-blue.

The collicky kangaroo
Asked, "Am I getting the flu?
I've never once wheezed
Or snorted or sneezed,
Or never once blew a ka-choo!"

The collicky kangaroo—
He sobbed with a loud "Boohoo!"
Said he, "I can't stand it,
I never once planned it,
How I got it, I haven't a clue!"

The collicky kangaroo—
They made him a powerful brew;
They boiled two fur coats
With the milk from two goats
And it warmed him through and through.

The collicky kangaroo—
They cooked him Australian stew;
They boiled cock-a-doodles
With plenty of noodles—
With a cupful of crinklies and moo.

Now the collicky kangaroo
Is the frolicky kangaroo,
He eats herbs and greens,
And pots of baked beans
And is happy the whole day through!

Do you suppose you could do something in that manner with a gnu or an armadillo, an anteater or a rhinoceros today? My little brother used to call a rhinoceros a "rhinosersosersos." Not a bad start for a verse about asinine animals, do you think?

Billy, Grade Eight, was challenged by the gnu:

Once there was a gnu,
Who wore a size ten shoe.
This was a most unusual practice,
Now he's the only gnu that dares step on a cactus.

He thinks he's very wise,
But he wears ear muffs on his eyes.
He wears nose plugs in his ears
To keep out boos and cheers.

One day he got a red and white shirt,
But the next day it got full of dirt.
But when he finally did die,
He had no more sorrows than a butterfly.

Billy, Grade 8

So was Donna in Grade Five:

THE GNU WITH THE FLU

I once knew a gnu
And this gnu I knew
Had the flu.
This gnu that had the flu
Was a very new gnu
This gnu was as sick as you
When it had the flu.

I once knew a gnu
And this gnu I knew—
This very new gnu
Once had the flu!

Donna, Grade 5

But for sheer fun, who can beat fifth-grade Larry's rhyme?

BABOON

There was a baboon
Who lived in a zoo
And waited and waited for
Something to do.
He looked at the window,
Took out a loose bar,
And jumped right out on top of a car.
He rode to the jungle,
Jumped on a tree.
When he saw his mama,
He shouted with glee.
The natives near by
Were cooking a man
They were so dumb
They put him in a pan.
They popped him like popcorn
The man flew up
Splashed in the dipper
Which looked like a cup.

Larry, Grade 5

Well, what's next on Dr. Joy's list of laughter looseners? *Pixilated puns,* I'll be bound. *Pixilated* here means so foolish as to appear drunken; and puns—you all know that puns are two-way words—words that make sense with one meaning and wit with the other.

Take this pun, for instance. *This Week Magazine* once described the dress of an Indian Maharanee as a *sarong* instead of a *sari.* In apologizing for the mistake, the magazine printed, "All we can say is that we are *sari* we were *sarong.*"

One of the punniest, funniest puns is the old one about the young fellow named Fisher:

There was a young fellow named Fisher
Who was fishing one day in a fissure;
When the cod with a grin
Pulled the fisherman in
Now they're fishing the fissure for Fisher.

Try your luck at weaving a pun into a rhymed verse today. Puns are only punishment to those not clever enough to make them. More of you, though, might have more luck with *"vici-verses"* or backwards writing than with puns.

This old English verse is a good example of a "vici-verse."

THE STRANGE MAN

His face was the oddest that ever was seen,
His mouth stood across 'twixt his nose and his chin;
Whenever he spoke it was then with his voice,
And in talking he always made some sort of noise.
Derry down.

He'd an arm on each side to work when he pleased,
But he never worked hard when he lived at his ease;
Two legs he had got to make him complete,
And what is more odd, at each end were his feet.

His legs, as folks say, he could move at his will,
And when he was walking he never stood still.
If you were to see him, you'd laugh till you burst
For one leg or the other would always be first.

If this whimsical fellow had a river to cross,
If he could not get over, he stayed where he was,
He seldom or ever got off the dry ground,
So great was his luck that he never was drowned.

But the reason he died and the cause of his death
Was owing, poor soul, to the want of more breath;
And now he is left in the grave for to molder,
Had he lived a day longer, he'd have been a day older,
Derry down.

Many riddles depend on puns for answers. Take for instance, that old, old riddle, "What's black and white and red all over?" Well, the answer depends on a pun on the word *red*. To answer the riddle, you must think of *red* as a form of *to read* instead of a color. The answer is a *newspaper,* as you probably know. I once asked a six-year-old, "What's black and white and red all over?" and she answered, "An embarrassed zebra." And I was the embarrassed one. Her wrong answer was much better than the right one.

Lewis Carroll, who wrote *Alice in Wonderland,* was a master hand at a pun. Remember his pun on lesson?

"And how many hours a day did you do lessons?" said Alice, . . .
"Ten hours the first day," said the Mock Turtle: "nine the next, and so on."
"What a curious plan!" exclaimed Alice.
"That's the reason they're called lessons," the Gryphon remarked: "because they lessen from day to day."

It would be fun to take the Alice book, chapter by chapter, and locate the puns—there're surely some zany ones there. But remember, puns are like any other form of wit, not good if you use too many of them.

Oh, you can have fun with a pixilated pun today especially if you weave it into a tongue twister. Note this one:

HOARSE HORSE

My horse had a hoarse throat. Every time he ran around the horse corral his hoarse throat got hoarser and hoarser, so I called a horse doctor. He fixed up my horse's hoarse throat. Now my horse can run around the horse corral any time he wants without getting a hoarse, horse throat.

Tom, Grade 6

Tom in Grade Five wove his puns into a story:

Once when I went deep-sea diving I saw a school of fish. I peeked in and saw fish learning readin', writin' and 'rithmetic. I was surprised to know that some of those fish are pretty shark (sharp). Next I went to another school. This was the North Side School (just for northerns). The fish live much like we do. They have banks to keep their money in (river banks). The traffic is so heavy that they need a traffic carp (cop). Some of the fish flounder around. They even have stars (Miss Star Fish). I still would rather be a human.

Tom, Grade 5

Sixth-grade Arthur has written a good "vici-verse":

A FUNNY MAN

I know a man, a funny man.
His coat is pink, his pants are tan,
One shoe is purple, the other one red.
He wears a hat when he goes to bed.

He never walks, but always skips,
With lipstick on his lips.
He sleeps all day and works all night
His nose glows like a yellow candle light.

His shoes are a blackish brown
He looks just like a clown
He is as happy as can be
And doesn't care what people see.

Arthur, Grade 6

Some of you will enjoy attempting vici-verses today—they're easy to write—just write them as if they were sense, but on second thought, the reader will discover their nonsense.

Instead of "vici-verses" a few of you today will want to write one of Dr. Joy's *silly stories*. Here's a fine one by fourth-grader David; this story is true monkey business:

Monkeys Loose in Cape Canaveral

One day in Miami, Florida, some monkeys got loose and ran out of the pet shop. (They had put the owner of the pet shop in one of their cages. They made a monkey out of him.) There were 100 monkeys in all. They headed straight for Cape Canaveral missile base where the soldiers were getting ready to launch a one-ton satellite. There was a place in the satellite that had to be patched and 99 monkeys climbed through the hole in the satellite and were inside the satellite. Just then a man came and patched the hole and the monkeys were trapped inside the satellite. Now you're probably wondering what happened to the 100th monkey. Well, he ran into the control and pressed the take-off button. Then the missile took off with the satellite and the 99 monkeys. Scientists came running into the control room wondering what happened. Then they saw how and what the monkey had done, but the scientists thought that they could listen to the "beep-beep" of the satellite on the radio but when they tried to listen to the "beep-beep" of the satellite, they heard the "chatter-chatter-chatter" of the monkeys. The scientists never did find out what happened to the one-ton satellite. And for all I know the 99 monkeys are still chattering away in the satellite in the middle of outer-space.

David, Grade 4

Stories can be told in rhyme, too, you know. Eighth-grade Charlotte has used an old gag in a new and droll rhyme:

THE UNUSUAL HAPPENING

A man was sitting
On a knoll
When up behind him
An Indian stole.

With hatchet raised
He took the man's scalp
The man jumped up
And ran for help.

The Indian was so startled
He dropped the scalp and fled
The man ran back
And calmly put it back on his head.

The man was hungry
So his false teeth stepped out
And do you know what?
They came back with a trout?

Charlotte, Grade 8

Before we leave Dr. Joy's office, we must sample a *loony limerick* or two. Limericks are stylized rhymes—always with five lines. The first two and the fifth lines rhyme; the third and fourth lines rhyme with each other and are shorter than the others. Have you heard this famous limerick?

A sleeper of the Amazon
Put nighties of his gramazon
The reason that
He was too fat
To get his own pajamas on.

And this chuckly one?

A cheerful old bear at the zoo
Said, "I never have time to be blue;
When it bores me, you know,
To walk to and fro,
I reverse it and walk fro and to."

Why not try your luck with limericks today? This excellent one was written by Lowell in sixth grade:

> There once was a dog named Rover
> Who talked to the purple clover,
> "Come on, let's play!
> You'll soon be hay!"
> Yelled Rover to the purple clover.

Lowell, Grade 6

Today your limericks must be funny, but they need not be punny.

> Loony, tuney limericks,
> Pixilated puns—
> Silly stories, nutty nice
> Vici-versi ones.
> Crazy characters that seem
> From a "luney bin."
> Asinine new animals
> Slithering out and in
> Loony laughter looseners
> Prescribed by Dr. Joy
> Should shake you up like popcorn—
> Every single girl and boy!

III. Just Plain Nonsense

I hope you're feeling full of nonsense because that's what we're interested in today—just plain nonsense. When writing time comes, we're going to put our April-Fool fun into writing.

I found an interesting verse about the first day of April. It's almost two hundred years old, and it asks a question you may have asked yourself. Here it is:

> The first day of April some do say
> Was set apart for All Fools' Day.
> But why the people call it so
> Nor I, nor they themselves do know.

If that verse is two hundred years old, people must have wondered for a long time how April Fools' Day came to be. Have you wondered too? Well, here's one story of how it all started.

April Fools' Day began in England about a hundred years after Columbus discovered America. In those days, the new year began in the spring and people celebrated New Year's Day with a holiday they called the Feast of Fools. Then the government changed New Year's Day to January 1. The people didn't like having their holiday changed, and to protest the change, they began playing tricks on the day that used to be New Year's Day. One of their favorite tricks was to send someone to buy a penny's worth of strap oil or pigeon milk, and when he found that these things didn't exist, they'd stand about laughing loud and long and calling out "April Fish" instead of "April Fool" as we do.

Well, you can see that April Fools' Day was not all nonsense when it began. There was a reason for jokes and tricks then; it was the people's way of telling the government that they did not like its changes.

Along with playing tricks, the people also made up stories about April Fools' Day, and although they were nonsense, the stories too had a lot of sense in them. Have your teacher read you "The Wise People of Gotham" in *Stories to Dramatize* by Winifred Ward. It is one of the funniest of these old tales.

In this old story the people of Gotham are protesting their high taxes which, they hear, are being raised even higher. They have a meeting to decide what to do. One of their number points out that men are often punished for being wise, but that fools are usually considered innocent.

Accordingly, when the king comes, he finds the villagers acting very foolish indeed. He asks one of their number why he is carrying his heavy house door on his back, and is told that the householder is going on a journey and fears that robbers will come while he is gone and break in his door, something which couldn't possibly happen if he carries the door with him. After a number of such inane replies, the king rides away, muttering that the men of Gotham are too foolish to punish.

It might be fun to write a modern-day story of this type protesting a situation you'd like to get rid of. Stories like this one that are funny yet serious—stories that mix sense and nonsense together. The stories of Tyll Ulenspiegel are very famous folk tales that make serious points. Telling stories of Tyll's merry pranks was one way the people of Germany talked back to their rulers. Tyll's nonsense always made sense. You'll have to read at least one of *Tyll Ulenspiegel's Merry Pranks* by M. Jagendorf.

Probably our foremost children's writer for talking nonsense without sense is Theodor Seuss Geisel, the famous Dr. Seuss who wrote *Horton Hatches the Egg, If I Ran the Zoo,* and many others. But this rollicking humorist is also a master hand at talking sense through nonsense. His messages to us about our democracy in such rhymed thrusts as *Thidwick, The Big-Hearted Moose* and *Yertle the Turtle* set us to wondering after the laughter.

Perhaps some of you can write nonsense stories to protest the things you don't like in our modern-life patterns.

Eighth-grade Clare has used this indirect method in her television program on tree delinquency. This is clever irony for a thirteen-year-old:

"Good evening, ladies and gentlemen. I'm certainly glad to see you all once again. Tonight we will have a panel discussion upon the subject of tree delinquency, a constant threat to our young, growing trees. Tonight's panelists are some of the world's best known authors, teachers, and lecturers. On my right is that distinguished author, Sir Cedric Poplar, and the famous lecturer and teacher, Mr. Richard S. Maple. On my left, is that also famous lecturer, John B. Oak, and his colleague, Henry W. Pine.

"Now, gentlemen, I would like your opinion upon this problem of tree delinquency. Which age group do you think is most destructive? Mr. Oak."

"I think that the young two-to-three-year-old blue spruce gangs are really the most dangerous."

"Why do you say that?"

"Because you see they have such savage instincts and are always ready to fight if a new gang comes into their territory."

"I beg to disagree with you, sir."

"Why, certainly, Sir Cedric."

"I don't think that any one group or person is the most dangerous. I think that it depends upon the surroundings."

"Although I agree with you on the point of danger, I don't agree that the surroundings affect our young trees so much, Sir Cedric."

"Well, I can't understand your thinking, Mr. Maple, but do explain your point, please."

"I believe that if the nature of the trees is once implanted, nothing can stop their instinct, even Elvis or Pat."

"Now, Maple my friend, let's not get technical. I think that if our young trees didn't have to grow so close together, and were separated and given a chance to plan clubs, there wouldn't be any delinquency."

"Perhaps you're right, Mr. Pine. Your theory seems quite sound."

"Thank you, Sir Cedric. Debating with you has been a pleasure."

"I'm dreadfully sorry gentlemen, to break up this discussion, but time is running out.

"Thank you ladies and gentlemen, and all young trees listening in. I hope that you've enjoyed our educational program. Next week we will have another interesting program about our teen-age trees—their pleasures, fashions, and their opinions on tree delinquency.

"I thank you. This has been another in the series of 'Tree Delinquency' programs."

Clare, Grade 8

Stories that get at a problem obliquely often are more effective than direct criticism.

In order to make your stories nonsense, they will probably involve impossible situations, something that couldn't possibly happen. In preparation for this sort of writing, you might play the game called "For Goodness Sake." It's a fine game for April Fools' Day. And what's more, it may help you to write funny stories.

Here's how to play "For Goodness Sake." Take a half sheet of paper and write the name of a *thing* at the top. You can write the name of any kind of thing—a balloon, a baboon, or a silly thing, maybe like a pig's tail or a hippopotamus or a leaky pan or a green cat. You write the name of just one thing, then you fold your paper so that you hide what you've written. Pass the paper to the person across the aisle from you.

The next person, without peeking at what's already written on the paper, writes the name of another thing, folds the paper, and passes it across the aisle to someone else. The third person writes down the name of a crazy place; for example, down the toe of a Christmas stocking or in the Arctic Ocean or in a bird's nest—just any place he can think of. The paper should be folded over again and passed on. The fourth person writes something that happened; for example, "there was a fight" or "the one ate the other" or "they decided to buy a car." Any happening will do. Now we're ready to open the paper and read the impossible situation. Of course, you can have any number of papers, being passed through the class at the same time—the more papers, the more impossible situations, and the more nonsense story starters.

I played this game one day not too long ago and this is the impossible situation that resulted: "A mouse and a school teacher in a box of chocolates, and they worked their arithmetic." Isn't that an impossible situation?

This situation gave me an idea for a nonsense story, too. The teacher whose name was Mary Nibbles loved chocolates and hated

very clever

mice. The mouse was named Little Math because he longed to be educated so he could do arithmetic and figure out his own mouse-holes—mathematically. There's a magic chocolate in the story that reduces Mary Nibbles to bite-size so that she's able to meet Little Math in the chocolate box and teach him how to do arithmetic.

Did you notice that in my story I tried to make it funnier by giving the characters funny names? The chocolate-eating school-teacher was named Mary Nibbles and the mouse who wanted to learn arithmetic was Little Math. See if you can think of funny names for all the characters in your story. Ogden Nash, a modern humorous poet, has used both fitting names and an impossible situation in his poem, "The Tale of Custard, the Dragon." What kind of dragon do you suppose Custard was? Does his name give you a clue? Well, he could very well be a spineless shaky dragon —a coward. And that's just what Custard is—or thinks he is—a cowardly dragon. Be sure to read about the impossible situation in which Custard is involved. It's as funny a poem as I've ever read. But there's real sense in between the nonsensical lines, and the rhymes are priceless.

Of course you may not want to put sense in your April Fools' Day writing. You may want to go all-out foolish and follow the leadership of Edward Lear, father of English nonsense, or Lewis Carroll, who wrote *Alice in Wonderland.*

These men could and did write sheer nonsense just for the fun of it. They made up words right and left and put them together in just plain nonsense poetry, as you may decide to do in writing time today.

The cleverest kind of silly story begins as if it were true. Richard in Grade Five has done an outstanding job writing a story that way:

Once my dog was doing a trick in our living room. She was doing somer-saults backwards. Suddenly something happened! There was a crash and a bang! There was a big hole in the floor and our dog wasn't there. We looked through the hole. Our dog wasn't in the basement, and there was a big hole in the basement floor! We went downstairs to look in the hole. It was so dark that we couldn't see a thing—even with a flashlight. Two months later a card came to us from the airport. We were supposed to get a package there. When we reached the airport we saw our dog in a cage. It came from China. There was a letter with it that said they found the dog by a big hole. Then we knew that our dog had gone through the world. Now we go to China for our vacation through that hole.

Richard, Grade 5

Of all stories that are fun to write, sheer nonsense gives the most release. I can almost hear eighth-grade Gordon's pen chuckle as he writes these words:

One day I was riding the calves. There was a lazy one that was too lazy to run. I hopped on him, I kicked him. He took off. We were about a mile from the moon when I fell off. I hit the earth with a bang; my neck was broken and my head was about three feet from me. I got up and carried my head to the house. I got some string and some paste. I tied my head on and pasted my neck together. I don't think I lost my brains because I'm just as stupid as I was before.

Gordon, Grade 8

But Mary Lou's story is my choice:

REVERSE REFRIGERATION

One day Mr. Coldspot, the refrigerator serviceman, came to fix our refrigerator. He must have gotten out of bed on the wrong side because he put the parts in backwards. He heated the refrigerator instead of making it cold.

Mother had just bought three dozen fresh eggs and they hatched into chicks. They were not a bit hungry because Mother keeps our popcorn in the refrigerator to keep it fresh and it popped and the chicks ate the popcorn.

Thanks to Mr. Coldspot we had chicken every Sunday.

Mary Lou, Grade 6

IV. Fish Stories

Hello, fishermen! Simple Simon with his bent pinhook, fishing for a whale in a pail has nothing on us today. We're out to get whales of stories from minnow-sized experiences, and it's going to be easy as well as fun to hook a story.

You know, the arithmetic of fishermen has always been an elastic kind of arithmetic—inches as long as feet, ounces as heavy as ordinary pounds, and ordinary pull-ins, a fight to the very finish. "Telling fish stories" probably started normally enough when the first cave man hated to tell his wife *why* he had caught no fish for dinner, and fish stories have become a part of the folklore of all peoples.

Today in writing time we're going to write fish stories. That will certainly be easy, since each of you has either gone fishing yourself, or has heard about someone's going fishing. Since that's the case— and I'm certain it is—we've plenty of material for hundreds of good fish stories, which you know are three-tenths fact and seven-tenths imagination. As a matter of fact, fish stories no longer have to be about fish at all—the expression "fish story" has grown to mean any story told for truth that sounds more false than true. We Applegates have a story in our family that is 100 per cent true, but I do not believe anyone actually believes it when we tell it:

My youngest brother, John, was at sixteen or seventeen the president of the De Molays for the section of the state of Iowa in which we lived. At one of the conventions—this one was held at Burlington, Iowa—the boys had worked in business sessions all day. Then in the evening the Burlington boys were putting on a dance in their honor. They had arranged for each three boys to call for three girls at one girl's home. This saved locating so many different addresses. When he rang the doorbell at the address he had been given, John presented himself and his two friends from home. "I am John Applegate," he said, "And these are my two friends, Jim Turnipseed and Don Beanblossom."

"Applegate—Turnipseed—Beanblossom." The girls thought the boys were playing a trick on them and had made up their names and were offended for most of the evening. As for the names, they were old respectable ones in the town in Iowa that I used to call home.

Now that fish story was a real one, but it has all the earmarks of a genuine "fish story." All that makes a fish story a "fish story," you know, is that it is told with the ring of truth and with a straight face (with a straight pencil in this case). The listeners usually know very well that you are spoofing them. Remember those directions when you write your story today, and remember, too, that a fish story doesn't necessarily have to be about fish or fishing—it's just a straight story that forgot to stay life-sized and grew too much.

The plots of a fish story can be much alike yet very different. These might be the steps:

Step 1. Getting ready for going fishing.

Step 2. Finding a spot and getting settled.

Step 3. What happened?

Those three steps could lead up to a wonderful fishing climax. The steps of any plot climb up, and on that third step—What happened?—the story slides down the banister to a quick finish. Plots climb up slowly and slide down fast.

What happened? Oh, so many things could happen. The fish could decide to boycott you altogether. You might in your quiet spot on the other side of those bushes hear two bank robbers burying their loot. You might get that first tug on your line and find that your "fish" was an old automobile part you needed for completing your hot rod. You might catch a large fish and find something inside it for which you got a reward. Oh, yes, and the fish might pull you in and you could go to a school of fish for a while. And of course, you might lead us up to a grand climax and then, with a laugh, let us down neatly with no real climax at all!

What happened? How on earth do I know? This is your fish story. For all I know, you went fishing and caught—well, something—a story, anyway. But I'm not going to try to keep up with your vivid imaginations.

Some of you might simply write the story your father told the last time he went fishing. Or isn't your father the kind of person given to "fish stories"? You take over then and finish his story. You writers don't really need any help today—fish stories come quite naturally to people, as you will see when you start to write.

Now it's writing time for those fish stories. They'll be good ones if they sound true, if they gradually get too big to be believed, and if you can tell the whole story without laughing yourself. Remember your stories today may be all true, half-true, or out-and-out whoppers.

Let's close with a riddle. How can today's writing prove that children do not stick to their writing topic?

Give up? Each of you started out to write about fish, but ended a "lion."

"Fish Story" Results

As I was fishing one day my diamond ring fell in the water. Such a fine diamond ring didn't belong at the bottom of the lake.

I dived in and went down, down. There was a sign saying School District 22. I peeked into the schoolhouse window. There was a blackboard with a worm drawn on it with the words "Do eat" at the top. On the other side was a hook with a worm and the words "don't eat" at the top. Now you know why you never catch any fish.

Then I saw something shining at the bottom. It must be my ring. Down I went—yes, there it was, but I certainly wouldn't take it now. There was a small church. Inside a wedding was on. The bride, Miss Star Fish, was too proud of her diamond. I mean mine. I couldn't bear taking it away from Mrs. Sunfish now.

Lynne, Grade 7

One day I went fishing. I saw a dogfish swimming after a cat fish; a sun fish after a rain fish. I saw a stone roller after a pebble roller. They all were going round and round. The wind was blowing from the East and you know when the wind blows from the east fish bite the least. And that day did not look good for fishing anyway.

Donald, Grade 6

Seventh-grade Ricky had real fun writing this sheer nonsense:

It was a hot summer day and so I thought I would go swimming. And as I dived into the water, I saw a funny fish. As I watched him I forgot to get more air from the surface and before I knew it, I was breathing underwater. I followed him a long way until I saw an old ship and started off toward it. And soon I was inside it. I took my flashlight out but I had no batteries. Soon I found an electric eel and used it for a battery. I found an old sword, cannons, and a treasure chest, too. When I tried to get the treasure back to land, I couldn't lift it so I got a sea horse and he carried it for me for a few ears of corn. I kept the eel with my gold fish but when I cleaned them I got a shock. I would have kept the sea horse but he did not like my Mom and Dad and tried to kick them. When I go swimming I shall also take them with me to see their old friends. The eel gets a new charge of electricity. The horse gets more sea weed to eat; he does not like hay. I have gone and found two other ships, of course, with their help, and I found a lot of treasures, too.

Ricky, Grade 7

One day our class went to see how vegetable soup was made. We hopped on the bus and set off.

When we finally were there, we had to wait for Sue-Ellen. Our class was very angry with her. She is always complaining just because she has to push her father's car to work every morning so they can save gas. Some people!

The man in the vegetable soup building explained how the soup was made.

Did you know every time somebody writes in a complaining letter, it is melted down and made into an alphabetical letter for the soup? The way they taste, some people must write on rubber. Jimmy L and M opened the door to the soup room. Then came the flood! Soup all over! The vegetables bobbed around like corks! We were washed out into the street.

That night, after my clothes had been washed, I told Mommy and Dad all about the trip to the vegetable soup factory.

Patricia, Grade 7

David in Grade Five had a surprise ending that added to the fun:

One day I said to my Dad, "Let's go fishing." But he said, "Aw, I'm too tired."

Just then Mom said, "Dear, will you help me with the dishes." By the time she got through talking, we were in the car with the tackle in the back seat. Soon we were at the old fishing hole. All dad said was, "Whew," and cast in his line. I put mine in, too. Soon Dad said, "What kind of bait are you using?" I said I was using my superduper fisher dipper. He said, "You won't catch anything with that." But I said I'd stick with it until I caught something. I was just lying there when my pole almost got out of my hand. I started to reel it in. When I got it in, I found a 77-pound trout on my line. By that time Dad had taken my bait and put it on his hook. We went home with a 77-pound trout. We left the whale there.

David, Grade 5

As Sue says herself, her story is "All Wet!"

ALL WET!

Up! Two-three-kick,
Down! Two-three-kick,
Side! Two-three-kick,
Around! Two-three-kick.

There I stood in the midst of the sea,
With a school of Barracudas all staring at me.

The teacher blew her whistle and down they went,
Everyone was perfect with their knees unbent.

A school of male Sturgeons passed by,
All the Barracudas got quite shy.

After all was settled, down they went,
They started again with their knees unbent.

In the Land of Pinney-Punny [6]

In the Land of Pinney-Punny
Talk is hardly ever funny.
Folk there hold an hour as worthless
That has not been wholly mirthless.
Pinney-Punnyians put reliance
Only in the strictest science;
Not a day but teacher hushes,
Laughter. (Must out-do the Russias)
Round and round like satellites—
Brittle days and curdled nights.
Someone else's goals pursuing—
Always man's and state's undoing.
Not a chuckle; not a chortle;
Many an unhappy mortal
Lives and knows not life is funny,
In the Land of Pinney-Punny.

Humor? Fun? What is it? What is it but the tying of one's life into a loose knot; a going to meet the day with a sense of adequacy; the feeling that there is time for sitting down and rocking? Once in Portland, Maine, after a long, hazardous winter plane flight, I found a rocking chair in my hotel room. Oh, how I rocked. Humor and laughter are the rocking chairs of the mind. Laughter loosens the spirit.

[6] Located in the state of mind.

CUPBOARD OF IDEAS   for Chapter Twelve

Laughter Loosens the Spirit ❖ ❖ ❖ ❖ ❖ ❖ ❖ ❖ ❖ ❖ ❖ ❖ ❖

Primary Shelf

I. (Gr. 1–3) Near the close of a cloudy, unsettled day, let second- and third-grade children write in a sentence or two the funniest thing that happened during the day. In first grade, make up the sentences together until the children can write their own. The humor clears the air, and school ends on a pleasant note.

II. (Gr. 2–3) Draw a crayon picture of a funny animal and make up a two-line rhyme about him.

> My Magookey is green—
> The funniest dog you've ever seen.

III. Whenever you find a humorous story in your school reader, let each child think of a funny happening in the same category as fun at a farm or a funny school happening, a funny sight you saw on the way to school. Make a funny book out of the stories you get.

IV. Have a class story time when you make together a weekly chapter of a child with an engaging grin whose picture hangs in front of the room. Name him (or her), and write his funny adventure every week. If you've a good artist in the room, let him make a life-size picture on cardboard so that the story pal can stand at the front of the room.

V. When something funny happens in a schoolroom like a dog or cat coming in, sometime during the day make a funny story together, or individually write the story about the unusual visitor, perhaps from its point of view.

VI. Make whole stories from one funny story seed written on the board:

Bennie dressed his sister's cat in doll clothes. The cat didn't like it.

The stuffing came out from Susie's doll. A mouse crawled in. His tail stuck out. The doll now had a long tail.

A cat discovered a mirror. What funny things happened when he looked at himself?

VII. Keep a stuffed or a live pet in the schoolroom. Every once in a while let the children pretend what funny thing happened over night.

VIII. Have on the board such a sentence as: "Oh, my! Oh, my!" laughed Sam. "That is the funniest thing I ever saw." What was Sam seeing? Write the story.

IX. Let each child choose a pair of rhyming words and write a funny story using them together. What might happen to a fat-cat; a bare-chair; a box-fox; an able-table?

X. (Gr. 2–3) Make a baby book of funny sayings and doings that little brothers, sisters, and cousins have said and done at home.

XI. Make a funny alphabet book with nonsense rhymes. Assign each child a letter, and let him illustrate his page:

The ape ate the tape.

The cat wore a new spring hat.

The duck rode a horse that could buck.

XII. Draw a funny picture and tell the story you have pictured.

XIII. Take a child or animal comic strip and write the sketch or story into a real one.

XIV. (Gr. 2–3) Think of humorous words such as *funny, giggle, silly, clown,* and *laugh* and get second and third graders to think of a rhyming word for each and concoct funny two-line rhymes such as:

I saw a bunny
Who looked funny.

I wonder if a giraffe
Can laugh.

Do puppies giggle
When they wiggle?

The road was hilly
So the car bounced silly.

The little fat clown
Danced up and down.

Intermediate and Upper-Grade Shelf

I. *Humorous Verse and Rhyme-Fun*

A. **Whofunits,** short, ridiculous verse about the things around
   the house that mysteriously disappear: Where's my baseball
   bat? Who ate the extra piece of cake?
B. **Scientist goose, reporting.** Make modern nursery rhymes about
   science or as comments on the current news.
C. **Swoops and oops,** the spills and thrills of sledding, skating,
   and skiing.
D. **Jingle-jangles.** Put five rhymable words on the board: *ocean,*
   pizza, merry, artistic, veranda, and ask each child to choose
   one; go down the alphabet to get ideas for words that rhyme
   with it and see how long a rhymed verse he can make and
   still make sense. Use two words if two make a better rhyme:
   household; "mouse-holed" (from Ogden Nash) .
E. **Pretend to be a homely animal in the zoo,** *a la* "The Plaint
   of the Camel" from *Davy and the Goblin* by Charles E.
   Carryl. Write your humorous reactions to your size and
   shape.
F. **Rhyming funny definitions**

A schoolteacher is a person who makes many suggestions,
But it's the children who answer the questions.

G. The teacher draws these objects on the board:

Children look at them with the eyes of imagination and write a funny verse about what one figure represents:

This bald man
Has just one hair
He's just being chased
By a very large bear.

This is the level of John's new hat
A lady just sat on it—
Was she fat!

This is the clean sheet
That with a thud
Last Monday fell in some
Beautiful mud!

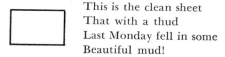

H. Imagine queer chicks that hatched out of Easter eggs and put the creatures into verse.

I. Ideas for humorous limericks

1. Funny happenings at school
2. Pairs of homonyms: great-grate; ate-eight
3. Pupils' last names
4. Alliterative words: a fly and a flea got caught in a flue.
5. Teachers' names
6. Family first names
7. Geographic names that strike the children as funny

II. Humorous Prose

A. For heaven's sake. Have conversations between the heavenly bodies showing their agitation at having their territory invaded by man and their concern, even to the point of discussing a possible Monroe Doctrine for outer space.

B. **Colossal fossil.** A huge skeleton in the museum comes alive and tells an adventure out of its past.

C. **Ben's spyglass specs.** On Benjamin Franklin's birthday anniversary, January 17, write stories about some special spectacles he invented that would see what people were thinking. Weave one funny episode that might have happened about the spectacles into a funny story.

D. **Look here, Revere.** Write monologues in prose or verse by Paul Revere's horse about that famous ride.

E. **Humorous conversations.** Write conversations between the shoes of noted people.

F. **The ghosts' lament.** In a monologue a ghost tells what a time he has had scaring people since they began to believe in the wonders of science.

G. **"I still chuckle" stories.** Write into a good story the funniest thing that ever happened to you or that you ever witnessed.

H. **Magazine covers.** Collect covers that suggest funny stories. Act out each story in groups. Then let each person write the story the cover suggested to him.

I. **Imaginagerie.** Concoct new animals by joining two others: leopalion; elecamel; kangarabbit, and so on.

J. **Funny outer-space stories.** Think through together a few plots that the children suggest to get the whole class writing, or put some funny titles on the board to spark the children's writing:

1. The Cat That Went on a Spaceship
2. Who Threw Those Flying Saucers?
3. Mr. Chase, What Is Space?
4. Mr. Donneville from Mars

CHAPTER THIRTEEN

For Those Unlucky Mortals
Who Need a Summary

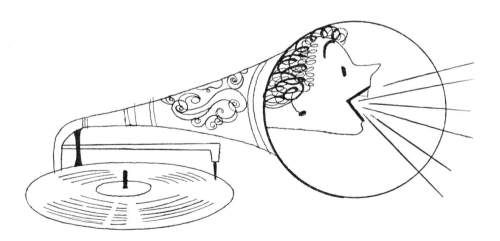

1st boy: Gee, she must think we're dumb or something. First she tells us what she's going to tell us, then she tells us, and ends up telling us what she's told us. Can ya imagine?

2nd boy: Maybe she's on a closed circuit 'er something!

THE CAIRN [1]

When I think of the little children learning
In all the schools of the world,
Learning in Danish, learning in Japanese
That two and two are four, and where the
    rivers of the world
Rise, and the names of the mountains and the
    principal cities,
My heart breaks.
Come up, children! Toss your little stones gaily
On the great cairn of Knowledge!
(Where lies what Euclid knew, a little grey stone,
What Plato, what Pascal, what Galileo:
Little grey stones, little grey stones on a cairn.)
Tell me, what is the name of the highest mountain?
Name me a crater of fire! a peak of snow!
Name me the mountains on the moon!
But the name of the mountain that you climb all day,
Ask not your teacher that.

Edna St. Vincent Millay

THE COCOON

Lying in a jar
Beside my bed,
Was a small cocoon
Not knowing fear or dread.

Inside this cocoon
Was a small furry thing,
And around its neck
Was a furry yellow ring.

Soon out of this thing
Of drab, dark gray,
Will creep a butterfly
Lovely and gay.

Barbara Russell, Grade 5

[1] By permission of Norma Millay Ellis. From *Collected Poems*, Harper & Brothers. Copyright 1923, 1951, by Edna St. Vincent Millay and Norma Millay Ellis.

I suppose, in a way, you could have expected it—a different kind of summary, I mean. I kept telling you—remember?—that I believed that the students, not the teacher, should do the summarizing; that there wasn't much use in the teacher's telling the students what he *hoped* they have learned. Besides, this book wasn't really written in the first place to teach; my real purpose was to open new vistas to some of you and get you to thinking about the language arts and what you might do about them in your school or home situation.

I have a feeling that neither you nor I are fully meeting the needs of our children in this field, but I for one am determined to keep on discovering until I find a better way than my present one —which really works very well for a great many children, but not well enough for all of them. My father used to say: "There's always a way to get at everybody—if we're smart enough to find it." —

I sometimes feel that we English teachers are like the ancient Negro who after the Civil War learned to read at the age of seventy. When asked by a friend what progress he was making, he replied, "When I come to a sign in the road I kin tell how fur, but I can't tell whar yit." I guess a teacher is lucky these days if among bristling clusters of signposts even his direction is right, let alone his "whar."

I am a little sorry (but, not very) if you are disappointed that this summary chapter doesn't review *Easy in English* in relation to the laws of learning. I have a feeling that if a great many of you were held up (singly, of course) on a dark corner by a thug who was once a teacher (but who had to give up the pursuit because of the inadequate remuneration) and he should stick a gun against your ribs, demanding, "Name the laws of learning or I'll shoot!" that most of you would have to say, "Shoot!" In case that situation possibly should arise, it might be wise to review the laws of learning yourself. It certainly would look bad for a teacher's epitaph to read:

> The reason he's consigned to burning—
> He didn't know the laws of learning.

Oh well, I can't imagine a teacher's turning thug anyway—the one thing to recommend thuggery to a teacher would be that it is night work, but a blessed relief from checking papers. Besides, such a career would hold far less security than pedagoguery and teachers want security, I'm told.

Dear me, I'm having fun again—I keep forgetting that this is an educational book—but as penance for my levity under such solemn circumstances, I'll tell you that there's a fine discussion of the laws of learning in these three books:

Human Development and Learning (Part IV) by Crow and Crow; American, 1956
Psychology and Teaching by Morse and Wingo; Scott, Foresman, 1955
Dynamics of Learning by Cantor; Paster and Stewart, 1946

It pays to check at intervals to see how things and emphases have changed since we graduated from college.

Seriously, I pondered deeply the problem of how to summarize this book in the light of the philosophy that the gathering must be different from the sowing. I believe that a summary is not a mere reiteration of facts; it is, rather, a rethinking of the essential facts at hand. I just don't believe that deepening a rut does other than wear away the springs of the educational vehicle.

Then in the middle of a sleepless night after a day when everything had gone wrong (one parking ticket; once being stopped by an officer for *hesitating* instead of *stopping* at a stop sign; one forgotten appointment), I got a real inspiration for Chapter Thirteen. Why not let poetry do my gathering for me? Poetry is capsule truth. Poetry talks to each of us in his own language. Poetry personalizes any problem. Why not summarize with poetry?

And why not, indeed?

What is the teacher's job? The poets know:

Then said a teacher, Speak to us of Teaching.
And he said:
No man can reveal to you aught but that which already lies half asleep in the dawning of your knowledge.
The teacher who walks in the shadow of the temple, among his followers, gives not of his wisdom but rather of his faith and his lovingness.
If he is indeed wise he does not bid you enter the house of his wisdom, but rather leads you to the threshold of your own mind.
The astronomer may speak to you of his understanding of space, but he cannot give you his understanding.

The musician may sing to you of the rhythm which is in all space, but he cannot give you the ear which arrests the rhythm nor the voice that echoes it.

And he who is versed in the science of numbers can tell of the regions of weight and measure, but he cannot conduct you thither.

For the vision of one man lends not its wings to another man.[2]

THE BEAN-STALK [3]

Ho, Giant! This is I!
I have built me a bean-stalk into your sky!
La,—but it's lovely, up so high!

This is how I came,—I put
Here my knee, there my foot,
Up and up, from shoot to shoot—
And the blessèd bean-stalk thinning
Like the mischief all the time,
Till it took me rocking, spinning,
In a dizzy, sunny circle,
Making angles with the root,
Far and out above the cackle
Of the city I was born in,
Till the little dirty city
In the light so sheer and sunny
Shone as dazzling bright and pretty
As the money that you find
In a dream of finding money—
What a wind! What a morning!—
Till the tiny, shiny city,
When I shot a glance below,
Shaken with a giddy laughter,
Sick and blissfully afraid,
Was a dew-drop on a blade,
And a pair of moments after
Was the whirling guess I made,—

---

[2] Reprinted from *The Prophet* by Kahlil Gibran with permission of the publisher, Alfred A. Knopf, Inc. Copyright 1923 by Kahlil Gibran; renewal copyright 1951 by Administrators C. T. A. of Kahlil Gibran Estate, and Mary G. Gibran.

[3] By permission of Norma Millay Ellis. From *Collected Poems*, Harper & Brothers. Copyright 1921, 1948 by Edna St. Vincent Millay.

And the wind was like a whip
Cracking past my icy ears,
And my hair stood out behind,
And my eyes were full of tears,
Wide-open and cold,
More tears than they could hold,
The wind was blowing so,
And my teeth were in a row,
Dry and grinning,
And I felt my foot slip,
And I scratched the wind and whined,
And I clutched the stalk and jabbered,
With my eyes shut blind,—
What a wind! What a wind!

Your broad sky, Giant,
Is the shelf of a cupboard;
I make bean-stalks, I'm
A builder, like yourself,
But bean-stalks is my trade,
I couldn't make a shelf,
Don't know how they're made,
Now a bean-stalk is more pliant—
La, what a climb!

Wisdom was never learned at any knees,
Not even a father's, ...

.   .   .   .   I am not one
Who must have everything, yet I must have
My dreams if I must live, for they are mine.
Wisdom is not one word and then another,
Till words are like dry leaves under a tree;
Wisdom is like a dawn that comes up slowly
Out of an unknown ocean.[4]

---

[4] From *Collected Poems*, "Tristram" by Edwin Arlington Robinson. By permission of The Macmillan Company, publishers.

When you are weary sometimes of your own
Utility, I wonder if you find
Occasional great comfort pondering
What power a man has in him to put forth?
'Of all the many marvelous things that are,
Nothing is there more marvelous than man,'
Said Sophocles; and he lived long ago; [5]

And for a moment take a hurried glimpse of this self you might
become, but—thank God—are not yet:

PETER PUTTER [6]

They called him Peter Putter from the way
He had of doing nothing with the air
Of straightening up the universe. Somewhere
In youth a fortune fell on him. They say
His house with forty rooms above the bay,
"Built upon slipping sand," was the despair
And byword of the villagers. And there
Cleveland once stopped to pass the time of day.

Now Peter trims, and tamps, and mends the stairs,
And pulls the burdock from his weedy lawn;
Content to come where any hole has gone,
Holding off time with pruning shears and prayers.
And while he struggles with his small repairs,
The large decays eat unconcernedly on.

Do you ever sit down and think about this sort of thing, teacher?

The prophet of dead words defeats himself:
Whoever would acknowledge and include
The foregleam and the glory of the real,
Must work with something else than pen and ink
And painful preparation: he must work
With unseen implements that have no names,
And he must win withal, to do that work,
Good fortitude, clean wisdom, and strong skill.[7]

[5] *Ibid.*, "Captain Craig"
[6] From *Selected Poems and Parodies of Louis Untermeyer,* copyright, 1935, by Harcourt, Brace and Company, Inc.
[7] From *Collected Poems,* "Octave XX" by Edwin Arlington Robinson. By permission of The Macmillan Company, publishers.

Grains of Sand That Might Become Pearls
If Irritating Enough

GRAIN 1: Is there any possible way by which we can return to child-hood of the space age, the capacity to wonder?

SATURDAY TOWN [8]

> So few years ago, the road
> Coiled through hills to town, adventurous
> As any road to Samarkand,
> And at the end was Saturday,
> Stores, and sodas, and the New York train,
> And a noble steed named Wonder Horse
> Flickering at the Orpheum.
> Now the road runs short and flat,
> A diesel slithers in that used to bellow
> Snorting steam, and no one runs to see.
> And children would not turn a hair, so numb
> Are they with wonders and spectaculars,
> If Wonder Horse Himself
> Planked himself in the next seat beside them
> At the tarnished Orpheum,
> To watch the spacemen blasting off for Mars.

GRAIN 2: Poetry is not a predigested cereal or a quick-mix. One must cook it slowly—slowly—on the back of the mind's stove. But give it to the young regularly, one small bowlful at a time, and how those spirit muscles will fill out. Raise kids without poetry? I'd as soon think of raising them without laughter or a sense of God's nearness.

Take just this one poem, for instance; it's a whole bottle of elixir.

---

[8] By permission of the author, Bianca Bradbury, and *The Christian Science Monitor.*

CLEAN HANDS [9]

It is something to face the sun and know you are free.
To hold your head in the shafts of daylight slanting the earth
And know your heart has kept a promise and the blood runs clean:
        It is something.
To go one day of your life among all men with clean hands,
Clean for the day book today and the record of the after days,
Held at your side proud, satisfied to the last, and ready,
So to have clean hands:
        God, it is something,
        One day of life so
    And a memory fastened till the stars sputter out
    And a love washed as white linen in the noon drying.
Yes, go find the men of clean hands one day and see the life,
    the memory, the love they have, to stay longer than the
    plunging sea wets the shores or the fires heave under the
    crust of the earth.
O yes, clean hands is the chant and only one man knows its sob
    and its undersong and he dies clenching the secret more to
    him than any woman or chum.
And O the great brave men, the silent little brave men, proud of
    their hands—clutching the knuckles of their fingers into fists
    ready for death and the dark, ready for life and the fight, the
    pay and the memories—O the men proud of their hands.

And these capsules of wisdom and beauty from many Sandburg
poems—what directions should accompany the capsules if any?

    The wind never bothers . . . a bar of steel.[9]

    (Washington, D.C.)
    There is . . . something . . . here . . . men die for.[9]

    Somebody loses whenever somebody wins.[9]

    Regrets fly kites in your eyes.[9]

    Bring in
        the handshake of the pumpkins.[9]

    The bridge says: Come across, try me; see how good I am.[9]

[9] From *Smoke and Steel* by Carl Sandburg, copyright, 1920, by Harcourt, Brace and Company, Inc.; renewed by Carl Sandburg. Reprinted by permission of the publishers.

In the night the cabbages catch at the moon, the
  leaves drip silver, the rows of cabbages are
  series of little silver waterfalls in the moon.[10]

He told himself, This may be
something else than what I
see when I look—how do I
know? For each man sees himself in the Grand Canyon—
each one makes his own Canyon
before he comes, each one brings
and carries away his own Canyon—
who knows? and how do I know? [10]

GRAIN 3: What "potted-plant" techniques have we parents and
teachers been using on the children we hoped would become pine
trees?

ADVICE [11]

A fir tree needs the sun and wind
To grow full strong and disciplined.

Think not to hover over
Your lad and lass
Lest you should cover clover
Or dim the grass
With your own shadow. Rather
Stand well apart,
Let their bravado gather
Now at the start
Sunlight for steady growing
And winds that bring
Concepts for ready knowing
Of everything.

A fir tree needs an open space
To grow in symmetry and grace.

[10] From *Good Morning, America,* copyright, 1928, 1955, by Carl Sandburg.
Reprinted by permission of Harcourt, Brace and Company, Inc.
[11] From *Stars of the Morning* by Hazel Harper Harris, copyright, 1957; by
permission of Exposition Press, Inc., publishers.

GRAIN 4: Is grouping the answer to individual differences in children? What *is* the answer? Is there *any* answer?

> You can work it out by Fractions or by simple Rule of Three
> But the way of Tweedle-dum is not the way of Tweedle-dee.
> You can twist it, you can turn it, you can plait it till you drop,
> But the way of Pilly-Winky's not the way of Winkie-Pop.[12]

GRAIN 5: "Children cannot create out of a vacuum," [13] says Natalie Cole. How must this philosophy affect our teaching of the creative arts? *Can* we teach the creative arts? *Should we?*

NOT EFFORT [14]

> Expression is a state, and not an act;
> In time of bloom
> Do not all flowers loose upon the air
> Their stored perfume?
>
> Can rain be granted to the thirsting fields
> Before the clouds gather?
> Expression is not effort of our powers
> Release, rather.

GRAIN 6: What are we doing to the dissenter? Is it only in science that men dare have a revolutionary idea? There are methods of crucifixion other than nailing to a wooden cross. What happens to our thinkers in the intermediate grades and junior high school? What is the scientific method and how can it be used in the humanities?

> And I honour the man who is willing to sink
> Half his present repute for the freedom to think,
> And, when he has thought, be his cause strong or weak
> Will risk t' other half for the freedom to speak,
> Caring naught for what vengeance the mob has in store,
> Let that mob be the upper ten thousand or lower.[15]

[12] From *The Jungle Book* by Rudyard Kipling. Reprinted by permission of The Macmillan Company of Canada, Ltd., Mrs. George Bambridge, and Doubleday & Company, Inc.

[13] From *The Arts in the Classroom* by Natalie Robinson Cole. By permission of The John Day Company, Inc.

[14] By permission of the author, Nora B. Cunningham, and *The Christian Science Monitor.*

[15] From *A Fable for Critics* by James Russell Lowell.

GRAIN 7: Imagination shows a clearer picture than a pedantic paragraph. "Nightmare Number Three" by Benét has a grim warning to thoughtful citizens of our day. When the heart and soul are gone from the lives of a generation, what will its children learn from adults? How can home and school counteract the effects of mechanized living? *We must find out!*

NIGHTMARE NUMBER THREE [16]

We had expected everything but revolt
And I kind of wonder myself when they started thinking—
But there's no dice in that now.
                              I've heard fellows say
They must have planned it for years and maybe they did.
Looking back, you can find little incidents here and there,
Like the concrete-mixer in Jersey eating the wop
Or the roto press that printed "Fiddle-dee-dee!"
In a three-color process all over Senator Sloop,
Just as he was making a speech. The thing about that
Was, how could it walk upstairs? But it was upstairs,
Clicking and mumbling in the Senate Chamber.
They had to knock out the wall to take it away
And the wrecking-crew said it grinned.
                              It was only the best
Machines, of course, the superhuman machines,
The ones we'd built to be better than flesh and bone,
But the cars were in it, of course . . .
                              and they hunted us
Like rabbits through the cramped streets on that Bloody Monday,
The Madison Avenue busses leading the charge.
The busses were pretty bad—but I'll not forget
The smash of glass when the Duesenberg left the show-room
And pinned three brokers to the Racquet Club steps
Or the long howl of the horns when they saw the men run,
When they saw them looking for holes in the solid ground . . .

[16] "Nightmare Number Three" by Stephen Vincent Benét. From *Selected Works of Stephen Vincent Benét*. Published by Rinehart & Company, Inc. Copyright, 1935, by Stephen Vincent Benét.

I guess they were tired of being ridden in,
And stopped and started by pygmies for silly ends,
Of wrapping cheap cigarettes and bad chocolate bars,
Collecting nickels and waving platinum hair,
And letting six million people live in a town.
I guess it was that. I guess they got tired of us
And the whole smell of human hands.

.   .   .   .

                              For a while, I thought
That window-cleaner would make it, and keep me company.
But they got him with his own hoist at the sixteenth floor
And dragged him in, with a squeal.
You see, they co-operate. Well, we taught them that
And it's fair enough, I suppose. You see, we built them.
We taught them to think for themselves.
It was bound to come. You can see it was bound to come.
And it won't be so bad, in the country. I hate to think
Of the reapers, running wild in the Kansas fields,
And the transport planes like hawks on a chickenyard,
But the horses might help. We might make a deal with the horses.
At least, you've more chance, out there.
                              And they need us too
They're bound to realize that when they once calm down.
They'll need oil and spare parts and adjustments and tuning up.
Slaves? Well, in a way, you know, we were slaves before.
There won't be so much real difference—honest, there won't.
(I wish I hadn't looked into that beauty-parlor
And seen what was happening there.
But those are female machines and a bit high-strung.)
Oh, we'll settle down. We'll arrange it. We'll compromise.
It wouldn't make sense to wipe out the whole human race.
Why, I bet if I went to my old Plymouth now
(Of course, you'd have to do it the tactful way)
And said, "Look here! Who got you the swell French horn?"
He wouldn't turn me over to those police cars;
At least I don't think he would.
                              Oh, it's going to be jake.
There won't be so much real difference—honest, there won't—
And I'd go down in a minute and take my chance—
I'm a good American and I always liked them—
Except for one small detail that bothers me
And that's the food proposition. Because you see,
The concrete-mixer may have made a mistake,
And it looks like just high spirits.
But, if it's got so they like the flavor . . . well . . .

GRAIN 8: What are our reading purposes in grades seven to twelve? Research says youth well taught in reading classes up to those grades lose their reading power before college entrance. Why? Let us look to our goals.

> 'T would be endless to tell you the things that he knew,
> All separate facts, undeniably true,
> But with him or each other they'd nothing to do;
> No power of combining, arranging, discerning,
> Digested the masses he learned, into learning;
>
> .   .   .   .
>
> A reading-machine always wound up and going,
> He mastered whatever was not worth his knowing,[17]

GRAIN 9: What is the best method of teaching correct usage? Filling out blanks in a workbook and learning rules have certainly proved to be ineffective. What shall we use instead?

AT WOODWARD'S GARDENS [18]

> A boy, presuming on his intellect,
> Once showed two little monkeys in a cage
> A burning-glass they could not understand
> And never could be made to understand.
> Words are no good: to say it was a lens
> For gathering solar rays would not have helped.
> But let him show them how the weapon worked.
> He made the sun a pin-point on the nose
> Of first one then the other till it brought
> A look of puzzled dimness to their eyes
> That blinking could not seem to blink away.
> They stood arms laced together at the bars,
> And exchanged troubled glances over life.
> One put a thoughtful hand up to his nose
> As if reminded—or as if perhaps
> Within a million years of an idea.
> He got his purple little knuckles stung.
> The already known had once more been confirmed
> By psychological experiment,
> And that were all the finding to announce
> Had the boy not presumed too close and long.

[17] From *A Fable for Critics* by James Russell Lowell.
[18] From *Complete Poems of Robert Frost*. Copyright, 1930, 1949, by Henry Holt and Company, Inc. Copyright, 1936, by Robert Frost. By permission of the publishers.

There was a sudden flash of arm, a snatch,
And the glass was the monkeys' not the boy's.
Precipitately they retired back cage
And instituted an investigation
On their part, though without the needed insight.
They bit the glass and listened for the flavor.
They broke the handle and the binding off it.
Then none the wiser, frankly gave it up,
And having hid it in their bedding straw
Against the day of prisoners' ennui,
Came dryly forward to the bars again
To answer for themselves: Who said it mattered
What monkeys did or didn't understand?
They might not understand a burning-glass.
They might not understand the sun itself.
It's knowing what to do with things that counts.

GRAIN 10: What shall we do about teaching foreign languages in
our elementary schools?

FIRST GRADER

She whispered, "Je t'aime," close to my ear;
I knew no French; my heart's ears could not hear;
I smiled, but there was no communication.
Is it like that when nation talks to nation?

GRAIN 11: How can an elementary teacher best help a child with
his problems?

A father sees a son nearing manhood.
What shall he tell that son?
"Life is hard; be steel; be a rock."
And this might stand him for the storms
and serve him for humdrum and monotony
and guide him amid sudden betrayals
and tighten him for slack moments.
"Life is a soft loam; be gentle; go easy."
And this too might serve him.
Brutes have been gentled where lashes failed.
The growth of a frail flower in a path up
has sometimes shattered and split a rock.
A tough will counts. So does desire.

So does a rich soft wanting.
Without rich wanting nothing arrives.
Tell him too much money has killed men
and left them dead years before burial:
the quest of lucre beyond a few easy needs
has twisted good enough men
sometimes into dry thwarted worms.
Tell him time as a stuff can be wasted.
Tell him to be a fool every so often
and to have no shame over having been a fool
yet learning something out of every folly
hoping to repeat none of the cheap follies
thus arriving at intimate understanding
of a world numbering many fools.
Tell him to be alone often and get at himself
and above all tell himself no lies about himself
whatever the white lies and protective fronts
he may use amongst other people.
Tell him solitude is creative if he is strong
and the final decisions are made in silent rooms.
Tell him to be different from other people
if it comes natural and easy being different.
Let him have lazy days seeking his deeper motives.
Let him seek deep for where he is a born natural.
Then he may understand Shakespeare
and the Wright brothers, Pasteur, Pavlov,
Michael Faraday and free imaginations
bringing changes into a world resenting change.
He will be lonely enough
to have time for the work
he knows as his own.[19]

Schoolteachers and parents—while they often do not realize it —are slowly but surely changing the world. Think on these things:

MEADOWS. Behind us lie
The thousand and the thousand and the thousand years
Vexed and terrible. And still we use
The cures which never cure.

. . . .

[19] From *The People, Yes* by Carl Sandburg, copyright, 1936, by Harcourt, Brace and Company, Inc.

DAVID. Corporal, the crowing son of heaven
   Thinks we can make a morning.
MEADOWS.   Not
   By old measures. Expedience and self-preservation
   Can rot as they will. Lord, where we fail as men
   We fail as deeds of time.

.   .   .   .

MEADOWS. The human heart can go to the lengths of God.
   Dark and cold we may be, but this
   Is no winter now. The frozen misery
   Of centuries breaks, cracks, begins to move,
   The thunder is the thunder of the floes,
   The thaw, the flood, the upstart Spring.
   Thank God our time is now when wrong
   Comes up to face us everywhere,
   Never to leave us till we take
   The longest stride of soul men ever took.
   Affairs are now soul size.[20]

GRAIN 12: How can a teacher help a child to push back the walls of
his environment and personality and to enlarge his world?

   The world stands out on either side
   No wider than the heart is wide;
   Above the world is stretched the sky,—
   No higher than the soul is high.
   The heart can push the sea and land
   Farther away on either hand;
   The soul can split the sky in two,
   And let the face of God shine through.
   But East and West will pinch the heart
   That cannot keep them pushed apart;
   And he whose soul is flat—the sky
   Will cave in on him by and by.[21]

[20] From *A Sleep of Prisoners* by Christopher Fry. Copyright 1951 by Christopher Fry. Reprinted by permission of Oxford University Press.
[21] Excerpt from "Renascence." By permission of Norma Millay Ellis. From *Collected Poems*, Harper & Brothers. Copyright 1917, 1945 by Edna St. Vincent Millay.

Index